English Pronunciation in the
Eighteenth Century

NEW SPELLING and PRONOUNCING

ENGLISH DICTIONARY.

A

A, An article, placed before names of the fingular number that begin with a founded confonant.

A'bacus, (⅃BIK⅃S) n. a counting table; the uppermoft member of a pillar.

Abáft, (IB⅃FT) ad. behind; to the ftern.

Abáifance, (⅃BAZINS) n. a bow or curtefy; refpect.

Abándon, (⅃B⅃NDIN) v. to forfake; to defert.

Abáfe, (⅃BAS) v. to bring down; to humble.

Abáfement, (⅃BASMINT) n. depreffion; humiliation.

Abáfh, (⅃B⅃SH) v. to put to the blufh.

Abáte, (⅃BAT) v. to diminifh; to leffen.

Abátement, ⅃BATMINT) n. an allowance made.

Abb, (⅃B) n. the warp threads of cloth.

A'bbacy, (⅃BISE) n. the rights, privileges, or jurifdiction of an abbot.

A'bbefs, (⅃BIS) n. the governefs of an abbey inhabited by women.

A'bbey, (⅃BE) n. a monaftery, governed by an abbot or abbefs.

A'bbot, (⅃BIT) n. the chief of an abbey inhabited by men.

A B B

Abbréviate, (⅃BREVEAT) v. to abridge; to fhorten.

Abbreviátion, (⅃BREVEASHIN) n. fhortening; a contraction.

Abbréviature, (⅃BREVEITUR) n. a mark ufed for the fake of fhortening.

A'bdicate, (⅃BDIKAT) v. to renounce; to refign.

Abdicátion, (⅃BDIKASHIN) n. refignation.

Abdómen, (⅃BDOMIN) n. the lower part of the belly.

Abdóminous, (⅃BDOMINUS) q. belonging to the abdomen; big-bellied.

Abdúce, (⅃BDUS) v. to draw away.

Abecedárian, (ABESEDAREIN) n. one who teaches the alphabet.

Abecédary, (ABESEDIRE) q. belonging to the alphabet.

Abèrrance, (⅃BERINS) n. an error.

Abérrant, (⅃BERINT) q. going wrong.

Abérring, (⅃BERING) part. going aftray.

Aberrátion, (⅃BIRASHIN) n. wandering.

Abét, (⅃BET) v. to aid, or affift.

Abétment, (⅃BETMINT) n. encouragement.

A 2

Frontifpiece: First dictionary page of the *Grand Repository*

English Pronunciation in the Eighteenth Century

Thomas Spence's *Grand Repository of the English Language*

JOAN C. BEAL

CLARENDON PRESS · OXFORD
1999

OXFORD
UNIVERSITY PRESS

Great Clarendon Street, Oxford OX2 6DP

Oxford University Press is a department of the University of Oxford
and furthers the University's aim of excellence in research, scholarship,
and education by publishing worldwide in

Oxford New York

Athens Auckland Bangkok Bogotá Bombay Buenos Aires Calcutta
Cape Town Chennai Dar es Salaam Delhi Florence Hong Kong Istanbul
Karachi Kuala Lumpur Madras Melbourne Mexico City Mumbai
Nairobi Paris São Paulo Singapore Taipei Tokyo Toronto Warsaw

and associated companies in Berlin Ibadan

Oxford is a registered trade mark of Oxford University Press

Published in the United States
by Oxford University Press Inc., New York

© Joan Beal 1999

The moral rights of the author have been asserted

First published 1999

British Library Cataloguing in Publication Data
Data available
Library of Congress Cataloging in Publication Data
English pronunciation in the eighteenth century: Thomas Spence's
Grand repository of the English language/Joan C. Beal.
Includes bibliographical references and index.
1. Spence, Thomas, 1750–1814.   Grand repository of the English
language.   2. English language—18th century—Pronunciation.
3. English language—18th century—Lexicography.   I. Title.
PE1617.S65B4   1998   423'.1–dc21   98-51328

ISBN 0-19-823781-2

1 3 5 7 9 10 8 6 4 2

Typeset by Joshua Associates Ltd., Oxford
Printed in Great Britain on acid-free paper by
Biddles Ltd., Guildford and King's Lynn

Acknowledgements

I am extremely grateful to Noel Osselton for all his help and encouragement and in particular for his clear guidance and meticulous attention to detail in the supervision of the Ph.D. thesis which formed the basis of this book. Thanks are also due to Tom Cain for his helpfulness in the latter stages of the thesis and to all my colleagues in the Department of English Literary and Linguistic Studies, University of Newcastle upon Tyne, for their moral and practical support. I am indebted to Charles Jones and Bev Collins for their constructive comments on the Ph.D. thesis, and to Richard W. Bailey and Gabrielle Stein for their equally helpful comments on the first draft of this book. It goes without saying that any faults or shortcomings are mine alone. I wish to acknowledge the assistance that I have received from the staff of the Robinson Library, especially the Inter-Library Loans section, and the Local Studies Section of Newcastle City Library. Thanks are also due to the latter for permission to reproduce the two pages of the *Grand Repository* which appear as the frontispiece and as figure 5.1.

Table 4.1 appears with the permission of Professor John Wells, and the list of words in Appendix 7*a* appears with the permission of Anthea Fraser Gupta (formerly Shields), to whom I am grateful for her helpful comments in the very late stages of this book's production.

Finally, my thanks and apologies are due to my husband, Ninian, and my daughters, Madeleine and Alice, for their patience and forbearance.

Contents

List of Figures and Tables

Abbreviations

CSED	*Collins Softback English Dictionary* (4th edn., Glasgow: HarperCollins)
DEMEP	*Dictionary of Early Modern English Pronunciation 1500–1800*
DNB	*Dictionary of National Biography*, ed. Stephen and Lee (1885–1901; repr. 1973)
EME	Early Middle English
ENE	Early Modern English
LNE	Later Modern English
ME	Middle English
NE	New English
OCP	Oxford Concordance Program
OED	*The Oxford English Dictionary*
OF	Old French
PDE	present-day English
RP	received pronunciation
SED	Survey of English Dialects

A Note about Bracketing

I have used throughout the normal conventions of phonemic (/ /), phonetic ([ ]), and orthographic (⟨ ⟩) bracketing. Phonemic bracketing and IPA symbols are used for the representation of Middle English phonemes—e.g. /ʊ/ is used for what earlier scholars would represent as ME ŭ. To avoid confusion between conventional orthography and the notations of eighteenth-century orthoepists, I have used 'curly brackets' ({ }) for the latter.

1. Thomas Spence: His Life and Works

1.1.1. *Family background and influences*

Thomas Spence was born on 21 June 1750 on the Quayside, then one of the poorest areas of Newcastle upon Tyne. His father was a Scot who had settled in Newcastle some eleven years previously, and who had followed the occupations of netmaker and shoemaker, later becoming a hardware dealer. Whatever he earned at these occupations would not have gone far, as there were besides Thomas eighteen other children to support. This places Spence, almost uniquely amongst eighteenth-century orthoepists and grammarians, firmly in the lower classes. Little is known about such formal education as Spence might have received: Ashraf (1983: 12) notes that he 'began his working life at his father's trade of netmaking at the age of ten after some schooling'. We do, however, know from Spence's own account in *The Important Trial of Thomas Spence* that his father had his own method of educating his sons. 'My father used to make my brothers and me read the Bible to him while working in his business, and at the end of every chapter, encouraged us to give our opinions on what we had just read. By these means I acquired an early habit of reflecting on every occurrence which passed before me, as well as on what I read' (Spence 1803: 65; quoted from Waters 1917: 65).

Spence's family moved in radical and dissenting circles: they joined the breakaway Presbyterian congregation of the Revd James Murray, a famous preacher at the time, and described by Ashraf (1983: 19) as 'well to the left of Whig tradition . . . an egalitarian democrat'. Later, Spence's father and brother Jeremiah were to join the Glassites, a millenialist Congregationalist group who advocated a return to the communal ownership of property practised by the early church. Bindman (1989: 198) describes the Spence family as 'leading members of the Glassite congregation at the Forster Street meeting house'. Whether Thomas Spence continued to adhere to this sect or not, he was undoubtedly influenced by their belief in common ownership of property, and Ashraf (1983: 20) suggests that 'possible Glassite tendencies were reflected in the millennial metaphor of Spensonia' in Spence's later writings.

1.1.2. *Newcastle in the eighteenth century: a radical city?*

Thomas Spence and his family were poor, but far from being intellectually impoverished. Nor was Spence born into an intellectual backwater: Shields (1973: 5) writes that 'Newcastle upon Tyne in the eighteenth century was an intellectually stimulating place'. It was a centre for printing and engraving (Thomas Bewick, a close friend of Spence, lived in nearby Cherryburn); it was well known for the production of children's books and a hotbed of educational publishing. Alston (1965–73: i. 110–11) shows that, in the eighteenth century, more grammars were printed in Newcastle than in any other anglophone city except London. Bookshops such as Barker's and Charnley's, and Sand's circulating library in the Bigg Market, were, according to Horsley (1971: 206), 'open for twelve hours a day' and 'the regular meeting place of the prominent citizens of the town'. There was ample opportunity for political debate in clubs such as the Constitutional Club and the Independent Club, both of which tended to take a reformist, even republican, stance. Newcastle in the eighteenth century was hospitable to radical thinkers: as well as being home to the likes of James Murray and the Glassites, between 1770 and 1773, and again for a brief spell in 1775, it was visited by Jean-Paul Marat, who chose to launch his revolutionary tract *The Chains of Slavery* (1774) in this provincial city.[1] In 1775 the Newcastle Philosophical Society was formed by a group of gentlemen with the intention of encouraging intellectual debate. Members of this Society included Thomas Spence, Thomas Bewick, and the Revd James Murray and, according to Horsley (1971: 206), it was attended by Marat during his visit to Newcastle.

1.1.3. *Spence in Newcastle: the birth of the 'Plan'*

So, by the time he was a young man, Spence was keeping company with the radical intellectuals of the Newcastle clubs. We know that by 1775 he was a schoolteacher, for the title page of *The Grand Repository of the English Language* (Spence 1775: sig. A1[r] refers to his 'School in the Keyside'. Indeed, the young Spence already had something of a following in Newcastle, for Bewick in his memoirs (1862: 71, quoted in Robinson 1887: 34) relates how Spence had 'got a number of young men together and formed into a debating society, which was held in the evenings in his schoolroom in the Broad Garth'. Bewick goes on to relate an entertaining tale about how he

---

[1] There has been much speculation about Marat's stay in Newcastle, and we have to be cautious in interpreting material in which the few facts have been embroidered. Horsley (1971), for instance, describes Marat as Spence's friend, but, as Ashraf (1983: 110) points out, there is nothing to connect Spence with Marat beyond the extraordinary coincidence that these two radical thinkers moved in the same circles at the same time and that in successive years (1774 and 1775) they each published a 'revolutionary' tract in Newcastle. I point out the connection here merely to show what a hive of radical activity Newcastle was in the later eighteenth century!

and Spence came to blows over the question of common ownership of the land: Bewick felt that this was impracticable except in a new colony, but Spence was not to be swayed from his firm belief that 'property in land is everybody's right', despite the beating he took at Bewick's hands.

On 8 November 1775 Spence read to the Newcastle Philosophical Society a paper to which he later (1793) gave the title *The Rights of Man*. Shortly after this, he was expelled from the Society, not, apparently, because of the content of this lecture, but for the heinous offence of having it published and selling it in the streets.[2] This lecture was to be reprinted several times, forming as it did the basis of Spence's political philosophy for the next thirty-nine years. According to Rudkin (1927: 229–30), the earliest extant version is the 1793 edition mentioned above, which was the fourth edition. It was published again in *Pigs' Meat* (Vol. 3 (1795)) and as *The Meridian Sun of Liberty* (Spence 1795*a*), in the Preface of which Spence writes: 'Read this Lecture which I have been publishing in various editions for more than twenty years.' The gist of the lecture, and the nub of what the author was to refer to later as 'Spence's Plan', was that, since Natural Right gives everybody an equal claim to what Nature provides, then all land should be the common property of those who live on it.

1.1.4. The Grand Repository of the English Language

In the same year that Spence read his lecture to the Philosophical Society, *The Grand Repository of the English Language* was published. Only two copies of this work survive—one in Boston, Mass., and the other in Newcastle Central Library—but it is also available on microfiche as no. 155 in the *English Linguistics 1500–1800* collection (Alston 1972). The Preface of the *Grand Repository* consists almost entirely of extracts from Thomas Sheridan's *Dissertation on the Causes of the Difficulties which Occur in Learning the English Tongue* (1761), which is the only source for the *Grand Repository* that is acknowledged by Spence. This Preface is followed by an advertisement for Spence's *Repository of Common Sense and Amusement*, then comes a very short Grammar (ten pages), almost certainly influenced by the works of the Newcastle grammarian Ann Fisher (see §4.2 for a fuller discussion of Spence's sources). The Dictionary part of the *Grand Repository* is preceded by three pages, each setting out the 'New Alphabet', the first of which is reproduced in Figure 5.1. Then comes 'An Accurate New Spelling and Pronouncing English Dictionary', in which the words are first spelt in traditional orthography, with the main stress marked, then in brackets in the

---

[2] However, the *Newcastle Chronicle* report on 25 November 1775 states that the members of the Newcastle Philosophical Society 'disclaim all patronage' of Spence's lecture, 'being informed that he . . . became a member, apparently, for the purpose of obtruding upon the world, the ERRONEOUS and dangerous levelling principles, with which the lecture is replete'. An early example of what the modern Labour Party would call 'entryism'!

capital forms of the new orthography (the first page of the dictionary is reproduced as the frontispiece to this book). This is a relatively short dictionary (14,536 entries on 342 pages), but that it was intended as a dictionary rather than just as a guide to spelling and pronunciation is shown by the fact that definitions, albeit brief ones, are provided.[3] Lastly, there is a section giving a list of 'Christian Names of Men and Women', which, like the dictionary entries, are given in both traditional orthography and Spence's 'New Spelling'. In the middle of these is placed a page of errata.

The Grand Repository of the English Language is, as the title suggests, intended as a guide to various aspects of the language and, given the brevity and simplicity of the grammar and the dictionary definitions, as a practical aid for those to whom Spence refers in the Preface as 'the laborious part of the people'. However, it is the 'New Alphabet' and Spence's intention to use the *Grand Repository* as a first step towards the reform of English spelling that have attracted such attention as Spence has received from scholars of language (Abercrombie 1948; Shields 1973, 1974) and that played the most important part in Spence's plans for society as a whole. As a teacher of English, Spence would have had first-hand knowledge of the difficulties which children experienced in learning to read. Just as he proposed a radical solution to the problems of politics in his plan for common ownership of land, his *Grand Repository* set out a radical reform of the alphabet which, like his political views, was in many ways ahead of its time. Although Shields (1973) suggests that Spence's later works in his phonetic alphabet do show slight alterations which involve a move away from the 'phonetic' ideal of the Grand Repository and a compromise with the contemporary reverence for 'correct' traditional spelling, Spence never abandoned his belief that a reformed alphabet was essential if the lower classes were to become sufficiently educated to gain political awareness.

1.1.5. *Other Newcastle works*

Spence was to remain in Newcastle until 1783. The only works published in Newcastle which are still extant are (apart from the *Grand Repository* itself): *The Real Reading Made Easy,* which illustrates the phonetic alphabet first developed in the *Grand Repository*, and two versions of *A Supplement to the History of Robinson Crusoe*, one in Spence's alphabet, the other in traditional orthography. All of these were published in 1782. However, we know from later references in *Pigs' Meat* that he also published a version of his 1775 lecture, entitled *The Poor Man's Advocate*, in 1779, and a song, *The Rights of Man in Verse*, in 1783. The *Grand Repository* also advertises the first issue of *The Repository of Common Sense and Innocent Amusement*, a

---

[3] Some of the definitions bear the hallmark of Spence's political ideas—e.g. *Whig*: 'a friend to civil and religious liberty'.

sort of Spencean *Readers' Digest*, with 'extracts from the best authors in which every word is spelled according to the best pronunciation by the new alphabet'. Since no copies of this are extant, we can only conclude that Spence was unable to find enough subscribers to make it viable.

Whilst in Newcastle, Spence also made his first attempt at another venture which he was to continue more successfully in London: the stamping of slogans on coins. These were produced to publicize 'Spence's Plan', for all those that have survived bear these words: for instance, a halfpenny is countermarked 'Spence's Plan you Rogues' (see Bindman 1989: 198). These were stamped with punches cut by Thomas Bewick, who also cut the punches for the *Grand Repository*.

1.1.6. *Spence moves to London*

There are no extant publications from Spence between 1783 and 1792, nor do we have any information as to his whereabouts during this period. What we do know is that by 1792 he was in London and already in trouble with weightier authorities than the committee of the Newcastle Philosophical Society, for his first London publication is *The Case of Thomas Spence, Bookseller* (1792), which relates how he was imprisoned for selling Thomas Paine's *Rights of Man*. The memoir of Spence in The *Newcastle Magazine*, January 1821, suggests that Spence 'became discontented with Newcastle, and resolved to seek the Metropolis. He was often heard to say that there was no scope for ability in a provincial town, and that London was the only place where a man of talent could display his powers.'

Certainly, Spence arrived at the capital in what were dangerous and exciting times for a man of his convictions: the French Revolution of 1789 had instilled in the Government and its institutions a dread of a similar uprising in Britain, leading to heavy repression of what we might loosely term 'radical' ideas. The works of Thomas Paine were especially singled out as likely to incite the lower orders to revolution and Paine was denounced and caricatured in what amounted to a 'propaganda war' of pamphleteers in the 1790s. More seriously, this decade saw the passing of a series of Acts suppressing freedom of expression: the suspension of Habeas Corpus in 1794, followed by the Two Acts of 1795, which extended the definition of High Treason to include acts of speech or writing, gave the authorities the power to imprison the likes of Spence without trial. Spence, far from being deterred by this danger, used every means at his disposal to propagate his message. He became a member of the London Corresponding Society, which was founded in 1792: according to Bindman (1989: 56), Spence 'was on the radical wing of the LCS; a "violent democrat", in the words of an informer, with "levelling" tendencies that worried the more moderate executive'. (Like Bewick, they disagreed with Spence on the question of common ownership of property and land.)

During his time in London, Spence made his living largely by selling books and pamphlets, as well as a drink called saloup, in the first instance from a street stall. He continued to publish pamphlets on the theme of his Plan, as well as the periodical *Pigs' Meat*. In 1793 Spence opened a shop called 'The Hive of Liberty', and began to sell tokens as well as printed material. Like the early tokens produced with Bewick's help in Newcastle, these always carried a radical message.[4] Bindman (1989: 57) notes that 'the printing of radical texts was always susceptible to laws against sedition; a token, on the other hand, could retain a certain immunity and could pass from hand to hand relatively inconspicuously'. Apart from using these tokens as a means of propagating his Plan, Spence became sufficiently interested in what was at the time the minor 'craze' of token collecting to produce a catalogue, *The Coin Collector's Companion* (1795*b*).

1.1.7. *Arrests, trials, and political writings*

Spence was arrested three times between 1792 and 1794, when, along with other members of the London Corresponding Society, he was arrested under the Suspension Act, imprisoned for seven months, charged with High Treason, and finally acquitted in December 1794. On his release, Spence resumed the publication of *Pigs' Meat* and went on to publish *The End of Oppression* (1795*c*), *The Meridian Sun of Liberty* (1795*a*), *The Reign of Felicity* (1796), *The Rights of Infants* (1797), *The Constitution of a Perfect Commonwealth* (1798), and *The Restorer of Society to its Natural State* (1801). The last-named publication led to Spence's arrest on a charge of seditious libel, for which he was sentenced to a year's imprisonment and a fine of £20. A full account of the trial is provided in *The Important Trial of Thomas Spence*, which Spence published, along with *The Constitution of Spensonia*, first (1803) in a version of the 'Spensonian' alphabet originally developed in the *Grand Repository* and later (1807) in conventional orthography.

1.1.8. *The last years: 'Citizen Spence' and his followers*

After his release from Shrewsbury Jail, Spence continued to promote his Plan through informal meetings. Ashraf (1983: 84–5) refers to a handbill dated 18 March 1801, in which 'well-wishers' are recommended to 'meet frequently . . . after a free and easy Manner to converse on the Subject [of Spence's Plan], provoke investigation, and answer such Objections as may be stated, and to promote the circulation of Citizen Spence's pamphlets'.

---

[4] Examples of Spence's tokens (described more fully in Bindman 1989) are one displaying a Red Indian with the inscript 'If Rent I once consent to pay, my liberty is passed away'; and Spence's favourite, which was buried with him, bearing on one side a picture of a cat and the inscript 'I among slaves enjoy my freedom' and on the reverse a dog and 'much gratitude brings servitude'.

These small, informal gatherings were difficult for the authorities to suppress and we can assume that 'Citizen Spence's' ideas were indeed being propagated, for Ashraf (1983: 87) points out that 'the Home Secretary drew the attention of the police to sayings like "Spence's Plan and Full Bellies" which had appeared on every wall in London'. (McCalman (1988: 3) considers the establishment of Spence's 'free and easy' as marking the beginning of the 'radical underworld' which is the subject of his eponymous work, and of which Spence was the father.) Apart from collections of the broadsides and songs sung at the 'free and easy', Spence's only other publication was *The Giant Killer, or Anti-Landlord*, of which three numbers are extant, all dated in August 1814. Spence died on 1 September 1814: at his funeral a week later, friends carried a pair of scales before his coffin, which was bedecked with white ribbons, the intention being to symbolize the justice and purity of Spence's life and ideas. Ashraf (1983: 92) notes that 'his tokens were distributed to mourners and onlookers, so that he literally went to his grave still spreading his immortal message'.

After Spence's death, his followers continued to meet as 'The Society of Spencean Philanthropists'. Their propagation of Spence's ideas led to the trial of four of its members on a charge of high treason in 1816, and in 1817 an Act was passed 'for more effectively preventing seditious meetings and assemblies', which explicitly prohibited 'all societies or clubs calling themselves Spencean or Spencean Philanthropists' (57 George III c. 19, quoted in Ashraf 1983: 98). McCalman (1988: 2) argues that, despite such draconian action on the part of the government, Spence's followers, 'a circle of radicals whom a variety of historians have dismissed as harmless cranks or destructive loonies', may be considered 'stalwarts of a small but *continuous* revolutionary-republican underground which runs from the mid 1790's to early Chartism'.

1.2. *THE GRAND REPOSITORY OF THE ENGLISH LANGUAGE*: A RADICAL WORK?

1.2.1. *Spence's two 'plans'*

The brief account above is sufficient to show that, throughout his adult life, Spence was zealously and fearlessly engaged in promoting the Plan first formulated in that ill-fated lecture to the Newcastle Philosophical Society in 1775.[5] What has been overlooked by some of Spence's biographers and political commentators is the extent to which Spence's other 'plan', for introducing a reformed system of spelling, was an integral part of Spence's reform of society and was likewise still being promoted up to the time of his

---

[5] Butler (1984: 190) comments that Spence was 'distinguished from other radicals by his single-hearted pursuit of his main doctrine, the parish ownership of land'.

death. Hyndman (1882, quoted in Shields 1973: 22) writes that the young Spence 'wasted much time and energy in his endeavours to establish a phonetic system of spelling. But the young man was an enthusiast, and soon turned his thoughts to more important matters.' Likewise Rudkin (1927: 229), whose biography of Spence otherwise has much to commend it, makes the mistake of asserting that 'except for an occasional broadside, Spence made little use of his phonetics in London'. Spence's own words give the lie to these dismissive statements. In *The Important Trial of Thomas Spence* (which, as noted in §1.1.4. above, was printed first in the 'Spensonian' alphabet), he explicitly links his two 'plans': 'When I first began to study, I found every art and science a perfect whole. Nothing was in anarchy but language and politics. But both of these I reduced to order, the one by a new alphabet, the other by a new Constitution' (Spence 1803: 59; quoted from Waters 1917: 59). Here we see Spence asserting, with a characteristic lack of false modesty, that in 1775 (at the age of 25) he had already formulated the solution to all society's ills. The part played by the New Alphabet in Spence's new society is first hinted at in the preface to the *Grand Repository* itself. Spence envisages his new spelling taking over from the traditional orthography and being used in books: as a start, he proposes a 'weekly miscellany', which he thinks should succeed 'especially among the laborious part of the people, who generally cannot afford much time or expence in the educating of their children, and yet they would like to have them taught the necessary and useful arts of reading and writing' (1775: sig. B2^r).

Indeed, the provision of such education was an integral part of his Plan for the reform of society, as becomes evident in Spence's later political works. In *A Supplement to the History of Robinson Crusoe*, Spence describes how the people of Lilliput, having been given the benefit of a phonetic alphabet (the *Crusonean* being one of Spence's names for his orthography), find it very easy to learn to read, with revolutionary consequences: 'As they could now learn as much in a Month, as formerly in a Year, the very poorest soon acquired such Notions of Justice, and Equity, and of the Rights of Mankind, as rendered unsupportable, every species of Oppression' (1782*a*: 40, quoted in Shields 1974: 44).

In Spence's view, the education of the lower classes was the key to the reform of society and the New Alphabet was the key to the education of the lower classes.[6] As well as facilitating literacy, Spence probably intended the *Grand Repository* as a guide to 'correct' pronunciation. In *The Giant Killer, or Anti-Landlord* (No. 1 (6 Aug. 1814)), the importance of attaining a

---

[6] Spence's opinion may seem naïve, but there are still those who would agree with him: a letter to *The Guardian* on 21 July 1987 puts the question 'what would be the effects on the distribution of power and influence brought about by large numbers of people suddenly becoming literate?' The correspondent, an Adult Literacy tutor, goes on to suggest that 'lots of practice is needed to learn to read and write, and the Establishment controls the subject matter for this'.

'correct' pronunciation, or, at least, avoiding a 'vulgar' one, is hinted at. 'Why should People be laughed at all their lives for betraying their vulgar education, when the Evil is so easily remedied. How ridiculous it is to hear People that can read saying *Any Think—A Horange—Idear—Noar.*' However, to Spence, the acquisition of such a pronunciation was not the only (or even the principal) purpose of his *Grand Repository* and subsequent works in phonetic spelling: he saw it rather as an essential means to the end of opening up education and opportunities for advancement to the lower classes, so that his radical Plan for the reform of society could be achieved. The two reforms, of spelling and of society, had always run parallel in Spence's thinking.

1.2.2. *Eighteenth-century attitudes to 'correct' pronunciation*

Spence's *Grand Repository* was published at a time when interest in fixing a standard for English pronunciation was reaching its height. As Holmberg (1964: 20) points out, 'it is in the eighteenth century that the snob value of a good pronunciation began to be recognised'. The recognition to which Holmberg refers here was part and parcel of what Leonard (1929) calls 'The Doctrine of Correctness': that Augustan emphasis on propriety and politeness which led to the outright condemnation of non-standard usage in all areas of language, and to a huge demand, particularly from the rising middle classes, for explicit and prescriptive guides to correct usage, guides which would help them to avoid betraying their 'vulgar' origins. With regard to pronunciation, this demand was largely met, especially in the latter part of the century, by the publication of numerous pronouncing dictionaries, each giving some indication, by the use of diacritics and/or phonetic or semi-phonetic respelling, of the 'correct' pronunciation of every single word. Social and political factors such as the beginning of the Industrial Revolution in the larger provincial towns and cities; the improvements in communications brought about by, for example, the introduction of the Turnpike trusts in the 1750s; and the Act of Union of 1707; all led to a greater awareness on the part of the middle classes in areas distant from London that their language was doubly damned for being 'provincial' as well as 'vulgar'.

It was by this time generally understood that the pronunciation which should act as a model for such guides was that of genteel society in London: the 'vulgar' (i.e. lower-class urban) and the 'provincial' alike were almost universally condemned. However, some of the earliest and most influential of these guides to 'correct' pronunciation were written by 'provincials', such as James Buchanan, who produced the *Linguae Britannicae Vera Pronunciatio* (1757), and Thomas Sheridan, author of the *General Dictionary of the English Language* (1780). As Crowley (1991: 73) points out: 'Sheridan was Irish, Buchanan was a Scot; it is no small irony that it is from the edges of the dominant culture that these two prominent elocution masters arrive with their prescriptions for "proper English".'

Both Sheridan and Buchanan were aware that their own countrymen were particularly in need of guidance in the matter of 'correct' pronunciation: Sheridan prefaced his dictionary with a set of 'Rules to be observed by the Natives of Ireland, in order to attain a just Pronunciation of English', whilst in the preface to the *Linguae Britannicae Vera Pronunciatio* Buchanan (1757: p. xv) states that 'the people of North Britain seem, in general, to be almost at as great a loss for proper accent and just pronunciation as foreigners', but he promises that, after studying his work, 'they may in a short time pronounce as properly and intelligibly as if they had been born and bred in London'.

Such altruistic concern for their fellow-countrymen earned little credit for these lexicographers: both were castigated for daring to presume that they could teach the English how to pronounce their own language. Sheridan had the dubious honour of being held up to ridicule by no less a man than Dr Johnson, who said: 'What entitles Sheridan to fix the pronunciation of English? He has in the first place the disadvantage of being an Irishman' (Boswell 1934: ii 161). Sheridan was able to survive such criticism because of his established reputation as a teacher of elocution. Buchanan, however, enjoyed no such cushioning from the attacks of the English: Sheldon (1947) points out that he was condemned in the *Monthly Review* (18 (1757), 82) because, being a Scot, he did not 'seem a competent judge of English pronunciation', and William Kenrick, in the preface to his *New Dictionary of the English Language* (1773: p. i), without mentioning names at this point, states that 'there seems indeed a most ridiculous absurdity in the pretensions of a native of Aberdeen or Tipperary to teach the natives of London to speak and read'. On the other hand, it was the duty of a well-bred Londoner to teach provincials the correct pronunciation, as can be seen in the announcement on the title page of John Walker's *Critical Pronouncing Dictionary* that it included 'Rules to be observed by the Natives of Scotland, Ireland and London, for avoiding their respective Peculiarities'. It is worth noting here that Walker saw 'the peculiarities of (his) countrymen, the Cockneys' as particularly reprehensible, because they, being 'the models of pronunciation to the distant provinces, ought to be the more scrupulously correct' (1791: p. xii). (See §3.3 for an evaluation of these pronouncing dictionaries.)

1.2.3. *Reactions to* The Grand Repository of the English Language

How does Spence fit into this picture? Although his *Grand Repository* never excited the attention given to Sheridan or even Buchanan, he was a provincial writer publishing in the most northerly city of England, and speaking a dialect which to the Londoner would probably be indistinguishable from Scots. The stigma of 'provincialism' must have been keenly felt in what was in the later eighteenth century becoming an increasingly important and wealthy city.[7] Although the *Grand Repository* attracted little or no attention in the press, there is anecdotal evidence that Spence himself encountered, and answered, the same kind of criticism as that extended to Buchanan and Sheridan. Welford (1895: 432–3) relates the following story:

When soliciting subscriptions to this curious work (*The Grand Repository*) he called upon the Rev. H. Moises, master of the Grammar-School, morning lecturer of All Saints' Church, for the purpose of requesting him to become a subscriber to the work. As Mr. Spence had a strong Northern accent, Mr. Moises enquired what opportunities he had had of acquiring a just knowledge of the pronunciation of the English Language. 'Pardon me,' said Spence, 'I attend All Saints' Church every Sunday Morning!'

Place's unfinished and unpublished biography of Spence, which survives in BL Add. MS 27,808, includes several letters from persons acquainted with Spence. The following extract is redolent of the kind of criticism more publicly aimed at Buchanan:

During the whole of his life, he was zealously engaged in propagating his plan of parochial partnership in land. He also published some works in what he termed the Spensonian dialect, being an attempt to render the orthography of the English Language identical with its pronunciation, like the Italian. This orthography was somewhat defective, as he spelled the words according to the Northumbrian idiom, Newcastle on Tyne being his birthplace.   (BL Add. MS 27,808, fo. 227)

1.2.4. *Conclusion*

Whether or not Spence 'spelled the words according to the Northumbrian idiom', we shall see in Chapter 5. Spence, like Buchanan before him and Sheridan after him, was concerned with 'correct' pronunciation, for the full title of his dictionary is *The Grand Repository of the English Language: containing, besides the excellencies of all other dictionaries and grammars of the English tongue, the peculiarity of having the most proper and agreeable pronunciation.* It would, however, be a mistake to think of the *Grand Repository* as just another book designed to help the middle classes in Newcastle to avoid the twin hazards of vulgarity and provincialism. The *Grand Repository* is in some ways in tune with the spirit of its age, but in other ways completely discordant. Whilst other pronouncing dictionaries, like the grammars cited by Leonard (1929), were intended to assist the middle classes and *nouveaux riches* in acquiring linguistic gentility, Spence's

---

[7] Horsley (1971: 220) writes that Newcastle in the eighteenth century 'was . . . a thriving manufacturing town and port, whose population rose during the century from 18,000 to 28,000, with a corresponding increase in revenue from £8,056 1*s.* 1$\frac{1}{4}d.$ to £25,699 0*s.* 10$\frac{1}{2}d$'.

was intended for the education of the lower classes, as the first step in a plan for spelling reform as well as a guide to pronunciation. Just as Spence's Plan was for a Radical reform of society, his *Grand Repository* was intended as part of a 'radical' reform of English orthography.

We shall examine the *Grand Repository* in more detail in Chapters 4 and 5. The question which I would like to pose here is: how is it that such a radical and innovative work as the *Grand Repository* has largely escaped the attentions of historical phonologists, despite Abercrombie's identification of Spence as a 'forgotten phonetician' worthy of serious attention? The answer lies partly in the inaccessibility of the text prior to the production of Alston's microfiche collection *English Linguistics 1500–1800*.[8] However, the scholarly neglect of Spence as a source of information on eighteenth-century pronunciation is part of a wider pattern. I intend to demonstrate in the next chapter that the eighteenth century, and most of all the *phonology* of eighteenth-century English, has been paid so little attention by scholars, at least until relatively recently, that this period can justifiably be termed the 'Cinderella' of English historical linguistics.

---

[8] It is perhaps significant that the only scholar to attempt a detailed study of the *Grand Repository*, Anthea Fraser Shields (now Gupta), was at the time (1972–3) based in Newcastle and so had access to the copy in Newcastle Central Library.

2. Eighteenth-Century English: The 'Cinderella' of English Historical Linguistics?

2.1. INTRODUCTION

The scholarly neglect of the Later Modern English (LNE) period has led Charles Jones (1989: 279) to describe the eighteenth and nineteenth centuries as 'the Cinderellas of English historical linguistic study'. A glance at the available textbooks for undergraduate courses alone would appear to confirm Jones's judgement: Görlach (1988: 211) refers to the study of Early Modern English variation as 'the Cinderella of English historical linguistics' and notes 'the neglect of the Early Modern English period', but his own (1991) textbook, along with other useful works such as Ronberg (1992), have done much to remedy the situation. Where LNE is concerned, no such general textbook exists: Partridge (1969) pays much more attention to the Tudor than to the Augustan English of his title and, whilst Richard Bailey (1996) has provided a long-needed guide to the English of the nineteenth century, there is, at the time of writing, still not a single textbook suitable for an undergraduate course on eighteenth-century English.

With the notable, and very recent, exception of Richard Bailey (1996), such works as have been devoted to the LNE period, and the eighteenth century in particular, tend to deal with single issues or specific areas of linguistic study. Thus there has been ample coverage of what Leonard in his eponymous (1929) work termed 'the doctrine of correctness', and of linguistic ideas in the eighteenth century, in Aarsleff (1983), Cohen (1977), and Crowley (1991), whilst eighteenth-century grammars are surveyed in detail in Michael (1970). Eighteenth-century lexical and semantic change have been dealt with by Susie Tucker (1967, 1972); whilst the lexicography at least of the first half of the century has its 'classic' work in Starnes and Noyes (1991, 1st edn., 1946). The notable omission here is of any work devoted to the phonology of eighteenth-century English, for it is in this area that the neglect of the eighteenth century by historical linguists has been greatest. This neglect is also apparent in general histories of English and in histories of English phonology. Where interest is shown in the eighteenth century, phonology is neglected, and where interest is shown in the history of English phonology, the eighteenth century is neglected. The only exceptions to this rule, apart from a small minority of general histories of English and of English phonology, are a number of monographs on eighteenth-century orthoepists and works devoted to the standardization of pronunciation, notably Holmberg (1964) and Mugglestone (1995).

2.2. GENERAL HISTORIES OF ENGLISH

Since the late nineteenth century, numerous histories of the English language have been published in Britain, the USA, and continental Europe. Given this time span and this geographical range, we can expect to find a diversity of theoretical approaches and viewpoints, from the neogrammarian approach of the late-nineteenth and early twentieth centuries; through the mid-twentieth century with the dominance of structuralist and transforma-tional-generative theories; to the later twentieth century, when some histories take a more socio-historical approach. The theoretical stance taken by an author can affect his or her attitude to the eighteenth century as a period worthy of study or otherwise. Generally speaking, the more important systematic and regular rule changes are to a theory, the less attention is paid to the eighteenth century by those who espouse it. For instance, compared to the Early Modern period, with its fine example of a chain shift, this later century has little to excite the interest of a structuralist, but scholars who take a socio-historical viewpoint or who work in the field of lexical phonology are ready to find order in the apparent chaos of eighteenth-century sound changes. The time span of these histories is also significant in itself: as Charles Jones (1989: 279) points out: 'There has always been a suggestion . . . especially among those scholars writing in the first half of the twentieth century, that phonological and syntactic change is only properly observable at a great distance and that somehow the eighteenth, and especially the nineteenth centuries, are "too close" chronologically for any meaningful observations concerning language change to be made.'

Thus, with the notable exceptions of Wyld (1927, 1936) and McKnight (1928), early histories of English, such as Lounsbury (1894), pay very little attention to the eighteenth century, and even less to the nineteenth, which, for Lounsbury, of course, was the present day! As the twenty-first century draws near, there is the sense of a 'respectable' distance between us and the eighteenth century and, indeed, scholars writing after about 1970 tend to say something about LNE even if, as in Freeborn (1992), it is confined to a discussion of prescriptivism and standardization. Geographical differences between the histories of English reviewed here are also apparent in that those written in the USA such as Pyles and Algeo (1982) and Peters (1968) understandably see the eighteenth century as the beginning of American English, and so pay little attention to developments in British English in this period. This is not to say that the American works have nothing of interest for us: rather, eighteenth-century developments are noted in so far as they contribute to the differentiation of British and American English. Thus, Pyles and Algeo (1982: 226), mention one of the sound changes which will be discussed in Chapter 5, but from an American point of view: 'What strikes most American ears most strongly is the modern standard British shift of an older [æ], which survives in American English except before *r* (as in *far*), *lm* (as in *calm*) and in *father*, to [ɑ] in a number of very frequently used words. Up to the very end of the eighteenth century, [ɑ] in such words was considered vulgar.' As we shall see in §5.2, the last sentence here over-simplifies a very complex issue, but at least the sociolinguistic significance of this sound change is recognized.

The vast majority of general histories of English include a statement to the effect that all the 'major' or 'grammatical' changes in the English Language were completed by 1700. For example, Freeborn (1992: 180) writes that 'the linguistic changes that have taken place from the eighteenth century to the present day are relatively few' and Bloomfield and Newmark (1963: 293) likewise assert that, 'after the period of the Great Vowel Shift was over, the changes that were to take place in English phonology were few indeed'. In all these cases, the neglect of the eighteenth century is presented as excusable, because there is simply nothing of interest happening in this period. As I suggested in §2.1, this opinion is expressed particularly by those who toe the structuralist (Nist 1966; Stevick 1968) or transformational–generative (Bloomfield and Newmark 1963) line. Nist's small section on eighteenth-century phonology is headed 'phonemic stabilization', Stevick is primarily interested in changes in the phonemic inventory of English, whilst Bloom-field & Newmark (1963: 288) dismiss changes in the language between the eighteenth century and the present day as 'due to matters of style and rhetoric . . . rather than to differences in phonology, grammar or vocabulary' and go on to state, rather dogmatically, that 'historical or diachronic linguistics, as such, is traditionally less concerned with such stylistic and rhetorical changes of fashion than with phonological, grammatical and lexical changes'.

Other general histories of English are less dismissive of the eighteenth century as a period of potential interest, but deal with it in terms of the single issue of 'correctness'. A telling example here is Bourcier (1981), in which the eighteenth century is dispensed with in five pages (204–8) on 'Post-Restoration social and intellectual attitudes' in which the words highlighted here tell the whole story: '*order and discipline . . . codification . . . a regulatory body . . . prescriptive grammar*'. The same point is made by Bryant (1962: 89–90): 'As progress was made towards a uniform standard in the English language, freedom decreased. Rules began to be formulated, efforts began to be made to fix the language, to determine what was right and what was wrong, to prescribe the goal to be attained. This attitude reached its height in the eighteenth century, the age in which reason and logic were uppermost.' This is, of course, a valid and important point, but it is not the only point of interest with regard to the eighteenth century. The handful of general histories which deal adequately with the eighteenth century acknowledge this and also share a recognition that a lack of large-scale structural changes such as the Great Vowel Shift does not mean that there were no changes of interest in the eighteenth century, merely that they were of a different nature. Thus Barber makes a statement rather like those quoted above, to the effect that 'by about 1700, the main changes in pronunciation that made up the Great Vowel Shift were all completed' (1993: 199), and then goes on to state that, apart from the coalescence of ME /eː/ and /ɛː/ 'there have been no really major changes in pronunciation since 1700, though there have been a number of minor ones' (1993: 210). However, Barber proceeds to give a fair, if somewhat over-simplified, summary of the sound changes which were occurring in the eighteenth century, recognizing, for instance, the loss of preconsonantal and word-final /r/ as the most important 'minor' change.

A few general histories of English go further than this, recognizing that the linguistic changes of the eighteenth century are not 'minor', but of a different and much more complex nature than those of preceding centuries. This point is made most forcefully by Strang (1970: 78–9):

Some short histories of English give the impression that changes in pronunciation stopped dead in the 18c, a development which would be quite inexplicable for a language in everyday use. It is true that the sweeping systematic changes we can detect in earlier periods are missing, but the amount of change is no less. Rather, its location has changed: in the past two hundred years changes in pronunciation are predominantly due, not, as in the past, to evolution of the system, but to what, in a very broad sense, we may call the interplay of different varieties, and to the complex analogical relationship between different parts of the language.

Strang appears here to be putting forward an argument which seems to contradict the basic tenet of neogrammarian (and later) theory now known as the 'uniformitarian principle'. She suggests that sound changes in LNE are of a different nature from those of earlier periods, a view that we shall see in §2.3. would be contested by Charles Jones (1989). What is significant, though, is that Strang recognizes that it is the sheer complexity and apparent irregularity of eighteenth-century sound changes that make this period so interesting. The same point is made, albeit less explicitly, by McKnight (1928: 458): 'The subject of eighteenth-century pronunciation is one of vast complexity of which the few details here given can give no perfect concep-tion. Many new influences were at work.' Schlauch (1959: 131), too, recognizes, for instance, that 'the group represented by ME *a* lengthened and modified in quality before special consonants and groups of consonants has a complicated history'. As we shall see in §5.2., this is, if anything, an understatement.

Wyld is perhaps the first historian of English to point out that this period has received little scholarly attention. He writes of the eighteenth and nineteenth centuries: 'This period offers ample scope for investigation. It is no exaggeration to say that a proper history of each of these centuries has yet to be written' (1936: 186). Wyld has recently been condemned by, for example, Richard Bailey (1996: 90) as 'a fierce language snob' who laid too much emphasis on the importance of RP, but he did recognize the part played by social influences in eighteenth-century sound change, and when we examine his works carefully we can even see precursors of Labovian terminology. For instance, Wyld (1927: 152) states, with reference to certain changes in LNE pronunciation, 'there is no doubt that all these alterations in the older Received Standard came originally *from below*, and represent attempts at greater correctness.' (emphasis added). Although Wyld here is actually referring to what Labov (1972: 123) would call 'change from above'—that is, above the level of consciousness—both Wyld's recognition of the role of the middle classes in linguistic change and the idea of 'change from below' have, with the benefit of hindsight, a very 'Labovian' ring to them[1]. A few other general histories likewise recognize the importance of social factors in linguistic change during the LNE period. Thus Strang (1970: 85) writes of the lengthening of ME /o/ before /r/: 'As usual, before 1800 social consciousness is at work in the distribution of the forms, and in 1791[2] the long vowel before /r/ is declared vulgar. Also, as usual, it persisted not only among the vulgar, but also among the most assured.' McKnight (1928: 453), too, notes social class as an important factor in the complex distribution of 'narrow' [æː] versus 'broad' [ɑː] pronunciations of ME /a/ in the eighteenth century:

The situation in the eighteenth century with relation to these two sounds seems to have been unsettled. . . . There was dialectal difference. There was also a difference corresponding with difference in social class. The differing judgements of Kenrick and Bayley should be recalled. The broad sound is often associated with the 'rustical'. The narrow or fronted sound, on the other hand, is referred to as 'mincing' and is often regarded as affected.

(See §5.2 for further discussion of this variation.)

Wyld (1927: 173) also seems to foreshadow recent theories of sound change in his recognition of the gradual nature of eighteenth-century sound change and of what we now call lexical diffusion: 'Our present pronunciation

---

[1] This, of course, with benefit of hindsight. It might be fairer to say that Labov's works have a rather Wyldian ring to them!

[2] Strang presumably refers here to Walker's *Critical Pronouncing Dictionary* (1791), but, rather annoyingly, she does not specify this.

[of ME /ɛː/ words] is the result of the gradual abandonment of one type, and the adoption, universally, of another. The process involved one word after another, and went on slowly during the seventeenth, more quickly in the following century.'

Wyld, McKnight, Schlauch, and Strang all recognize that the eighteenth century is an important period in the history of English because the overtness of the censure of stigmatized forms in works like John Walker's *Critical Pronouncing Dictionary* (1791) gives us a window on the socio-linguistic forces influencing sound change at this time and because the very complexity of these changes is a challenge to the historical linguist. With hindsight, we can see the operation of social and lexical diffusion through their accounts of eighteenth-century sound change. Between them, these scholars also make use of a wide range of evidence to discuss a number of eighteenth-century sound changes. Obviously, this varies with the avail-ability of evidence at the time of writing: none of these authors had the easy access which we now enjoy thanks to Alston's microfiche editions. Schlauch, writing in Warsaw in 1954, relies mainly on 'indirect' evidence and, as far as direct evidence goes, seems to have had access only to the works of the Scottish orthoepist and grammarian James Buchanan and that not directly but through Meyer (1940). However, she gives a substantial amount of information on eighteenth-century sound changes despite these shortcom-ings. Strang appears to have used a number of secondary sources, notably Wyld (1936) and Jespersen (1909–49), both of which, as we shall see, make use of a wide range of direct evidence. She therefore provides a reasonable amount of detail on a number of eighteenth-century sound changes, but cites dates without giving the direct sources to which those dates refer. For example, she writes of the variation in this period between a long and a short vowel in words such as *leisure, pleasure, treasure* 'of two commentators writing almost simultaneously one, in 1787, describes the long vowel as "affected", the other, in 1791, prefers it' (Strang 1970: 84) The dates presumably refer to James Elphinston's *Propriety Ascertained in her Picture* and John Walker's *Critical Pronouncing Dictionary*, but the reader is not informed of this. Wyld (1927, 1936) and McKnight (1928), on the other hand, make extensive reference to a wide range of direct evidence from the eighteenth century. These works have their flaws: Wyld's remarks on earlier orthoepists like Gil would be actionable if made about a living person, and he takes too literally Walker's account of the vowel in *put, bull,* etc., suggesting that the rounded vowel was 'restored when there is an initial lip-consonant' (1927: 185), whereas, as we shall see in §5.4, the reverse process probably occurred. McKnight likewise makes mistakes, citing, for instance, the 'well known rimes of the Scotch Marjorie Fleming' as evidence for 'the Northern English pronunciation of *a*' (1929: 455–6) not realising, presumably, that evidence from Scots might point to the operation of the

Scottish Vowel Length Rule rather than the general northern lack of lengthening. However, despite these flaws, the works of Wyld and McKnight provide a wealth of information from the direct evidence of the eighteenth century. Now that this evidence is more readily available, these early scholars at least point their modern counterparts in the right direction. McKnight refers to sources not mentioned in the other general works: particularly interesting from the point of view of this study is his citation of G. Wright's (1774) grammar, written in Sunderland. Wyld's wide trawl of orthoepistic sources likewise nets some treasures: note, for instance, his observation of an early instance of one of the features typifying what is now known as 'Estuary English', i.e 'fronting' of /θ/ to /f/: 'Elphinston (1787) speaks of a tendency of the "low English" to say *Redriph* for *Rotherhithe* and *loph* for *loath* . . . At the present time this substitution appears to be rather a personal idiosyncrasy than a dialect feature, though it does appear to be very frequent in a rather low type of Cockney English' (Wyld 1927: 209). When the history of twentieth-century English is written, this will be a valuable piece of evidence for 'change from below'.

This review of the general histories of English has shown us that, the more a scholar is willing to recognize the importance of socio-historical factors in linguistic change and the existence of gradual (in the sense of 'socially and lexically diffusing') changes as opposed to the apparently more systematic sound laws and changes of phonemic inventories beloved of the neogrammarians and structuralists, the more he or she will see the eighteenth century as an important and intriguing period for study. The most useful of these texts for the modern scholar are those which use a wide range of direct and indirect sources to present the true complexity of this era. We shall now go on to review the histories of English phonology according to the same criteria.

2.3. HISTORIES OF ENGLISH PHONOLOGY

In this section, I include works such as Sweet (1888) and Horn and Lehnert (1954), which deal chronologically with the sound changes that have occurred in English, and also more theoretical works such as Chomsky and Halle (1968), Anderson and Jones (1977), and Charles Jones (1989), which are primarily concerned with phonological theory, but use some of the major sound changes of English, including Modern English, to illustrate and/or test out their theories.

If we look first at the more 'philological' histories of English sounds, we find that most of these, unlike the general histories above, pay some attention to eighteenth-century sound change, with the exception, of course, of works like Dobson (1957), which does not pretend to cover the whole history of English. Apart from such works, which advertise themselves as stopping before or at 1700, the only work reviewed here which provides hardly any information on eighteenth-century sound changes is Moore (1960). This devotes only ten out of 176 pages to the development of modern English sounds, and, like some of the American works reviewed in §2.2, deals with this period in terms of American rather than British English. Thus at the end of the section on 'special developments before r', Moore (1960: 137) notes:

These special developments of vowels before **r** have been stated in terms of their results in the speech of those who pronounce a retroflex **r** before consonants as well as before vowels . . . In the speech of those who do not pronounce **r** when it is followed by a consonant, the same vowels have developed except that [ɝ] is replaced in some varieties of English by [ɜ], and that there is a tendency to the development of a glide [ə] sound after the vowel, or to compensatory lengthening, resulting in [ɑə], [ɑː], [ɛə], etc.

As we shall see in §§5.2 and 5.8, this is a gross oversimplification of the very complex intertwined history of 'compensatory lengthening' and loss of rhoticity in British English.

The other works of this nature vary in their usefulness according to the extent to which they make use of the wide range of direct and indirect evidence to be discussed in Chapter 3. The earliest authors, notably Ellis (1869) and Sweet (1888), did not have access to the range of direct evidence that is available today. Jespersen (1909–49: 13) points out that, whilst Ellis's work 'is highly meritorious both for the vast quantity of material collected for the first time and for its discussion of an enormous variety of questions from a phonetic as well as a historical point of view . . . his extracts are not always reliable'. Sweet (1888) is not only highly reliant on Ellis, but uses as his 'phonetic authorities' for what he terms the 'third modern period' (1700–1800) a small and eclectic set of works: *The Expert Orthographist* (1704); *A Short and Easy Way for the Palatines to Learn English* (1710); Thomas Dyche's *Guide to the English Tongue* (1710); Thomas Lediard's *Grammatica Anglicana Critica, oder Versuch zu einer vollkommenen Grammatic der Englischen Sprache* (1725); James Buchanan's *Essay Towards Establishing a Standard* (1766); Benjamin Franklin's *Scheme for a New Alphabet* (1768); and Thomas Sheridan's *General Dictionary of the English Language* (1780). Of the last three, Sweet is slightly dismissive; thus of Buchanan he writes: 'the author was a Scotchman, and there are Scotticisms in his pronunciation'; of Franklin 'the pronunciation here given is, of course, affected by American provincialisms'. Sheridan fares slightly better: 'the author was an Irishman, but familiar with the standard pronunciation' (Sweet 1888: 207). The patchy nature of Sweet's evidence naturally leads to shortcomings in his account of sound changes in the 'third modern period'. For example, on the lengthening of ME /a/ before voiceless fricatives, Sweet gives a full account of the very useful evidence from Christopher Cooper's *Grammatica Linguæ Anglicanæ* (1685)[3], but has nothing to say about the very complex variation between /a/ and /ɑː/ throughout the later eighteenth and at least the early nineteenth centuries. This is, of course, because his only evidence for the later eighteenth century comes from Sheridan, who, as we shall see in §5.2., does not recognize a separate 'long' sound in, for example, *father*, giving the stressed vowel in this word the same notation as that in *hat*.

Perhaps the most useful and reliable of these early works is the first volume of Jespersen's *Modern English Grammar* (1909–49). After his criticism of Ellis, Jespersen (1909–49: 14) writes: 'I have as a rule left Ellis's word-lists alone and have trusted chiefly to my own copies or extracts from the phoneticians and grammarians themselves.' He includes in his list of 'authorities' from the eighteenth century several not used by Ellis: William Johnston's *Pronouncing and Spelling Dictionary* (1764); Elphinston's *Principles of English Grammar* (1765) and *Propriety Ascertained in her Picture* (1787); and Robert Nares's *Elements of Orthoepy* (1784). He also includes Walker's (1775) rhyming dictionary and (1791) *Critical Pronouncing Dictionary*, which were inexplicably omitted from Sweet's list. As Jespersen points out, the 'most valuable authors' for the eighteenth century are 'Jones, Elphinston, Nares and Walker': from this list all but Jones, whose *Practical Phonography* (1701) was included in the list of authorities for the 'second modern period', were ignored by Sweet. As we might expect from his more extensive list of sources, Jespersen's coverage of eighteenth-century sound changes is more thorough than those of his predecessors. He has a substantial chapter (pp. 355–87) entitled 'Eighteenth-Century Changes', dealing mainly with consonantal changes and the vowel changes associated with loss of rhoticity, but he also deals with the continuation into the eighteenth century of seventeenth-century vowel changes in the chapter with that title, and includes evidence from Nares and Elphinston in his chapter X on 'Loss of Consonants and Rise of (aˑ, ɔˑ).[4] Jespersen devotes thirteen pages (pp. 297–310) to the rise of /ɑː/ alone, including a wide range of sources from the seventeenth to the nineteenth centuries. In the chapter on eighteenth-century changes *per se* he includes many interesting points of detail from his 'authorities'. An example of this is his section 13.16, in which he writes: 'Some words may be added here about the distribution of [n] and [ŋ] before [g] and [k]. E 1765 gives the general rule that [n] not [ŋ] is to be spoken in the "prepositives" *in* and *con*; but W 1791 has *con* with [ŋ] when stressed, as in *congress, congregate, concourse,* [n] when not stressed, as in

---

[3] These passages are less useful in an age when a classical education is the exception rather than the rule, as Sweet leaves them untranslated in Latin. Angry marginilia in the library copy which I consulted testify to this.

[4] Jespersen uses what appears to be a half length mark to represent a long vowel. I shall use Jespersen's notation in actual quotes from his work, but elsewhere I shall use IPA notation. Thus, my /ɑː/ is equivalent to Jespersen's [aˑ].

congratulate, congressive, concur' (Jesperson 1909–49: 357). Such fine detail as this will prove invaluable, both in pointing towards the sound changes that should be investigated in Chapter 5 and in providing material for comparison with the evidence from Spence.

One of the most detailed surveys of the history of English sounds to include the later modern period is Horn and Lehnert (1954). They include in their sources of evidence the better-known pronouncing dictionaries of the eighteenth century and make the interesting observation that these had been, until recently, a peculiarly English phenomenon. They also make good use of the testimony of 'foreign' grammars and guides to pronunciation, noting, for instance (1954: 343), the remark of Georg Christoph Lichtenberg, who lived in England in 1770 and 1774–5, that 'zierlichen Mädchen' (dainty young ladies) pronounced the ⟨a⟩ in *nasty* so high that it sounded almost like *nehstï* and his comment that this was in order to avoid the 'vulgar' [ɑː]. Such insights add to the picture of the sociolinguistic complexity of variation between 'long' and 'short' reflexes of ME /a/ in the later eighteenth century.

The histories of English sound changes which remain to be reviewed are somewhat less useful because they are less comprehensive. Ekwall (1975), consults an impressive list of eighteenth-century authorities, but his account of English sound changes is brief. Nevertheless, this work would be useful as a first port of call for a scholar with an interest in eighteenth-century sound changes, for he does at least point towards the more important developments. For example, on what we have already seen to be a highly complex matter, the lengthening of ME /a/, he first writes: 'A long vowel is certainly recorded in all positions . . . in the 18th century', but goes on to qualify this rather bald statement, by admitting to variation between /æ/ and /ɑː/ in the RP of his own day, and to write: 'This variation is an old one. 18th century orthoepists (such as Perry 1776, Scott 1788, Walker 1791) frequently give [æ] in words of this kind. This [æ] may be to [ɑː] as Pres. E. [ɔ] is to [ɔː] in words like *cross, lost*. [æ] may in part be explained as a reaction against the new pronunciation' (Ekwall 1975: 26). There is not a great deal of detail here, but there is enough to alert us to the interesting complexity of this sound change, and also its possible parallelism with that of lengthened ME /o/.

Prins (1972) likewise covers the whole of the Modern English period and outlines all the important sound changes, but evidence from the eighteenth century is scanty and often relegated to footnotes. An example of this is Prins's section on the change of ME /iu/ to present-day English (PDE) [juː]:

The pronunciation [juː] began to develop in the late 16th c. and was getting fairly common after 1640, though as late as Cooper (1685) *iu* was still preferred in careful speech (Dobson II, 187). The intervening stages are not clear, for the *i* may have fronted *uː* to *üː*: . . . *juː* after consonants in many cases became *uː*. Thus *dūk, tūzdi* were fashionable at one time, though now vulgar and AmE.[2] *juː* is now commonly retained initially after consonants, except after *r, ʃ, tʃ, dʒ* and consonants + *l*. After *l* usage still fluctuates: *luːt, ljuːt* 'lute'.

Note 2. Scott's *Pronouncing Dictionary* (1768) gives *duk, sut*.

Formerly, *j* was still pronounced after *r* and consonant + *l*, e.g. *rjūd, bljū, fljū*, but this is now old-fashioned or provincial.

Note 3. Ledyard (1725) gives evidence of the loss of *j* after consonants like *r, ʃ, tʃ, dʒ*, but also after *d, l, n, r, s, t*, e.g. *steward, lewd, new, suit*.

There is less detail here than in Jespersen (1909–49), but enough to alert the reader that this sound change is worthy of further investigation, as we shall see in §5.6.

If we move on to the more theoretically oriented works, we find here, as in the works of a similar orientation discussed in §2.2, that the 'messy' eighteenth century is sometimes overlooked. Chomsky and Halle (1968) is in no sense a historical phonology of English, but demands a mention here because of its importance as a seminal text for generative phonology. It includes a chapter on 'the evolution of the Modern English vowel system', in which the authors' stated purpose is 'to trace the evolution of the pivotal rules of the modern English Vowel system . . . and to provide some explanation for the remarkable stability of the underlying system of representations' (Chomsky and Halle 1968: 249). They have made no attempt to be exhaustive in their coverage of the 'authorities' on early and later Modern English, but have taken the accounts of just four orthoepists: Hart, Wallis, Cooper, and Batchelor. The explanation for this choice is as follows:

They illustrate the main steps in the evolution. They do not, of course, constitute a single line of descent from the earliest to the latest, nor is any of them necessarily the lineal ancestor of the dialect of modern English that is described in the main part of this book. The dialects are, however, sufficiently closely related so as to provide us with a reasonably clear picture of the main lines of development. (Chomsky and Halle 1968: 249)

This highly selective approach to evidence is excusable within the theory of generative phonology: since it is grammars that change, not sounds, and since that change is held to take place in a discontinuous manner by the reconstruction of a 'new' grammar by each child, there is no need for exhaustive coverage, and any reasonably reliable orthoepist can represent a 'grammar' of his time. However, in jumping from Cooper (1687) to Batchelor (1809), Chomsky and Halle ignore the eighteenth century, with all its messy variation. Thus they do not even see ME /ɛː/ as a problem, for the evidence of variation between /iː/ and /eː/ pronunciations in the Early Modern English (EME) reflexes simply does not arise.

Anderson and Jones (1977) likewise are primarily interested in establishing a theory of phonology, in this case dependency phonology, and so discuss a number of large-scale processes from various periods of English, for they are 'primarily interested in what an attempt to characterize the processes tells us about the nature of phonological structure' (1977: p. v). However, they do pay more regard to empirical evidence than Chomsky and Halle, and so, for instance, in accounting for the distribution of /ʊ/ versus /ʌ/ in PDE conclude, in contradiction to Chomsky and Halle, that 'a distinct process of centralization is involved' (Anderson and Jones 1977: 85).

Having developed the theory of dependency phonology, Charles Jones (1989) puts it to work on a more comprehensive history of English phonology. The title of this chapter is taken from Jones (1989), who fully recognizes the 'Cinderella' status of the study of eighteenth-century phonology and takes some noteworthy steps to remedy the situation. Interestingly, Jones contradicts the received view that eighteenth-century sound changes are different in nature from those of earlier periods and attempts 'to show how the eighteenth and nineteenth centuries manifest the same types of phonological processes we have met at earlier historical "moments"' (1989: 281). In this regard, his accounts of the later 're-enactment' of the English Vowel Shift, and of 'compensatory lengthening' of vowels before /r/ after loss of rhoticity, provide the best combination to date of linguistic theory and proper attention to evidence, and will prove most useful for our investigations in Chapter 5.

2.4. MONOGRAPHS AND OTHER WORKS ON EIGHTEENTH-CENTURY PRONUNCIATION

I have already indicated in §2.1. that, whilst eighteenth-century phonology tends to have been paid relatively little scholarly attention, the exceptions to this rule are a number of monographs and articles on eighteenth-century orthoepists and works primarily concerned with the standardization of English pronunciation. These works are perhaps the most important for the purposes of this study, as, in the absence of any comprehensive study of eighteenth-century phonology, they provide vital points of comparison between the pronunciation described in the *Grand Repository* and that of Spence's contemporaries. It would be far too ambitious to attempt in a study like this to compare Spence's recommended pronunciations on a word-by-word basis with those of a large number of other eighteenth-century orthoepists, but the works reviewed in this section provide vital comparative information on the areas of eighteenth-century pronunciation which will be discussed in Chapter 5. Several of the works reviewed here deal with orthoepists who, like Spence, had northern or Scottish origins: information from these sources will be particularly valuable in helping us to determine whether, when Spence's account differs from that of, say, Walker, that divergence can be attributed to 'northern' influences on Spence. In other cases, these sources, northern or otherwise, will help us to see whether Spence is alone in diverging from Walker, or whether there is supporting evidence from his contemporaries.

Before dealing with comparative evidence, though, we should perhaps consider the few scholars who have recognized the importance of Spence's works as evidence for eighteenth-century pronunciation. Abercrombie (1965) was the first to 'discover' Spence as one of his 'forgotten phoneticians' and so deserves priority here. He refuted Emsley's (1942) claim that the first 'phonetic' dictionary of English was that of Dan Smalley (1855), pointing out that the *Grand Repository* was 'a dictionary in which the pronunciation was "parenthesized" . . . in a genuine, scientific, phonetic alphabet with seventeen new letters' (Abercrombie 1965: 68). Abercrombie has little to say about the actual pronunciations represented in the *Grand Repository* other than the following: 'There are, however, traces of Spence's northern origin in some of the pronunciations he gives in his dictionary . . . Most noticeable is the predominance of the vowel he represents by ĭ, or Ŧ in its upper-case form, in unstressed syllables. *Sycophant*, e.g. is rendered sĭkĭfĭnt, *haddock* hădĭk; *swallow* swălĭ' (1965: 73). Whether this use of what appears to be /ɪ/ in unstressed syllables is an indication of 'northern' origin, or of a lack of acuity on Spence's part, has been, as we shall see in §5.7, a matter of some controversy amongst the few scholars to have studied Spence's linguistic works in any detail. We have Abercrombie to thank for the fact that they (or should I say we) were alerted to Spence in the first place. Of course, Spence was not the only 'forgotten phonetician' of the eighteenth century to be discovered by Abercrombie in this article: he also discusses *Magazine* by G. W. (1703); an anonymous work entitled *The Needful Attempt to Make Language and Divinity Plain and Easie* (1711), both works of spelling reform, and Abraham Tucker's *Vocal Sounds* (1773), in which a phonetic script is advocated, not for general use, but for the study of language. The first two of these are interesting exceptions to the generally accepted rule that spelling reform was no longer a 'live' issue in the eighteenth century: Abercrombie (1965: 60) remarks that the authors of these 'are the only spelling reformers I have come across in the first half of the eighteenth century'. If we include Elphinston, even without considering the Americans Franklin and Webster, we begin to see that Spence, whilst certainly in a minority, was not entirely alone in advocating spelling reform in the eighteenth century. It is, however, Abercrombie's section on Abraham Tucker that is the most useful as evidence for eighteenth-century pronunciation. Here we see that Tucker, like Spence, invented a new symbol for /ŋ/, thus recognizing its phonemic status, and that Tucker gives testimony both to breaking before /r/ and weakening or loss of preconsonantal /r/, predating Walker, who is said by

Jespersen (1909–49: 360) to be 'the oldest Englishman to admit the muteness'. Apart from these nuggets of information, Abercrombie is important largely because he alerted scholars to the importance of these hitherto neglected eighteenth-century sources.

   The most thorough studies of Spence's linguistic works so far have been carried out by Anthea Fraser Shields (now Gupta). Her (1974) article 'Thomas Spence and the English Language' is more accessible than her unpublished (1973) dissertation on Spence, and it summarizes her most important findings on the pronunciations represented by Spence in the *Grand Repository* and other works in his alphabets. I shall therefore concentrate on Shields (1974) here, although reference will be made to the more comprehensive Shields (1973) in Chapter 5. In both works, Shields is mainly concerned with what she calls Spence's 'linguistico-political views' (1974: 34) and the changes in Spence's alphabets from the *Grand Repository* to his later works produced in London. She does not attempt a comprehensive study of the pronunciations represented in these works, but does make some important points, not least of which is to refute the suggestion made by Abercrombie and by Spence's contemporaries that his 'northern origin' is evident in these. At times, the lack of any consistent comparison with Spence's contemporaries leaves her slightly wide of the mark: for example, one of the few 'smaller features of Spence's spelling' which she admits 'may represent northern pronunciations' is the use of a vowel equivalent to present-day /uː/ in e.g. *good* and *book* (Shields 1974: 58). What Shields fails to recognize here, and what we shall see in §5.5., is that the long vowel here, especially in words like *book*, was not unequivocally 'northern' in eighteenth-century English: *book* has a long vowel even in Walker (1791). This is a minor criticism of a work that did not set out to make such thorough comparisons, and my correction only strengthens Shields's case against those who assume that the pronunciations represented in Spence's works will be 'northern'. Shields recognizes the complexity of the distribution of variant pronunciations at this time. Her comment on the distribution of [uː] and [juː] variants is particularly perceptive:

There are other areas in which opinion was divided at this period, and although Spence may differ in detail from any one orthoepist, say Sheridan, the distribution of one sound as opposed to another in certain groups of words seems to be, as Jespersen described it (1909 p. 381) 'seemingly without any principle'. This is particularly true of */uː//juː/. For instance, Spence distinguished *rude* ('rud') from *rood* ('rood'): Sheridan has both as 'roᵌd'. If anything, Spence has his 'u'[5] more extensively than any one of the phoneticians listed by Jespersen (p. 381) has its equivalent: Spence has what might be described as the maximal distribution of */juː/. It might be that here we really have to do with the gradual distribution of change through the lexicon

---

[5] By this, Shields means the {U} 'as in *tune*', a symbol which represents [jū].

(Wang 1969): Spence's 'u' is very stable throughout the texts, and distinct from 'oo'/'w': in no more than a few cases can the t.o [traditional orthography] spelling be said to have any influence on his choice.   (Shields 1974: 59)

As we shall see in §5.6, Spence's is not the 'maximal distribution of */ju:/' in the eighteenth century: that honour goes to the Scots orthoepist John Burn, but Shields deserves credit here for pointing out the importance of works like Spence's as evidence for lexical diffusion. From the point of view of the present study, Shields's conclusion is particularly encouraging:

In conclusion, I fail to see that there is anything in Spence's system, or in his spellings, to shock his contemporaries, and little to show his northern origin. Compared to the casual and irregular transcriptions of Franklin, or to the unsatisfactory spelling systems of Johnston or Elphinston, Spence's work is good—consistent, following a definite convention, and apparently fairly reliable, at least phonemically, and some-times even phonetically.   (Shields 1974: 60–1)

Shields's work, then, provides important pointers towards areas of interest, and confirmation that Spence is a 'reliable' phonetician, worthy of study. No other scholar has so far looked at Spence's work in any detail as evidence for eighteenth-century pronunciation. Weinstock (1976), in a review of sources for the then projected 'Dictionary of Early Modern English Pronunciation 1500–1800' (henceforth DEMEP), writes somewhat dismissively of Spence, that 'although he managed to transcribe vocalic phonemes and allophones, and to distinguish voiceless /θ/ . . . from voiced /ð/ . . . he missed to indicate consonantal allophones like clear or dark l̠[6] as well as the various articulations of r̠' (1976: 33). Given, as we shall see in Chapter 4, that Spence's script was essentially phonemic, to criticize him for failing to make such allophonic distinctions, which would not be necessary in an alphabet intended for reformed spelling, seems rather unfair. Neither Sheridan, nor Walker, nor any other eighteenth-century orthoepist that I know of, made such distinctions in their transcriptions, unless we count, for example, Mather Flint's use of r for weakened preconsonantal /r/.

More recent works have tended to at least pay lip-service to Spence without necessarily going into any detailed study of his works. Thus, he is mentioned in Charles Jones (1993, 1995) as a northern parallel to the Scottish orthoepists discussed there, and Mugglestone (1995) sees fit to include the *Grand Repository* in her bibliography, although Spence, unlike Sheridan, fails to merit an inclusion in her index and indeed a specific mention anywhere in this work.

[6] If it had been usual for eighteenth-century orthoepists to make such a distinction in their representations, Spence's failure to show this allophonic distinction might provide evidence of 'northern' influence, for present-day Tyneside and Northumbrian English lacks 'dark' /l/. Clear / l/ appears in e.g. *milk* and an epenthetic [ə] appears in e.g. *film, Alnmouth* between /l/ and a following nasal.

Mugglestone (1995) is, however, important as the most recent of three major works dealing with the issue of standards and standardization of pronunciation in the Modern English period. The earliest of these, and perhaps the most useful of all for our purposes, is Sheldon's (1938) unpublished dissertation on standards of pronunciation in the orthoepists of the sixteenth, seventeenth, and eighteenth centuries. It is very unfortunate that this dissertation is not readily available, containing as it does a wealth of information from a wide range of eighteenth-century sources, including a complete reproduction of *A Vocabulary of Such Words in the English Language as are of Dubious or Unsettled Accentuation* (1797). Despite its inaccessibility, this dissertation has been extremely influential: it was used as a source by Holmberg (1964) and by the authors of several of the monographs discussed below, although not by Mugglestone (1995). Given the resources available at the time (Spence had not yet been 'discovered' for instance), Sheldon (1938) is remarkably thorough, and recognizes the socio-historical significance of pronouncing dictionaries. Commenting on Walker's remarks on the Cockneys, she writes:

As soon as people had the idea that pronunciation could be a social shibboleth as well as a regional one, it was natural that the social aspect should become more important than the geographical. Thus vulgar pronunciation becomes a thousand times more offensive and disgusting than provincial pronunciation. When we consider how, especially after the industrial revolution, social aspirations operate, this is exactly what we should expect to happen. By Walker's time, there is no doubt that this attitude was felt pretty generally.   (Sheldon 1938: 359)

Sheldon's comment's here, like those of Wyld discussed in §2.2., seem to foreshadow the works of modern sociolinguists like Labov. Indeed Mugglestone, writing with the benefit of the insights of Labov and James and Lesley Milroy, makes exactly the same point in her second chapter, entitled 'Images of Accent: Prescription, Pronunciation and the Elegant Speaker' (1995: 58–106). If Sheldon can be criticized, it is because in her dissertation and in her later (1946, 1947) articles on pronouncing dictionaries, she is perhaps responsible for the demonization of Walker as an arch-prescriptivist who was overly influenced by the spelling of words. Her comparison of Sheridan and Walker in her 1947 article is typical. Here, she asserts that, with regard to unstressed vowels, 'Sheridan in general represents these vowels honestly, as they were pronounced in normal speech' whilst 'Walker often enters, for unstressed sounds, pronunciations that do not reflect the actual speech of his time' (Sheldon 1947: 137–8). Her conclusion is 'that while Sheridan reflects the speech of his time better, Walker satisfies the temper of his time better, and its demand for linguistic regulation and reform' (Sheldon 1947: 146). There, is, of course, some truth in this: as we shall see in Chapters 4 and 5, Walker was often guided by 'analogy' to prescribe pronunciations different from those recommended by some of his contemporaries, and he was reluctant to recommend pronunciations which involved the 'loss' of a sound represented in the spelling (see, for instance, the discussion of preconsonantal /r/ in §5.8), but, as we shall see, he could be a very acute observer, and some of the distinctions noticed by him and dismissed by scholars in the earlier part of this century as 'influenced by the spelling' have since been vindicated. This criticism apart, we must hail Sheldon as a pioneer in the field of eighteenth-century phonology: her paper co-authored with Bronstein (Bronstein and Sheldon 1951), in particular, is a small-scale example of exactly the sort of study which will be undertaken in Chapter 5: a close comparison of the reflexes of ME /oː/ in the relevant entries from a number of eighteenth- and nineteenth-century pronouncing dictionaries.

Holmberg (1964) is the first published work specifically devoted to standardization of pronunciation and, as such, is quite heavily indebted to Sheldon (1938), although Holmberg had already produced his own (1956) monograph on James Douglas. Holmberg, unlike many of the general works reviewed in §2.2, devotes more space to the eighteenth century than to any other period. His justification for this is twofold and highly relevant for this study. First, he recognizes that 'it is in the eighteenth century that the snob value of a good pronunciation began to be recognized. In this century we find the beginings of the present outlook' (1964: 20). Secondly, he is aware of the neglect of eighteenth-century phonology which is the theme of this chapter: 'The phonology of late Modern English, which I take to mean the English from about 1700, has attracted relatively less interest in scholarly discussion than early Modern English pronunciation' (1964: 36). Here Holmberg confirms our findings in §2.2 concerning both the 'Cinderella' status of eighteenth-century phonological studies and the interest of this area for socio-historical linguists. Holmberg's work is very important in providing a summary of eighteenth-century attitudes to the pronunciation of English and he recognizes the complexity of eighteenth-century sound changes: for instance, on the matter of reflexes of ME /a/ lengthened to /ɑː/ in present-day RP, he writes 'it is a remarkable fact that about 1800 there was much hesitation as to the proper pronunciation of this vowel' (1964: 37). However, like Sheldon, he tends to be too dismissive of evidence, particularly that of Walker. On the matter of the coalescence of ME /eː/ and /ɛː/ he writes:

There can be no doubt whatever that ME $\tilde{e}$ and ME $\bar{e}$ were identical about 1800 . . . However, as late as the beginning of the nineteenth century attempts were being made to keep up the difference between ME $\tilde{e}$ and ME $\bar{e}$. Thus both in 1791 and 1806 Walker wrote that the vowel in *flee* and *meet* was 'distinguishable to a nice ear' from the vowel in *flea* and *meat*, the former having 'a squeezed sound of long open *e* formed by a closer application of the tongue to the roof of the mouth, than in that vowel singly'. . . . It is evident that Walker . . . was influenced by the spelling when he tried to keep up the difference. Many later writers have proved to be prejudiced in the same way.   (Holmberg 1964: 40–1)

In fact, recent work employing more sophisticated techniques of analysis such as Labov (1975) and Milroy and Harris (1980) has shown that the kind of distinction only 'distinguishable to a nice ear' is in fact consistently produced by speakers in cases such as this when a 'merger' has been reported. Contrary to what Holmberg says, we must bear in mind that Walker could well have had such a 'nice ear'. This apart, though, Holmberg provides a good summary both of attitudes to 'correct' pronunciation in the eighteenth century and the most important features of this pronunciation, at least as far as stressed vowels are concerned. His work provides an important starting-point for any study of English pronunciation in the eighteenth century.

Indeed, Holmberg is cited in one of the newest works in this area, Mugglestone (1995). Drawing on standard works in sociolinguistics and the social psychology of language, as well as orthoepistic and literary sources from the eighteenth and nineteenth centuries, Mugglestone presents the most comprehensive work to date on the standardization of pronunciation in British English. Although she concentrates mainly on that other 'Cinderella' of historical linguistics, the nineteenth century, with information from such gems of prescriptivism as *Poor Letter H: Its Use and Abuse* (1854–66) and *Mind Your H's and Take Care of Your R's* (1866), Mugglestone provides interesting material from the latter part of the eighteenth century. In her Introduction, she points out that 'five times as many works on elocution appeared between 1760 and 1800 than had done so in the years before 1760' (Mugglestone 1995: 4), whilst the first chapter puts into context the importance of pronouncing dictionaries in the process of standardization:

The pronouncing dictionary was, in a number of ways, to be of fundamental importance in furthering . . . notions of 'proper' speech. Trading on the popularity of the dictionary in a post-Johnson age, and on a public increasingly habituated to consult, and defer to, its authority on all matters of doubt, writers such as Kenrick, Johnston, Walker, Browne, Longmuir, and Nuttall, amid many others, all yolked Johnson's definitions to increasingly complex systems of transcription. Their work often met an audience which seemed to subscribe all too readily to the ideologies of a standard manipulated within the prescriptive tradition.   (Mugglestone 1995: 34–5)

Her insights into the reception of eighteenth- (and nineteenth-) century pronouncing dictionaries and the workings of laws of supply and demand governing their proliferation are particularly interesting. As far as specific pronunciations are concerned, Mugglestone (very much in the 'Labovian' tradition) concentrates on a few key variants which became shibboleths in the course of the period under consideration: 'h-dropping', i.e. /h/ vs. zero, in e.g. *hat*; 'g-dropping', or /ŋ/ vs. /n/, in e.g. *hunting, shooting, fishing*; loss of preconsonantal and word-final /r/ in, e.g. *cart, car*; and the rise of the present-day RP /ɑː/ in e.g. *laugh, basket*. Some of these features will be discussed in Chapter 5, and in every case Mugglestone provides useful information, not only on the continued diffusion of certain sound changes into the nineteenth century, but also on their sociolinguistic significance in the eighteenth century. Thus she notes with regard to 'h-dropping' that Sheridan 'is the first writer to record' this 'in terms which reveal a negative sensitization to its use' (1995: 39).[7] Mugglestone is particularly useful on the vexed and complex question of lengthening of ME /a/, taking the socio-historical view that language change involves changes in norms 'and in the conflicting claims of individual writers and speakers at this time about the "proper" use of ɑ, this is precisely what can be seen to be in operation' (1995: 91).

The works of Sheldon, Holmberg, and Mugglestone are, then, the closest antecedents of this study, combining as they do an examination of eighteenth-century sources with a broadly socio-historical view of linguistic change in this period. Significantly, though, none of them uses Spence as a source, and indeed, with the possible exception of Sheldon, none of them provides a thorough account of any *one* source. For complete investigations of single sources we must turn to the monographs and dissertations produced at various times in the course of this century. Many of these were produced outside the UK and some are not readily available, so I cannot pretend that this survey is comprehensive, but I would claim that it is representative. Many of the monographs reviewed here are of particular relevance to the present study in that they deal with orthoepists who were geographically close to Spence—that is, Scots, such as Elphinston, James Douglas, and Sylvester Douglas, or northern-born, such as Mather Flint, Granville Sharp, John Kirkby, and Robert Nares. Others are interesting in that they deal with those who (like Flint and Sharp) wrote grammars for foreign learners of English and therefore make interesting and illuminating comparisons with other European languages. These monographs tend to have been produced in 'waves' under the influence of certain scholars or schools of thought. Thus a large number, including Bendix (1921), Kern (1913), Müller (1914), and Stichel (1915), were produced in Germany in the first quarter of this century and under the influence of Wilhelm Horn.[8] These

[7] Of course, as we shall see in Chapter 5, Spence records [h] at the beginning of all words in which it is orthographically signalled except for a number of words of French origin such as *hour, honour, herb*. Spence in 1775 is unlikely to have been aware of the stigma of 'h-dropping', as this has never been a feature of Tyneside speech. It is mentioned as a vulgarism in *The Giant Killer*, but, by the time of its publication in 1814, Spence had spent many years in London.
[8] This point is made explicitly by Pollner (1976: 2), who refers to the previous study of Nares by Bendix as one of a number of works appearing in the first third of this century 'die . . . auf Anregung von Wilhelm Horn unternommen wurden' (which . . . were undertaken at the suggestion of Wilhelm Horn.)

all tend to follow the same pattern, dealing systematically with each phoneme of ME and its reflexes as evidenced in the source under investigation. This means that any one historical source is easy to find and follow up, but, as Pollner (1976: 2) points out, has the disadvantage of making it difficult for the reader to get an overall picture of the particular orthoepist's system. Pollner, on the other hand, belongs to what we might call the 'DEMEP school' and, like Rohlfing (1984), presents his findings in terms of his source's system rather than that of ME and compares that system with those of the source's contemporaries rather than with earlier ones. Thus the aim is to present a fuller picture of later Modern English pronunciation rather than a continuous development from ME. Where an earlier and a later monograph have been devoted to the same source, such as Müller (1914) and Rohlfing (1984), both on Elphinston, the later source is generally more useful, if only because the author has had access to a wider range of material. Thus Müller has studied only *The Principles of the English Language Digested, or English Grammar Reduced to Analogy* (1765), volume I of *Propriety Ascertained in her Picture* (1787), and *Inglish Orthoggraphy Epittomized* (1790) and, like Elphinston's contemporaries, complains about the difficulty of reading the latter work, written as it is entirely in Elphinston's reformed spelling. Rohlfing, on the other hand, is able to present a much fuller picture, drawing as he does on all the above plus volume II of *Propriety Ascertained* (particularly interesting as this deals specifically with 'Scotticisms'); *A Minniature of Inglish Orthoggraphy* (1795), *A Dialogue, Contrasting . . . dhe Practice and Propriety of Inglish Speech and Spelling* (1797), and Elphinston's correspondence, written in his reformed spelling (1791–4). This provides Rohlfing with a much wider range of examples: on the matter of the lengthened reflex of ME /a/, for instance, Rohlfing provides a large number of words with and without Elphinston's '*a* shut protracted' (probably [æː]) including *staves* in which the plural has this 'protracted' vowel, contrasting with short [æ] in the singular *staff*. If we saw this piece of evidence in isolation, we might be tempted to disregard it as a 'mistake' or a 'spelling-pronunciation', but Rohlfing shows that the same contrast is found in Johnston (1764, 1772) and Buchanan (1762).

Apart from these monographs of the 'Horn' and 'DEMEP' schools, there are a number of interesting works from other sources. Malone (1924) and Bergström (1955) each deal with 'northern' sources, and provide insights into the attitudes to 'northern' pronunciation which prevailed in the eighteenth century. Bergström's account of the Cumbrian John Kirkby provides early evidence of the salience of the 'unsplit' short /ʊ/ sound as a marker of northern pronunciation, later confirmed by, for example, Kenrick and Walker. Of his 'seventh vowel', Kirkby writes that it 'has only a short sound' and is represented by '*u* wherever it is short, as in *Skull, Gun, Supper,*

Figure, Nature' (quoted in Bergström 1955: 71). Kirkby goes on to explain in a note that 'this sound is scarce known to the Inhabitants of the North, who always use the short sound of the eighth vowel instead of it' (Kirkby's 'eighth vowel' is long in *too, woo, Food*, etc., short in *good, stood, Foot*, etc.)

Malone's (1924) account of Granville Sharp shows that, whilst Sharp recognizes the English of London as 'perhaps in general the best' (quoted in Malone 1924: 210), in several places where northern pronunciation accords better with the spelling, he points out that this is more 'according to rule'. For instance, although he admits that ⟨o⟩ has 'the short sound of *u*' in *Affront, Attorney, Bomb*, etc., 'in the dialects of Lancashire and some other places, the *o* is pronounced according to rule, in many of these words' (Malone 1924: 214). It is interesting to see that 'provincial' as opposed to 'vulgar' pronunciations were not always condemned at this stage: Rohlfing (1984) shows that Elphinston likewise is not always condemnatory of Scots dialects in volume II of *Propriety Ascertained.*

Kökeritz (1944) provides a reprint and an extensive commentary on the work of another northerner, Mather Flint, whose *Prononciation de la Langue Angloise* was published in Paris in 1740 and 1754. Written as it was for foreign learners of English, Flint's work provides comparisons between the contemporary pronunciation of English and French, which in some cases provide early evidence of changes which are firmly attested in English works later in the century. Thus, Flint's account of ME /a/ before /r/ shows evidence of lengthening of the vowel and weakening of the consonant: '*A* suivi de *r* est un peu long sans être ouvert, & l'*r* est prononcé moins rudement qu'en françois' (repr. in Kökeritz 1944: 11). As we shall see in §§5.2 and 5.8, such evidence can be vital in reconstructing the chronology of a sound change, especially where, as in the case of weakening/loss of preconsonantal /r/, works written for native speakers display a reluctance to recommend a pronunciation which might not accord with the spelling.

The last two monographs to be noted are from different eras, but both deal with the works of Scots orthoepists: Holmberg (1956) and Charles Jones (1991). The former reproduces and provides an extensive commentary on the unpublished manuscripts (*c.*1740) of James Douglas, a doctor who was born in Midlothian but spent most of his adult life in London. According to Holmberg, Douglas was describing the 'correct' English of London but probably spoke a 'modified' Scots. This work provides useful evidence, for instance, of a separate vowel, a 'fourth *a*-sound' in, for example, *hard*; *glass*; *fast*; *advance*: according to Holmberg (1956: 39), Douglas 'was apparently one of the first to recognize it as a separate sound'. Jones (1991) is an edition of Sylvester Douglas's *Treatise on the Provincial Dialect of Scotland* (1779). Sylvester Douglas was born near and educated in Aberdeen, but, like James Douglas, spent his later years in London. According to Jones (1991: 4), Douglas 'like many eighteenth-century writers on "good" pronunciation . . . is not concerned to correct the habits of those who profess "the grosser barbarisms of the vulgar scotch jargon", but addresses himself to the removal of the *vestigia ruris* from those Scots who otherwise speak with at least some of the characteristics of a refined, standard (by which is meant polite London) dialect'. Jones's Introduction to this edition of Douglas provides an interesting perspective on the status of the speech of 'refined' Scots, confirming the impression that we receive from other Scots like Elphinston and James Adams, as well as northerners like Granville Sharp, that 'provincial' usage was not always condemned outright in the eighteenth century, and was certainly seen as preferable to the 'vulgar' usage of London[9]. Jones's commentary, like Jones (1989), is couched in the terms of dependency phonology and likewise provides an interesting combination of close historical observation and phonological theory. In many areas, not least that of the 'labial vowels', Jones (1991) has provided comparative information which will play a key part in our discussions in Chapter 5.

2.5. CONCLUSION

The publication of Jones's monograph, along with other very recent works such as Mugglestone (1995) and Jones (1995), perhaps signals the fact that the 'Cinderella' status of eighteenth-century historical linguistic studies will soon be a thing of the past. The publication of the relevant volumes of the *Cambridge History of the English Language* (volume iii, covering 1476–1776 and volume iv, covering 1776 to the present day) should finally redress the balance where general works are concerned, although there is still no sign of an undergraduate textbook equivalent to Görlach (1991) for the eighteenth century. Despite the lack of general works on our period, though, there is certainly enough in the way of monographs and other works on individual eighteenth-century orthoepists, as well as the works on the historical phonology of this period, to give a general idea of what sound changes were in progress in the later eighteenth century. However, given the current fragmented state of this knowledge, and especially in the light of the apparent collapse of the DEMEP project, there is still a crying need for new work, particularly in the area of eighteenth-century phonology. Given the current emphasis amongst historical phonologists on the lexical diffusion

[9] Both Elphinston and Adams, for instance, condemn the Londoners' 'suppression of *h* when it ought to be sounded after *w*' (Adams 1799: 144), whilst Douglas writes of a 'most capricious defect' amongst 'some individuals in England . . . that in words where others pronounce the *h*, at the beginning, they do not; and where others suppress it, or where it is not written, they pronounce it' (Douglas 1779, quoted in C. Jones 1991: 128).

of sound changes and the place of the lexicon in phonological change (see §3.4 and Labov 1994), the most urgent need is for a study of evidence that provides an account of the pronunciation of a whole 'lexicon'. We shall consider in the next chapter to what extent Spence's *Grand Repository* and other pronouncing dictionaries of the eighteenth century provide such evidence.

3. Evidence for Eighteenth-Century Pronunciation: The Value of Pronouncing Dictionaries

3.1. INTRODUCTION

The question which we shall address in this chapter is whether the *Grand Repository* and other eighteenth-century pronouncing dictionaries provide useful information for the historical phonologist: how much information do these pronouncing dictionaries provide, how reliable is this information, and how does it compare with other available sources of information on the pronunciation of English in the eighteenth century? Before considering the pronouncing dictionaries themselves, we should perhaps review the other types of evidence available to historical phonologists[1] engaged in reconstructing the pronunciation of an earlier period of English.

3.2. RECONSTRUCTING THE HISTORICAL PHONOLOGY OF MODERN ENGLISH: AN OVERVIEW OF THE DIFFERENT TYPES OF EVIDENCE

Those who study the phonology of present-day English, or even of English from the late nineteenth century onwards, have an abundance of data at their disposal in the form of tape recordings (or phonographic recordings from the earlier part of this period), and, in discussions about the nature of this data, are largely concerned with the problem of capturing 'vernacular' or unselfconscious speech in an interview situation. For instance, Labov (1972: 209) writes of the '*Observer's Paradox*: the aim of linguistic research in the community must be to find out how people talk when they are not being systematically observed; yet we can only obtain these data by systematic observation'. The problems encountered by the historical phonologist are of a different nature: as Wyld (1936: 1) points out:

---

[1] Here I am using the term 'historical phonologist' somewhat loosely and with no implications regarding the theoretical orientation of the scholars concerned. Many of those whom I place under this 'umbrella' term would have described themselves as philologists. I mean the term to include all those, from H. C. Wyld to Morris Halle, who are concerned with the pronunciation of English in centuries previous to the present one.

It is an unfortunate circumstance for students of the history of a language, but one from which there is no escape, that they are dependent upon written documents for a knowledge of all but the most recent developments, since, in the nature of things, they can gain no direct and personal access to the spoken language earlier than the speech of the oldest living person they may know.

Written documents, however, contain various kinds of evidence concerning the pronunciation of their authors and/or their authors' contemporaries, which need to be evaluated. We can divide these types of evidence broadly into two categories: those which provide *direct* or overt evidence and those which provide *indirect* or covert evidence. Into the former category we will place statements about the language by the orthoepists, grammarians, and elocutionists of the day and into the latter such evidence as is provided by spellings, rhymes, and puns. When dealing with indirect evidence, the historical linguist has to extract information which the author did not necessarily intend to convey. For instance, Shakespeare rhymed *war* with *jar* and *warm* with *harm* in *Venus and Adonis* (ll. 98/100 and 193/195 respectively) because he was writing within a tradition which demanded end-rhymes and because those words fitted in with the theme of his poem, not because he wished to record for posterity the fact that /w/ had not yet exerted a rounding influence on the following /a/. Historical phonologists such as Wyld (1923) and Kökeritz (1953) have, however, used such rhymes as evidence for exactly that. On the other hand, those who provide direct evidence do so consciously, but not necessarily for posterity: the orthoepists of earlier centuries are writing for their contemporaries and each has his (or in the eighteenth century perhaps her) own axe to grind, about spelling reform, 'analogy', or 'correct' speech. Historical phonologists differ in the extent to which they are prepared to take such evidence on trust. Davies (1934), Wyld (1923, 1927, 1936), and Kökeritz (1953) tend to prefer indirect evidence, whilst Dobson (1957), Chomsky and Halle (1968), Cercignani (1981), and Charles Jones (1989) give more credence to the works of the orthoepists. Jespersen (1909–49) takes a fairly balanced view, conceding that 'the spellings of more or less illiterate persons are often very instructive' and that 'much may be learnt from the versification of poets', but concluding that 'of infinitely greater value is the direct information given in the works of old phoneticians, grammarians and spelling-reformers' (1909–49: 4–6).

Direct evidence is almost[2] non-existent before the sixteenth century, so that the accounts of Old and Middle English pronunciation on which the philological categories used by Dobson, Wyld, etc. are based have been constructed entirely from orthographic (indirect) evidence found in manu-

---

[2] The exception here is, of course, the thirteenth-century *Ormulum*, which, according to Charles Jones (1989: 12) 'provides us with what are fairly direct indications of approximate graphic/phonological correspondence, a type of evidence which is more often associated with the grammarians and phoneticians of the sixteenth and later centuries'.

scripts. For the period with which we are concerned, direct evidence becomes more widely available with the advent of the sixteenth-century orthoepists, just at the point in history when standardization of spelling in printed materials makes indirect evidence from prose texts in Standard English less useful. Let us consider these types of evidence in turn.

3.2.1. *Direct evidence*

The richness of evidence available for the pronunciation of English from the sixteenth century onwards is noted by Charles Jones, who finds it 'especially noticeable that the level of "direct" evidence increases dramatically during this era and there survive extensive data compiled by scholars some of whom, by any set of standards, show sophisticated and advanced views on the speech habits of real speakers' (1989: 196). It would appear that the historical phonologist has only to study these works in order to reconstruct the pronunciation of ENE but, of course, it is not so simple. Even the strongest advocates of 'direct' evidence admit that the early orthoepists and grammarians vary in terms of accuracy and reliability. Jones (1989: 197) asks his readers to resign themselves to the fact that, 'despite the detail and variety of the evidence left to us . . . we shall remain confused and perplexed over many important matters of fact and interpretation'. Dobson (1955: 33) concedes that 'each case must be treated on its merits, and we must be guided by internal evidence revealed by detailed and critical examination, not by *a priori* assumptions'.

By *a priori* assumptions, Dobson is here referring to the assumption that an orthoepist born in London will be more reliable as a source of evidence for 'standard' pronunciation than one born outside Puttenham's much quoted sixty-mile radius,[3] but *a priori* assumptions based on the historical phonologist's theoretical orientation can likewise cloud the judgement when the lack of any agreed method of representing the sounds of English at the time means that so much of the evidence from the orthoepists of the sixteenth, seventeenth, and even the eighteenth centuries is left open to interpretation. An example of this can be found in Chomsky and Halle (1968). These two generative linguists base their account of the evolution of the modern English vowel system entirely on evidence provided by four orthoepists: Hart, Wallis, Cooper, and Batchelor. They provide no detailed evaluation of these sources, but simply state that they 'review the vowel systems of four English dialects spoken in earlier centuries' and that these dialects 'were chosen because they illustrate the main steps in the evolution' (Chomsky and Halle 1968: 249). In the case of Hart, Chomsky and Halle construct rules which account for the shift of ME $\bar{\imath}$ and $\bar{u}$ to [ēy] and [ōw]

---

[3] 'Ye shall take the usual speech of the Court, and that of London and the shires lying about London within lx miles and not much above' (Puttenham 1598, quoted in Dobson 1955: 28).

(Chomsky and Halle's notation), but note that Dobson (1957) denies that such reflexes ever existed:

It is important to note that Dobson's conclusions concerning the pronunciation of these sounds in the sixteenth century are not based on evidence from the sources, but are rather inferences drawn on the assumption that sound change is a gradual process. Since what Dobson terms 'the usual view' concerning the facts of sixteenth century pronunciation of ME tense /i/ and /u/ cannot be reconciled with a view of sound change as a gradual process, Dobson feels justified in interpreting away the statements and transcriptions to be found in sixteenth century sources. (Chomsky and Halle 1968: 255)

Chomsky and Halle, of course, do not believe in the gradual nature of sound change: for them the source of linguistic change lies in the discontinuous creation of new grammars by each generation of language learners, and, for the linguist attempting to reconstruct such a grammar, the 'best' grammar is the 'simplest' or the one that can generate all and only the grammatical sentences of the languages with the smallest number of rules. Thus, they point out the mote in the eye of the unenlightened Dobson, but fail to notice the beam in their own which is evident in their interpretation of Hart's evidence. Noting that Hart sometimes represents ME /ɔw/ as [ōw] and sometimes as [ō], Chomsky and Halle find themselves 'faced with the question of whether the vacillations in Hart's transcriptions of ME /ɔw/ represent actual vacillations in his speech or instead result only from certain inadequacies in his observations' and 'take the position that the latter was the case—that early in Hart's career he was unable to tell whether or not a tense [ō] was followed by a homorganic glide, whereas later he was able to distinguish between [ō] and [ōw]' (1968: 261). They go on to discuss how they would have to modify their analysis if they did take Hart's evidence at face value but conclude that 'these modifications do not shed any new light on the evolution of the English vowel system. . . . Our main purpose is as well served by the simpler facts as by the more complex facts that face us if we take Hart's transcriptions at face value' (1968: 262).

Dobson in turn had accused his neogrammarian predecessors of ignoring evidence that did not fit their theories: 'Nothing is more false than to regard modern Standard English as a uniform dialect developing solely in accordance with its own sound-laws; and the misconception that it is to be so regarded has led older scholars to many errors of interpretation—the impatient rejection or neglect of perfectly genuine evidence' (1955: 35).

The lesson to be learned from this is that every generation of historical phonologists has accused the previous one of what Dobson terms 'the impatient rejection or neglect of perfectly genuine evidence': every scholar works within some theoretical framework and is tempted to dismiss evidence that does not fit in with that theory, but what criteria can be used to favour the evidence of one orthoepist over that of another?

One criterion that is often used when discriminating between orthoepists is that of how good they were as phoneticians. There seems to be a general consensus that John Hart and Christopher Cooper are 'good' phoneticians, largely because of the clarity and accuracy of their descriptions of articulations, but opinions of other orthoepists vary. Here again, we find that the theoretical orientation of the twentieth-century scholar may affect the evaluation: Dobson (1957: 102), for instance, considers that William Bullokar 'can hardly be said to have any remembrance in the list of English phoneticians'. One instance which Dobson gives of Bullokar's lack of acuity is his description of the consonants /l/, /m/, /n/, /r/, /l/, and /s/ as 'half-vowels': Dobson (1957: 102) dismisses this as 'a conception which, it seems, is a muddle of several distinct ideas'. Charles Jones (1989: 249), on the other hand, sees Bullokar's classification of 'half-vowels' as of particular interest, because these very consonants cluster together in Jones' 'sonority hierarchy' as being, in the case of /l/, /m/, /n/, and /r/, sonorant and, in the case of /s/, a continuant, and therefore more 'vowel-like' than, for instance, /t/, /p/, and /k/. Thus one man's muddle is another's prescient insight and we must constantly re-evaluate the work of the orthoepists according to the current state of our knowledge of phonetics and phonology.

Another criterion which could be used in judging the relative merits of orthoepists is that of consistency. However, as we shall see when considering eighteenth-century evidence, what appears to be an internal inconsistency in the account of a particular orthoepist may in fact be a faithful recording of contemporary pronunciations when a sound change was in progress. Labov (1975) shows that, when a sound change is in progress, any detailed examination of the usage in a speech community will reveal what appears at first sight to be random or 'free' variation between the 'old' and the 'new' sounds, but that, on closer examination, there is found to be a strict order in which the 'new' sound appears in certain phonetic environments before others. The specification of these environments may be very detailed, with sounds occurring before and after the one involved in the change creating in combination an environment more favourable to the change than either of them would in isolation. Labov's studies, and others to which we shall refer in §3.4, have shown that, in the middle stages of a sound change, ordered variation is the norm, with consistency across the lexical set being found only when a sound change has completed its course: 'This spacing out of phonetic subclasses is characteristic of the intermediate stages of change in progress like the spacing out of runners in a race: at the beginning they are all bunched together; in the midst of the race they are strung out according to their individual abilities and speeds; at the finish, they are brought together again, (Labov, 1975, repr. in Baldi and Werth 1978: 292). To their credit, scholars such as Dobson (1955, 1957) and Sundby (1953) have recognized the significance of statements like that of Cooper, who writes that '*A* is formed by the middle of the tongue a little rais'd to the hollow of the Palate. In these *can, pass by, a* is short; in *cast, past* for *passed*, it is long' (Sundby 1953: 4). Here, Cooper might be seen as inconsistent, but, as we shall see in §5.2, his evidence provides vital information concerning the diffusion of lengthened ME /a/ in the seventeenth century.

Internal consistency, then, is not a good criterion by which to judge an orthoepist. When Dobson writes, in defence of orthoepistic evidence, that it is 'far too consistent to be artificial or unreal' (1955: 38), he is referring to consistency *between* orthoepists of the same period. Whilst it is generally acknowledged that there are differences between the accounts of various orthoepists (Dobson 1957 would be a much shorter work if this were not the case), historical phonologists are generally wary of the 'lone voice' and are more likely to give credence to the evidence of one orthoepist if others back him up. Thus the statement of Cooper quoted above is seen by Dobson as reliable, not only because of Cooper's reputation as 'a good phonetician, and a systematic, careful and honest observer' (Dobson 1957: 310) but also because it is consistent with evidence provided earlier by Daines and Coles. No evidence of this nature can be considered in isolation—as Aitchison (1981: 34) says of linguistic reconstruction in general, 'each individual piece of evidence is of little value on its own. It is the cumulative effect that counts. When a linguist finds several clues all pointing in the same direction, he can be more confident that his reconstruction is a plausible one.'

Dobson is quoted above describing Cooper as 'honest', suggesting that he told us the truth about the state of the language in the late seventeenth century. 'Honesty' is another criterion by which orthoepists have been judged, with scholars like Wyld being particularly reluctant to take the descriptions of sixteenth- and seventeenth-century schoolmasters on trust. The problem here is that many of the orthoepists were conservative in their attitudes to linguistic change, and, as Holmberg (1964: 10) points out 'they were sometimes more anxious to teach what they believed was correct than to record the pronunciation they actually heard or used'. Dobson acknowledges the conservative tendencies of many of the orthoepists, but considers that the 'Standard English' of the sixteenth and seventeenth centuries was 'a taught language, and the teaching of pronunciations as correct preserves them' [i.e. those pronunciations] (1955: 38). Indeed, if we were to take account only of the evidence of orthoepists, our datings of many sound changes would be considerably later than if we also consider the indirect evidence to be discussed below. Take, for instance, the case of ME /ai/ as in *maid, tail*, etc.: indirect evidence from rhymes, puns, and spellings suggests that this sound had become monophthongal and merged with ME /aː/ as in *made, tale* by the early sixteenth century, yet Gil (1626) ridicules the monophthongal pronunciation as typical of the speech of those he refers to contemptuously as 'Mopsae'. Wyld (1936: 169) concludes that 'Gil seems to be a cantankerous and rather ridiculous person, who, if he lived up to his theories, must have spoken a detestable kind of English'. Dobson (1955: 41–2), on the other hand, takes a more balanced view:

Gil's duty was that of a schoolmaster, and from the point of view of his own generation he was right; to retain the diphthongs had hitherto been one of the criteria of the educated language . . . it is both natural and right that resistance to neologisms should be strongest and most vocal when they have already become widely current, i.e. when they are on the verge of acceptance, even if in retrospect it appears an unavailing pedantic opposition to the prevailing tendency of the language.

Once again, the lesson to be learned from this is that we should sift such evidence carefully. At any stage of the language, there will be conservative and innovative pronunciations in use: the pronouncements of conservative orthoepists like Gil need to be taken alongside those of his more liberal colleagues and the indirect evidence from rhymes, puns, and spellings, if a complete picture is to be achieved.

Of course, conservatism and prescriptivism were even more powerful forces in the eighteenth century, when standards of pronunciation were being explicitly codified by elocutionists like John Walker. When we go on to consider the value of pronouncing dictionaries as evidence for eighteenth-century pronunciation, we shall need to bear in mind that the authors of these works may be prescribing an ideal pronunciation rather than describing a real one, but, as with seventeenth-century orthoepists such as Gil and Cooper, as much can be learnt from the pronunciations which are proscribed as from those which are recommended.

3.2.2. *Indirect evidence*

Having considered the advantages and disadvantages of direct evidence for earlier pronunciations of English, we should now consider the alternatives. Of all historical phonologists, Wyld is perhaps the most vehement in his dismissal of orthoepistic evidence, concluding that 'the path of progress lies in the minute study of the letters and books written in the periods under consideration, rather than in that of reiterated torturing and weighing of the descriptions given by the writers on pronunciation' (1936: 115). Wyld places highest value on the evidence from what he calls 'occasional spellings': spellings which deviate from the current orthographic 'norm'. The argument is that such deviations are almost always in the direction of 'phonetic' spelling,[4] and can alert us to changes in pronunciation at an early stage.

---

[4] This certainly seems to be the case with such examples of semi-literate usage as can be found today: one gem which I found on a discarded shopping list in Kwik Save was '3 Lasanyas'— exactly reflecting the pronunciation of this Italian delicacy on Tyneside.

Once spelling becomes more codified, particularly from the eighteenth century onwards, such evidence becomes rarer and largely confined to private letters and journals, such as the Wentworth Papers, but Wyld makes a great deal of use of these sources, particularly from the fifteenth and sixteenth centuries. Of course, these spellings need to be interpreted in the light of the usual values of letters at the time of writing. Some information is relatively unambiguous, such as the omission of consonants: when in a letter by Margaret Paston[5] we read ⟨nex⟩ for *next* and ⟨kepyn⟩ for *keeping*, the spellings indicate fairly clearly that the /t/ was not pronounced in the first word and that the final nasal in the second word was alveolar rather than velar. On the other hand, when we see spellings of ⟨dipe⟩ for *deep*, ⟨spiche⟩ for *speech*, etc. from Queen Elizabeth I, we need to bear in mind that the 'conventional' value of ⟨i⟩ at that time was /iː/, and that these spellings point to the fact that the shift of ME /eː/ to /iː/ was well established by this time. 'Inverted spellings' are also hard to interpret: Jespersen (1909–49: 4) suggests that 'no one would think of writing *delight* instead of the older form *delit, delyt* (> OF *delit*) till after the *gh* of *light* had become mute'. In this case, he is almost certainly right, but how are we to interpret the instances of unetymological initial ⟨h⟩ that we find alongside 'dropped' ⟨h⟩ in spellings such as ⟨hanswered⟩ for *answered* and ⟨elmet⟩ for *helmet* in the sixteenth-century diary of Henry Machyn? (cited in Wyld 1936: 144). Are these, too, 'inverted spellings', indicating that initial ⟨h⟩ has no phonetic value and Machyn simply adds or deletes it at random, or should we, like Charles Jones (1989: 265–74), take this evidence at face value and consider that /h/ was being added in syllable-initial position?

Apart from these problems of interpretation, other objections have been raised to the use of 'occasional spellings' as evidence. There is the question of whether the 'occasional spellings' are those of the named author or of a scribe or clerk. In the case of earlier collections of letters, such as the Paston Letters, this problem is particularly widespread, and needs to be addressed carefully. Norman Davis, who has produced the definitive edition of the Paston Letters, concludes that 'only about half of the letters are in the handwriting of the authors . . . some of the women's letters are among the most interesting and important of all, but they do not give as precise linguistic evidence as the men's; for it does not appear that any of them are autograph' (1954: 120). This statement of Davis puts into question much of Wyld's evidence, for the latter asserts that 'the letters of women . . . are far less carefully spelt than those of men, and tell us more concerning their actual mode of speech' (1936: 113). Of course, even if the 'occasional spellings' are the work of clerks, they still reflect

---

[5] I use this example to illustrate a point about the interpretation of occasional spellings. As we shall see, Margaret Paston almost certainly had this letter written by a clerk, and so the 'occasional spelling' is his.

somebody's usage, but whether that of the clerk himself or the lady dictating is impossible to tell.

In later periods, notably the eighteenth century, we can be more confident that a woman's letters are written in her own hand, but the advances in education that made these ladies literate, along with the codification of spelling by this time, meant that 'occasional spellings' become less common by this time. However, there are still collections such as the Wentworth papers, which provide useful evidence: for instance, a letter from Lady Wentworth[6] to her son, written in 1706, has the spellings ⟨hard⟩ and ⟨sartainly⟩ for *heard, certainly*, corroborating the statement made by John Walker (1791) that the first syllable of the word *merchant* had been pronounced march 'about thirty years ago' (see §3.3.2. for a fuller examination of Walker's statement).

Another question raised by 'occasional spellings' is that of what kind of English they exemplify. Dobson (1955: 46) suggests that they cannot give evidence of Standard English because 'aberrant spellings necessarily come from persons who have not mastered the orthography and are therefore imperfectly educated, and who in consequence cannot be accepted, whatever their social status, as reliable witnesses to educated speech'. This sounds a reasonable argument, until we remember that some of the 'occasional spellings' cited above are attributed to Queen Elizabeth I, who, apart from being of the highest social status possible (who could be more likely to speak 'the Queen's English' than the Queen herself?) was very well educated.[7] Given that standards of spelling were not so rigid in Elizabeth's time as in later centuries, Dobson's comment here does not seem valid.

Spellings, then, are problematic because their interpretation is not always straightforward, but mostly because their authorship is not always clear. However, where there is clear evidence that they are written in the hand of the named author, they can provide useful information if only as a supplement to direct evidence. In the case of the other two kinds of indirect evidence that have been used by scholars such as Wyld and Kökeritz, the question of authorship is less problematic,[8] for they tend to come from the printed works of established authors and involve information to be gleaned from rhymes and puns.

Where rhymes are concerned, one obvious problem is that they can only tell us that certain pairs of words had the same vowel or diphthong, not what

---

[6] These examples are taken from Davies (1934: 141).

[7] Wyld (1936: 104) quotes Ascham, writing in 1550 about the then Princess Elizabeth: 'She talks French and Italian as well as English; she has often talked with me readily and well in Latin, and moderately so in Greek. When she writes Greek and Latin, nothing is more beautiful than her handwriting.'

[8] Less problematic, but not wholly unproblematic: Cercignani (1981) points out that some of the rhymes used as evidence of 'Shakespeare's Pronunciation' by Kökeritz (1953) in fact occur in passages which are of dubious authorship.

that vowel or diphthong was. Take the following extract from *A Midsummer Night's Dream*, II. ii. 9–12:

> You spotted snakes with double *tongues*
> Thorny hedge-hogs, be not seen;
> Newts and blind-worms, do no *wrong*;
> Come not near our fairy queen.

Does this indicate that the words in italic are pronounced /tɒŋ/ and /rɒŋ/ or /tʊŋ/ and /rʊŋ/? Dobson (1957: 584) suggests that either is possible, since ME /o/ was often raised to /ʊ/ before ⟨ng⟩ and a pronunciation of *tongue* with /o/ by lowering of /ʊ/ was also current. Rhymes can only be used to corroborate evidence from other sources: if we know from direct evidence that two originally distinct vowels have merged, then a rhyme involving those vowels may produce an earlier date for the merger than the more conservative evidence of orthoepists.

Poets were not always innovative in their rhymes, however. Dobson (1955: 48) makes the point that mergers provide new rhymes, which poets would naturally adopt as soon as possible, but phonemic splits or, as Dobson terms them, divergent developments, are not attested so quickly by poets, for the simple reason that they deprive them of established rhymes. In cases where poets continue to employ rhymes long after the sounds involved have diverged, we have what are known as 'eye-rhymes', which give no reliable information about contemporary pronunciation. Cercignani, however, accords with Wyld in asserting that poets must be assumed 'innocent' of eye-rhymes until proved guilty, quoting Wyld as follows:

It is suggested that however 'bad' a rhyme of the age of Shakespeare, Dryden, and Pope may appear when judged simply by the standards of our own usage, we are not justified in dismissing it as imperfect and careless until we have tested it in the most searching way, and by every means at our disposal. If all these fail to establish the actual existence, or even the probability, of such a pronunciation in the poet's own day as would make the rhyme a good one, then, and not until then, are we entitled to say that the rhyme is faulty.   (Wyld 1923: 6, quoted in Cercignani 1981: 8–9)

Of course, what this does confirm is that rhyme evidence cannot stand alone, but must be tested against direct and other kinds of indirect evidence. From the point of view of this study of late eighteenth-century usage, rhymes will be of little value, because the later a poem is written, the longer a tradition of 'eye-rhymes' there is for the poet to draw on: Wyld's (1923) study, significantly, ends with Pope, and can therefore help us only with a picture of early eighteenth-century usage.

Puns, of course, were much more favoured in the sixteenth and seventeenth centuries than in the eighteenth: in the earlier period, they were viewed as instances of the classical rhetorical device of *paranomasia*, 'a play on words that sound identical (homophones) or similar, but have different meanings' (Ronberg 1992: 164), whereas in the age of Dr Johnson they were regarded with contempt as Shakespeare's 'fatal Cleopatra'. Kökeritz, more than any other scholar, set great store by the evidence provided by puns, largely because, whilst rhymes may be traditional, puns rely for their effect on using contemporary pronunciations. The problem, of course, lies in knowing whether a pun was intended when the words concerned are no longer homophonous. Cercignani (1981: 12) accuses Kökeritz of 'a decided laxity in admitting instances that are not so obviously intended as to justify their use as dependable sources of information'. There are, of course, instances in Shakespeare where a line would be incomprehensible if a pun were not intended, such as the following exchange from *Twelfth Night*, I. ii. 96 ff.

ANDREW. What is purquoy? Do, or not do? I would I had bestowed that time in the *tongues*, that I have in fencing, dancing, and beare-bating: O had I but followed the Arts.

TOBY. Then hadst thou an excellent head of hair.

This would make no sense unless *tongues* was homophonous with *tongs* (for curling the hair): a reading which is, of course, supported by the rhyme from *A Midsummer Night's Dream* cited above. As it is, these two pieces of evidence support each other and are in turn supported by the direct evidence of Elisha Coles (1674), who has *tongs* and *tongues* listed under *o*. Other instances cited by Kökeritz are, however, more dubious, so that it would appear that puns can be used only with caution and where they are supported by other kinds of evidence. In any case, as we have seen, they will be of little use for a study of later modern English.[9]

This survey of the various types of evidence used by historical phonologists points to one conclusion: the reconstruction of earlier pronunciation is a jigsaw puzzle, with each type of evidence providing part of the picture. Only direct evidence is clear and explicit enough to stand alone, and, even then, a single orthoepist cannot be relied upon to give a true picture, but must be judged in terms of the consistency of his account with those of his contemporaries. As we have seen, indirect evidence becomes less plentiful in the eighteenth century, when puns fall out of favour and spelling becomes more standardized. We will, therefore, have to rely more than ever on the direct evidence of writers on pronunciation for an account of eighteenth-century pronunciation. If Dobson is to be believed, we have a hopeless task on our hands, for he asserts that 'the eighteenth century produced no writers

---

[9] This is not to say that puns disappeared after Shakespeare's time: in the unlikely event of all audio material being lost to posterity, future scholars might gain insights into the pronunciation of late-twentieth-century English from advertising jingles: e.g. 'It asda be Asda' attests 'h-dropping' and prevocalic voicing of /t/.

to compare either with the spelling reformers who are our main source up to 1644 (Hodges) or with the phoneticians who, beginning with Robinson (1617) carry us on from 1653 (Wallis) to 1687 (Cooper's *English Teacher*)' (1957: 311). Dobson's study, of course, ends at 1700, so he has no need to justify what appears a cavalier neglect of such great eighteenth-century phoneticians as Elphinston, Jones, Nares, and, of course, Walker, all of whom, as we saw in §2.3., are acknowledged by Jespersen (1909–49. 9). What we shall see in the next section is that the later eighteenth century saw the emergence of a particularly valuable resource for the historical phonologist: the pronouncing dictionary.

3.3. PRONOUNCING DICTIONARIES AS EVIDENCE OF EIGHTEENTH-CENTURY PRONUNCIATION

3.3.1. *Evaluating eighteenth-century pronouncing dictionaries: an overview*

When we consider the number of pronouncing dictionaries and other works on pronunciation produced in the eighteenth century, Dobson's dismissive remark (quoted above) seems extraordinary. However, as we saw in Chapter 2, Dobson was writing at a time when the study of eighteenth-century English was neglected even more than it is today: the prevailing attitude in the first half of the twentieth century was that the study of English philology stopped at 1700. To a certain extent, this neglect of eighteenth-century orthoepists is understandable: access to the texts was difficult before the publication of Alston's (1965–73) bibliography and the production of his (1972) microfiche collection. Some pronouncing dictionaries, notably the *Grand Repository* itself, had not even been 'discovered' at this time. Quite apart from these practical obstacles, perhaps the intellectual climate was not yet right for the study of eighteenth-century phonology: despite his side-swipes at the neogrammarians (see §3.2.1), Dobson was, above all a philologist, interested in tracing the course of sound changes in the 'standard' language and, as Charles Jones (1989: 279) points out, there is no great phonological 'event' like the Great Vowel Shift associated with the eighteenth century. As we saw in Chapter 2, the eighteeenth century is interesting above all from a socio-historical point of view.

Sociolinguistics, of course, had not been invented in 1957 when Dobson produced his *magnum opus* and it is perhaps significant that Wyld and Kökeritz, who did see the importance of eighteenth-century orthoepists, have been hailed by Weinreich, Labov, and Herzog (1968) as Ur-socio-linguists: as we shall see, it is only with access to the methods and theories developed by Labov and his successors that the 'orderly heterogeneity' (Weinreich *et al.* 1968: 100) of eighteenth-century pronunciation can be seen as significant. Of course, this explanation has been compiled with benefit of hindsight: what we need to consider here is whether Dobson's dismissal of eighteenth-century orthoepists was justified in terms of the criteria used by him and applied in his (1957) work to the orthoepists of the sixteenth and seventeenth centuries.

The evidence provided by eighteenth-century orthoepists is, if anything, even more 'direct' than that of their predecessors, for, whilst the sixteenth and seventeenth-century writers often provide descriptions of contemporary pronunciation in order to illustrate problems in the conventional orthography, those of the eighteenth century are specifically concerned with describing and prescribing in great detail what they consider to be the 'correct' pronunciation of English. Because their main purpose is to provide a clear and foolproof guide to this 'correct'[10] pronunciation, eighteenth-century pronouncing dictionaries provide more detail than the orthoepistic works of the preceding centuries, and because their authors are able to build on the foundation provided by the seventeenth-century orthoepists, the descriptions of sounds are often easier for us to understand, but we still need to approach these works with caution. We must ask about the eighteenth-century orthoepists the same three questions posed in §3.2.1, regarding those of the sixteenth and seventeenth centuries: how 'good' were they as phoneticians; how 'honest' were they; and how 'consistent' are their accounts both internally and with each other? We shall deal with the last question in §3.4, since, as we hinted in §3.2.1, this is inextricably tied up with the question of lexical and social diffusion of sound changes, but, in judging the merits of authors who took on the task of laying down the standards of 'correct' pronunciation, we must also ask a fourth question: how familiar would they have been with the 'standard' that they were prescribing?

3.3.2. Were eighteenth-century pronouncing dictionaries written by 'good' phoneticians?

Let us deal first with the matter of whether the authors of eighteenth-century pronouncing dictionaries were 'good' phoneticians or not. We can examine their credentials as phoneticians with reference to biographical information (where would they have learnt to observe and describe pronunciation?) and in terms of 'the proof of the pudding' (how convincing are their descriptions?), although in both cases we must take care to avoid the *a priori* assumptions outlined in §3.2.1.

Biographical information on the eighteenth-century orthoepists varies according to their subsequent fame and influence. The *DNB* has substantial entries on Sheridan, Walker, William Kenrick, and even Spence, but nothing

---

[10] I use the word 'correct' here to cover a number of different words used in the eighteenth century to describe the pronunciation aspired to by readers of pronouncing dictionaries. Spence, for instance, refers on his title-page to 'the most proper and agreeable pronunciation'.

on John Burn or William Johnston,[11] for instance. Sheridan is also the subject of two biographies (Benzie 1972; Sheldon 1967). From these sources, the credentials of Sheridan and Walker are fairly clear: both were actors at some time in their lives and both were leading lights in the elocution movement of the later eighteenth century. In this respect, as with their pronouncing dictionaries, Sheridan led the way and Walker followed but was ultimately to have more success because of the clearer and more prescriptive rules that he laid down (Benzie 1972: 49). Both these men seem to have learnt from their experience on the stage the importance of clear enunciation, and both seem to have become keen observers of differences in 'accent' (stress and intonation) and pronunciation. In Sheridan's case, we can see where this acute observation was learnt, for he had as a teacher no less a man than Swift: Benzie (1972: p. vii) points out that in Sheridan's own biography of Swift 'he recalls how much the Dean taught him about the art of oral expression by making him read aloud for him two or three hours each day' and goes on to relate 'how every time a visiting clergyman occupied his pulpit, the Dean of St. Patrick's produced pen and paper to record any deviation from orthodox orthoepy on the part of the preacher. After the sermon, Swift never failed to admonish the culprit for his errors.' Sheridan certainly learnt from his mentor the art of careful observation, as the following anecdote of James Beattie shows:

Mr. Sheridan, in those elegant Lectures which I heard him deliver at Edinburgh about twenty years ago, distinguished . . . the English interrogatory accent from the Irish and the Scotch, in this manner. His example was, 'How have you been this great while?'—in pronouncing which, he observed, that towards the end of a sentence an Englishman lets his voice fall, an Irishman raises his, and a Scotchman makes his voice first fall and then rise. (Beattie 1783: 296, quoted in Benzie 1972: 32)

If public acclaim is any measure of worth, then both Sheridan and Walker were 'good' elocutionists. According to the *DNB*, Sheridan 'lectured on elocution with great success in London, Bristol, Bath, Oxford, Cambridge, and Edinburgh', whilst of Walker it is stated that 'during a professional tour in Scotland and Ireland he met with great success, and at Oxford the heads of houses invited him to give private lectures in the university'. Their pronouncing dictionaries likewise were extremely successful and influential: even though Sheridan was castigated by the author of *A Caution to Gentleman Who Use Sheridan's Dictionary* (1790), and Walker often disagreed with him concerning specific pronunciations, the author of his obituary in the *Public Advertiser* of 22 August 1788 felt moved to write: 'there are few men, perhaps, if any, to whom the English Language owes more than to the late Mr. Sheridan. His Dictionary

---

[11] Horn and Lehnert (1954: 105) write of Johnston that 'über sein Leben ist nichts bekannt' (nothing is known about his life.)

has formed an invaluable standard for the just pronunciation of our language . . . the want of which in England, was heretofore so much lamented by Dean Swift, in his representation to Lord Oxford' (quoted in Benzie 1972: 117).

Of course, this notice was written before the publication of Walker's *Critical Pronouncing Dictionary* (1791), which was to overshadow every other pronouncing dictionary for over a century: Mugglestone (1995: 41) writes that 'by the end of the nineteenth century, John Walker had . . . become a household name . . . He had in effect become one of the icons of the age, commonly referred to as "Elocution Walker"', just as Johnson had come to be labelled "Dictionary Johnson" in the public mind.' So, in terms of their experience as actors and elocutionists and of their success with the public, we might expect Sheridan and Walker to be 'good' phoneticians, and, as we shall see later in this section and in Chapter 5, their observations are often acute and detailed.

What, though, of the other, slightly less famous, authors of eighteenth-century pronouncing dictionaries? Kenrick, like Sheridan and Walker, was associated with the stage: not as an actor, but as a writer. The *DNB* entry for Kenrick hardly inspires confidence. 'He was brought up as a scalemaker, or in some such employment, but early became a hack writer. . . . He became the enemy of every decent and successful person, and so notorious a libeller that few condescended to answer him. His vanity led him to fancy himself equal to any task without serious study.' Yet this entry goes on to state that 'though a superlative scoundrel, he was clever. Kenrick was the first in England to use a system of superscripted numerals to indicate different vowel sounds, but in doing so, he may have been, with a true hack's instincts, jumping on a bandwagon. He is accused of this in the *Monthly Review* :

Mr. Sheridan was the first among the moderns who conceived the idea of establishing a certain standard of pronunciation by visible marks. Having thrown out this idea many years since, when he first laid open his plan of his Grammar and Dictionary, the thought was greedily seized on by the late Dr. Kenrick, who resolved to forestall our author's work. (*Monthly Review* 63 (July–Dec 1780), 245, quoted in Benzie 1972: 102 n. 20)[12]

So Kenrick was a hack, but a clever hack, and as such his pronouncements on language and the pronunciations indicated in his *New Dictionary of the English Language* (1773) should perhaps be treated with caution, but not dismissed entirely, for, as we shall see, his recommendations are not out of line with those of Sheridan and Walker, and his remarks on 'incorrect'

---

[12] In fact neither Kenrick nor Sheridan was the first to use this system: that honour goes to the Scot John Warden, whose *A Spelling Book* (1753) used just such a system (Charles Jones 1995: 55–7).

provincial pronunciations show that he was a keen observer of these, if only to lampoon them.

Of other authors of pronouncing dictionaries, less is known. For instance, little is known of John Burn apart from what he tells us himself in the introduction to his *Pronouncing Dictionary of the English Language* (1786; 1st edn., 1777), yet the dictionary must have enjoyed some success to have gone into a second edition. Burn tells us (1786: 2) that he 'has made the English Language a particular part of his study for more than forty years, and given all the attention he was capable of to the best speakers: yet he thought it highly expedient to compare his ideas of pronunciation with those of others, who have written before him on this subject'. As we shall see in Chapter 5, Burn's introduction shows both an awareness of current debates on matters of language, such as spelling reform (which he is against), and a sensitivity to linguistic change and variation.

Spence had, as far as we know, no connections with the stage. His interest in pronunciation was, as we saw in Chapter 1, largely fuelled by his desire for spelling reform, but he would almost certainly have come across works on pronunciation in the course of his early career as a teacher. In the Newcastle classrooms of the 1770s, Spence could not have avoided the works of the highly successful local grammarian Ann Fisher,[13] whose *Practical New Grammar* contains a chapter on Orthography in which the 'sounds' of each 'letter' are described, as well as a list of 'Words the same, or nearly alike, in Sound, but different in Signification and Spelling'. This is not an innovation on Fisher's part: indeed, the vast majority of eighteenth-century grammars follow this pattern, but, since we know that Fisher's grammar was written for, and used in, the classroom, it provides evidence that some attention was paid to 'orthography' by English teachers in the late eighteenth century, and that the 'sounds' of the letters would be taught along with the correct spelling of words. This is not to say that Spence used Fisher as a source of 'correct' pronunciation: indeed, he improves on Fisher, for, whereas she, like Sheridan, gives only three 'sounds' of ⟨a⟩ (short, as in *hat*, long as in *hate*, and 'open, full and broad' as in *call*), Spence has four, including the long sound in *father*. However, it does indicate that a teacher of English in the late eighteenth century would have a direct professional concern for, and experience in, teaching pronunciation. In this respect, Spence's credentials are as good as those of the earlier schoolmaster–orthoepists such as Mulcaster and Gil.

Such biographical information as we have on the authors of eighteenth-century pronouncing dictionaries suggests, then, that they learnt their trade either on the stage or in the classroom, and the later works, such as those of

---

[13] Indeed, we shall see in Chapter 4 that Spence almost certainly used an early edition of Fisher's grammar as the model for the short grammar prefacing the *Grand Repository*.

Burn and Walker,[14] make reference to earlier ones, suggesting that the provision of guides to 'correct' pronunciation had become something of an industry by the end of the century.[15] To judge whether or not these authors were 'good' phoneticians, though, we need to consider the consistency and clarity of the works themselves. We shall examine their accounts of certain sounds in detail in Chapter 5, but here we need to look at some extracts from the pronouncing dictionaries in order to establish that such an exercise is worthwhile. As we shall see in §4.2 with respect to Spence's New Alphabet, the systems of notation provided in these pronouncing dictionaries tell us about the phonemic inventory of the recommended accent—that is, how many phonemes there are (we can, for instance, easily tell that Sheridan has three sounds—whilst Spence and Walker have four) whilst we can find out about the incidence of those phonemes from the dictionary entries themselves. What we cannot tell from a dictionary such as *The Grand Repository* is the phonetic nature of those phonemes: how do we know that the sound in *father* was [ɑː] rather than [æː] or even [ɛː]? The answer is that we can know no such thing from Spence alone, but must put together information from the *Grand Repository* with that gleaned from other dictionaries, in which the sounds are described, along with that gathered by scholars such as Dobson from earlier sources.[16]

Fortunately, Walker, Sheridan, Kenrick, and Burn preface their pronouncing dictionaries with accounts of how the letters are pronounced, and with remarks about 'incorrect' pronunciations which are to be avoided. In addition, Walker has extensive notes in the body of his *Critical Pronouncing Dictionary* whenever there is controversy over the 'correct' pronunciation of a word, thus giving us a great deal of insight into the variability of pronunciation at the time even as he attempts to eradicate such variability. An example of this is Walker's (1791) note on the word *merchant*:

Mr. Sheridan pronounces the *e* in the first syllable of this word, like the *a* in *march*; and it is certain that, about thirty years ago, this was the general pronunciation; but since that time the sound of *a* has been gradually wearing away;[17] and the sound of *e*

---

[14] Walker seems to have studied a large number of orthoepistic works of the seventeenth and earlier eighteenth centuries: in the Preface to his *Critical Pronouncing Dictionary* he refers to Elphinstone, Nares, Jones, Kenrick, Sheridan, and Watts, whilst in his discussion of the 'Organic Formation of the Letters' he refers to Holder's *Elements of Speech* (1669).

[15] Mugglestone (1995: 36) suggests as much when she writes that, 'once the pronouncing dictionary was instituted, demand for the instruction it claimed to offer was high and, together with attendant texts on the same subject, it too was seemingly assimilated within the consequences of that "consumer revolution" documented by Neil McKendrick'.

[16] Because it is so difficult to establish the phonetic nature of the sounds represented in eighteenth-century pronouncing dictionaries and because, as we shall see in Chapter 4, Spence's system is essentially a phonemic one, I have chosen, except where discussing possible phonetic distinctions, to employ phonemic bracketing throughout in my discussion of eighteenth-century pronunciation.

[17] Walker's use of words is interesting here, in view of the discussion of the diffusion of sound

is so fully established, that the former is now become gross and vulgar, and is only to be heard among the lower orders of the people. It is, indeed, highly probable, that, however coarse this sound of *e* may now seem, it was once, not only the common pronunciation, but the most agreeable to analogy. We still find, that the vowel *i* before *r*, followed by another consonant, takes the short sound of *e*, which is really the short sound of slender *a*, as *virgin, virtue*, &c.; and it is a similar alteration which takes place in the *e* before *r*, followed by another consonant, in *clerk, Serjeant, Derby*, &c. where this vowel falls into the sound of the Italian *a. Sermon, service, vermin* &c. are still pronounced by the vulgar, as if written *sarmon, sarvice, varmint* &c.; and this was probably the ancient manner of pronouncing every *e* in the same situation. This analogy is now totally exploded; and except *clerk, serjeant* and a few proper names, we have scarcely another word in the language where this *e* has not its true sound. But instead of saying with Mr. Nares, that *Merchant* has returned to the proper sound of *e*, we may with greater probability assert, that this and every other word of the same form have acquired a sound of *e* which they never had before, and which, though a feebler and a shorter sound, conduces to the simplicity and regularity of our pronunciation.

Here, Walker not only tells us how the word *merchant* should be pronounced, but gives us a window into the sociolinguistic salience of the alternative pronunciation and an insight into the process of linguistic change that was in progress: in the middle of the eighteenth century, the /ˈmɑːrtʃənt/ pronunciation was acceptable, as the spellings from the Wentworth Letters cited in §3.2.2 confirm, but by 1791, this pronunciation is acceptable only in the words *clerk, serjeant, Derby*, and other proper names, whilst in all other words, such as *merchant, servant*, it is considered 'vulgar'. As we shall see in Chapter 5, such comments are extremely useful in tracing the diffusion of sound changes through the eighteenth century and often point to areas of interest and controversy.

The note cited above also gives some indication of how we can tell from eighteenth-century pronouncing dictionaries what the quality of the sound indicated by a particular symbol, or combination of symbol and diacritic, might have been (as we shall see, words like *slender* by this time had an established meaning in orthoepistic literature). Most of these dictionaries (though not the *Grand Repository*) have extensive prefaces in which the sounds are described, the most useful of these being Walker's *Critical Pronouncing Dictionary* with its 545 'rules'. Some of these rules are of a prescriptive nature, but others simply describe the 'sounds' of the 'letters' in ways which, like the descriptions of the earlier orthoepists, are often open to different interpretations, but which nevertheless provide useful clues about

---

change which appears in §3.4. Either he means that it is disappearing gradually as older people die off, 'wearing away' as they do; or that it is going out of fashion: people use it less; or that it is wearing away lexically: used in fewer words. In any case, Walker recognizes the gradual nature of linguistic change here, and, since he appears to present a 'phonetically abrupt' choice between /ɑː/ and /ɔː/ here, the gradualness must be lexical and/or social.

eighteenth-century pronunciation. As an example, let us look at Walker's rules 31–59 on the 'Organic Formation of the Letters'. These rules alone establish Walker's credentials as a 'good' phonetician, showing as they do his awareness of articulatory processes and the fact that he has studied the works of earlier phoneticians, notably Holder, whose *Elements of Speech* (1669) he acknowledges as the source of his distinction between voiced and voiceless consonants. Rule 41 states:

The best method of shewing the organic formation of the consonants will be to class them into such pairs as they naturally fall into, and then by describing one, we shall nearly describe its fellow, by which means the labour will be lessened, and the nature of the consonants better perceived. The consonants that fall into pairs are the following:

p	*f*	*t*	*s*	*sh*	*th*	*k*	*ch* chair
b	*v*	*d*	*z*	*zh*	*dh*	*g*	*j* jail

(Walker 1791: 6)

Whilst in rule 43 he goes on to explain the distinction:

This difference in the formation of these consonants may be more distinctly perceived in the *s* and *z* than in any other of the letters; the former is sounded by the simple issue of the breath between the teeth, without any vibration of it in the throat, and may be called a hissing sound; whilst the latter cannot be formed without generating a sound in the throat, which may be called a vocal sound. The upper rank of letters, therefore, may be called breathing consonants; and the lower, vocal ones.   (Walker 1791: 6)

These rules do not tell us anything particularly interesting about eighteenth-century pronunciation, but they do indicate that Walker was able to describe sounds accurately. It is when we look at his descriptions of vowel sounds that the information becomes significant. In this section on the 'Organic Formation of the Letters', Walker describes vowels in terms of the aperture of the mouth and the position of the tongue and lips, again building on work done by the seventeenth-century phoneticians. His descriptions of the ⟨a⟩ sounds are as follows:

32. It will be necessary to observe, that there are three long sounds of the letter *a*, which are formed by a greater or lesser expansion of the internal part of the mouth.
33. The German *a*, heard in *ball, wall* &c. is formed by a strong and grave expression of the breath through the mouth, which is open nearly in a circular form, while the tongue, contracting itself to the root, as to make way for the sound, almost rests upon the under jaw.
34. The Italian *a*, heard in *father*, closes the mouth a little more than the German *a*, and by raising the lower jaw, widening the tongue, and advancing it a little nearer to the lips, renders its sound less hollow and deep.

35. The slender *a*, or that heard in *lane*, is formed in the mouth still higher than the last; and in pronouncing it, the lips, as if to give it a slender sound, dilate their aperture horizontally; while the tongue, to answer this narrow emission of breath, widens itself to the cheeks, raises itself nearer the palate, and by this means, a less hollow sound than either of the former is produced.   (Walker 1791: 5)

Although these descriptions are wordy to those of us used to the binary descriptions of twentieth-century phonology, these 'rules' tell us that the 'German *a*' is back, open, and rounded; the 'Italian' is unrounded and less open; and the 'slender' less open still, higher, and unrounded. When we look at Walker's rules 72–85 on the different 'sounds' of ⟨a⟩, we glean even more useful information: rule 72 simply states '*A* has three long sounds and two short ones'. Rule 73 then deals with the 'first sound . . . which among the English is its name. This is what is called by most grammarians its slender sound (35) . . . It exactly corresponds to the sound of the French *ê* in the beginning of the words *être* and *tête*' (1791: 10). Here, Walker uses two strategies to indicate this sound of ⟨a⟩: first, he uses the terms defined in the rules on 'Organic Formation of the Letters' quoted above, terms which in any case by the end of the eighteenth century must have become conventional: as he acknowledges, 'most grammarians' use these terms. The contemporary readership probably had a fair idea what was meant by 'slender', just as twentieth-century British readers know what is meant by the 'flat' *a* of Northern English however annoying such terms are to phonologists. These same terms—'slender' *a*, 'Italian' *a*, and the 'Broad German' *a*—were used by Dr Johnson in his *Dictionary*, and Walker quotes Dr Johnson's observation on the last of these in rule 79. Walker also compares the English sounds to similar ones in foreign languages, thus the 'slender' *a* is like the *ê* in French *être*. This information is very valuable to the twentieth-century reader, as, providing the pronunciation of French has not changed radically since 1791, this tells us that the sound was still a monophthong, and more open than [e:]—probably something like [ɛː]. Likewise, 'Italian' *a* is the sound used by Italians in *Toscano*, *Romana*, and this, along with the description in rule 34, suggests [ɑː] or [aː].

The above examples should suffice to show that Walker was a 'good' phonetician, who had studied earlier works on phonetics, was an acute observer, and was able to describe the nature of sounds in a way that is reasonably clear even to the twentieth-century reader. His immediate predecessors do not give anything like the same amount of detail, but still provide clear enough articulatory descriptions. Take Sheridan's (1780: 6) description of his ⟨a⟩ sounds, for example: 'a^3 is the fullest sound, made by the greatest aperture of the mouth, and the voice strikes upon that part of the palate which is nearest to the passage by which the voice issues: a^1 is formed by a gradually less aperture, and the stroke of the voice more advanced; a^2 in like proportion still more so and in sounding e^3 the mouth is almost closed.' (Note that Sheridan uses a^3 as in *hall*; a^1 as in *hat*; a^2 as in *hate*; e^3 as in *see*. Sheridan did not recognize the 'Italian' *a* sound.)

So, eighteenth-century pronouncing dictionaries provide us with descriptions of sounds which build on, and are as good as, those of the seventeenth-century orthoepists. These descriptions reassure us that the authors are 'good' phoneticians and supplement the phonemic (inventory and incidence) information provided in the notation systems and the dictionary entries themselves.

3.3.3. *Eighteenth-century pronouncing dictionaries: descriptive or prescriptive?*

We must now consider how 'honest' the authors of these dictionaries were in providing descriptions of 'good' eighteenth-century pronunciation rather than prescriptions for an idealized pronunciation not necessarily used by anybody. In this respect, Walker has come under more criticism than any other eighteenth-century orthoepist, simply because he was so successful in laying down the 'rules' for correct pronunciation. The note on *merchant*, quoted above, recommends the retention of /ɑː/ in exactly those words which have that pronunciation in present-day RP: is this because Walker was such an accurate observer of the 'best' pronunciation in 1791, or is it simply the case that he was so influential that subsequent generations have adopted his rules?[18] What came first: the chicken or the egg? Sheldon (1947: 146) considers Walker less reliable than Sheridan in this respect: 'While Sheridan reflects the speech of his time better, Walker satisfies the temper of his time better, and the demand for linguistic regulation and reform. . . . there can be no doubt that, if any one single person were to be named as the greatest influence on English pronunciation, that person would have to be Walker.' Alston (1972: EL 155), in his introduction to the microfiche text of *A General Dictionary of the English Language*, seems likewise impressed by Sheridan's 'honesty': 'A curious but nonetheless evident fact, is that though the tone of his Preface suggests an authoritative and prescriptive reformer, Sheridan's pronunciation appears to be much more typical of the last half of the eighteenth century than one might expect.'

This, of course, begs the question: how do we know what was typical if pronouncing dictionaries like Sheridan's and Walker's are our major source

---

[18] Matthews provides evidence that suggests the former. He concludes from a comparison of earlier eighteenth-century 'occasional' spellings and later eighteenth-century orthoepists' 'phonetic' spellings of vulgarisms 'that the pronunciation of [ɑː] and [ɜː] in words which originally contained *er*, *person*, *star*, *hard*, *clerk*, *Hertford*, etc., had been practically settled in London speech, the distribution being the same as that which now obtains in Standard' (1937: 325).

of information? What seems to tip the scales in Sheridan's favour is that the criticisms levelled at him, particularly by the author of *A Caution to Gentlemen Who Use Sheridan's Dictionary*, seem to advocate a pronunciation which must have been very stilted if it existed at all by 1780. Sheridan is criticized above all for admitting that vowels in unstressed syllables are pronounced differently from those in stressed syllables, something that even Walker allows, as we shall see in §5.7. Sheldon notes that the author of this tract

disapproves of the fact that Sheridan makes no distinction in the pronunciation of unstressed syllables, writing <u>cavurn</u>, <u>comuner</u>, <u>culpuble</u> all with the same sound. And he explains that people of credit say BE-STOW, BEEN, CITIZEN, SPIRIT, ARETHMETIC, ENFORCE, ENJOY, not, as Sheridan, <u>bisto</u>, <u>citizn</u>, <u>sperit</u>, <u>arithmetic</u>, <u>inforce</u>, <u>injoy</u>.[19] In the case of <u>champion</u>, the pronunciation is not TSHAM-PYUN as Sheridan has it; the last syllable must be pronounced -PEUN.   (Anon. 1790: 31, quoted in Sheldon 1938: 308)

Harking back to Wyld's criticism of Gill for suggesting that ME /ai/ was still a diphthong in 1611, Sheldon points out that the author of *A Caution* is still criticizing Sheridan for advocating a monophthongal pronunciation as late as 1790:

Particularly amazing, at this late date, is the caution given to Sheridan's readers to pronounce <u>ai</u> as a diphthong. For over a century, various grammarians had been pairing <u>ai</u> and long <u>a</u> (<u>pane</u> and <u>pain</u>) in their lists of words pronounced alike. Yet there still hangs on in the minds of some of the most puristic, the idea that a distinction should be kept between these two groups, and that the two letters in <u>ai</u> should be shown by the diphthongal sound . . . the significant point of the criticism is clear; Sheridan regards <u>ai</u> as a single vowel; 'people of rank and education' always pronounce it as a diphthong.   (Sheldon 1938: 310)

Sheldon's comments show what a 'bad' phonetician the author of *A Caution* must have been: Sheridan is seen as 'honest' because his critics are so misguided, but many of the criticisms in *A Caution* could equally have been applied to Walker, who, like Sheridan, states that the sound of ⟨ai⟩ in *pain*, *gain*, *stain* is the same 'slender *a*' as in *lade*, *trade*, *spade*, etc. (Walker 1791: 10). They were not because, as Sheldon suggests, Walker was respected and influential, whereas, as we saw in §1.2.2, Sheridan was Irish, and therefore fair game. Why, then, has Walker been regarded as somehow less authentic than Sheridan in his representation of late-eighteenth-century pronunciation? Apart from the authoritative and prescriptive tone which was, as Sheldon suggests, the secret of Walker's success, we should perhaps be wary of his pronouncements because of his predilection for 'analogy'. Although Walker in his preface pays lip-service to the idea of letting 'custom' (i.e. the consensus of educated speakers in London) dictate the 'correct' pronunciation, we see, particularly in those notes in which he takes

---

[19] The pronunciation of *been* is omitted from the list in *A Caution to Gentlemen*.

issue with his fellow orthoepists, that his favourite criterion is 'analogy'. Take, for example, his note on *soot*:

Notwithstanding I have Mr. Sheridan, Mr. Nares, Dr. Kenrick, W. Johnston, Mr. Perry, and the professors of the black Art themselves, against me in the pronunciation of this word, I have ventured to prefer the regular pronunciation to the irregular. The adjective *sooty* has its regular sound among the correctest speakers, which has induced Mr. Sheridan to mark it so; but nothing can be more absurd than to pronounce the substantive in one manner, and the adjective derived from it by adding *y*, in another. The other Orthoepists, therefore, who pronounce both these words with the *oo* like *u*, are more consistent than Mr. Sheridan, though, upon the whole, not so right.   (Walker 1791)

Here, we see that Walker regards /uː/ as the 'regular' sound of ⟨oo⟩, so that, except for a small number of words spelt this way for which the short vowel is acceptable, this long sound should be used. Moreover, he sees it as ridiculous to have a base word pronounced differently from its derivatives, and so decides on /suːt/ and /'suːtɪ/. We shall see in §3.4 and in Chapter 5 that, when a sound change is in the process of lexical diffusion, as the shortening of ME /oː/ in *look*, *foot*, etc. certainly was in the late eighteenth century, a base word may well be pronounced differently from its derivatives, because of the different phonetic environments involved. So, despite Walker's credentials as a 'good' phonetician, we must always be wary of his tendency to impose regularity where it may not have existed. He was, after all, in the business of laying down strict guidelines for a 'standard' pronunciation' and 'standard' has been defined by Milroy and Milroy (1985: 23) as 'an idea in the mind rather than a reality—a set of abstract norms to which actual usage will conform to a greater or lesser extent'. In testing the 'honesty' of eighteenth-century orthoepists, we are engaged in a somewhat circular process, for, apart from the 'occasional' spellings, and evidence from rhymes, which become less reliable as time goes on, we are wholly dependent on these orthoepists for our understanding of eighteenth-century pronunciation. What we must do is compare them with each other and beware the 'lone voice', particularly when that voice articulates the principle of analogy.

3.3.4. *The evidence of 'provincial' authors*

It was hinted in the previous section that Sheridan was vulnerable to criticism above all because he was Irish. Sheridan had the dubious honour of being held up to ridicule by no less a man than Dr Johnson, who said: 'What entitles Sheridan to fix the pronunciation of English? He has in the first place the disadvantage of being an Irishman' (Boswell 1934: ii. 161).[20] The author of *A Caution* is not above mentioning this either: 'The errors

[20] Like many of Dr Johnson's pronouncements, this should perhaps be taken with a pinch of salt. The *DNB* entry on Sheridan tells us that he was given a pension of £200 to write his dictionary by Lord Bute, one of Johnson's patrons. Johnson saw this as an affront.

which exposed his System to the censure and ridicule of the learned, I attribute to habitual influence. He was an *Irishman*; and to the last period of his life, his Origin was obvious in his pronunciation' (Anon. 1790: 4, quoted in Sheldon 1938: 306). This brings us to the last question that we must consider in evaluating the evidence of eighteenth-century pronouncing dictionaries: how would the authors have had access to what was by then agreed to be the 'best' pronunciation—that is, that of well-educated and well-bred people in London?

All 'provincial' authors, including Spence, were subjected to the same criticisms in the eighteenth century (and later). The attitudes expressed in the quotations above suggest a 'knee-jerk' reaction on the part of southern English critics which may seem to us typically eighteenth-century, typically Augustan,[21] but, even with the hindsight of late-twentieth-century tolerance, the question has to be asked: how could a person in the late eighteenth century who had spent all his or her life in, say, Newcastle or Glasgow or Dublin be conversant with the 'correct' pronunciation of English current amongst educated and refined Londoners? In the case of Sheridan, of course, this question does not really apply: he was educated at Westminster for a short while and on returning to Dublin came under the influence of Swift. It is highly unlikely that, with this education, and his acquaintance with the stage, Sheridan would be unaware of the 'best' speech, even if he spoke with a slight 'brogue' himself. His awareness of the 'correct' way to speak and the 'incorrect' features of Irish pronunciation are proved by his inclusion of 'Rules to be observed by the Natives of Ireland' in his *General Dictionary*, a set of rules upon which even Walker could not improve. Walker, although not of genteel stock, was born in Middlesex and spent much of his life in London, so he, too, would have been well acquainted with 'correct' speakers. What, though, of those, like Spence, who were 'provincial' in the sense of having been born, bred, and educated outside London and/or 'vulgar' in the sense of belonging to the lower classes? We have seen in §1.2.3 that Spence, when asked how he might have access to 'correct' punctuation, replied that he attended 'All Saints' Church every Sunday morning'.

The serious point here is that Spence regarded the clergy in Newcastle as providing a model of correct pronunciation, a point which he made again in *The Giant Killer* (1814), where, in an article entitled 'An infallible way to correct Provincialisms and other Vulgarisms in Speech', he exhorts his readers to 'pay attention to the Clergy in the Pulpit, from whom they will

---

[21] Twentieth-century philologists have been known to level the same kind of criticism at 'provincials'. Thus Wyld (1936: 179) writes of Elphinston: 'The first thing which occurs to us with regard to Elphinston is that he was a Scot, not in itself a drawback in the ordinary affairs of life, but a fact which produces some misgivings in connexion with one who is to act as a guide to English speech in the second half of the eighteenth century.'

have language which may be depended upon'. Buchanan also saw the clergy as having an important role in the dissemination of his unifying national standard. 'With respect to the inhabitants of North Britain . . . let gentlemen at the bar, and those that minister in holy things, be especially exemplary . . . and let both clergy and laity enjoin the schoolmasters over that part of the united kingdom, to acquire and teach a proper Pronunciation to the rising generation' (Buchanan 1766, quoted in Crowley 1991: 79).

Charles Jones (1993) suggests that, in late-eighteenth-century Scotland, the usage of the Church and the Bar may already have constituted a kind of regional or 'modified' standard, not necessarily *identical* with the usage of London as described by, for example, Walker, but none the less acceptable in polite society within Scotland, and distinct from 'vulgar' usage. Evidence that some kind of modified, 'genteel' variety was already recognized by this time is provided by Sylvester Douglas, who makes a distinction between 'the grosser barbarisms of the vulgar Scotch jargon' and the language of his target readership, those 'whose language has already been in a great degree refined from the provincial dross, by frequenting English company, and studying the great masters of the English tongue in their writings'. He aims to help these readers to rid themselves of 'those *vestigia ruris* which are apt to remain so long' (Douglas 1779, quoted in C. Jones 1991: 101). Likewise, James Adams, in his *Pronunciation of the English Language Vindicated from Imputed Anomaly and Caprice* (1799), makes a distinction between 'the broad dialect' and 'the tempered medium, still retaining its characteristic distinction of Scotch' (quoted in C. Jones 1991: 7). That there is some continuity between this 'tempered medium' of the late eighteenth century and the language of middle-class Scots today is suggested by Aitken (1979: 96), who, with reference to the eighteenth century, writes that 'some of the features which differentiate the accents of present-day middle-class Scots from those of working-class Scottish speakers were introduced on an English model at this time'. Later Aitken (1979: 99) goes on to refer to the 'anglicising Scots' of the eighteenth century and suggests that they attempted to teach a model of pronunciation identical to that of London and, understandably, failed. The question that I wish to address is whether this was really the case, or whether the model presented in eighteenth-century pronouncing dictionaries produced by Scots and, indeed, northern English writers was already the 'tempered medium' referred to by Adams, rather than what we might call the 'proto-RP' of educated London usage. To answer this question fully would require a detailed examination of *all* the pronouncing dictionaries and other works on pronunciation written by Scots and northerners in the eighteenth century, a monumental task comparable to that performed by Dobson (1957).[22] What we need to recognize

---

[22] Such an account, at least of the Scots orthoepists, is provided in Charles Jones (1995).

here is that 'modified' standards may well have existed in the eighteenth century, and that what counted as 'refined' and 'correct' or, to use Spence's words, 'the most agreeable' pronunciation in Edinburgh or Newcastle may have been different from the 'proto-RP' developing in the capital and described (or rather prescribed) by Walker. We shall see in §3.4. and in Chapter 5 that such differences may shed light on the geographical diffusion of sound changes in the eighteenth century, and that to dismiss the works of 'provincial' orthoepists would be to ignore potentially valuable information.

3.4.1. *Pronouncing dictionaries as a record of lexical diffusion*

We have seen in §3.3. that the pronouncing dictionaries of the eighteenth century can be judged in the same terms as the orthoepistic works of the two preceding centuries and that, in these terms, they can be seen to provide a wealth of valuable information on the pronunciation of eighteenth-century English. We have yet to consider the one overwhelming advantage that the pronouncing dictionary has over any other kind of orthoepistic work: it provides a record of the pronunciation of every word in the lexicon. By 'the lexicon', I mean, of course, the nomenclature of any one dictionary and not the 'inner' lexicon that forms part of any one speaker's grammar. No dictionary is ever a complete record of any one person's, or even any language's, active and/or passive vocabulary, and some eighteenth-century pronouncing dictionaries (notably the *Grand Repository*) have much shorter word-lists than others, but even relatively short dictionaries like the *Grand Repository* provide a great deal more information concerning the incidence or distribution of particular sounds than even the most detailed orthoepistic works of the sixteenth and seventeenth centuries. For example, Christopher Cooper is one of the earliest orthoepists to provide information about the lengthening of ME /a/ before fricatives and /r/, and, in the examples he gives, provides hints that the process of lengthening was conditioned by the phonetic environment. First, Cooper tells us that 'in these *can, pass by, a* is short; in *cast, past* for *passed*, it is long' (1687, quoted in Sundby 1953: 4). Then, he goes on to write: '*A* Hath three sounds . . . the first of these, for the most part, is pronounced long in its own sound before *nch* and *s* when another Consonant follows, and before *r* unless *sh* follows' (1687, quoted in Sundby 1953: 34)[23] and to give a list of pairs of words with 'a short' in the first of each pair, and 'a long' in the second. These are: *bar, barge*; *blab, blast*; *cap, carking*; *car, carp*; *cat, cast*; *dash, dart*; *flash, flasket*; *gash, gasp*; *grand, grant*; *land, lance*; *mash, mask*; *pat, path*; *tar, tart*.

---

[23] Cooper also provides information on, and examples for, the 'slender *a*' here, but I have omitted them, as the point of interest here is the contrasting environments for 'long' and 'short' *a*.

Here, Cooper provides a total of twenty-nine different lexical examples, giving the clear impression of a 'rule' for the lengthening of ME /a/ in the late seventeenth century which could be stated as follows: ME /a/ is lengthened before /r/ followed by another consonant (/-rC), before /s/ followed by another consonant (/-sC) and before /θ/ (/-θ). Cooper provides us with enough information to make the first two generalizations, although he does add that ME /a/ is not lengthened before /rʃ/. However, we have only one word, *path*, as evidence for the last. We cannot tell from Cooper's evidence alone whether this lengthening was general in the environment /-θ/—that is, whether it also occurred in *bath* or not. Moreover, Cooper's twenty-nine examples are not really enough to predict with any confidence whether the exception noted by Cooper (that of words like *marsh*) is isolated or not. Cooper's exemplification is full by the standards of seventeenth-century orthoepistic works, but pales by comparison with the amount of information on the lexical distribution of sounds provided by even a relatively modestly sized pronouncing dictionary such as the *Grand Repository*. As we shall see in §5.2, the *Grand Repository* provides 412 words in which ME /a/ appears in the environment /-rC and it is not the case that all these realizations of the vowel are long. Nor is Spence alone amongst writers of eighteenth-century pronouncing dictionaries in having this 'lexical set' split between long and short realizations of ME /a/. What appears, from Cooper's relatively sparse evidence, to be a clear case of an environmentally conditioned sound change becomes much more complicated when we inspect the much fuller evidence provided by eighteenth-century pronouncing dictionaries. What we have to consider here is whether this fuller evidence is a blessing or a curse: will we be able to see the wood for the trees and, even if we can, is the ability to scrutinize so many individual 'trees', or words to abandon the metaphor, an advantage to the historical phonologist?

3.4.2. *Lexical diffusion and sound change*

Until the late 1960s, the sparsity of exemplification in orthoepistic works has not been seen as a problem, largely because of the dominance within historical phonology of theories incorporating the basic tenet of what has come to be known as the 'Neogrammarian Doctrine', stated clearly by Osthoff and Brugmann in 1878: 'Every sound change, inasmuch as it occurs mechanically, takes place according to laws that admit no exception' (Lehmann 1967: 204). Labov (1994: 422) points out that 'the obverse of this "exceptionlessness" is lexical regularity: that when a sound changes it affects every word in which that sound change occurs in the same phonetic environment'. If we accept the Neogrammarian view of the regularity of sound change, then a few lexical examples providing us with the environments in which the sound change does or does not occur should suffice: if Cooper, for example, tells us that ME /a/ is lengthened in *tart* but not in *tar*;

in *carp* but not in *car*, then this should be more than enough to allow us to reconstruct the sound change set out in §3.4.1 above, with perhaps some further refinement of the phonetic conditioning to allow for the prohibition of this sound change in words like *marsh*. Cooper himself, without the benefit of Neogrammarian theory, goes a long way towards constructing such a 'rule'. Likewise, this theory of 'exceptionlessness' would lead us to believe that, if ME /a/ was lengthened in *path*, then it would also be lengthened in *bath*. Where 'exceptions' to a regular sound change are apparent, Neogrammarian theory would explain them in terms covered by the rider 'inasmuch as it occurs mechanically'. The non-mechanical or irregular processes invoked to explain exceptions were *analogy* and *dialect borrowing*. However, these explanations have always appeared *post hoc* and to have something of the *deus ex machina* about them. This point is made clearly by Wang (1969: 10), who suggests that, 'contrasted with the sweeping scope of phonetic laws, which have direct or indirect physiological motivation when internally induced, these suggestions appear unsatisfyingly ancillary and particularistic. In some cases, such suggestions are completely ad hoc and unconvincing, but they remain in the literature mainly for lack of alternative explanations'.

Of course, careful philologists such as Dobson and Jespersen would never reconstruct a sound change on the basis of a few examples from a single source: the size of Dobson (1957) alone is testimony to the fact that he has painstakingly collated and compared all the available evidence. However, both these distinguished scholars keep firmly within the Neogrammarian tradition, explaining irregularities or exceptions as caused by either analogy or dialect borrowing. Indeed, the assumption of regularity is so strong that they are unable to take at face value Cooper's evidence for the phonetic conditioning on lengthening of ME /a/ before /r/ outlined in §3.4.1 above. Dobson, noting that Daines as well as Cooper shows the lengthened vowel before /r/ followed by another consonant, writes that 'Daines appears to have [aː] in *bars* and one would think it unlikely that the singular *bar* would not have the same vowel' (1957: 518).

Here, Dobson is invoking the principle of 'analogy' even when there is no evidence for it: he simply cannot believe that analogy would not operate in such circumstances. Likewise, Jespersen explains Cooper's short *a* in *pass by* as due to weak sentence stress and, after suggesting that Cooper has a short vowel in *bar, car, tar* because these words might occur before a word beginning with a vowel, goes on to write: 'Cooper, of course, says nothing about *bar, car, tar* having "a longa" before words beginning with a consonant, but we must be allowed to suppose that such was the case' (Jesperson 1909–49: 310). Indeed, Jespersen explicitly invokes the principle of 'preservative' or 'preventative' analogy in his introduction: 'A general tendency to change a sound in a certain direction may be checked in the case of some words, if there exists some other closely related form (of the same or some other word) in which the sound exists under such circumstances that it is not affected by the change' (Jesperson 1909–49: 18).

On the other hand, Dobson could be seen as invoking 'dialect borrowing' or at least 'dialect mixture' on a massive scale, when he writes that the 'central theme' of his book 'is that many elements went to make up the developing standard spoken language of the ENE period; that there were many variant pronunciations, many levels and styles of speech, co-existing at any time' (1957: p. v). Indeed, he often explains exceptions to ENE sound changes by reference to variant forms in ME.[24]

Of course, analogy and dialect borrowing might well provide convincing explanations for certain sets of exceptions to otherwise regular sound changes, and, without the Neogrammarian assumption of regularity, the discipline of historical phonology would never have been founded: the problem is that even the most 'regular' sets of changes, such as the Great Vowel Shift, appear to leave 'residues': irregular forms which are difficult to explain even with recourse to analogy and dialect borrowing. One notorious set of 'exceptions' to the Great Vowel Shift is the set of words which did not take part in what Charles Jones (1991: 283) terms the '[ee] > [ii] vowel shift re-enactment', which changed earlier /mɛːt/ to present-day RP /miːt/ etc. Apart from words with /r/ after the ME /ɛː/, these exceptions are *great*, *break*, *steak*, *drain*, and (less convincingly, because archaic) *yea*. Labov (1978) uses evidence from a study of a similar sound change in the north-eastern cities of the USA to show that, when spectrographic analysis is used, it becomes apparent that the phonetic conditioning of sound change is in fact much finer than could have been perceived by earlier philologists, or, indeed, orthoepists. He finds that a combination of preceding and following consonants may act together to favour or disfavour a certain change, and that in the case of this particular vowel-raising, a preceding postconsonantal /r/ and a following voiceless stop both disfavour raising. He goes on to state that 'not only are *great* and *break* preceded by post-consonantal /r/, but they are followed by voiceless stops so that both initial and following environments disfavor the change—if the EME raising of ēā operated on the same general principles as our late twentieth-century raisings', and proceeds to explain the unraised vowel in *great*, *break* as opposed to the raised one in *treat*, *creak*, by virtue of the fact that 'voiced clusters . . . have the heaviest effect' (1978: 294). *Yea* is explained partly by analogy with *nay* and partly because 'such discourse particles ranged over five-sixths of the vowel spectrum, whilst *Drain* shows other irregularities in its history . . . which make it a special case. This leaves *steak* . . . as a true exception which we

---

[24] An example of this occurs in the discussion of shortening of ME /ɛː/ where Dobson (1957: 503) writes: 'in the word *jet*, adopted from OF, ModE ĕ may either represent a ME variant in ĕ or be by shortening of ę̄'.

cannot give any rationale or probabilistic account for. Since this was [eː] in the sixteenth century, it should now have a high vowel' (1978: 294). Here Labov, with benefit of modern techniques of research and analysis, and drawing on the Neogrammarian principles of regularity of sound change, analogy, and the 'uniformitarian principle', goes a long way towards explaining what he quotes Samuels (1965) as calling 'those *enfants terribles* of traditional *Lautlehre*' (1978: 290), but even he is left with the one 'true' exception of *steak*.

In a more recent survey (1994), Labov reviews the vast amount of research carried out to date on the 'tensing' of short /æ/ in the same north-eastern cities of the USA. Again, he finds that a fine phonetic conditioning is operating, favouring tensing after /m/, /n/, /f/, /θ/, and /s/ in Philadelphia. However, there are certain sets of 'exceptions'.

- Normally, this tensing occurs only when the /æ/ is in a closed syllable, so that *ham*, *hand* would be tense but *hammer* lax. Where the following syllable is a level 2 inflexional suffix, the vowel becomes tense: thus *hamming* as in *hamming it up* has a tense vowel. This could be explained by 'analogy' with the base form of the verb *ham*.
- If the /æ/ occurs in a word in which it is the only vowel and it can be realized as schwa, then it remains lax: thus *can* (= 'tin can') is tense, but *can* (modal verb) remains lax. This too could be explained by 'analogy', since schwa is lax and so 'the marked stressed form can be said to be lax by analogy with the unstressed forms' (Labov 1994: 431).
- If a level 1 derivational suffix follows, then tensing is variable: *Lassie* and *plastic* are variable: 'The variability of the first may be said to reside in the variable identification of the isolated word *lass* in the first part of *Lassie* . . . But there is no free form *plast* that might support the same argument for *plastic*' (1994: 431).[25]
- 'Strong verbs ending in nasals remain lax, contrary to the general rule' (Labov 1994: 431). According to Labov, grammatical information of this kind cannot be accounted for by any of the Neogrammarian principles, yet the findings here are not isolated: Toon (1976) found the same class of words in Old English resisted the raising of West Germanic short /a/ before nasals. This is not 'analogy' in the Neogrammarian sense, but can be explained if we allow grammatical as well as phonetic conditioning.
- 'All vowels followed by voiced stops are lax, except for those of *mad*, *bad* and *glad* which are always tense' (Labov 1994: 431). Labov considers that this might be explained by the above words all being

---

[25] Of course, *plastic* is also variable in RP. Labov does not seem to consider the possibility of analogy with *plaster*, or, indeed, that some speakers might consider *plast* as in *Elastoplast* to be a base form. But the latter are, of course, called *Band Aids* in the USA.

'affective adjectives', but that *sad* with a lax vowel disproves this hypothesis. 'This is massively regular for the entire Philadelphia speech community—a clear case of lexical diffusion, arrested in mid-career at some point in the past' (Labov 1994: 431).

So, as in the earlier study of raising, Labov concludes here that, whilst many apparent 'exceptions' to regular sound changes can be explained by fine phonetic conditioning (a regularity more subtle than had earlier been realized) or by analogy, there are still cases that can be explained only as lexical exceptions. In the 1994 study, Labov examines the claim, first stated in Wang (1969) that sound change is not, as the Neogrammarians stated, phonetically gradual and lexically abrupt, but proceeds by lexical diffusion—that is, it is phonetically abrupt but lexically gradual. Thus, when a sound change is in progress, we can expect the kind of split in a lexical set that we in fact find in §5.2.3, when examining ME /a/ before rC, and, even when a change is complete, a 'residue' may remain as a result of two (or more) changes competing for the same lexical items. Labov comes to the conclusion that lexical diffusion is a factor that needs to be taken into account in the study of sound change, but that the regular 'Neogrammarian' type of sound change also occurs.

Similar conclusions, though within a different theoretical framework (that of lexical phonology) are reached by Kiparsky (1988), McMahon (1991), and Harris (1989). Both Labov and Harris see lexical diffusion as a process operating typically at a certain stage in the life cycle of a sound change. According to Labov (1994: 542):

- *Regular sound change* is the result of a gradual transformation of a single phonetic feature of a phoneme in a continuous phonetic space. It is characteristic of the initial stages of a change that develops within a linguistic system, without lexical or grammatical conditioning or any degree of social awareness ('change from below').
- *Lexical diffusion* is the result of the abrupt substitution of one phoneme for another in words that contain that phoneme. The older and newer forms of the word will usually differ by several phonetic features. This process is most characteristic of the late stages of an internal change that has been differentiated by lexical and grammatical conditioning, or has developed a high degree of social awareness or of borrowings from other systems ('change from above').

Harris, on the other hand, sees the same sequence of 'events' as 'a continuous process whereby individual changes can percolate deeper and deeper into a linguistic system' (1989: 55). He explains that 'A typical progression is for sound changes to begin life as modifications to low-level output rules and then over time to penetrate deeper and deeper into the linguistic system. From the perspective of Lexical Phonology, this process can be viewed as the progressive infiltration of lexical structure by phonological rules' (1989: 37).

So, both Labov and Harris see the gradual phonetic modification traditionally viewed as regular or Neogrammarian sound change as typical of the early stages of a change and lexical diffusion as occurring at a later stage—in Labov's view, when the change has been noticed by the speech community and may be subject to extension or correction because of its 'social' meaning. Harris sees a typical progression whereby the sound change will eventually affect the phonology of the language: 'the lexicalization of a phonological rule thus represents a potential intermediate stage between the inception of a change as a post-lexical rule and its eventual demise when and if the contrast comes to be phonemicized' (1989: 55).

The place of lexical diffusion in sound change is still very much a 'live' issue: Labov's formulation has, for instance, already been challenged by Milroy (1993), as not taking sufficiently into account the complexity of variation in 'vernacular' as opposed to 'standardized' languages. Milroy makes a very valid point, but the data examined by, for instance, Labov (1994) and Harris (1989) certainly show that lexical diffusion exists. Moreover, Labov (1972, 1994) demonstrates that, even where sound change is 'regular', the phonetic conditioning may be so fine as to appear like lexical diffusion—the *great*, *break*, *drain* examples being a case in point.

The consequence of these developments in historical linguistic theory is that the level of exemplification provided by pronouncing dictionaries becomes very important. If we can view what is, in a sense, a whole lexicon at a point in history at which a sound change is in progress, then any lexical diffusion will become apparent in a 'split' in that lexicon between words exhibiting the 'old' sound and those with the 'new'. Furthermore, if we compare the 'lexicons' of dictionaries from earlier and later in the century, and from different parts of the country, we may well find patterns of diffusion through time and space. Lastly, if, as Labov suggests, lexical diffusion is typically involved in 'change from above', a stage at which speakers become aware of the sociolinguistic salience of the change, then the pronouncing dictionaries, written as they were with the express purpose of prescribing 'correct' usage, should show evidence of this. Indeed, there are explicit references in some of the pronouncing dictionaries to the minefield that had been created for speakers by lexically diffusing changes. Take, for instance, Kenrick's comment on what has been seen by linguists as theoretically impossible (see Labov 1972): the reversal of the previously attested merger of ME /oi/ and /iː/ in *toil*, *tile*; *loin*, *line*, etc.: he writes that it 'would now appear affectation' to pronounce *boil*, *join*, otherwise than *bile*, *jine*, but that the same pronunciation in *oil*, *toil* is 'a vicious custom' which 'prevails in common conversation' (Kenrick 1773 quoted in Jespersen 1909–49: 330). For the eighteenth-century reader, caught between the Scylla of vulgarity and the Charybdis of affectation, the pronouncing dictionary became an indispensible guide, but, for the twentieth-century historical phonologist, it provides invaluable detailed evidence of lexical diffusion at a time when 'change from above', in Labov's sense, was certainly in progress with regard to several sound changes, some of which are still diffusing today.

In Chapter 5, we shall examine Spence's *Grand Repository* and other eighteenth-century pronouncing dictionaries for detailed evidence of the lexical diffusion discussed above. However, since the *Grand Repository* is the main focus of our attention here, we should first look more closely at the nature of Spence's notation. This we shall do in Chapter 4.

4. Spence's *Grand Repository of the English Language*

We have seen in the previous chapter that the pronouncing dictionaries produced in the later eighteenth century constitute a potentially very valuable source of information on the pronunciation of English in that period, not least because the respelling of each dictionary entry provides enough instances of any sound for patterns of variation and hence of the diffusion of sound changes, to be observed. What I intend to consider in this chapter is why Spence's *Grand Repository* deserves particular attention.

4.1. THE FIRST 'PHONETIC' DICTIONARY OF ENGLISH?

It has to be stated at the outset that by 'first phonetic dictionary of English' I mean the first to adhere consistently to the 'phonetic' principle of *one sound = one spelling*.[1] In the literature on eighteenth-century pronouncing dictionaries, several works are cited as being the first to provide information of various kinds regarding the pronunciation of English. Up to a certain point, there is a progression here, from the first appearance of accentuation in a dictionary in Dyche's spelling dictionary of 1723, through Benjamin Martin's (1749) indications of the number of syllables in certain words, of silent letters. and of 'double' (i.e. geminated) consonants, to Buchanan's (1757) indications of vowel quantity and respelling of certain words whose traditional spelling deviated considerably from the phonetic (e.g. *enough*, respelt *enuff.*) In these cases, each dictionary improves on its predecessors, giving more phonetic information. Buchanan's *Vera Pronunciatio* is said by Emsley (1933: 1156) to be 'perhaps the first English pronouncing dictionary', and by Alston (1972: EL 39) to constitute 'the first attempt to provide a "standard" of pronunciation for the vocabulary of English'. Buchanan's is not the first 'phonetic' dictionary, because his notation provides information only about accentuation and vowel quantity for every word. On the other hand, it is certainly the first to provide any information about the segmental phonology of English, and as such can be said to constitute the first attempt

---

[1] Thus, when I use the term 'phonetic' in quotation marks, I mean this in the sense of *one sound = one spelling* and not in the more narrow linguistic sense of making allophonic distinctions. Indeed, I conclude in this chapter that in the linguistic sense, Spence's system is *phonemic.*

at a pronouncing dictionary of English. Dyche and Pardon (1735), on the other hand, can take credit for setting the ball rolling, for, according to Starnes and Noyes (1991: 129), 'it is to be remembered not only that Dyche did give the initial impetus to the study of pronunciation but that the stress of the title-page and the introduction of the *New General English Dictionary* on pronunciation was largely instrumental in establishing this department as a requisite of an English dictionary'. There comes a point, though, when several dictionaries are produced, all of which give a fairly clear indication of the phonetic quality of each word: what distinguishes them from each other, and leads me to suggest that none of them can lay claim to the title of first 'phonetic' dictionary, is the manner in which the phonetic information is presented.

Abercrombie (1981: 207) points out that the Roman alphabet has never been satisfactory for the representation of the European vernaculars, all of which devised orthographies by the use of digraphs and a few additional letters, and that 'for at least the last four centuries these orthographies have been under attack as unsatisfactory makeshifts which fail to do justice to the languages they represent'. Abercrombie goes on to categorize the various remedies suggested for the orthographical problems of English, as proposed by orthoepists and spelling reformers from the sixteenth century onwards. These remedies are:

1. *New alphabets.* The remedy here is to abandon the Roman alphabet altogether, and devise a totally new script capable of representing all the phonemic distinctions made in English. Examples of such scripts are those devised by Wilkins, Lodwick and Robinson. According to Abercrombie, the problem with such scripts is that the symbols are often too similar to each other to allow the appearance of words as wholes to be sufficiently distinct.

2. *Augmentation of the Roman alphabet.* Abercrombie (1981: 209) suggests that 'our orthography is one of the least successful applications of the Roman alphabet. The unjust treatment of English sounds by our traditional spelling probably accounts for the particular fertility of this country in schemes for augmenting the Roman alphabet.'

He then divides such schemes into two main categories, according to the method of augmentation. These are:

(*a*) *Diacritics.* In a diacritic scheme, dots, dashes, and other marks are placed under or over the letter, usually with minimal disruption to the actual orthographical form of the words. The supreme example of a diacritic system of spelling is that devised for Hodges's *English Primrose* (1644) which Abercrombie (1981: 209) describes as 'an ingenious spelling-book, which carried this device to an extreme: it must have been a nightmare for printer and proof-reader'. Abercrombie also places William Johnston's

(1764) pronouncing dictionary in this category, noting that Johnston made use of italic and black letter characters as well as diacritics.

(*b*) *Extended alphabets.* Abercrombie suggests that this is the most successful expedient of all, involving the introduction of new letters to make up for the deficiencies of the Roman alphabet.These letters can either be borrowed from, e.g. Anglo-Saxon or Greek, as were the {ð}, {θ}, and {ʒ} used by Hart, Thomas Smith, and William Thornton respectively, or newly invented. Invention of a totally new letter is difficult, because 'an apparently satisfactory new character will often turn out, in use, to be ill-suited to mixture with the rest of the alphabet, or to be too like letters which already exist' (1981: 210). According to Abercrombie, the best way of augmenting the Roman alphabet, and the best way of remedying its deficiencies with regard to English, is by modification of existing letters. This modification can take several forms: inversion; reversal; structural modification, such as the removal of the dot from ⟨i⟩; the addition of bars or dashes to letters; and ligaturing. The latter was much used by Spence, who produced ten new letters by this means.

None of the dictionaries of the eighteenth century uses a new alphabet, but those that provide a guide to pronunciation can be usefully placed in Abercrombie's categories of diacritics and extended alphabets. Abercrombie makes no evaluation of these categories with regard to the 'phonetic' nature of the works produced by the various means, but he does see the use of an extended alphabet, particularly one produced by the modification of existing letters, as the most useful and practical expedient.

Bert Emsley categorizes pronouncing dictionaries from the eighteenth to the twentieth centuries according to their 'phonetic' nature, and sees a progress towards the phonetic ideal, culminating in the use of IPA script in the twentieth century. Emsley never mentions Spence, but this could have been an oversight rather than a deliberate omission, as his articles were written in 1933, 1940, and 1942, with Abercrombie's discovery of Spence as a 'forgotten phonetician' not being made public until 1948. This may account for what seems an outrageous assertion by Emsley: that Dan S. Smalley's (1855) dictionary was the first phonetic dictionary of English. Emsley's categories of pronouncing dictionary are as follows:

1. No respelling. Dictionaries such as Dyche and Pardon's involve no respelling at all, but merely give information concerning accentuation, etc.
2. Diacritic respelling. In Emsley's definition, 'diacritic' respellings involve the omission of silent letters; the use of different letters and type forms for different sounds—e.g. Webster's use of italics for unstressed vowels; and diacritic marks which indicate quality as well as quantity.
3. Phonetic (not international) respelling.
4. International phonetic respelling.

Emsley suggests that type 1 is typical of the earlier eighteenth century, and is exemplified by Dyche; type 2 of the later eighteenth century, as exemplified by Buchanan; type 3 of the nineteenth century, and type 4 of the twentieth. We have already seen that the earlier eighteenth-century dictionaries, up to Buchanan's, are indeed of Emsley's type 1, involving as they do no attempt to represent the pronunciation of each word. Buchanan's, as the first real 'pronouncing' dictionary, does indeed fit into Emsley's type 2. What remains to be seen is whether the dictionaries of the late eighteenth century are also of this type, and whether Spence's *Grand Repository* fits into Emsley's scheme, or, as Abercrombie's categorization might suggest, stands out as atypical. The dictionaries to be considered, all published within sixteen years of the *Grand Repository*, are: William Johnston's *Pronouncing and Spelling Dictionary* (1764); William Kenrick's *New Dictionary of the English Language* (1773); William Perry's *Royal Standard English Dictionary* (1775); Thomas Spence's *Grand Repository of the English Language (1775); Thomas Sheridan's General Dictionary of the English Language* (1780); and John Walker's *Critical Pronouncing Dictionary* (1791). Since Spence's work was published in 1775, only Johnston and Kenrick out of this list could challenge him for the title of first compiler of a 'phonetic' dictionary, but it will be useful, in the light of Emsley's claim, to have an overview of guides to pronunciation in late-eighteenth-century dictionaries. Let us consider these dictionaries in turn.

4.1.1. *William Johnston's* Pronouncing and Spelling Dictionary (*1764*)

This dictionary could be seen as 'phonetic' in so far as it provides a very clear indication of how each word is to be pronounced: however, Johnston does not introduce a new phonetic alphabet, but achieves his end by the use of 'observations', i.e. remarks on the 'rules' of English spelling such as they are, and 'signs', which consist of italic and black letter forms. Although Johnston does not use diacritics as such, this system puts him firmly in Emsley's (1940: 55) 'diacritic' category, in which 'different letters and type forms signify different sounds'. Johnston even aligns himself with Buchanan, stating in his preface that, just before publishing, he acquired a copy of Buchanan's work, which he considered 'a laudable effort of the same nature with this of mine' (1764: p. vii), but, since he felt that he had himself 'hit upon many things necessary for conveying a right pronunciation by the letters, which are not mentioned in his, nor, for what I know, in any other author's' (1764: p. vii), he decided to go ahead and publish anyway, giving us what Alston (1972: EL 95) regards as 'one of the most valuable sources for the study of mid-eighteenth-century pronunciation'.

Johnston's work was certainly the first to give a complete account of the pronunciation of English, and as such had a moderate degree of success: Buchanan repaid the compliment by basing much of his (1766) *Essay towards Establishing a Standard for an Elegant and Uniform Pronunciation of the English Language* on Johnston, and the dictionary was reprinted in 1772 and *c.*1795. However, since Johnston does not devise a phonetic script for his dictionary, and does not adhere to the principle of 'one sound=one spelling', his dictionary is not 'phonetic'. What Johnston does is to set out the 'rules' of English spelling, in so far as they give indications of pronunciation. In cases where these rules are not followed, he uses different types to distinguish the sounds indicated: italic type indicates that the letter is sounded in a way which deviates from the spelling rule, whilst black-letter type is the 'sign of quiescence', indicating that the letter is silent. Thus a letter in italics could have several phonetic values, depending on the spelling rule concerned. For example, Johnston cites the rule that ⟨s⟩ between vowels is usually pronounced /z/ in English. Since this is the norm, no further indication of pronunciation is needed in such cases and so the orthographic ⟨s⟩ is left undisturbed. In cases where this environmental rule is not followed, Johnston indicates the pronunciation by an italicized {*s*}. Thus in 'generosity', where an intervocalic ⟨s⟩ is pronounced /s/, in contravention of the first rule mentioned above, an italicized {*s*} is used to indicate this pronunciation. Conversely, in 'baptism', where the orthographic ⟨s⟩ is pronounced as /z/ in an environment other than that specified by the rule, the same italicized {*s*} is used by Johnston to represent the /z/ sound. In cases where the deviation from the spelling rules is so extreme that it cannot be encapsulated in his system, Johnston resorts to Buchanan's expedient of respelling: thus 'beaux' is respelt {bōs}; 'laugh', {l*a*ff}.

Johnston's system is ingenious and very well executed, building as it does on the traditional orthography of English and making good its defects. Johnston's reader would learn as much about the rules of English spelling as about pronunciation, but the effectiveness of this work as a pronouncing dictionary would be reduced by the need for the reader to digest all these complicated rules before being able to understand the entries. Johnston's dictionary does, as Alston suggested, contain much valuable phonetic information, but it is not in our sense or in Emsley's a phonetic dictionary.

4.1.2. *William Kenrick's* New Dictionary of the English Language (*1773*)

Kenrick[2] is cited by Holmberg (1964: 29) as being, along with Sheridan, 'the first to introduce a practicable transcription system'. Kenrick certainly did indicate the phonetic quality of each word, but his system involves even less interference with the traditional orthography than Johnston's: indeed, his system can hardly be called one of 'transcription' at all. Minimal disruption

---

[2] I am indebted to the Librarian of Ushaw College, Durham, for allowing me access to this work, which is not readily available.

of the traditional orthography is precisely what Kenrick aimed for: far from sharing Johnston's esteem for Buchanan, Kenrick hardly attempts to disguise his contempt for that 'North Briton'. This contempt is aroused not only by Buchanan's nationality, but also by his attempt to provide a phonetic representation of words, which Kenrick felt would cause problems with spelling. This was, after all, an age in which 'correct' spelling was revered to such an extent that the pronunciation of certain words was changed to reflect the spelling more closely: the final /f/ was restored in *handkerchief* and the /h/ in *forehead*, for instance. Dr Johnson, in the preface to his dictionary (1755: sig. A2^v) formulated the principle that 'for pronunciation, the best general rule is to consider those as the most elegant speakers who deviate least from the written word', and subsequently a great deal of store was set by the 'correct' spellings provided in Johnson's dictionary.

Kenrick used a series of numbers placed over syllables to indicate the precise quality of the vowels. Thus *cur*, *fir*, *her*, *earth* would all have the number 1 placed above, with the orthography left intact, and so {u^1}, {i^1}, {e^1}, and {ea^1} all indicate the same sound. This is certainly not a 'phonetic' system, even though the numeral always indicates the same sound, for, although any one combination of letter and numeral is unambiguous, more than one combination can represent the same sound, so the phonetic ideal of 'one sound=one spelling' is not adhered to. Kenrick acknowledges 'the celebrated Mr Sheridan' as the source of his idea for distinguishing 'the sounds of words by certain typographical marks to be placed over particular syllables'. If we are to take Kenrick's acknowledgement at face value, then the source of his inspiration must have been Sheridan's *Dissertation on the Causes of the Difficulties, which Occur in Learning the English Tongue* (1761), for it is here that Sheridan sets out for the first time his system of numerical marks. Sheridan's dictionary, when it finally arrived, did use superscripted numbers, but in a manner slightly different from that adopted by Kenrick. In the intervening years, Kenrick's dictionary attracted some admiration, especially from John Burn, whose *Pronouncing Dictionary of the English Language* (1786) copied Kenrick's system exactly.

Thus no dictionary before Spence's could be called 'phonetic', either in Emsley's sense, or in our sense of conforming to the ideal of 'one sound=one spelling'. The next dictionary we have to consider was printed in the same year as Spence's *Grand Repository*, and so cannot be seen as a precedent for Spence's work, but may help us to build up a picture of what was 'typical' in such dictionaries as provided guides to pronunciation in the later eighteenth century.

4.1.3. *William Perry's* Royal Standard English Dictionary (*1775*)

Perry, like almost every other lexicographer of this period who shows an interest in pronunciation, refers to Sheridan, who 'in his lectures on the art of reading Prose, promised shortly to present the public with a rhetorical grammar and pronouncing dictionary'. Perry is referring here to Sheridan's *Lectures on the Art of Reading* (1775), the first part of which dealt with prose. Since the above quote comes from Perry's second edition of 1788, Perry could well have read the published work by then. However, it is also likely that Perry attended the lectures, for Benzie (1972: 68) points out that Sheridan gave a course of the readings usually accompanying his lectures in Edinburgh in 1764, and that 'in order to make himself known in Edinburgh, William Perry, the lexicographer, in 1777 gave public readings of prose and verse and a course of lectures on reading, all closely following the model of Sheridan'. Perry found Sheridan's projected scheme preferable to Buchanan's, in which 'the sounds of words are expressed by varying their orthography' (1788: pp. iv–v). Perry, however, feels that he has improved on Sheridan's projected scheme, in which there are 'several duplicates of the same sound, differently marked. Thus the second sound of a and e as in *hate*, *there*, are the same. The third sounds of e and i in *here*, *field* are also the same.'

So, although Perry aligns himself with Kenrick in his condemnation of Buchanan, and his intention not to disrupt the orthography, he criticizes Sheridan for not adhering to the 'one sound=one spelling' principle, which Sheridan, incidentally, was the first to articulate, but not the first to put into practice. Perry's scheme, like Johnston's and Kenrick's, would be termed 'diacritic' according to both Emsley's and Abercrombie's definitions: in fact, it combines the numerical system used by Kenrick and proposed by Sheridan with the use of different types such as we find in Johnston. Charles Jones (1995: 63) considers Perry's to be 'the most elaborate system of diacritic marking'. Perry leaves the orthography undisturbed, using a combination of diacritics proper and numerals to distinguish the vowel sounds, and using commas and cedillas to distinguish between consonantal sounds. For silent letters, and for 'indistinct vowels', he uses italics. Perry also indicates 'flat and slowly accented syllables' by the use of a grave accent, and 'sharp and quickly accented syllables' by the use of an acute accent. He adds in a note below his key that ' a, e, i, o and u without any of the above characters either alone, or before or after a consonant, have a shorter sound than a, e, i, o and u, though of the same quality, in the same proportion as a in *wash* is to a in *hall* or o in *not* is to o in *soft*.' Sheldon (1946: 34) suggests that this is a device borrowed from Kenrick, originally used to indicate long versus short vowels, and that Perry is here marking a 'mid' length not bearing the main stress of the word, such as that represented by the ⟨o⟩ of *bravado.* Jones (1995: 66), however, suggests that Perry's marking of words such as *border, warning* with grave accents, and such as *better, washing* with acute, indicates that 'the former might correlate with syllable structures where vowel length . . . might correspond . . . to Sylvester Douglas's distinction between long and short syllables'. Perry does seem to be a fairly acute observer of phonetics, calling Sheridan to task for not noticing the separate ⟨a⟩ sound in e.g. *part*, but his is not a phonetic dictionary, for he uses more than one spelling for the same sound: *try* and *pine, now* and *out* are pairs of words which exemplify this.

4.1.4. *Thomas Spence's* Grand Repository of the English Language (*1775*)

The above consideration of William Perry's *Royal Standard English Dictionary* brings us chronologically to the date of publication of Spence's *Grand Repository*. The latter did, indeed, use a system of notation which was 'phonetic' in the sense of 'one sound=one spelling'. Abercrombie was the first to point this out, explicitly contradicting Emsley's attribution of priority to Smalley, stating that 'in 1775 there appeared a dictionary in which the pronunciation was "parenthesized" . . . in a *genuine, scientific, phonetic* alphabet with seventeen new letters' (1965: 68, emphasis added). Some doubt has been cast on the phonetic accuracy of some of Spence's representations (see e.g. Weinstock 1976: 32–3), but that his system is a phonetic one in the sense of 'one sound = one spelling' is beyond dispute. Spence clearly states at the foot of the page on which his alphabet is set out: 'in reading what is printed in this alphabet, nothing is required but to sound every letter, and but one way; for each letter represents but one sound, and that invariably in whatever position' (1775: sig. C1ᵛ). (It should be stated at this point that the alphabet under consideration here, and, indeed, throughout this book, is the one used in the actual dictionary entries for the *Grand Repository*. At the beginning of this work, Spence actually sets out three alphabets: one based on upper-case letters; one based on lower-case letters; and a copperplate version. The latter two are not used in the dictionary part of the *Grand Repository* and so lie outside the scope of this work.)

Spence's note as quoted above is as clear a statement of the 'phonetic' principle of 'one sound=one spelling' as one could hope for. This principle had been articulated before, by Sheridan in his 1761 *Dissertation*, but Sheridan had yet to put this into practice, and, as we shall see, never really did. However, even to cite this 'phonetic' principle as an ideal was unusual in the eighteenth century: as Emsley suggests, 'diacritic' respelling is indeed typical of that century precisely because the traditional orthography was held in such esteem that lexicographers were loath to depart from it. To find a system similar to Spence's—that is, one which is 'phonetic' rather than 'diacritic' in Emsley's sense, and which achieves this by means of what Abercrombie would term an 'extended alphabet' rather than a new script—we have to go back to the spelling reformers of the sixteenth and early seventeenth centuries, such as

Hart, Smith, Gil, and Butler, or forward to the 'phonetic' dictionaries of the nineteenth and twentieth centuries such as those of Daniel Jones.

Considering the sixteenth-century parallels, it is interesting to note that Spence, too, was a spelling reformer: both his pedagogical aims and his approach to the task of representing the pronunciation of English look back to a time when spelling reform was seen as an attainable end. Dobson (1957: 310) characterizes the phoneticians of the seventeenth century as 'abandoning as a proved failure the attempt to reform English spelling alone and to evolve an alphabet on phonetic principles (unless for international use, as Robinson, Wilkins and Lodwick do)' and concentrating instead 'on the study of phonetics for its own sake'. The eighteenth-century phoneticians were, on the whole, preoccupied with 'correctness', as were the grammarians of that century, and would view spelling reform as undesirable as well as impracticable. Spence probably knew nothing of Hart's or Smith's work, or for that matter of any phonetician in the intervening period. The only source we can be sure of for his *Grand Repository* is Sheridan's *Dissertation*: Spence's work resembles that of the earlier orthoepists because Spence simply does not see, or dismisses, the objections of the intervening century, starting as he does with a clean slate and a radical plan. Spence's work is Janus-like, looking back to the sixteenth century in its optimistic view of the attainability of spelling reform, and forward to the nineteenth century in the 'phonetic' nature of the script devised.

We shall consider Spence's script in detail in §4.2: here, a few examples should suffice to show its 'phonetic' nature in contrast to the respellings of Johnston, Kenrick, and Perry. For example, for /iː/, Spence uses the symbol {E}, no matter what the orthographic representation: thus *feed* is transcribed as {FED}, *feat* as {FET} and *field* as {FELD}. Certain consonantal phonemes are represented by ligatured symbols: thus /ʃ/ = {SH}; /ʒ/ = {ZH}; /tʃ/ = {CH}; /θ/ = {H}; /ð/ = {H}; /ʍ/ = {WH}; and /ŋ/ = {NG}. This contrasts with the 'diacritic' expedients of Spence's predecessors, who would use superscripted symbols or numbers to distinguish vowels, and different types, such as italic, to distinguish consonants. Spence seems not to be concerned about disrupting the traditional orthography: if he perceives a different sound, then he uses a different symbol, the only concession to the traditional orthography being that his script is based on it and seeks to extend it rather than start from scratch with a totally new set of symbols. Spence was undoubtedly the first to compile a 'phonetic' dictionary of English.

4.1.5. *Thomas Sheridan's* General Dictionary of the English Language (*1780*)

Why did the *Grand Repository* excite so little comment at the time, if it was such a revolutionary departure? Spence was an obscure figure in 1775, before his move to London and subsequent political activity brought him a certain notoriety. However, even if Spence had been better known and had published in London, his work would probably have been overshadowed by the dictionary that had been eagerly awaited since it was first promised in 1761: Thomas Sheridan's *General Dictionary of the English Language*. We have already seen how Kenrick, Perry, and Spence all acknowledged Sheridan as in some way giving impetus to their work, and, indeed, that Sheridan had been the first to articulate the 'phonetic' principle with regard to a pronouncing dictionary. The long time-lapse between his *Dissertation* (1761) and his *Dictionary* (1780) means that, as far as the compiling of a 'phonetic' dictionary is concerned, Sheridan was not the first to *do* anything, except perhaps to sell his dictionary in large numbers! Sheridan's *General Dictionary* was certainly very influential: Holmberg (1964: 30) wrote of Sheridan: 'by his *Dictionary*, which was to appear in many editions during the nineteenth century, he undoubtedly most effectively contributed to his aim of creating an accepted standard of pronunciation.' Benzie (1972: p. v) suggests that 'Thomas Sheridan mixed with the leading figures of his time, and had a considerable influence on social and literary culture in the 18th century'. His *Lectures on Elocution*, published in 1762, but delivered from 1758 onwards in London, Oxford, Cambridge, Bath, and Edinburgh, created such a stir in polite society that he was satirized in two farces by Samuel Foote: *The Orators* (1762) and *The Mayor of Garret* (1764). Small wonder that his work was taken more notice of than that of an unknown schoolteacher from Newcastle upon Tyne. Sheridan's *General Dictionary* combines the numerical system taken up by Kenrick with the respelling used by Buchanan. As such, it comes closer to the 'phonetic' ideal than any previous dictionary except Spence's, but, in the end, Sheridan does use more than one notation for the same sound, and his system is essentially a 'diacritic' rather than a 'phonetic' one. Furthermore, Sheridan departs from the 'phonetic' ideal in, for instance, using forms of ⟨i⟩ and ⟨y⟩ interchangeably, according to the accepted spelling: thus the /ɪ/ of *fit* is transcribed as {i¹}, but the same sound in the final vowel of *lovely* is given as {y¹}; the /aɪ/ of *fight* is transcribed as {i³}, but the same diphthong in *lye* is given as {y³}. Where consonants are concerned, Sheridan also tends to be inconsistent and influenced by spelling: *abscond* is transcribed as {a¹bsko¹nd} but *absconder* as {a¹bsco¹ndu¹r}.

4.1.6. *John Walker's* Critical Pronouncing Dictionary (*1791*)

Influential though Sheridan's *General Dictionary of the English Language* was, before the eighteenth century had ended it was to be supplanted by the most influential pronouncing dictionary before that of Daniel Jones: John Walker's *Critical Pronouncing Dictionary* (1791). Walker freely admitted that, as far as the system of notation was concerned, 'Mr. Sheridan . . . not only divided the words into syllables and placed figures over the vowels as

Dr. Kenrick had done, but by spelling these syllables as they are pronounced, seemed to complete the idea of a Pronouncing dictionary' (1791: p. iii). The system used by Walker is, therefore, virtually identical to that devised by Sheridan: improvements needed to be made, not in the system, but in the actual pronunciations recommended, for in this respect Walker felt that Sheridan fell far short of the ideal. Indeed, Walker, along with other critics such as the author of *A Caution to Gentlemen Who Use Sheridan's Dictionary* (1790), found numerous instances of 'impropriety, inconsistency, and want of acquaintance with the analogies of the language' (1791: p. iii).

Walker's aim was to provide a set of rules which would give a precise and prescriptive guide to correct pronunciation. Taking his cue from Nares, who, in his *Elements of Orthoepy* (1784), linked an index of 5,000 words to a list of rules for pronunciation, Walker prefaced his *Critical Pronouncing Dictionary* with no less than 545 rules covering the definition and classification of vowels and consonants; the organic formation of the letters (articulation); the pronunciation of each letter; accent; quantity; and syllabication (*sic*). The majority of these rules (nos. 63–485) deal with the different pronunciations of each letter: items in the dictionary have cross-references to these rules in cases of difficulty or controversy, and, where the pronunciation recommended by Walker differs from that given by Sheridan or others, Walker provides arguments to back up his recommendation in the prefaced rules and in the individual entries. For instance, rule 454 expounds the general principle that, if a syllable is stressed, then the 'true' sound of the letters is preserved, whilst the sounds of unstressed syllables are liable to alteration: thus the ⟨x⟩ of *'exercise* is pronounced with /ks/, the 'true' sound, whilst *ex'ert* has /gz/. Walker (1791: 54) goes on to state that

this analogy leads us immediately to discover the irregularity of *sure*, *sugar*, and their compounds, which are pronounced *shure* and *shugar*, though the accent is on the first syllable, and ought to preserve the s without aspiration, and a want of attending to this analogy has betrayed Mr. Sheridan into a series of mistakes in the sound of s in the words *suicide*, *presume*, *resume*, etc. as if written shoo-icide, pre-zhoom, re-zhoom, etc.

In setting out such rules, Walker sets himself up as the ultimate authority on correct pronunciation and his *Critical Pronouncing Dictionary* as the acme of pronouncing dictionaries. Such confidence is apparent in his Preface, where, after an appraisal of his predecessors, he writes: 'I have endeavoured to unite the science of Mr. Elphinstone, the method of Mr. Nares, and the general utility of Mr. Sheridan, and to add to these advantages have given critical observations on such words as are subject to a diversity of pronunciation' (1791: p. iv).

Walker's confidence certainly convinced the public: his *Critical Pronouncing Dictionary* was reprinted over 100 times between 1791 and as late as 1904, and inspired many imitators. One such was Stephen Jones, who, in his

Sheridan Improved (1798), has been shown by Sheldon to rely heavily on Walker for his 'corrections' of Sheridan, and who had a great influence on Noah Webster, and hence on American pronunciation. Sheldon (1947: 146) suggests that Walker became more popular than Sheridan because, 'while Sheridan reflects the speech of his time better, Walker satisfies the temper of his time better, and its demand for linguistic regulation and reform. . . . There can be no doubt that, if any one single person was to be named as the greatest influence on English pronunciation, that person would have to be Walker.' However, Walker achieved this influence without improving on Sheridan's *system*: Walker's notation, like Sheridan's, is essentially 'diacritic', and not consistently phonetic even in its own terms. For instance, Walker, in rule 85, states that ⟨a⟩, when followed by ⟨ll⟩ or ⟨l⟩ plus any other consonant except ⟨p⟩, ⟨b⟩, ⟨f⟩, or ⟨v⟩, is pronounced as the 'broad' sound, {a³} in Walker's notation. In the dictionary, both *all* and *awl* are spelt {a³ll}, but *ball* is spelt {ba³wl}. The presence of the {w} is not explained in his rules, and must simply be an instance of inconsistency on Walker's part.

It would appear that, were it not for the appearance of Spence's *Grand Repository* in 1775, Emsley's assessment of eighteenth-century pronouncing dictionaries as typically 'diacritic' would have been perfectly accurate. Charles Jones (1995: 80) cites Spence's *Grand Repository* as the 'one exception to this general trend'. Although the *Grand Repository* is one of a number of pronouncing dictionaries produced in response to the growing demand for a guide to correct pronunciation in the late eighteenth century, it stands apart from all the others both in its purpose and in the means of executing that purpose. On the one hand, it is intended as the first step in a programme of spelling reform as well as a guide to correct pronunciation, and, on the other hand, it is the only eighteenth-century (and therefore the first) dictionary of English to provide a 'phonetic' system of transcription by means of an extended alphabet. All other eighteenth-century lexicographers were, of course, inhibited from producing new or extended alphabets other than by diacritic means by their reluctance to depart from the traditional orthography. Spence, however, was always the radical, and had no such inhibitions: the traditional orthography had no more right to impede his plan for the reform of spelling than did the traditional landlords to stand in the way of his plan for the reform of society. The nature of Spence's alphabet, and its effectiveness as a phonetic script, will be considered more closely in the next section.

4.2. SPENCE'S NOTATION AND ITS SOURCES

We have seen in the previous section that Spence's *Grand Repository* was the first pronouncing dictionary of English to employ a truly 'phonetic' system for representing the pronunciation of the words entered. What I intend to do in this section is first to consider the nature of Spence's notation and its effectiveness for the purposes of representing the pronunciation of the words that were entered, and then to look at the phonemic system represented by the New Alphabet as it compares with that of the present-day RP as described by Wells (1982).

Figure 4.1 shows sig. C1^v of the *Grand Repository*, on which the New Alphabet is set out along with examples of words in which each symbol is used. An examination of the layout of Spence's New Alphabet reveals that, above all, it is based on the traditional alphabet and the most usual values of letters in traditional orthography.

In the case of the vowels, the first symbol listed is in each case identical with the upper-case form in traditional orthography and it represents the sound which is nearest to the name of that letter: thus {A} represents the sound used by Spence in *mane*; {E} represents that used in *mete*; {I} represents that used in *site*; {O} represents the sound in *note*; and {U}

The NEW ALPHABET.

Capi-tals.	Small Letters.	Names.		Capi-tals.	Small Letters.	Names.	
A	ʌ	a	as in mane, (MAN)	Y	y	yï	as in young, (YUNG)
ʌ		ă	as in man, (MAN)	Z	z	iz	
ʌ		ah	as in father, (FAHIR)	Ꟁ		oo	as in moon, (MꟀN)
Ʒ		au	as in wall, (WAUL)	OI		oi	as in oil, (OIL)
B	b	ib or bï		OU		ou	as in houfe, (HOUS)
D	d	id or dï		SI		iſh	as in fhell, (SIEL)
E	ɛ	ē	as in mete, (MET)	ZI		izh	as in vifion, (VIZIN)
ɛ		ĕ	as in met, (MET)	CI		itch	as in child, (CIILD)
F	f	if		TH		ith	as in think, (THINK)
G	g	ig or gï		H		ith	as in they, (HA)
H	h	hä		WH		whï	as in which, (WHICI)
I	i	ī	as in fite, (SIT)	NG		ing	as in loving, (LUVING)
		ĭ	as in fit, (SIT)				
J	j	idge or jï					
K	k	ik or kï					
L	l	il					
M	m	im					
N	n	in					
O	o	ō	as in note, (NOT)				
		ŏ	as in not, (NOT)				
P	p	ip or pï					
R	r	ir					
S	s	iſs					
T	t	it or tï					
U	u	ū	as in tune, (TUN)				
		ŭ	as in tun, (TUN)				
V	v	iv					
W	w	wï	as in way, (WA)				

⁎ The vowels in this alphabet are A ʌ ʌ Ʒ E ɛ I I O Ɔ U Ꟁ OI OU; and the confonants B D F G H J K L M N P R S T V W Y Z SI ZI CI TH H WH NG.

☞ To read what is printed in this alphabet, nothing is required but to apply the fame found immutably to each character (in whatever pofition) that the alphabet directs.

N. B. In the following work, n. ſtands for name, or fubftantive;—q. for quality, or adjective;—v. for verb;—part. for participle;—ad. for adverb;—conj. for conjunction;—prep. for prepofition;—interj. for interjection.

A

Figure 4.1. Spence's New Alphabet

represents that in *tune*. In each case, the other vowel sounds most usually represented by that letter are listed immediately after it and are all formed by modifying the conventional upper-case letter. Thus the 'a sounds' are listed together: the right-hand half of {A} is used to represent the vowel used by Spence in *man*; {A} without the cross-bar to represent that in *father*; and a ligatured {A} and {U} to represent the sound in *wall*. The vowels used by Spence in *not* and *tun*, like that in *man*, are each represented by a symbol formed by cutting the conventional upper-case letter in half vertically. This would not be practicable for {E} and {I}, so, in these cases, the 'short' values are represented by symbols in which a cross-bar is added to the conventional upper-case letter.

As far as possible, the order in which Spence's symbols are listed follows that of the traditional alphabet: the four 'a sounds' are followed by {B} and so on. After {Z}, Spence lists the symbols for sounds which are not represented by a single symbol in traditional orthography and for which he has created new symbols by ligaturing. In most cases, these ligatured symbols are formed by joining together the two letters which usually represent the sound in traditional orthography: thus /ŋ/ is represented by ligaturing {N} and {G}; /ʍ/ by ligaturing {W} and {H}; and the diphthongs /ɔɪ/ as in *oil* and /aʊ/ as in *house* by ligaturing {O} with {I} and {U} respectively. The only exception to this is the ligaturing of {Z} and {H} to create a symbol for /ʒ/ as in *vision*, but, since Spence represents /s/ as {S} and /z/ as {Z} it would seem logical to use this ligatured symbol for the voiced equivalent of /ʃ/ as in *shell*, which in turn is represented by ligaturing {S} and {H}. Unfortunately, Spence did not use the same reasoning in devising symbols for /θ/ as in *think* and /ð/ as in *they*: instead of differentiating this voiceless/voiced pair by ligaturing {H} with {T} and {D} respectively, Spence uses two ligatures of {T} and {H}, taking the bar right across the top for /θ/ but not for /ð/. These two symbols are extremely difficult to distinguish from each other in the *Grand Repository* and Spence's Errata page contains fourteen words in which the wrong symbol for /θ/ or /ð/ has been printed out of 104 errata altogether.

The ligature of two ⟨o⟩ symbols for /uː/ as in *moon* might seem out of place here, representing as it does what to the phonetically trained mind is a 'u sound', but once again Spence has created a symbol by ligaturing the two letters which most usually represented that sound in traditional orthography. (As we shall see in §5.5, many more words with ⟨oo⟩ in traditional orthography were pronounced with a long vowel in eighteenth-century English than in present-day RP.) Spence has placed this symbol at the end of his alphabet probably because it fits neither with the 'o sounds' nor with the 'u sounds' in his sequence.

What this brief examination of Spence's New Alphabet reveals is that, although, as we concluded in §4.1.4, it is a truly 'phonetic' system in that any one symbol always and only represents a single sound, it is very much based on the traditional alphabet. This is a practical, 'user-friendly' system. Given the simplicity of Spence's New Alphabet and his reputation as a self-taught, working-class thinker, one is tempted to assume that Spence's notation has no precedents or sources, that Spence simply invented it. However, taking the biblical precept that 'there is nothing new under the sun', we must search for any sources that Spence might conceivably have used in devising his New Alphabet.

We have already seen in §4.1.4 that the only acknowledged source for Spence's *Grand Repository* is Thomas Sheridan's *Dissertation on the Causes of the Difficulties which Occur in Learning the English Tongue* (1761). Spence quotes at length from this work in the Preface to the *Grand Repository*, and acknowledges his debt to Sheridan as follows:

Having, since the proposals for publishing the following work were delivered to the public, met with Mr. Sheridan's Dissertation on Language &c. and finding that he was so much in my mind with regard to the difficulties in learning English, and the methods which ought to be taken to remove them, that he has expressed almost everything I would or could say on the subject, *and as it cannot but be to the credit of any design that different persons, unknown to each other, should think equally well of it*, I beg leave to give here some part of his Dissertation on the causes of the difficulties which occur in learning the English tongue. (Spence 1775: sig. A2^r, emphasis added)

The part that I have emphasized perhaps gives a clue as to why Spence acknowledges Sheridan when no other source for the *Grand Repository* is mentioned. We have already seen in §4.1.2 that Kenrick, too, acknowledged 'the celebrated Mr Sheridan' as the originator of the system of superscripted numbers which was, in fact, used by Kenrick himself before Sheridan's dictionary was published. Kenrick's acknowledgement of Sheridan is uncharacteristically gracious, for, according to the entry for William Kenrick in the *DNB*, the latter, far from being a humble, self-effacing individual, was a notorious libeller. Perhaps 'Mr Sheridan' was so 'celebrated' that works like Spence's or Kenrick's would be endorsed by citing him as a source of inspiration: after all, the emphasized extract above could easily be paraphrased by the twentieth-century cliché 'great minds think alike'.

However, Spence uses Sheridan's *Dissertation* very selectively in his Preface, omitting Sheridan's conclusion, which differs radically from Spence's ideas on spelling reform. The last paragraph quoted from Sheridan is as follows:

But to this it will be immediately objected, that however right the design might appear in theory, it would be impossible to carry it into execution. That to follow the example of the latter Hebraeans, the whole graphic art must be changed; that new characters must be introduced into the alphabet, to mark all the differences of the vowels, both in quantity and quality; that there would be no use of these if they were not transferred into our books, which must be all reprinted according to the new alpabet (*sic*); and that people must be taught their alphabet anew to enable them to read such reprinted books.   (Spence 1775: sig. B1^r)

Sheridan at this point goes on to write: 'indeed any design of that sort must prove to the last degree impracticable, and consequently fail of its end. Nor could a thought of this enter into the head of any one, who knows that, the whole power of a Roman Emperor, was in vain exerted, to introduce a single letter into their alphabet . . . though such a character was confessedly wanting' (1761: 29). Spence, on the other hand, without informing his readers why he has done so, parts company with Sheridan at this point and instead argues as follows:

That many of the books would be reprinted in this new method of spelling, I make no doubt, if it was pretty generally used and approved of; yet I cannot see how this could be made an objection. For who would suppose any body would throw the books he at present reads into the fire because there were new editions of them in a new method of spelling? Might he not still read them, and if he would have his children to read them might he not learn them, or get them learned to read them as well as at present?   (Spence 1775: sig. B1^r)

In using 'the celebrated Mr. Sheridan' only as far as it suits his purpose, Spence indicates that he is perhaps not so ingenuous as some of his biographers would have us believe. In fact, if we look more closely at Spence's Preface, we can see that he in fact uses his arguments in favour of spelling reform as a thinly disguised 'plug' for his *Repository of Common Sense and Innocent Amusement*. He goes on to suggest that, 'whilst the public may by their encouragement get a book or books printed if they chuse in any language or manner; may they not also by their encouragement get the same done in this new method of spelling? For instance, if they chuse to encourage sufficiently, a weekly miscellany printed so, it will certainly be done' (Spence 1775 sig. B1^v). Such a 'weekly miscellany' Spence already had in mind in his *Repository of Common Sense and Innocent Amusement*, an advertisement for which appears on the page following this last page of the Preface. There are striking similarities between the wording of the Preface and of this advertisement. At the end of the former, Spence writes: 'I cannot but think it possible such a method of spelling may take place, *especially among the laborious part of the people, who generally cannot afford much time or expence in the educating of their children*' (1775: sig. B2^r, emphasis added), whilst, in the advertisement facing, he suggests that the *Repository of Common Sense and Innocent Amusement*, for which he is soliciting subscriptions is '*designed chiefly for those who cannot spare time, expence, and patience sufficient for learning to read in the usual way*' (1775, emphasis added). This perhaps explains why the *Grand Repository*, which is essentially a pronouncing dictionary employing a 'phonetic' notation as a guide to pronunciation, is prefaced by a tract on spelling reform: Spence wishes to kill two birds with one stone, perhaps cashing in on the demand for pronouncing dictionaries and using the *Grand Repository* as a launch pad for his reformed spelling.

Just because Spence does not acknowledge any source except Sheridan's *Dissertation*, this does not mean that no other sources exist for his *Grand Repository*. Shields (1973) makes a very convincing case for the English Grammar which appears at the beginning of the *Grand Repository* being closely modelled on one of the grammars produced by another Newcastle schoolteacher, Ann Fisher. Shields's appendix 7 (1973: 112–14) shows striking parallels between Spence's English Grammar and Fisher's *A Practical New Grammar* (1787).[3] For example, Spence's rule 1 is 'A VERB must agree with its Nominative in NUMBER and PERSON' (1775: sig. B2ᵛ), whilst Fisher's Rule I is 'A Verb must agree with its Nominative Word, in Number and Person' (1787: 106). Spence's Rule II is as follows. 'Such Names as want the Singular number, are mostly joined to a verb singular; as, the news is barren; your wages is small; the compasses is broken; the wages of sin is death' (1775: sig. B4ʳ). Fisher's Additional Remark 1 looks remarkably similar: 'SUCH Names as want the singular Number are mostly joined to a Verb singular; as, The News is barren. The Wages is small. The Compasses is broken. The Wages of Sin is Death' (1787: 111).

Obviously, this 1787 edition used by Shields could not be the source of Spence's 1775 English Grammar, but it was the 23rd edition of a work which was first published in 1748 under the title *The Pleasing Instructor.* This or any of the subsequent editions up to 1775 could easily have been used by Spence in the classroom and as a source for the Grammar in his *Grand Repository*. Shields goes on to speculate that Ann Fisher's 'lost' *Dictionary and Grammar* (?1774) is the source of both Spence's *Grand Repository* and Sheridan's *General Dictionary of the English Language* (1780). Shields's argument is based on a comparison of words (and definitions) from *Effort* to *Ejection* in seven eighteenth-century dictionaries, which shows that Spence's and Sheridan's entries are more like each other than either of them is to any of the other five. Since Sheridan's dictionary is so much longer than Spence's, Shields concludes that the former cannot be based on the latter, but that both must share some common source: 'Dictionary X'. Shields concludes that 'Dictionary X' could be Fisher's *Dictionary and Grammar* on the basis of the similarity between Spence's and Fisher's grammars already demonstrated; on the inclusion of a list of Christian Names in both Spence's and Sheridan's dictionaries as well as Fisher's Grammar; and on the emphasis on the marking of stress in all seven

---

[3] According to Alston (1965–73: i. 29) 'no copy of a 23rd edition has been located'. However, the copy of this edition consulted by Shields is still available for consultation in Newcastle City Library.

dictionaries compared by Shields as well as in the advertisement for Fisher's *Dictionary and Grammar* which appears in the 1787 edition of her Grammar. Shields has carried out an impressive piece of detective work here, and the lure of a 'lost' dictionary is entirely understandable, but, unless a copy of Fisher's *Dictionary and Grammar* is found, the case cannot be proved. What makes me slightly sceptical is the presence in the *Grand Repository* of certain words such as *antarctic*, *Magna Carta*, which do not appear in Sheridan. Given Spence's eclectic reading habits as witnessed in the compilations put together in *The Repository of Common Sense* and *Pigs' Meat*, it is just as likely that he used more than one source for his *Grand Repository*, perhaps basing the word-list on 'Dictionary X' but adding to this words that he had encountered elsewhere.

Fascinating though these speculations concerning the sources of Spence's grammar and word-list may be, our main concern in this section is to discover any possible sources for Spence's New Alphabet as used in the *Grand Repository*. With regard to the halved upper-case letters used for /æ/ as in *man*, /ɒ/ as in *not*, and /ʊ/ as in *tun*, Shields (1973: 62) writes that 'the particular means of mutilating the upper case type seems to be in its detail entirely Spence's own'. In so far as this refers to the *systematic* use of half-letters outlined above, Shields is probably right. However, some of Spence's half-letters had been used before, notably in seventeenth-century shorthand systems. A symbol for ⟨o⟩ similar to {C} had been used by Willis (1602), Shelton (1630), William Hopkins (1670), Lawrence Steel (1678), and in *The Alphabet of Reason* (1763). As a teacher of English with an interest in spelling reform, Spence might have been familiar with any or all of these and could well have taken the logical step of halving the capital {A} and {U} in the same way to represent the 'short' sounds of these letters. All of these shorthand systems, as well as that of Henry Dix (1633), make use of the {A} without the cross-bar, whilst the ligatured {A} and {U} as a symbol for the vowel in *wall* was used by Abraham Tucker (1773).

These are the only symbols in Spence's New Alphabet for which any precedents can be found (apart, of course, from those which are identical with upper-case forms in traditional orthography). Shields (1973: 62) indicates that Sheridan (1762: 5) had suggested a combination of ⟨z⟩ and ⟨h⟩ to represent the consonant in *osier*, but Sheridan does not ligature the letters as Spence does. Indeed, apart from the ligaturing of {A} and {U}, all Spence's ligatured forms seem to be entirely of his own invention.

A brief overview of attempts to create a symbol for the velar nasal is instructive in this regard. The need for a separate symbol for this sound is recognized as early as 1619 by Gil, but the ligatured form used by Spence and later by Batchelor (1809) does not appear before 1775. Shields (1973: 65) points out similarities between the alphabet produced by Benjamin Franklin (1768) and the cursive forms used in the copperplate of Spence's New

Alphabet. However, Franklin's alphabet first appeared in private correspondence and was not published in Britain until 1779, and, as Shields rightly points out, had Spence been aware of Franklin's system in 1775, he would almost certainly have adopted the latter's cursive form for the velar nasal in his copperplate instead of the curiously anomalous {Q} form that does appear.

So, whilst there are precedents, mainly in shorthand systems, for some of the symbols used in the *Grand Repository*, the alphabet as a whole, with its systematic use of half-letters, cross-strokes, and ligaturing, would appear to have been invented by Spence. In creating this notation, Spence kept as close to the traditional alphabet as was consistent with his desire to produce a system in which 'nothing is required but to apply the same sound immutably to each character' (1775: sig. C1^v). He achieved this by: grouping together in his 'alphabet' symbols for sounds normally represented by the same letter (e.g. the four ⟨a⟩ sounds); representing each member of such a group by some variant on that letter (in this case the upper-case {A}, the same form halved, the form without a cross-bar, and the form ligatured with {U}); consistently using the 'traditional' upper-case form of a letter for the sound closest to the traditional name of the letter (e.g. {I} for /aɪ/); and creating new forms by ligaturing the letters usually representing those sounds in digraphs (e.g. the ligatured {N} and {G} for the velar nasal).

In following these principles, Spence created what is for the most part a practical, easy-to-learn 'phonetic' system. The only symbols in Spence's notation which are unsuccessful are the two formed by ligaturing {T} and {H}. Spence's use of these rather than the {θ} and {ð} used earlier by Thomas Smith and later by the IPA, or the {th} and {dh} used by Elphinston, perhaps indicates that, when he devised the New Alphabet, Spence was operating according to the principles outlined above, rather than picking up ideas from his fellow orthoepists.

4.3. SPENCE'S NEW ALPHABET: A PHONEMIC SYSTEM?

If the *Grand Repository* was, as we have discussed in §4.2, intended primarily as a pronouncing dictionary and only secondarily as an introduction to reformed spelling, then we need to consider the New Alphabet in terms of its effectiveness as a means of indicating to the reader the 'correct' pronunciation of each word. On the title-page (1775: sig. A1^r), Spence boasts that the *Grand Repository* has 'the Peculiarity of having the most proper and agreeable Pronunciation of the alphabetic words denoted in the most intelligible manner by a New Alphabet'. Spence indicates at the outset that his New Alphabet represents sounds consistently and in a manner that the reader should find easy to understand. In producing his 'New Alphabet', Spence followed the principles set down by Sheridan in his *Dissertation*:

1. No character should be set down in any word, which is not pronounced.
2. Every distinct simple sound, should have a distinct character to mark it; for which it should uniformly stand.
3. The same character should never be set down, as the representative of two different sounds.
4. All compound sounds should be marked only by such characters, as will naturally and necessarily produce these sounds, upon being properly pronounced, in the order in which they are placed.   (Sheridan 1761: 8–9, quoted in Spence 1775: sig. A3^v)

We have already seen in §4.1 that Sheridan did not exactly succeed in putting these principles into practice in his *General Dictionary*, whereas Spence does adhere to the ideal of 'one sound = one spelling' in the *Grand Repository*. What we have not considered yet is how Spence's readers might know which sound was being represented by any one character in the 'New Alphabet'.

Most of the pronouncing dictionaries considered in §4.1 have extensive prefaces which provide detailed information concerning the articulation and distribution of the sounds represented by each letter of the alphabet, as well as a description and exemplification of the system of notation used in the dictionary proper. Walker gives 545 rules which provide such details, as well as specific hints to the Irish, Scots, Welsh, and northerners as to which pronunciations they should avoid. This, as we saw in Chapter 3, makes the *Critical Pronouncing Dictionary* an invaluable source of information for the historical phonologist and no doubt played a great part in its commercial success. Spence, however, provides none of this information: the only clues that the reader of the *Grand Repository* is given about the pronunciation and distribution of the sounds represented by the characters of the New Alphabet are in the layout of the system; the keywords provided; and the distribution of symbols in the *Grand Repository* itself. Walker, like Sheridan, was an elocutionist and took an intellectual interest in the articulation of sounds. Spence was writing for the 'laborious part of the people', who would not have had the time to work their way through such rules or to practise elocution exercises as did the fashionable young ladies in the wake of Sheridan's lecture tours. The *Grand Repository* was intended as a quick and easy guide to pronunciation and as an introduction to Spence's reformed spelling. The quotes above from Spence's title and 'Alphabet' pages stress the simplicity of the system and the ease with which it can be understood.

Spence must have assumed that the reader would know which sound was represented by, for example, {A} as in *mane* and would then simply reproduce this sound whenever the symbol {A} appeared. Keywords are provided only for the vowels and the sounds represented by ligatured letters in the New Alphabet. In addition, Spence provides a keyword for {Y} in the first version of the New Alphabet, whilst, in the second version, one is also provided for {W}: presumably, Spence realized that it was necessary to let the reader know that these symbols represented the consonantal values of the letters in traditional orthography, i.e. /j/ and /w/ rather than /ɪ/ and /ʊ/. Spence must have considered it self-evident that {F} would always and only represent /f/; {V} always and only /v/, etc. The only letters not represented by keywords which could possibly be misinterpreted are {G} and {J}, but here the names of the letters, 'ig or gi' and 'idge or ji' respectively, give a fairly clear indication that {G} represents /g/ and {J} represents /dʒ/. The New Alphabet is laid out as essentially a broad phonemic system, with no indication given as to the precise phonetic nature of the sounds represented. There is, for instance, no attempt on Spence's part to prescribe or even suggest a particular articulation of /r/, although we know from Walker (1791: 50) that several pronunciations of this 'letter' existed at the time, including that reportedly used by Spence himself and proscribed by both Walker and Kenrick, the uvular or 'Northumbrian burr'. Either Spence saw no reason to proscribe this, perhaps, like the Northumbrians encountered by Defoe on his journey, being proud of it, or, since at least one of his main purposes in writing the *Grand Repository* was to introduce his new spelling system, he felt that differences of articulation which affected neither the inventory nor the incidence of phonemes were not important.

As far as the quantity of vowels is concerned, Spence does, as we have seen above, have a systematic method of representing short vowels by either cutting the upper-case letter in half, or adding a cross-bar. In addition, in the lower-case version of the alphabet printed alongside the upper-case forms on both the New Alphabet pages, but not used in the dictionary itself, Spence marks a long vowel with a macron and a short vowel with a breve: thus, it is clear that the vowel of *mane* is long and that of *man* is short. What is not clear from this is whether the sound represented by {A} is monophthongal or diphthongal. Spence does seem to work from the principle that diph-thongs should be represented by ligatured letters and placed at the end of the alphabet, for, apart from {I}, the only other clearly diphthongal sounds in his system, /ɔɪ/ as in *oil* and /aʊ/ as in *house*, are treated in this way. The vowel in *wall* is ligatured, but placed amongst the other 'a sounds', so we can assume that it had something like the monophthongal, rounded vowel used in present-day RP. Since the first clear evidence of diphthongization in words like *mane* comes from Batchelor (1809), we can assume that this simply was not an issue for Spence or his readers: the sound was something like /eː/, whether more or less open we just cannot tell.

What emerges from this brief examination of the very scanty information provided on the 'alphabet' pages of the *Grand Repository* is that Spence either assumed a great deal of shared knowledge between himself and his readers as to the 'true' pronunciation of his keywords or he was concerned with the distribution rather than the exact quality of the sounds. Spence's system is a phonemic rather than a phonetic one: we, like Spence's eighteenth-century readers, can tell that the vowel in *mane* contrasts with that in *man*; that in *tune* contrasts with that in *tun* (note Spence's use of minimal pairs as keywords), but the exact quality of these vowels is left unspecified. Likewise, with regard to consonants, we can tell that the pronunciation described in the *Grand Repository* is rhotic, for instance, because the symbol {R} appears after, as well as before, vowels: *air* is respelt {AR}, for instance, but, as we have already seen above, we have no idea as to the articulation of /r/ favoured by Spence. The New Alphabet pages provide us with the phonemic inventory of the pronunciation recommended by Spence, whilst the entries in the *Grand Repository* provide information on the incidence or distribution of these phonemes. We have seen in Chapter 3 that such information can be extremely useful to the historical phonologist: to the eighteenth-century reader, assuming that, for example, the vowel in *mane* was understood and not a matter of controversy, this information would prove helpful in avoiding the more obvious linguistic gaffes such as h-dropping and r-insertion (mentioned by Spence in the extract from *The Giant Killer* quoted in §1.2.1) and would provide a useful guide to the pronunciation of the more learned words more often encountered in writing than in speech.

Since the New Alphabet is essentially a phonemic system, it might be useful at this stage to have an overview of Spence's system and to compare it with that of present day RP. For this purpose, I have chosen to use the description of RP and other varieties of present-day English provided by Wells (1982), because this work, like the *Grand Repository*, uses keywords. In Wells's case, each keyword 'stands for a large number of words which behave the same way in respect of the incidence of vowels in different accents' (1982: 120): in some cases, two or more keywords might represent the same phoneme in RP, but each represents a different historical lexical set and so may represent a different phoneme in other accents. For example, PALM and START both represent /ɑː/ in RP, but, because START represents the lexical set in which an /r/ follows the historically short /a/, this keyword may represent a different phoneme in, for instance, rhotic accents. The use of keywords thus allows Wells to give a clear and uniform account of several different accents, using reference points which are easily recognizable and do not require the reader to be a philologist (although he does provide a very useful account of the sound changes which led to the differences between accents and uses the keywords in the titles which he gives to these changes— for example, the FOOT-STRUT split separating northern accents with the same vowel for both these keywords from southern ones with two different vowels). It suits our purpose to extend this comparison into the diachronic realm: just as Wells is able to provide a clear comparative account of accents of contemporary English by using his keywords, so we will be able to use the same keywords to compare the system described by Spence in the *Grand Repository* with that of RP and/or other accents of present-day English. This comparison will highlight areas of interest for closer examination in Chapter 5.

Like Spence, Wells provides keywords only for the vowels and diphthongs. In fact, Spence's approach to the use of keywords seems justifiable when we see Wells's (1982: 123) explanation for his choices: 'the keywords have been chosen in such a way that clarity is maximized: whatever accent of English they are spoken in, they can hardly be mistaken for other words.' Spence could well have made the same claim, but what Wells fails to realize is that recognition of the sounds exemplified in the keywords depends on a knowledge of either RP or General American on the reader's part. I can personally vouch for the fact that this can cause confusion, for, as a first-year undergraduate learning phonology for the first time, I spent a good ten minutes puzzling over the fact that Strang (1968: 48) had *cub* and *put* as keywords for two separate phonemes, until I realized that this book was not designed for northerners. As we shall see, with regard to the *cub/put* problem, Spence's *Grand Repository was* designed for northerners. Wells's method is probably not as foolproof as he thinks, but it does provide a very useful point of comparison with the system described in the *Grand Repository*. Since Wells provides, in addition to the main keyword, several examples of other words in which the same phoneme occurs, I have been able to compare the incidence of phonemes in present-day RP with Spence's system, as well as the inventories of these systems. In Table 4.1 I have set out a comparison between these two systems. I have listed first the phoneme of RP represented by each of Wells's lexical sets. The columns then list the number and main keyword of each of Wells's lexical sets and the symbol used by Spence in the same word. Finally I have indicated any cases where, in the *Grand Repository*, the other examples provided by Wells have a different phoneme from that of Wells's keyword. In these cases, I indicate the number of the equivalent phoneme in Wells' system. For instance, Wells's vowel 3 is RP /æ/ and can be seen as equivalent to Spence's {ʌ}, for Spence has this symbol in the keyword TRAP and in almost all of the other examples given by Wells: *tap, cancel, badge, back,* but, in *scalp*, Spence has {ʌ͡U}, which is equivalent to Wells 13 THOUGHT, so I have marked this (scalp > 13). This shows us that the two systems have an equivalent phoneme in their inventories, but that the incidence of the phoneme is different.

If we consider the inventories of the two systems first, what emerges from Table 4.1 is that there are five vowel/diphthong phonemes in RP which were not present in Spence's system (by Spence's system, I mean that described in the *Grand Repository*, not his own accent). These are Wells's number 5 STRUT, number 9 NURSE, number 19 NEAR, number 20 SQUARE, and number

Table 4.1. *Wells's and Spence's systems*

RP	Wells	Spence	Keywords
ɪ	1. KIT	{Ɨ}	kit, ship, sick, milk, myth, busy, bridge
ɛ	2. DRESS	{E}	dress, edge, friend, neck, ready, shelf
æ	3. TRAP	{A}	trap, tap, (scalp > 13), cancel, badge, back
ɒ	4. LOT	{C}	lot, dodge, possible, (quality > 3), romp, sock, stop
ʌ	5. STRUT		> 6
ʊ	6. FOOT	{U}	foot, full, (good, look > 15), put, wolf, bush
ɑː	7. BATH	{Λ}	(bath, brass, ask > 3) calf, (dance, sample > 3), staff
ɒ	8. CLOTH	{C}	cloth, cough, cross, broth, (Boston n.a.), long
ɜː	9. NURSE		(nurse, burst, hurt, lurk, urge > 6), (jerk, term > 2)
iː	10. FLEECE	{E}	fleece, creep, feel, key, leave, people, speak
eɪ	11. FACE	{A}	face, cake, day, (raid n.a.), steak, tape, veil
ɑː	12. PALM	{Λ}	palm, psalm, father, (bra, spa n.a.)
ɔː	13. THOUGHT	{AU}	(thought > 14), taught, sauce, (broad > 14), hawk, jaw
əʊ	14. GOAT	{O}	goat, home, joke, know, roll, so, soap
uː	15. GOOSE	{ꟾꟾ}	goose, (loop n.a.), shoot, tomb, (view, mute > Spence's ⟨U⟩), (huge n.a.)
aɪ	16. PRICE	{I}	price, ripe, write, arrive, buy, high, try
ɔɪ	17. CHOICE	{CI}	choice, adroit, join, noise, toy, royal
aʊ	18. MOUTH	{CU}	mouth, house, loud, out, count, cow, crowd
iə	19. NEAR		(near, beer, fear, sincere > 10), (beard, serum n.a.)
ɛə	20. SQUARE		(square, care, fair, scarce, vary, where > 11), (pear >10)
ɑː	21. START	{Λ}	(start > 3), sharp, bark, carve, (far, farm > 3), heart
ɔː	22. NORTH	{AU}	(north, for, born, short, scorch > 4), war, warm
ɔː	23. FORCE		(force > 4), (four > 14), (bourne n.a.), (porch, sport > 4), (story > 14), (wore n.a.)
ʊə	24. CURE		(cure, pure, plural > Spence's ⟨U⟩), (tour > 18), (jury > 15)

Note: n.a. = not applicable, i.e. this particular item was not found in the *Grand Repository*.

24 CURE. All of these except number 5 developed in RP as a result of the loss of rhoticity and we have already seen that Spence's system is rhotic. In this respect, Spence's system is much closer to that described by Wells as Scots. The vowel of STRUT is, of course, the one that caused me such difficulties in my early undergraduate days and is still notably absent from all northern accents. Spence also appears to have one vowel phoneme which does not appear in Wells's inventory: that represented by {U} as in *tune*. Here, I think the difference is one of definition: as we shall see in Chapter 5, Spence and his contemporaries tended to view what was probably a diphthong /iu/ or a sequence of glide + vowel /juː/ as a single sound, most probably because the

sound is identical to the name of the letter ⟨u⟩ in the traditional alphabet. Wells, on the other hand, sees it as a sequence of two phonemes /j/ and /uː/ (see §5.6 on 'yod-dropping'.)

With regard to consonants, the one difference in inventory concerns the presence of the phoneme represented by {WH} as in *which* in Spence's system. Wells describes the sound at the beginning of *which* as /hw/ and accents which have /w/ in these words as subject to 'Glide Cluster Reduction'. He does acknowledge that some accents may have a single phoneme here: 'the phonetic realization of /hw/, in accents not subject to Glide Cluster Reduction, may be a sequence representable as [hw], or alternatively a single segment [ʍ], a voiceless labial-velar fricative. In Scottish English, for example, [ʍ] seems to be the norm. An alternative phonemicization is then possible: we can recognize an additional phoneme /ʍ/ in the system' (Wells 1982: 228). Spence's system, like present-day Scots, clearly has the extra phoneme: as we shall see in §5.10, what Wells calls 'Glide Cluster Reduction' was condemned by Walker as a Cockneyism and probably never encountered in the north: Wells points out (1982: 228) that 'the only local accents in England which retain /hw/ are those of Northumberland and nearby'.

Differences in the incidence of phonemes between Spence's system and that of RP as described by Wells are more numerous and complex than those of inventory, but they can be summarized as follows:

1. Where Wells has *good, look* with vowel 6 FOOT, Spence has {ꟙ} for these words, which is equivalent to Wells's vowel 15 GOOSE. Even today, many northern accents have /uː/ in such words, particularly *look, book*, etc. These differences are due to the 'later' shortening of ME /oː/ in present-day RP, which in RP contrasts with unshortened ME /oː/ in GOOSE, etc. This 'later shortening' was still in the process of lexical diffusion in eighteenth-century English, a matter which we shall consider in §5.5.

2. Where Wells has *scalp* with vowel 3 TRAP, Spence has {ʌ}, equivalent to Wells's vowel 13 THOUGHT, and where Wells has *quality* with vowel 4 LOT, Spence gives it {ʌ}, equivalent to Wells's vowel 3. Both these words involve ME /a/ before /l/, the normal development of which involved first diphthongization to /au/, then monophthongisation to either /ɑː/ as in *half* or /ɔː/ as in *ball*. However, according to Dobson (1957: 553), this only occurred when the /a/ was followed by a 'dark' /l/—i.e. orthographically ⟨ll⟩ or ⟨l⟩ followed by another consonant. The rounding in *quality* was due, not to the following /l/, but to the preceding /w/, which, in words such as *wasp, wand, quantity*, etc., led to a short /ɒ/ in RP. The former rounding does not occur in present-day Tyneside English, where, in more traditional accents, *ball* is pronounced /baːl/, and *all right* /aːˈriːt/; whilst the latter was variable in the eighteenth and nineteenth centuries. The sound changes involved, and their diffusion in eighteenth-century English, will be discussed in §5.3.

3. *Bath, brass, ask, dance, sample* have vowel 7 BATH in Wells, but the short vowel {\}, equivalent to Wells's vowel 3 TRAP, in Spence. The short vowel in this lexical set is still one of the most salient features of northern accents. However, even northern accents (at least the non-rhotic ones) have a long vowel in the words in Wells's 21 START set, but here Spence has the short vowel in START itself, *far* and *farm*, but the long one in *sharp, bark,* and *carve*. The diffusion of this lengthening of ME /a/ in these lexical sets was a complex matter and will be discussed at some length in §5.2.

4. This set of differences in incidence involves the distribution of the sounds represented by Spence's {ÆU} and {O} as against Wells's number 13 THOUGHT and number 14 GOAT. Spence has {ÆU} for *taught, sauce, hawk* and *jaw*, all in Wells's THOUGHT set and for *war, warm* from Wells's NORTH set (number 22), as well as for *scalp*, discussed above. For THOUGHT itself and *broad*, from Wells's THOUGHT set, and for *four* and *story* from Wells's FORCE set (number 23, but with the same vowel as NORTH in RP), Spence has {O}, equivalent to Wells's number 14 GOAT. For NORTH itself, as well as for *born, short,* and *scorch* from Wells's NORTH set, and for *force, porch,* and *sport* from the FORCE set, Spence has short {C}, equivalent to Wells's number 4 LOT. The short vowels in Spence's distribution can be explained by the rhoticity of his system, as lengthening of /o/ before historical /r/, like that of /a/ in the same environment, is tied in with loss of rhoticity. The distribution of *thought, broad, four,* and *story*, as against *taught, sauce, hawk* and *jaw*, may be connected with Spence's perception, suggested in the layout of the New Alphabet, that {ÆU} is essentially an ⟨a⟩ vowel, and so words with orthographic ⟨a⟩, ⟨aw⟩, or ⟨au⟩ could be seen as belonging here. (See §5.3.3.)

As far as the consonants are concerned, the most striking difference in inventory between Spence's system and that of RP is in the distribution of /r/. Spence's system is, as we have already indicated, rhotic. The loss of rhoticity in eighteenth-century English was mentioned by Walker (1791), who saw it as essentially a London phenomenon. As we shall see in §5.2 and §5.8, it was not seen as prestigious and had certainly not reached as far north as Newcastle by 1775, so that Spence's distribution of /r/ would be seen as 'correct' at the time.

Spence's distribution of /h/ is slightly different from that of RP, but only in that he has 'h-dropping' in a larger number of words derived from French (e.g. *herb*) than RP has. As we shall see in §5.9, Spence's distribution of initial /h/ is entirely in line with that of his contemporaries: in any case, 'h-dropping' except in French words was condemned as a cockneyism in the eighteenth century and is still unknown north of Sunderland (Beal 1993*a*: 167).

This examination of Spence's New Alphabet has shown that it is essentially a system in which the reader is given an account of the phonemic inventory of the recommended pronunciation but has to work out the actual pronunciation represented by any one symbol from the keywords. The entries in the *Grand Repository* then show the incidence, or distribution of these phonemes across the lexicon. A comparison of Spence's system with that of RP as described in Wells (1982) has revealed differences of inventory and incidence between the two systems, which provide pointers to the areas to be investigated in detail in the next chapter.

5. The Phonology of Eighteenth-Century English: Evidence from Spence's *Grand Repository* and Contemporary Pronouncing Dictionaries

5.1. INTRODUCTION

We saw in §3.4 that pronouncing dictionaries such as the *Grand Repository* are a particularly valuable source of evidence for linguistic changes which were in progress in the eighteenth century, since, in providing a full 'lexicon', they allow us to trace the lexical diffusion of those sound changes. Wherever the entries in the *Grand Repository* show two or more different realizations of what was a single phoneme in ME or even ENE, then we may suspect that lexical diffusion is at work, particularly if those realizations correspond to what we know from other sources (e.g. seventeenth-century orthoepists) to be 'older' and 'newer' or conservative and innovative sounds. A thorough examination of the *Grand Repository* entries will allow us to ascertain whether the diffusion is phonetically (i.e. environmentally) rather than strictly lexically conditioned, whilst a comparison of these entries with the same words in other contemporary pronouncing dictionaries will enable us to judge whether Spence is so far out of line with the other orthoepists as to be the 'lone voice' I warned against in §3.2, or whether his distribution of the variants is simply more conservative (closer to that of earlier sources) or more northern (closer to that of other northern or Scots sources) than others.

Of course, examining a whole lexicon is a daunting task, which probably explains why, despite the obvious importance of pronouncing dictionaries as evidence, there has, to my knowledge, hitherto been no study of an eighteenth-century pronouncing dictionary which has examined the whole lexicon for evidence of particular changes. For this study, I have made use of the Oxford Concordance Program (henceforth OCP) to enable me to obtain quickly lists of all the words in which Spence uses a particular symbol. Given that, as we saw in Chapter 4, Spence's *New Alphabet* is a phonemic one in which one sound = one symbol and vice versa, any one of these lists will provide an exhaustive account of the distribution of a particular phoneme in the pronunciation described in the *Grand Repository*. Since OCP would not be able to 'read' the *New Alphabet*, I had the *Grand Repository* recoded into alphanumeric symbols, as shown in Table 5.1.[1] Appendix 1 gives examples of the output from OCP, when programmed to provide all the words from the *Grand Repository* with the symbol which Spence used for /ɔɪ/, in this case recoded as 3. Taking lists like this, I have then looked up the same words 'manually' in other pronouncing dictionaries for comparison. Obviously, in some cases, the other dictionaries simply do not include a word found in the *Grand Repository*, and, given that Spence's is a relatively short dictionary, there will be many more examples of words in the same lexical sets found in, say Walker, that do not appear in my output files. Nevertheless, these files do provide a good starting point for comparison of the lexical distribution of phonemes in eighteenth-century English on a scale far greater than has been attempted before.

I have chosen to compare the word-lists from the *Grand Repository* systematically with the equivalent entries in Walker (1791), Sheridan

Table 5.1. *Spence's New Alphabet with alphanumeric coding used for OCP file*

New Alphabet	Recoding	IPA	New Alphabet	Recoding	IPA
{A}	A	eː	{P}	P	p
{ᴧ}	a	æ	{R}	R	r
{Λ}	1	ɑː	{S}	S	s
{ᴁ}	2	ɔː	{T}	T	t
{B}	B	b	{U}	U	juː
{D}	D	d	{ʮ}	u	ʊ (/ə/?)
{E}	E	iː	{V}	V	v
{Ɇ}	e	ɛ	{W}	W	w
{F}	F	f	{Y}	Y	j
{G}	G	g	{Z}	Z	z
{H}	H	h	{ꟻ}	w	uː
{I}	I	aɪ	{ɑ}	3	ɔɪ
{Ɨ}	i	ɪ	{ᴔ}	4	aʊ
{J}	J	dʒ	{SI}	s	ʃ
{K}	K	k	{ƵI}	z	ʒ
{L}	L	l	{CH}	C	tʃ
{M}	M	m	{Ħ}	5	θ
{N}	N	n	{H}	6	ð
{O}	O	oː	{WH}	7	ʌ
{C}	o	ɒ	{NG}	8	ŋ

[1] This work was made possible by means of a grant from the Small Grants Committee of the University of Newcastle upon Tyne

(1780), and Burn (1786), with Johnston (1764) substituting for Sheridan in §5.2, because Sheridan does not recognize the 'fourth sound of *a*' (= /ɑː/) under discussion in that section. Other pronouncing dictionaries and orthoepistic works have been referred to in the discussions in §§5.2–5.10 where they provide evidence that sheds further light on the sound changes concerned. I chose the pronouncing dictionaries named above for the following reasons: Walker, because, as discussed in §3.3.2, he provides such a wealth of information in his introduction, and because he was the self-styled voice of authority; Sheridan, because he is closer to Spence in time and because his *Dissertation* (1761) is, as we saw in §4.1.4, the only acknowledged source for the *Grand Repository*; Johnston, because he is slightly earlier than Spence and will provide time depth; and Burn because, as a Scot, he might show similarities with Spence which point to the existence of common norms in a 'North British' modified standard. These comparisons will allow us, in some measure, to trace the lexical, geographical, and social diffusion of sound changes in progress through the second half of the eighteenth century.

The lists of lexical items chosen for comparison in §§5.2–5.10 will be those output from OCP as containing the relevant symbol (and therefore the relevant sound) in the *Grand Repository*: for instance, in §5.2, we consider all the entries which contain {Λ}, the equivalent of PDE /ɑː/, in the *Grand Repository*, and then look more closely at a subset in which this symbol occurs before {R}. All these cases involve lengthening of an earlier (mainly ME, but later in the case of loanwords and neoclassical formations) /a/, and so the set of words with a particular symbol in the *Grand Repository* coincides with a philological set.

In other cases, this correspondence is not so neat and, to a certain extent, the list output from OCP has to be further refined by hand. For instance, §5.3 deals with the change of ME (and later) /a/ to /ɔː/ before an /l/ which is sometimes, but not always, vocalized, and in either case remains in the orthography. Examples of this in PDE are *talk* with vocalization of /l/ and *alter* without. The variability of /l/ vocalization as evidenced in eighteenth-century pronouncing dictionaries is interesting in itself, but, since Spence does not include 'silent' sounds in his New Alphabet entries, and since it is only the (recoded) New Alphabet entries which were input to OCP, it cannot be programmed to produce a list of words with Spence's {ÆU} symbol, before a vocalized ⟨l⟩. In this case, therefore, I have had to produce a list of all words with {ÆU} and then check back with the *Grand Repository* itself to see which of these have a following ⟨l⟩ in the traditional spelling. In other cases here, the /ɔː/ may be the result of monophthongization of ME /au/ and so should not be considered along with reflexes of ME /a/. (Examples of the two sources of PDE /ɔː/ and, indeed, Spence's {ÆU} are *caul* and *call* respectively.)

Since these are homophones, the OCP output would show them as two instances of the 'same' word. Since so much sifting of the OCP output is needed, I have not, except for exemplificatory purposes in Appendix 1, provided the raw output. Instead, I give lists, as Appendices 2–10, showing all the words in the relevant set (e.g. reflexes of /a/ before ⟨l⟩) for which Spence has a certain symbol, and then, for each word, either the IPA equivalent of the symbol used in each of the pronouncing dictionaries examined, or the contrasting feature (e.g. 'long' versus 'short'.)

We saw in §2.4 that, whilst most scholars, but especially those writing in the first half of the twentieth century, use the phonemes of ME as their starting point for the study of eighteenth-century phonology, others, notably those of the 'DEMEP school', prefer to take what they call a more 'synchronic' approach, taking as a starting point the system used by the particular orthoepist under examination. I have already had occasion to use the term 'ME (and later) /a/', which is perhaps an indication that I intend to compromise between these two approaches. It is useful for historical phonologists to use the ME system as a starting point, as it provides a certain time depth to the study, allowing us to make use of information from, for examples, Dobson (1957), which may reveal the beginnings of the sound change in question in ENE. On the other hand, as studies such as Chomsky and Halle (1968) show, the phonological system of eighteenth-century English is not that of ME, but has undergone restructuring, not least as a result of the Great Vowel Shift. Perhaps more immediately relevant to this study is the fact that the lexicon of eighteenth-century English is not that of ME: a word like *plastic* cannot be said to have ME /a/ because the word did not exist in ME (first citation 1598 in *OED*), but it is cited in eighteenth-century pronouncing dictionaries, it has (originally) a short /a/ before a voiceless fricative, like *plaster*, and, if a phonology has a rule lengthening earlier /a/ before voiceless fricatives, then *plastic* will have to be lexically marked as not subject to this rule in order to avoid it. When a sound change is still diffusing, such late additions to the lexicon are liable to get caught up in it eventually, as we can see from the fact that RP varies between /plæstɪk/ and /plɑːstik/ today, and, unless the innovation is from a language whose phonology is known and respected (e.g. French, from which later loanwords like *police* (1535) escape the effects of the Great Vowel Shift), loanwords and other innovations are subject to analogy.[2] Writers of pronouncing dictionaries would tend to include relatively recent additions to the lexicon, as, particularly when these are of a learned nature, they would be the very words about whose pronunciation the readers would be most uncertain. Thus, I have elected to include in my word-lists not only words with a certain sound in ME, but also later additions to the lexicon which could have been caught

---

[2] Note, for instance, the variation in pronunciation of the word *pasta*: British English so far continues to use the short vowel of the Italian original, but Australian English has [pɑːstə] with the same vowel as e.g. *past*.

up in the same sound changes in the eighteenth century: when I refer, for example, to ME (and later) /a/, it is to be understood that this covers both the stressed vowel of e.g. *plaster* and that of e.g. *plastic*.

This study will involve a detailed and systematic comparison of fairly large numbers of lexical items from the *Grand Repository* and three other eighteenth-century pronouncing dictionaries, in order to establish patterns of diffusion. It would be beyond the scope of a work such as this to examine the entire phonology of eighteenth-century English. I have therefore chosen to look at certain areas of the phonology which were involved in sound changes at the time. These areas were chosen according to the following criteria:

1. There is evidence that the sound changes concerned were still diffusing (socially, geographically, lexically, or any combination of the three) in the eighteenth century. We saw in Chapter 2 that many of the scholars who recognized the value of the eighteenth century as a period worthy of the historical linguist's attention also recognized the complexity of eighteenth-century sound changes. The testimony of these scholars, as well as the authors of the monographs reviewed in §2.4, will alert us to areas in which diffusion was causing this 'complexity'.

2. The variability caused by this diffusion was 'salient' (in the sense used by Labov 1966). We have seen in §3.3.4 that many eighteenth-century orthoepists make explicit reference to the 'vulgar' or 'provincial' nature of certain pronunciations. Walker, in particular, both in his Preface and in the notes to certain entries, pulls no punches in condemning such usages: his notes are an excellent litmus test of the 'salience' of a particular variant. Of particular interest will be those features which are condemned (or, in rare cases, even defended) as either Scots or northern, as investigation of these features may reveal the extent of northern influence in the *Grand Repository*, but we might also expect to find a lack of 'vulgar' Cockney features in the northern pronouncing dictionaries, so these, too, are worth investigating.

3. The sound changes should be characteristic of the eighteenth century, either in that they are innovations which mark this period as distinct from ENE, or in that they contrast with present-day RP. In the latter case, differences will tend to be of incidence rather than inventory, but, as we saw in §4.3, there are also, particularly in the area of vowels affected by loss of rhoticity, significant differences between Spence's inventory and that of RP.

Using these criteria, I have chosen to examine the *Grand Repository* and other eighteenth-century pronouncing dictionaries for evidence of the following sound changes (the section in which each of those changes is examined is indicated at the end of the appropriate paragraph below):

- Lengthening[3] of ME and later /a/ in various environments (before voiceless fricatives, word-final and preconsonantal /r/, and before /l/ or before /n/ + consonant in cases where the eighteenth-century pronunciation is with /ɑː/ rather than /ɔː/, e.g. *half, dance*, as opposed to *halt, haunt*). This group of changes satisfies all three criteria: the incidence of long versus short variants in eighteenth-century sources shows all the evidence of lexical diffusion, it is salient, then as now, but, as we shall see, for rather different reasons, and it is an innovation first evidenced in the late seventeenth century. (See §5.2.)

- ME (and later) /a/ becoming /ɔː/ or /ɒ/ before (sometimes vocalized) /l/ and after /w/. These again are innovations of late ENE (Shakespeare rhymes *war* and *far*): they are two different sound changes, but both produce rounded reflexes, and in both cases those reflexes are represented by Spence's {*Æ*}. They are 'salient' in a slightly different way from the other sound changes discussed here in that, whilst the unrounded variant is not identified as a northern feature by eighteenth-century orthoepists, pronunciations such as [baːl] [waːk] for *ball, walk* are characteristic of present-day 'broad' Tyneside speech.[4] As we shall see, there is also enough variation between the different sources to suggest some kind of diffusion was occurring in the eighteenth century. (See §5.3.)

- 'Splitting' of ME (and later) /ʊ/. As we saw in §4.3, one of the most striking differences in inventory between Spence's system and that of present-day RP as set out in Wells (1982) was the lack, in the former, of a vowel corresponding to RP /ʌ/, so that, for Spence, *put, cup* have the same vowel and *pus* ('the matter of a sore') and *puss* ('a cat; a hare') are homophones. This 'unsplit' /ʊ/, then, as now, was a highly salient northern feature, and is condemned as such by, e.g. Walker and Kenrick. Since this is a difference of inventory rather than incidence, there is less scope for lexical diffusion: Spence does not have the /ʌ/ at all, so there is nothing to diffuse. There is, however, a certain amount of variability in the pronunciations recorded in the eighteenth century for the later /ʊ/ from 'early shortening' of ME /oː/ in e.g. *soot*. This feature is really important because, above all, it identifies Spence as northern. (See §5.4.)

- Later shortening of ME /oː/. We have already seen that some reflexes of ME /oː/ vary between /ʌ/ and /ʊ/ in our eighteenth-century sources. In these cases, /ʌ/ is the result of earlier shortening of ME /oː/, already

[3] I use the umbrella term *lengthening* here, because the final outcome in RP, and, indeed in several eighteenth-century sources, is a long vowel: [ɑː] or [aː]. As we shall see, some of these changes involve breaking/diphthongization as an intermediate stage.

[4] An interesting repetition of the absence of (southern) rounding of OE *ā* in e.g. *stān, hām* giving [steːn] [heːm] in present-day Scots, and evidenced in northern place-names such as *Stanley* (= Stone lea) in County Durham.

shifted to /uː/ by the Great Vowel Shift, to /ʊ/. If this shortening took place early enough, the resulting /ʊ/ would fall together with ME /ʊ/ and be subject to the unrounding to /ʌ/ first evidenced in the late seventeenth century. If the shortening took place later, when unrounding was no longer operative, then the result would be /ʊ/. Present-day RP shows the result of early shortening in e.g. *blood* /blʌd/; later shortening in e.g. *book* /bʊk/ and no shortening in e.g. *boon* /buːn/. The results of these chronologically overlapping sound changes in RP are in themselves evidence of the kinds of competing sound change and lexical diffusion described in Wang (1969), and the eighteenth-century sources provide evidence of an earlier stage of this diffusion. Today, absence of later shortening in e.g. *book* is characteristic of some northern accents (Wells 1982: 133),[5] and we might expect to find the same in our eighteenth-century sources, but, as we shall see, this is not the case, for even Walker shows the long vowel in *book* etc. (See §5.5.)

- 'Yod-dropping', or, as Wells (1982: 206) terms this, 'Early Yod Dropping', involving the loss of /j/ in e.g. *rude*, *blue*. This change was an innovation of the eighteenth century and its diffusion created complex patterns of variation at that time. It appears to have been an innovation which began in London, and which was not approved of by e.g. Elphinston, who writes of the 'vulgar indolence' of those who 'sink the liquefaction'. We might expect to find less evidence of yod-dropping in the northern/Scots sources, as well as a complex pattern of lexically and/or phonetically conditioned variation even in the London sources. (See §5.6.)

- Reduction of unstressed vowels to /ə/. This sound change will be handled rather differently, as there would be far too many instances of unstressed vowels in the *Grand Repository* for a complete list to be examined. However, this area does merit our attention, because it was highly salient at the time: as we have seen in §3.3.3, one of the main criticisms of Sheridan put forward by the author of *A Caution to Gentlemen Who Use Sheridan's Dictionary* was that he substituted ⟨u⟩ for other vowels in unstressed position. As we shall see, ⟨u⟩ is the letter most often used by eighteenth-century orthoepists to represent schwa, but Spence often uses {ɪ}, the same symbol which he uses for /ɪ/ in *tin*, etc. It will, therefore, be interesting to compare a selection rather than an exhaustive list of entries from the *Grand Repository* and other eighteenth-century pronouncing dictionaries, to see whether Spence's

---

[5] Even here, though, the diffusion is still occurring: I said /buːk/ as a child, but my younger siblings (fourteen years younger) say /bʊk/. Coming from Lancashire (Wells's 'middle north'), we have accents usually characterized as retaining the unshortened vowel here, but observation not only of my family, but of numerous students from the same area, shows that the shortening is still diffusing geographically. Further north, in County Durham, the long vowel is still used even by younger speakers.

use of {ɫ} for some unstressed vowels is so out of line as to suggest a departure from his 'phonetic' ideal, or whether there is evidence from other Scots/northern orthoepists to suggest that the variety described by Spence really could have had this sound. (See §5.7.)

The above sound changes deal with vowels, whilst the remaining ones are concerned with consonantal features. There is, inevitably, a certain amount of overlap here, as, for instance, the vocalization of /r/ and /l/ is so closely linked to the lengthening of /a/. Once again, the consonantal features chosen for detailed examination have been selected according to criteria 1–3 above.

- Loss of rhoticity. We saw in §4.3 that many of the differences in inventory between Spence's system and that of RP as outlined in Wells (1982) were attributable to the rhotic nature of Spence's system: Spence, for instance, lacked the /ɜː/ of Wells's NURSE set, and the centring diphthongs /ɪə/, /ɛə/, and /ʊə/of NEAR, SQUARE, and CURE, all of which owe their origin in RP and other non-rhotic accents to weakening and loss of /r/ after the vocalic sounds concerned. In this respect, Spence's system is much more similar to present-day rhotic accents such as Scots than to RP. Once again it will not be practicable to carry out a comparison of full lexical sets here, mainly because all the pronouncing dictionaries concerned mark /r/ as present in their transcriptions whenever it is present in traditional orthography. This section will, rather, examine the evidence for weakening/loss of final and preconsonantal /r/ in the eighteenth century and its salience at the time. (See §5.8.)
- 'H-dropping'. Although there is evidence of 'h-dropping' and, conversely, 'h-insertion' from as early as the sixteenth century (see e.g. evidence from Henry Machyn in Wyld 1936), it is not until the eighteenth century that this becomes salient: Mugglestone (1995: 113) suggests that Sheridan 'was the first to record this new . . . sensitization to the loss of [h]' in his *Course of Lectures on Elocution* (1762). In the course of the eighteenth and nineteenth centuries it was to become, as Mugglestone so thoroughly proves, *the* shibboleth of 'vulgar' speech. It might seem, from this, that the pronouncing dictionary entries themselves will tell us nothing about 'h-dropping', since educated Londoners like Walker would avoid it at all costs, and Scots/northern (and, indeed, Irish) writers would have no cause to be influenced by 'h-dropping', since their native accents, to this day, are 'h-ful'.[6] However,

[6] Visitors to Newcastle from further south find it hard to believe that the outlandish accent of this extreme northern outpost is, in this respect, more 'correct' than their own. I advise them to visit St James' Park (home of Newcastle United FC), where they will hear the h-ful roar 'Howay the lads!'. Incidentally, the good citizens of Newcastle are aware and proud of their h-fulness: they believe that this is another instance of their inherent superiority to the 'Mackems' (citizens of Sunderland).

there is a subset of words with initial ⟨h⟩ which has been variably subject to 'h-dropping' since the eighteenth century: words such as *herb, honour, hotel* which are of French origin. We shall, therefore, examine the small list of words of French origin with initial ⟨h⟩ in traditional orthography to see which have or do not have /h/ in the *Grand Repository* and other eighteenth-century pronouncing dictionaries, in order to find out whether, perhaps as a 'hypercorrection', h-fulness was spreading to French words, as it certainly has in PDE (but not American) *herb*. (See §5.9.)

- Merger of /ʍ/ and /w/. This can be seen as parallel with the last feature, especially if, as the eighteenth-century orthoepists did, we analyse /ʍ/ as a sequence /hw/, for, in this case, the change of e.g *which* from /hwɪtʃ/ to /wɪtʃ/ becomes another case of 'h-dropping'. Like 'h-dropping' it is seen in the eighteenth century as a Cockney 'vulgarism', and Scots writers like Elphinston see it as an English (as opposed to Scottish) fault. I do not expect to find much evidence of lexical diffusion here, but it is worth examining the small set of words involved to see whether the Scots/northern orthoepists are more consistent in their adherence to /ʍ/. This phoneme is also of interest according to criterion 3, as it is one which is present in Spence's inventory, but not that of RP as outlined in Wells (1982), and again marks out Spence's system as closer to present-day Scots. (See §5.10.)

Each of these sections §§5.2–5.10 will begin with a brief summary of the state of our knowledge concerning the progress of the sound change(s) concerned up to the eighteenth century. Then, the salience of the pronunciations concerned in the eighteenth century, as indicated by, for instance, comments from orthoepists such as Walker, will be discussed. Finally, except where the discussion above has indicated that this is not practicable or appropriate, the detailed comparison of word-lists from the *Grand Repository* and in each case three other eighteenth-century pronouncing dictionaries will be discussed. Bringing in evidence from other eighteenth-century orthoepists where appropriate, we will then discuss whether the comparison shows evidence of lexical, geographical, or (less likely because only Spence was truly working class) social diffusion. It will be particularly interesting to see whether Spence and the Scots orthoepists (Burn and possibly Johnston in our detailed comparisons, but we shall also look at evidence from Elphinston, James Douglas, and Sylvester Douglas) tend to be closer to each other than to Londoners such as Walker and Kenrick, perhaps showing evidence of a 'northern' standard. For the detailed comparisons, I have, for the reasons outlined above, chosen Walker, Sheridan, and Burn, substituting Johnston for Sheridan in §5.2.[7]

---

[7] I have not listed these dictionaries chronologically because, as we shall see, the most

5.2. LENGTHENING OF ME /a/

5.2.1. *Sources of present-day English (RP) /ɑː/*

The /ɑː/ phoneme of present-day English is very interesting in terms of its regional and social distribution: although ⟨a⟩ before final ⟨r⟩, before ⟨r⟩ followed by another consonant, before ⟨lf⟩, and before ⟨lm⟩ is pronounced long, albeit with variations in quality, throughout England, the long vowel in other environments—namely, before ⟨f⟩, ⟨s⟩, ⟨th⟩ particularly when pronounced /θ/, ⟨nt⟩, ⟨ns⟩, and ⟨nd⟩—is, in strictly geographical terms, confined to the south (i.e. south of Birmingham). RP speakers everywhere have a long vowel in these environments, and educated middle-class northerners (modified RP speakers) may also use the long vowel in some or all of them. However, Wells (1982: 354) sums up the sociolinguistic salience of this vowel for northerners very accurately when he writes: 'Retention of a short vowel in BATH words extends much further up the social scale than does the retention of unsplit /ʊ/. . . . There are many educated northerners who would not be caught dead doing something so vulgar as to pronounce STRUT words with /ʊ/, but who would feel it a denial of their identity as northerners to say BATH words with anything other than short [a].'

Wells's category of BATH words includes the lexical set in which ME (and later) /a/ has been lengthened before a following fricative. This is only one of the sources of present-day /ɑː/; the others are:

1. Lengthening before word-final and preconsonantal /r/, as in *bar*, *cart*, etc.
2. Monophthongization of ME /au/ from Old French /ã/ in *aunt*, *command*, etc.; at an earlier stage, this monophthongization varied between /ɑː/ and /ɔː/, and present-day RP has reflexes of both, but, with the exception of *aunt*, words with orthographic ⟨au⟩ are pronounced /ɔː/ (e.g. *jaundice*) whilst those with orthographic ⟨a⟩ are pronounced /ɑː/. Doublets such as *stanch* /stɑːnʃ/ vs. *staunch* /stɔːnʃ/ occur in PDE. In the eighteenth century, the /ɑː/ pronunciation of orthographic ⟨au⟩ was more widespread, occurring in *jaundice*, etc.;
3. Monophthongisation of earlier /au/ associated with loss of /l/ in words such as *palm*, *half*, etc.
4. Attempts to reproduce foreign values in relatively recent loanwords—e.g. *banana*, *pyjamas*, *sonata*.

In all cases except 4, the long vowel is an innovation of the seventeenth and eighteenth centuries: a long /ɑː/ distinct from ME /aː/ could not have

conservative dictionary is not always the oldest, and, in any case, the dates of birth of the authors (Sheridan 1719, Walker 1732, Spence 1750, Burn not known) would give us a different order again. Spence has to be listed first, because his lexicon forms the basis for comparison: thereafter, the order is geographical, moving from the Londoner Walker, through the London-based Irishman, Sheridan, to the Glasgow-based Scot, Burn.

developed before the seventeenth century, for it is only then that, for the most conservative speakers of English, ME /aː/ was raised to /eː/. Had ME /a/ been lengthened before this date, then it would have been caught up in this raising, so that the present-day pronunciation would be /eɪ/ as in *mate*. Indeed, there is evidence that, for some speakers at least, sporadic early lengthenings of ME /a/ did lead to identification with ME /aː/ and subsequent raising: according to Dobson (1957), Bullokar, writing between 1580 and 1586, shows a long vowel identical with ME /aː/ before ⟨rn⟩ and ⟨rl⟩, as in *barn*, *warn*, *yarn*, and *carl*, and Wright (1905) shows dialectal pronunciations such as /meɪstə/ and /feɪðə/ for *master* and *father*. The reflexes in present-day RP must have their origins in the later lengthenings, but, as we shall see, the history of these sound changes is complicated and even today there are lexical exceptions in most cases: before fricatives, RP has /ɑː/ in *pass*, but /æ/ in *gas* before /n/ it has /ɑː/ in *command* but /æ/ in *expand*, and so on. Only the set with orthographic (but not intervocalic) ⟨r⟩ following the ⟨a⟩ has the lengthened vowel in all cases except those in which it is unstressed and reduced to schwa (e.g. *anarchy*) but an examination of the evidence from the seventeenth and eighteenth centuries will show that even this lengthening has not always been categorical.

The first writers to give evidence of a long vowel distinct from ME /aː/ are Daines (1640), Coles (1674), and Cooper (1685, 1687). (Dates refer to the year(s) in which the relevant works were written). Daines shows the new long vowel before ⟨r⟩ followed by another consonant in the words *barn*, *carp*, *sharp*, *smart*, *art*, and *marsh*. Coles writes that the ⟨a⟩ of *arm*, etc., is like that of *father*, and has a sound midway between *all* and *ale* (the other two 'long' realizations of ⟨a⟩). Cooper, as well as saying that ⟨a⟩ always has the value of a lengthened version of short /a/, i.e [aː] or [æː], when it occurs before preconsonantal /r/, except when the following consonant is /ʃ/, is the first to show evidence of the new long vowel occurring before voiceless fricatives, specifically stating that *past* (= *pass* + *ed*) has a long vowel but *pass* (as in *pass by*) a short one. Cooper also shows the long vowel in *path*, but does not suggest that this is generalized to other words in which ⟨a⟩ is followed by /θ/. Evidence for a lengthened vowel before final /r/ is much more scarce: Cocker (1696) has it only in *war*, whilst Dobson (1957: 519) cites foreign observers as recording a long vowel in *far* in 1672 and 1678.

By the beginning of the eighteenth century, in what was regarded as polite usage as recorded by the orthoepists and phoneticians of the day, a long vowel from ME /a/ would occur in the following environments:

- /-rC[8] (not /-r#)
- /-sC (not /-s#)

[8] Here / means 'in the environment of, - marks the position of the sound concerned, and C stands for 'any consonant'. Thus /-rC means 'before /r/ followed by any other consonant'. The hache symbol represents a morpheme boundary.

- /-θ
- before /ð/ in some words where other factors favourable to lengthening exist—namely, *father, rather, lather, paths*;
- (varying with /ɔː/) /-nC; /-lf; /-lm; /-lv.

(In the last three, lengthening may depend on loss of /l/, in which case the phonetic environments would be a following nasal or a following fricative. However, as we shall see, some eighteenth-century writers show a long vowel with the /l/ still realized.)

Between 1700 and the present day, there would appear to have been an extension of the environments in which the long vowel from ME /a/ occurred, to include /-r#, /-s#, /-f#, and /-fC. Wells (1982) deals with the present-day reflexes of these sound changes in two groups: the BATH set, including reflexes of ME /a/ before fricatives, ⟨l⟩ plus consonant, and /n/ plus consonant; and the START set, involving reflexes of ME /a/ (and /ɛ/ in e.g. *heart*) before ⟨r⟩.[9] I deal with these two sets separately here because, as indicated in the quote from Wells above, except for the *half* subset, BATH words rarely have /ɑː/ in northern accents of present-day English, whereas START words do have a long vowel (nearer to [aː]).

5.2.2. *Lengthening in* BATH *words*

The diffusion of this sound change, or set of changes through the eighteenth and nineteenth centuries, has been by no means straightforward. As we shall see, orthoepists such as Walker, writing in the late eighteenth and early nineteenth centuries, suggest that the sound change had been reversed in some contexts, notably before fricatives, and RP still has variation between words in which ME /a/ occurs in similar environments, such as *pass* /pɑːs/ versus *mass* /mæs/[10] and variable realizations of individual words such as *alabaster, bastard, paragraph, plastic*. As mentioned above, the lexical set with ME /a/ before /n/ is split today between /ɔː/ and /ɑː/, but within RP, with the exception of *aunt*, which always has /ɑː/ in RP, and *launch* and *staunch*, which usually have /ɔː/ but for some (conservative?) speakers can have /ɑː/, words with orthographic ⟨au⟩ are now pronounced /ɔː/. There is, however, some variability between /æ/ and /ɑː/ in words with orthographic ⟨a⟩ in this environment, with RP speakers having /æ/ in *cant, rant, finance, romance, expand, random*, but /ɑː/ in *can't, plant, dance, demand*.

Ekwall (1975, 1st edn. 1914) notes the variation between /æ/ and /ɑː/ in the RP of his own day, and goes on to write: 'this variation is an old one. 18th century orthoepists (such as Perry 1776, Scott 1788, Walker 1791) frequently

---

[9] I use angled brackets here to indicate that the sound concerned is in present-day English sometimes only present orthographically.

[10] *Mass* in the religious sense can be pronounced /mæs/ or /mɑːs/ in RP.

give [æ] in words of this kind. This [æ] may be to [aː] as Pres. E. [ɔ] is to [ɔː] in words like *cross*, *lost*. [æ] may in part be explained as a reaction against the new pronunciation' (1975: 26). Walker suggests just such a reaction when he states (1791: 10) that, although the long vowel referred to by him as 'Italian *a*' was previously heard in words such as *glass*, *fast*, 'this pronunciation of *a* seems to have been for some years advancing to the short sound of this letter, as heard in *hand*, *land*, *grand*, &c. and pronouncing the *a* in *after*, *answer*, *basket*, *plant*, *mast*, &c. as long as in *half*, *calf*, &c. borders very closely on vulgarity'. Walker's evidence for the 'previous' pronunciation could well have come from Nares, whose 'method' he so admired and imitated. In his *Elements of Orthoepy*, Nares (1784: 3–4) describes an 'irregular' pronunciation of the letter ⟨a⟩ which he calls 'open A': '*A* frequently has a sound which by many writers has been called its *open* sound. It is the sound proper to that vowel in Italian, and frequently given to it in French, as in the termination -*age*, and in many other instances. In the old orthography of our language, it was often represented by *au*; as in *daunce*, *graunt*, &c'. Holmberg (1956: 41) suggests that, 'if we accept Nares' comparison with French -<u>age</u> as correct we should transcribe the vowel [aː]'. Walker's description of 'Italian *a*' is very similar to that of Nares's 'open A'. Walker describes it as one of the 'three long sounds of the letter *a*' distinguished from each other by degrees of openness: the sound of ⟨a⟩ in *father* is more open than the 'slender' sound in *lane* but less open than the 'broad German' sound in *hall*, suggesting probably [aː] rather than the more open and retracted [ɑː] of present-day RP.

Nares goes on to give what he considers to be an exhaustive list of the words in which this 'open A' occurs, amounting to 140 in all (see Appendix 2*a*), and to comment:

A slight review of the above list will shew that this effect is chiefly produced by combinations of particular letters. The consonants *f*, *l*, *n*, and *s*, appear to be principally concerned in it: and the words might, for the most part, have been arranged from such considerations; thus, words in -*sk*, *ask*, *bask*, *cask*, *flask*, *mask*; words in -*ss*, *ass*, *brass*, *class*, *glass*, &c. &c. But the whole number of words is so inconsiderable, that classification seemed unnecessary.   (Nares 1784: 6–7)

Nares describes here almost exactly the set of environments involved in Wells's BATH set, so it would appear that Walker's reaction against the long 'Italian *a*' in words such as this is reversed in present-day RP. Nares's 'open A', probably [aː], falls out of favour in the later eighteenth and early nineteenth centuries, but is found again in a more open and retracted form [ɑː] in the RP of the twentieth century. Since there is such a close match between the words cited by Nares as having 'open A' and those with RP in PDE, we are probably dealing here not with a straightforward progression of the lengthening of ME /a/ to more environments and/or lexical items (indeed, some of the words cited by Nares as having 'open A', such as *alas, ant, blaspheme, transit*, do not have the long vowel in RP), but with a much more sociolinguistically-motivated set of changes involving words of this set.

The comments of eighteenth- and nineteenth-century writers on the pronunciation of BATH words certainly indicate an awareness of their salience. On the one hand, we have Walker condemning the use of 'Italian *a*' in words such as *basket, plant*, etc., and suggesting that the short vowel of *hand* is more acceptable, whilst, on the other hand, as we saw in §2.3, Lichtenberg noted during his stays in England between 1770 and 1775, the tendency of young girls to pronounce *nasty* with an exaggeratedly high vowel to avoid the vulgarity of [ɑː]. Mugglestone (1995: 90–7) shows that the 'Italian ⟨a⟩', the long vowel described by Walker as correct in *father* but vulgar in *basket*, &c., was widely condemned as a vulgarism right through the nineteenth century. This lengthening was most probably a 'change from below', starting without stigma as reported by the seventeenth-century orthoepists, and possibly at that time a lengthened, but not retracted [æː].

If we compare the pronunciation of Nares's 140 words with 'open' or 'Italian A' in other dictionaries of the eighteenth century, we find considerable variation. Appendix 2*a* shows that Spence has {ʌ} in only 18 of these words, Walker has his 'Italian *a*' in only 30 of these words, Johnston has his 'long acute a'[11] in 37, but Burn comes very close to both Nares and present-day RP with his equivalent long vowel in no less than 99 of the words in Nares's list, with another two (*contrast* and *gallant*) given as either long or short by Burn. Johnston's very conservative use of 'long acute a' may be explained by the fact that, written as it was in 1764, his is the earliest of the dictionaries compared here. On the other hand, if we look at the distribution of 'long' and 'short' variants in terms of phonetic environments rather than total numbers of words, Johnston seems mainly to avoid the lengthening after fricatives, with only *father, master*, and *shaft* having 'long acute a' in this context. Johnston does not mention any fricative consonant except /ð/ ('soft th') in his list of the very restricted (orthographic) environments in which 'long acute a' could occur. Walker's sparse use of 'Italian *a*' in many of the contexts represented by Nares's 140 words can, of course, be explained by his belief that such pronunciations were, by 1791, to be considered 'vulgar'. Before fricatives, Walker has 'Italian *a*' in only *bath, father, lath, master*, and before /n/ only in the context of /nd/, as in *chandler, command, countermand, demand, remand, reprimand, salamander*, and in the isolated instances *courant, prance*, and (alternating with the spelling *jaunty*

---

[11] Johnston describes the 'long acute' vowels as each having 'the long sound of its short vowel'. He goes on to say 'I find this long acute a seldom occurs but before l, m, n, r, followed by some other consonant; and before soft th, u and w; and when accented in the end of words'. (1764: 26).

pronounced /dʒɔːnti/) *janty*. So far we have Johnston (1764) and Walker (1791) more or less agreeing that the long 'acute' or 'Italian' a should be used sparingly before fricatives, though Johnston is more liberal with its use before nasals. In between these dates we have Nares (1784), and Burn (1786) both giving a much more liberal distribution, closer to present-day RP. What of Spence's *Grand Repository* (1775)? Spence certainly has four distinct '*a* sounds', as we saw in Chapter 4, and the sound represented by {Λ} is phonemically distinct from that represented by {ʌ}, for there is at least one minimal pair: *pam* {PʌM} (the knave of clubs) contrasting with *palm* {PΛM}. However, Spence has very few instances of {Λ} other than before /r/: out of the list of 140 words provided by Nares, only the following have this vowel in the *Grand Repository*: *ah, aha, alms, amen, blanch, branch, calf, calm, father, ha, half, mamma, master, palm, papa, psalm, salve, staff*. Of these, only *father, master*, and *staff* have a following fricative, and it is worth noting that the first two of these words have the 'long' vowel in all the dictionaries compared here. Even today, Tynesiders who, like most northerners, do not use the long vowel except before /r/, in the *half* subset, and in loanwords such as *pyjamas*, do have /ɑː/ in *master* (see Beal 1985 for an explanation of Tyneside /ɑː/ in *master* and *plaster*). *Father* was so universally established as a word in which this vowel occurred that most lexicographers and phoneticians, like Spence, used it as their example of this long 'a' sound when enumerating the distinctive sounds of English. The concensus of all the dictionaries studied here on the use of the 'long' vowel in *master* and *father* might indicate that the vowel was lengthened at such an early stage in these words as to have been lexicalized before the stigma of 'vulgarity' set in. Spence's isolated use of {Λ} in *staff* could perhaps be explained by analogy with its plural *staves*, which has a long vowel in Johnston and is also given a long 'a' sound by the Scottish orthoepist Elphinston. As a child of Scottish parents living in Newcastle, and attending the congregation of the Scottish preacher James Murray, Spence may well have been aware of this Scottish pronunciation of *staves*.

Before preconsonantal /n/, Spence uses {Λ} in *blanch* and *branch*, where Nares, Johnston and Burn agree in using the long vowel, but Walker has a short vowel. Spence's use of the long vowel in *blanch* could perhaps be explained as a reflex of earlier /au/ from French /ā/, but, as *branch* is the only other word with the same phonetic environment after the ⟨a⟩, since *lanch* is not included in the *Grand Repository*, we could equally be dealing with very fine phonetic conditioning here. This is supported by the fact that *Stanch* also has {Λ} in the *Grand Repository*: in Nares, this word is spelt *staunch* but included in a list of 22 words in which 'open A' is spelt with ⟨au⟩.

Spence, like the other four eighteenth-century sources here, also uses the long vowel whenever ⟨a⟩ is word final and stressed. Other eighteenth-century sources show this, although it was never mentioned in the seventeenth century: possibly the words involved were all too colloquial to be worth mentioning: *papa, mama, ah*, etc. In so far as these words are used in present-day English, they, like the *half* subset, have /ɑː/ even in northern English accents and so it is not surprising to see such agreement amongst our eighteenth-century sources.

In words of Wells's BATH set, it would appear that the pronunciation described in Spence's *Grand Repository* is barely affected by the 'vulgar' lengthening which goes in and out of fashion in the London English of the later eighteenth and the nineteenth century. This is not because Spence fails to recognize the 'new' long sound, for he has a separate symbol for it and uses it where northern English accents have it today: in word final position, in isolated words like *father* and *master*, and in the *half* subset. It is more likely that the pronunciation of the *Grand Repository*, like that of Johnston (1764), is conservative in this respect. Nares (1784) and Burn (1786) would appear to be recording a lengthened sound which they at least do not yet perceive as 'vulgar', whilst Walker (1791) shows the reaction setting in against the lengthened sound in BATH words.

5.2.3. *Lengthening in* START *words*

We have found in our examination of the lengthening of ME /a/ in BATH words that, although seventeenth-century sources such as Cooper and Daines provide evidence of a phonetically conditioned sound change, far from progressing straightforwardly in the eighteenth century, the lengthening before nasals and fricatives is complicated by sociolinguistic factors, for the lengthened sound is, at least by 1791, stigmatized as 'vulgar'. Where START words are concerned, there does seem to be a pattern of progress through the eighteenth century in that the change is attested before /r/ and another consonant (/-rC) much earlier than before word final /r/ (/-r#). Mather Flint, who produced editions of a guide to English pronunciation for French speakers in 1740 and 1754, describes the pronunciation of ⟨a⟩ when followed by final /r/ as short, but he also describes the vowel as short when followed by /rl/ or /r/ + a voiceless consonant, except for the words *art, cart, dart, tart, part*, in which it is 'un peu long' (quoted in Kökeritz 1944: 84). When it comes before /r/ followed by /b/, /d/, /m/, /n/, /nd/, or /t/, however, the vowel is described as long. What we seem to have here, then, is an account of a sound change subjected to very fine conditioning: not only is the vowel lengthened in the environment (/-rC) but not (/-r#), but lengthening in the former environment also seems to depend on the nature of the consonant following /r/. Moreover, there is a set of lexical exceptions in which the vowel is slightly lengthened. The only contradiction between Flint's evidence and that of the seventeenth-century orthoepists seems to be that Daines has a long vowel in some words with a voiceless consonant following the /r/, whilst Flint has a short vowel in this environment. What all these orthoepists agree on is that there is no lengthening of /a/ in the environment (/-r#).

As well as giving us this valuable information concerning the distribution of 'long' and 'short' reflexes of /a/, Flint provides a possible explanation in his description of the pronunciation of /r/ in these environments. The lengthening of /a/ before orthographic ⟨r⟩ is often explained as 'compensatory lengthening' following loss of rhoticity. Since there is evidence of lengthening in this environment from 1640 and the first clear observations of loss of rhoticity comes from the eighteenth century (Jespersen (1909–49: 360) gives Arnold, writing in 1718, as the first to speak of a 'mute r' in *mart*, *borough*, *parlour*, *scarce*), this explanation seems less than adequate. There is, however, evidence from the seventeenth century that /r/ had different allophones, and that some of these were perceived as 'weaker' or less consonantal than others. Jespersen (1909–49: 318) cites Ben Jonson (1640)[12] as being the first to recognize this, stating that /r/ was 'sounded firme in the beginning of the words, and more liquid in the middle and ends'. Flint is perhaps the first to associate this 'weakening' of /r/ in certain positions with the lengthening of /a/: under the heading A, Flint writes: '*A* suivi de *r* est un peu long sans être ouvert & l'*r* est prononcé moins rudement qu'en françois' (quoted in Kökeritz 1944: 11). Flint goes on to cite as examples: *hard*, *harm*, *barn*, *quart*, *war*, *warm*. For each of these words except *war*, Flint transcribes the /r/ in italics, which, as he explains in the preface, is a signal that a consonant is 'adouci'. Since the word final ⟨r⟩ of *war* is not italicized, it is presumably not 'adouci', so the lengthened /a/ may in this case not be associated with 'weakening' of /r/. Elsewhere Flint writes, under the heading R: 'ressouvenez vous que dans plusieurs mots l'*r* devant une consonne est fort adouci, presque muet & rend un peu longue la voyelle qui le précède. *barb*, *guard*, *arm*, *yarn*' (in Kökeritz 1944: 41). Later, he contrasts the Irish and English pronunciations of /r/: 'Les Irlandois . . . prononcent l'*r*, lettre presque muette en Anglois, extremement rude' (in Kökeritz 1944: 75). Flint's words are very like those of Walker (1791), who is cited by Jespersen (1909–49: 360) as being 'the oldest Englishman to admit the muteness'. Jespersen, however, quotes selectively from Walker: if we look at his remarks on /r/ in full, it becomes clear that Walker 'admits . . . the muteness' rather reluctantly. Walker starts the section of his preface devoted to the letter ⟨r⟩ by stating 'this letter is never silent' (1791: 50), but goes on to write at length about its different values:

As this letter is but a jar of the tongue, sometimes against the roof of the mouth and sometimes at the orifice of the throat, it is the most imperfect of all the consonants . . . There is a difference in the sound of this letter, never noticed by any of our writers on

[12] 1640 is the date of publication of Jonson's *Grammar*, but it must have been written earlier, as he died in 1639.

the subject, which is, in my opinion, of no small importance; and that is the rough and the smooth *r*. The rough *r* is formed by jarring the tip of the tongue against the roof of the mouth near the fore teeth: the smooth *r* is a vibration of the lower part of the tongue, near the root, against the inward region of the palate, near the entrance of the throat. This latter *r* is that which marks the pronunciation of England, and the former that of Ireland. **In England, and particularly in London, the *r* in *lard*, *bard*, *card*, *regard*, is pronounced so much in the throat, as to be little more than the middle or Italian *a* lengthened into *baa*, *baad*, *caad*, *regaad*** while in Ireland, the *r* in these words is pronounced with so strong a jar of the tongue against the fore part of the palate, and accompanied with such an aspiration or strong breathing at the beginning of the letter, as to produce that harshness we call the Irish accent. But if this letter is too forcibly pronounced in Ireland, it is often too feebly pronounced in England, and particularly **in London**, where **it is sometimes entirely sunk**; it may, perhaps, be worthy observation that, provided we avoid too forcible a pronunciation of the *r*, when it ends a word or is followed by a consonant in the same syllable, we may give as much force as we please to this letter at the beginning of a word, without producing any harshness to the ear. Thus *Rome*, *river*, *rage*, may have the *r* as forcible as in Ireland, but *bar*, *bard*, *card*, *hard* &c. must have it nearly as soft as in London.   (extracts quoted in Jespersen in bold)

When we look at Walker's remarks in full, the similarity with Flint's account is even more striking: the 'weaker' /r/ is found in preconsonantal position and the 'stronger' or 'harsher' trill in prevocalic position. Even the contrast between English and Irish pronunciation is the same. Where they differ is in Walker's extension of the 'weak' or 'soft' /r/ to word final position: by including *baa* presumably for *bar* in his second list, Walker appears to be saying not only that /r/ has by 1791 been weakened in word final position as well as in the preconsonantal position attested by Flint, but also that the lengthening of /a/ attested by Flint before /r/ followed by a voiced consonant has also been extended to this position. Elsewhere, Walker (1791: 10) states quite categorically that 'the long sound of middle or Italian *a* is always found before *r* in monosyllables, as *car*, *far*, *mar* etc'. Jespersen is not quite correct in naming Walker as the first English writer to give evidence of the loss of word final and preconsonantal /r/: as we saw in §2.4, that honour goes to Abraham Tucker. In any case, the extracts quoted by Jespersen refer only to the most advanced dialect of Walker's day, colloquial London English. Walker is not *recommending* the pronunciation with /r/ 'entirely sunk', for at the beginning of this extract he writes that /r/ is 'never silent' and his actual transcriptions of words all indicate that /r/ is pronounced in all positions. Walker was an accurate observer, but his *Critical Pronouncing Dictionary* was intended to be normative, to provide a detailed account of 'correct' pronunciation. That the vocalization of /r/ was stigmatized at the time can be seen from remarks made in the early nineteenth century, when it had become more established, especially in London speech. Jespersen (1909–49: 360), for instance, quotes the Birmingham schoolmaster Thomas Wright Hill (1821) as saying that /r/ 'ought more carefully to be preserved for posterity, than can be hoped if the provincialists of the Metropolis and their tasteless imitators are to be tolerated in such rhymes as *fawn* and *morn*, *straw* and *for*, *grass* and *farce*, etc. etc. to the end of the reader's patience'. (We shall look at the question of weakening and loss of preconsonantal and word final /r/ in more detail in §5.8.)

What this seems to indicate is that the lengthening of /a/ before pre-consonantal, and, later, before word final /r/ is associated with weakening rather than total loss of the following /r/: the 'correct' pronunciation recommended by Walker has a lengthened /a/ followed by what he describes as a 'soft' /r/ (cf. Flint's 'adouci'). The association of the lengthened /a/ with a 'weakened' /r/ is also evidenced by the fact that Thomas Sheridan, a famous elocutionist and often regarded as a more faithful observer than Walker (see e.g. Sheldon 1947), failed to recognize this 'fourth sound of the letter ⟨a⟩' in his *General Dictionary of the English Language* (1780), for Sheridan was an Irishman, and would therefore use the 'harsh' or 'rude' /r/ described by Walker and Flint.

Putting aside, for the moment, the question of the causation of this lengthening of /a/ before /r/, let us examine the progress of the sound change through the eighteenth century. In the early to mid-century, according to Flint, the lengthened vowel is found before /r/ followed by a voiced consonant, not before word final /r/, and not before /r/ followed by a voiceless consonant, although there are lexical exceptions to this last condition. By the end of the century, according to Walker, a long vowel is *categorical* in all these environments. We know this, not only because Walker states it as a categorical rule in his preface, but also because he provides us in the *Critical Pronouncing Dictionary* with such a wealth of evidence that lexical exceptions would be apparent if there were any. We might expect sources written between the dates of Flint (1740) and Walker (1791) to show evidence of the gradual diffusion of lengthening in this environment. The *Grand Repository* (1775) comes between those dates, as do the dictionaries of Johnston (1764) and Burn (1786).

Appendix 2*b* shows all the words in the *Grand Repository* in which ME /a/ occurs before word-final /r/, with an indication of the pronunciation of the vowel in these words ('long' or 'short') in the four dictionaries compared here. In all these dictionaries except Walker's, instances of the long vowel before word final /r/ are found only sporadically: Spence has no instances of {Λ} before final /r/, whilst Johnston has his 'long acute a' only in *far* (the word in which a long vowel was attested by two foreign grammarians in the seventeenth century), and Burn has his long a sound in *jar*, *mar*, *tar*. For Walker, of course, the long vowel is categorical in this environment, and his dictionary entries bear this out. We are dealing here with a small number of words, but already there seems to be a progression which is not entirely chronological between these sources: Spence with the short vowel categorical in this environment is the most conservative; Johnston comes next with one instance of the lengthened vowel; then Burn with three, and, finally, Walker is the most advanced with the lengthened vowel already categorical. The lengthening before word final /r/ seems to be an innovation of the later eighteenth century and even then to be most advanced in the London pronunciation recommended by Walker.

Before preconsonantal /r/ the lengthening was not categorical for Flint: he described it as occurring 'dans plusieurs mots' (quoted in Kökeritz 1944: 41) more regularly when the following consonant was voiced. Johnston writes that his 'long acute ⟨a⟩' occurs 'generally before r and some other consonant', but an examination of his dictionary entries reveals that this rule is not yet categorical in the dialect described by Johnston. Appendices 2*c* and 2*d* provide lists of all the words in which either the long (2*c*) or the short (2*d*) vowel occurs in Spence's *Grand Repository*, with an indication of the vowel (short versus long) used by Johnston and Burn for the same word. The words were also checked in Walker's *Critical Pronouncing Dictionary*, to establish whether there were any exceptions to Walker's rule on lengthening before /r/ and, in fact, Walker did have a short vowel in two of them: *antarctic* and *rampart*. The latter may be short because it is unstressed: although stress usually makes no difference to the vowel used by Walker, as we shall see below it is significant for the distribution of long and short variants for the earlier writers. *Antarctic* is a mystery, especially since Walker records the long vowel in *arctic* and he is usually such a stickler for 'analogy' that exceptions to his rules are explained with lengthy notes. Perhaps this minor inconsistency on Walker's part just goes to show that, in late eighteenth-century usage, the lengthening was not quite as categorical as Walker's rule would lead us to believe. Certainly, the figures for Spence, Johnston, and Burn suggest that it was by no means categorical before 1791: of the 412 words from Spence's *Grand Repository* in Appendices 2*c* and 2*d*, 283 are recorded in Johnston and 374 in Burn. Spence has a short vowel in 231 of these words (56.31 per cent); Johnston in 101 (35.68 per cent), and Burn in 51 (13. 63 per cent). What is immediately apparent is that the writers are in the same order as they were for the distribution of long versus short variants before word final /r/, with Spence as the most conservative, then Johnston, then Burn, and then Walker as the most advanced. This suggests that the sound change concerned was still in progress in the second half of the eighteenth century. By looking more closely at the entries in these pronouncing dictionaries, we may be able to see how the change was being diffused. The phonological constraints suggested in Flint's account seem no longer to be in operation. For instance, both Spence and Burn have a long vowel in *barbarous* but a short one in *barbecue*, where the immediate environment is identical. For Johnston and, to a lesser extent, Spence, there does seem to be a correlation between vowel length and stress in these words: for Johnston, 75.5 per cent of the words in Appendices 2c(i) and 2d(i), in which the syllable with ⟨ar⟩ is stressed have a long vowel and 94.33 per cent of the words in Appendices 2c(ii) and 2d(ii), in which the ⟨ar⟩ is unstressed, have a short vowel, whilst for Spence the correlation between unstressed syllables and the short variant is strong (79.06 per cent), but, where the ⟨ar⟩ occurs in stressed syllables, the distribution of long and short variants is more or less 50/50. In other words, one could predict that, for both Spence and Johnston, preconsonantal ⟨ar⟩ in unstressed syllables is likely to be realized with a short vowel, and for Johnston that it is likely to be realized with a long vowel in stressed syllables.

In fact, the rule is more or less categorical for Johnston, for almost all of his short realizations in stressed syllables can be explained by their occurrence in polysyllabic words (of the 50 words in Appendices 2c(i) and 2d(i) for which Johnston has a short vowel in a stressed syllable, 31 have three or more syllables—e.g. *harlequin*, *carpentry*, *protomartyr*). The fact that the earlier sources mention only the lengthening in monosyllables may have no significance: it could simply be the case that monosyllables spring to mind more readily. However, English does have a tendency to shorten vowels in polysyllabic words (Middle English trisyllabic shortening in *holiday*, etc., for instance) and the same condition here could have been a constraint on lengthening. In the dialect described by Johnston, however, the constraint must already be weakening, as he has several examples of polysyllabic words with the lengthened vowel—for example, *carpenter* has a long vowel whereas, as we have seen above, *carpentry* has a short one. In a further three instances (*parboil*, *starboard*, *charcoal*), the vowel occurs in the first half of a compound and so the /r/ is followed by a word boundary, an environment in which, as we have seen above, the ⟨a⟩ is almost always realized as short for Johnston anyway. This leaves only 14 instances for Johnston of a short stressed realization of ⟨a⟩ before preconsonantal /r/ for which there is no obvious explanation. For Burn, the long vowel is much nearer to being categorical in this environment, but, even so, such short instances as he has seem to occur under the same conditions as for Johnston: out of 51 words with a short vowel, 29 have the ⟨a⟩ in an unstressed syllable and, of the other 22, 11 are polysyllabic and 4 have the ⟨a⟩ in the first half of a compound (Johnston's list plus *farfetched*, a word not in Johnston's dictionary).

What, then, does this close examination of the distribution of long and short variants of ME (and later) /a/ in these pronouncing dictionaries tell us about the progress of lengthening of /a/ in the second half of the eighteenth century? First, the phonological constraints suggested by Flint seem no longer to be operating, for in all three sources the long vowel is found whether the consonant after /r/ is voiced or voiceless. Secondly, stress seems to act as a constraint at the beginning of the period under consideration, but to weaken as the century progresses: the long variant is found in stressed syllables earlier and more frequently than in unstressed syllables (or those with secondary stress), but towards the end of the century it is found more frequently until, in Walker's account, stress is no longer a constraint at all. Thirdly, it is found in monosyllabic and disyllabic words earlier than in polysyllabic words, although once again Walker's evidence shows no such constraint. Fourthly, in all accounts except Walker's there is some element of distribution that is purely lexical: for instance, both Spence and Burn have the long vowel in *barbarism*, *barbarous*, but the short variant in *barbecue*. Sometimes the differences seem arbitrary—for example, Spence has *archbishopric* with a short vowel in the first syllable, but *archdeaconship* with a long one. Further evidence that the rule is lexical at this stage can be found in the treatment of compounds: if the lengthening was applied after compounding, then words like *starboard* would be more likely to have a long vowel, for the ⟨a⟩ occurs before /rb/, but if it is applied at the lexical level to the root words, then, in the dialects described by Spence, Johnston, and Burn, *star* would not be subject to lengthening. In fact, the progress of this sound change follows quite closely the pattern set out in Harris (1989: 37): 'A typical progression is for sound changes to begin life as modifications to low-level output rules and then over time to penetrate deeper and deeper into the linguistic system. From the perspective of Lexical Phonology, this process can be viewed as the progressive infiltration of lexical structure by phonological rules.' The seventeenth-century evidence suggests that the lengthening rule is post-lexical, for the long vowel occurs in *bars* but not *bar*—that is, the lengthening applies at a stage after the plural morpheme is attached. At this point, the rule is also subject to phonetic constraints, appearing only when the following /r/ is itself followed by certain consonants. In the early eighteenth century, the rule seems to have lost its phonetic constraints, but to be applied after stress and syllabification, for it is subject to constraints in these areas. These constraints are, however, being lost by the last quarter of the century, the rule seems to be lexical if we take account of the behaviour of the reflexes of /a/ in compounds, and lexical diffusion is taking place. By the time Walker's evidence comes into play, the rule has been fully lexicalized and has spread so far by lexical diffusion that it is categorical: moreover, it has been extended to word final /r/. This last stage may have more to do with the more advanced nature of /r/ vocalization in Walker's dialect than with lexical diffusion *per se*: if, as seems to be the case, the trigger for this lengthening was vocalization/loss of /r/, then the northern/Scots 'modified standards' described by Spence and Burn and the earlier 'standard' of Johnston would have neither the vocalization nor the subsequent lengthening in this position. If the varieties described by these three had no vocalization or even weakening of /r/ even in preconsonantal position, why do they show the lengthening of /a/ at all? Here we must go back to our discussion of the status of /r/ vocalization: provincial writers viewed this vocalization in London speech as vulgar and so would have no reason to recommend it in their pronouncing dictionaries. On the other hand, a lengthened /a/ might have been used by those (clergymen, lawyers, etc.) who provided a model of 'good' speech in provincial cities such as Newcastle and Edinburgh. Harris (1989: 44–5) points out that, with regard to a similar sound change, *æ*-Tensing in Belfast, 'non-natives have difficulty in acquiring the tensing pattern' and refers to Payne (1980), writing on *æ*-Tensing in Philadelphia, who 'demonstrates how children from out-of-state families have less than complete success in learning the Philadelphia pattern. This is explainable if we assume that acquisition in this case involves learning a categorical contrast on a word-by-word basis rather than a general rule of allophony.' The sound change under consideration here may have started in southern varieties as a rule of allophony: [a] or possibly [æ] was, in the varieties described by Daines, Cooper, etc., tensed before the 'weakened' preconsonantal /r/. By Walker's time, the contrast has, effectively, been phonemicized: once the /r/ is fully vocalized, as it is in the most advanced variety described by Walker, we have pairs like /pæt/ versus /pɑːt/ (Walker's long 'Italian *a*' could have been either [aː] or backed to [ɑː] as in present-day RP). In between, we have, in the works of Spence, Johnston, and Burn, a series of dialects which, like those of Payne's 'out-of-state families', show the results of an attempt to acquire the lengthening without the phonetic trigger that caused it in southern dialects. This leads to the lexical distribution that we see in Appendices 2*c* and 2*d*: the distribution is not totally random, for we can see a consistency between the three accounts, but there is a strong lexical element. Certainly, there must have been a great deal of variation in the pronunciation of these words in the eighteenth century, for Sheridan does not even recognize a separate lengthened sound for orthographic ⟨a⟩ and Nares gives no evidence of 'open A' before /r/.

5.3. DEVELOPMENT OF ME AND LATER /a/ BEFORE ⟨l⟩ + CONSONANT AND AFTER /w/

5.3.1. *Introduction*

Apart from the lengthening already discussed in §5.2, ME /a/ has been subjected to two other environmentally conditioned changes in the NE period. These are:

1. diphthongization to /aʊ/ and subsequent monophthongization to either /ɔː/ or /ɑː/ before ⟨ll⟩ or ⟨l⟩ followed by another consonant, as in *tall*, *balm*.

2. rounding and lengthening to /ɔː/ after /w/ or /ʍ/, as in *water*, *quart*, *swarthy*, *wharf*, in some cases, such as *wash*, *squad*, *what*, either rounding occurs without lengthening, or the long rounded vowel is subsequently shortened, in either case giving /ɒ/ in PDE.

According to Dobson (1957), both these changes began before the eighteenth century, but, as we shall see, eighteenth-century sources vary with regard to the pronunciations recommended for words in these lexical sets and, indeed, there is still some variation within RP: the *CSED* gives alternative pronunciations for *waft* as either /wɑːft/ or /wɒft/; and *scallop* as either /ˈskɒləp/ or /ˈskæləp/.

With regard to the changes set out in 1 and 2 above, detailed examination of Spence's evidence in comparison with that of other eighteenth-century pronouncing dictionaries may provide insights into the progress of the sound changes involved in the late eighteenth century. Appendices 3*a* and *b* provide lists of all the words in the relevant lexical sets from the *Grand Repository*: 3*a*(i) and 3*b*(i) list words in which Spence has {ʎ} (= /ɔː/); 3*a*(ii) and 3*b*(ii) those for which Spence has {ʌ} (= /æ/), and 3*a*(iii) those for which Spence has {Λ} (= /ɑː/). In each case, the appendix gives the IPA equivalent of the sound recommended for ME or later /a/ in the same entries in the pronouncing dictionaries of Walker (1791), Sheridan (1780) and Burn (1786).

5.3.2. *Reflexes of ME or later /a/ before ⟨l⟩*

Dobson (1957: 553–4) suggests that around 1400 ME /a/ was diphthongized to /au/ before a back (dark) /l/—that is, before orthographic ⟨ll⟩, or ⟨l⟩ followed by another consonant. These reflexes subsequently shared the development of ME /au/, eventually becoming either /ɔː/ or /ɑː/. The orthoepists studied by Dobson show failure of this diphthongization in certain circumstances. These are:

1. Diphthongization fails before a single ⟨l⟩ in intervocalic position and before NE ⟨ll⟩ where ME had ⟨l⟩, as in *alley*, *allegory*. The undiphthongized ME /a/ also appears where original ⟨ll⟩ has a following bilabial, as in *shallow*, *mallow*, *tallow*.
2. Before /l/ followed by a bilabial consonant there is evidence of variation in the works of sixteenth- and seventeenth-century orthoepists. In *scalp*, PDE has /æ/ but Daines and Hodges both show reflexes of ME /au/. Conversely, in *almighty*, *always*, PDE has /ɔː/ but Hart has /æ/.
3. Before /l/ followed by an /f/ which begins a new syllable, failure of diphthongization is shown in PDE, as in *Alfred*, *alpha*, *alphabet*. (The last, being first recorded in 1513, may be explained under 6, below.)

4. There is occasional failure of diphthongization before /l/ followed by a voiceless consonant. Smith has /æ/ in *salt*; Hart has /æ/ in *chalk*; and Wallis suggests that it is more correct to pronounce /æ/ in *walk, talk*.

5. 'In unstressed syllables, the pronunciation in which the diphthongization failed was common and eventually displaced that in which it occurred' (Dobson 1957: 554). This explains PDE /æ/ in *shall*, presumably developed from the weak form. However, as we shall see below, many words with initial unstressed /al/ are learned words adopted in the sixteenth century or later, and so can be explained under 6. Even words like *alchemy*, first cited in 1362, could well have been readopted in NE, as they would rarely occur in speech.

6. Dobson (1957: 554) writes that 'diphthongization naturally fails in words adopted after the process was complete'. We shall come across many examples of such words, since by the late eighteenth century many of these words had become assimilated, at least in dictionaries. One interesting item discussed by Dobson which was also subject to variation in the eighteenth century is *halberd*. This was first recorded in the late fifteenth century—that is, just about the time when diphthongization of ME /a/ was taking place. Gil shows failure of diphthongization in this word and PDE has /æ/, but the *OED* records that the pronunciation was formerly /ɔː/. Dobson suggests that the variation in this instance could be for one of two reasons: either it was adopted in ME and varies because of the following bilabial, like the cases discussed in 2, above, or it was a later adoption and 'the *au* pronunciation is a deliberate anglicisation' (1957: 554). Presumably such 'anglicization' involves some analogical process, which could well operate with regard to other late adoptions in which /a/ occurs before ⟨l⟩.

There is a special development to /ɑː/ rather than /ɔː/ in words such as *half, calm*. Dobson suggests that the two monophthongizations of /au/ < ME /a/ were quite separate, educated Standard English at first having only the development to /ɔː/. 'The combinative development to [aː] must have been characteristic of some other form of English, probably vulgar London speech (Cockney) or the Eastern dialects from which, a century or more after its development, it made its way into educated St.E. Then followed a conflict between the originally vulgar [aː] (later [ɑː]) developed combinatively, and the hitherto normal [ɒː] developed isolatively'. (1957: 790–1) As we shall see, words with ME /a/ before ⟨lm⟩ were variable in the eighteenth century, although words such as *half, calf* seem to have had /ɑː/ (or /æ/) universally by then.[13]

---

[13] John Jones's *Practical Phonography* (1701) has *au* in *calf, a* in *half*. Ekwall (1975: 24) points out that 'till about 1650 our authorities . . . give the same diphthong or vowel [au, ɔː] in *calf, balm, calm*, etc., as in *talk*', probably showing that the sound indicated by Jones is really a

From Dobson's account, then, we can see that there was, under certain circumstances, variation between /æ/ and /ɔː/, and elsewhere between /ɔː/ and /ɑː/ in the sixteenth and seventeenth centuries. Appendices 3*a*(i), (ii), and (iii) provide a comparison of Spence's distribution of the symbols {*Æ*U}, {ʌ\}, and {ʌ} respectively, where the traditional orthography has ⟨al⟩, with Walker's, Sheridan's, and Burn's recommended pronunciations of the same words. This reveals that such variation continued into the eighteenth century. The most striking thing to emerge from this comparison is that Spence uses {*Æ*U} far more than Walker, Sheridan, or Burn use their equivalent notations for the rounded vowel. This is particularly noticeable with regard to words beginning with ⟨al⟩ followed by another consonant. For twenty-five of these words, Spence has {*Æ*U}, whilst Walker, Sheridan, and Burn each have their short ⟨a⟩ symbol. Examples of these words are *alchemist, algebra, alcove*. For one word, *alb*, Spence has {*Æ*U}, whilst Walker has his notation for the sound equivalent to RP /eː/, and Sheridan and Burn have their notations for the sound equivalent to RP /æ/. In almost all of these cases, the pronunciation recorded in the *OED* and in the *CSED* is /æ/. The exceptions are words beginning with ⟨alter-⟩, for which the *OED* records variation between /æ/ and /ɒ/, whilst the *CSED* has /ɔː/. In these cases, there seems to have been a fairly recent move towards the use of a rounded vowel, probably by analogy with *alter*, which has a rounded vowel in all four of the eighteenth-century sources investigated here. The words concerned are: *altercate, alternate, alternation,* and *alternative. Alternity* is not cited in the *CSED*, but the *OED* shows variation between /æ/ and /ɒ/ for this word, and so it probably belongs with the other four. *Altimetry* and *altitude* seem so far to have escaped this move towards /ɒ/, since neither the *OED* nor the *CSED* give pronunciations with the rounded vowel: possibly the orthographic distinction (⟨alti-⟩ rather than ⟨alter-⟩) means that the forces of analogy are not so strong here. What we have here is a number of words for which Spence's recommended pronunciation is closer to that of Collins for the late twentieth century than to those of his contemporaries in the late eighteenth century. It is very difficult to resist the temptation to see this as evidence of great foresight on Spence's part, but resist it we must, for there are far more words for which Spence has {*Æ*U} but neither Walker, Sheridan, Burn, nor any account of PDE shows the rounded vowel. Spence even has, in the word *aluminous*, one instance of {*Æ*U} when the following /l/ is intervocalic,[14] an environment in which diphthongization of ME /a/ never took place.

For the most part, the words with initial ⟨al⟩ for which Spence has {*Æ*U} whilst Walker, Sheridan, Burn, and PDE have an unrounded vowel are

survival into the very early eighteenth century of an essentially seventeenth-century pronunciation.

[14] Unless, of course, we analyse the /j/ of the following /ju/ sequence as a consonant, in which case it becomes closer phonologically (but not lexically) to e.g. *always*.

learned words of relatively recent (i.e. post fifteenth-century) adoption. Examples are *alcohol, alcoholization*, first cited in 1543 and 1678 respectively; *algebra, algebraical, algebraist*, first cited in 1541, 1571, and 1673 respectively, and *algid, algific*, first cited in 1626 and 1692 respectively. Dobson suggests that words such as these should retain, not ME /a/ as such, since they did not exist in ME, but a comparable /a/ from the source language, usually Latin, because, by the time they were adopted, the late ME diphthongization was completed. In a sense, however, the process is still not complete today, for the *alter-* and *alti-* words discussed above have been subjected to rounding by a process of analogy, bypassing the stage of diphthongization. In these cases the analogy is well motivated, but the other words with initial ⟨al⟩ for which Spence has {ÆU} whilst his contemporaries and PDE have an unrounded vowel are far too diverse for such a process to be in operation. Spence was a self-taught man and probably read these learned words without hearing them pronounced: indeed, the only place in which he would have any opportunity to hear learned discourse before 1775, apart from in church, would have been the Philosophical Society and other Newcastle clubs, where his fellow-members, although of a higher social standing than Spence, were still Newcastle men and may well have been speakers of modified standard English. Spence's use of {ÆU} in these words could have been a spelling pronunciation, for the use of a rounded vowel before /l/ was sufficiently well established for him to use *wall* as his example for the {ÆU} sound. On the other hand, it could be a 'hypercorrect' form and as such it may have been in use amongst Spence's acquaintances in Newcastle. The latter suggestion is plausible because, even in present-day Tyneside English, [aː] is heard in words with ME /a/ before /l/, such as *ball* [baːl] and *walk* [waːk], and Wright (1905) gives the unrounded vowel for South Northumberland. Sylvester Douglas bears witness to the fact that the unrounded vowel in such words was also used in 'northern' dialect, when, under *alter*, he writes: 'The *a* has, in this word, and in *halt* and *halter* its long broad sound, as in *all, hall*. The Scotch give it its short open sound' (1779, quoted in C. Jones 1991: 162). Douglas makes a similar remark under *bald*: by the 'long broad sound' of *a* he must mean /ɔː/, whilst by the 'short open sound . . . as in *pallid*' (1779, quoted in C. Jones 1991:162) he presumably means /æ/. If Spence was aware that /ɔː/ was the 'correct' alternative to his native Northumbrian /ɑː/ ([aː]) in these more common words, then he may well have overcompensated by using {ÆU} for the more learned words, not knowing that more metropolitan speakers such as Walker would use the unrounded vowel in some of these.

Turning now to those words in which the ⟨al⟩ is not word-initial, we find that there is in these cases less contrast between Spence's account and those of Walker, Sheridan, and Burn, but that it is still the case that Spence uses {ÆU} where the others have the unrounded vowel more often than the reverse. Some of these discrepancies may be explained in the same way as those discussed above: the words concerned are learned and so subject to spelling pronunciation and/or hypercorrection. This is particularly noticeable where the ⟨al⟩ is followed by a vowel, which, as we have seen, is an environment in which the late ME diphthongization never took place. The words concerned are *calefaction*, *calefactory*, and *calefy*, and, since they all share the same prefix, we can assume that analogy is operating within this group: having chosen {ɅU} for one of them, Spence is highly likely to use it for them all. However, there is no support for the use of the rounded vowel in these words in any source I have examined from this or any other period, and so we must assume that the decision to use {ɅU} in the first of these represents spelling pronunciation and/or hypercorrection. Spence is similarly alone in his use of a rounded vowel in *falcated*, first cited in 1704, but in this case the motivation could have come from analogy with *falchion* and *falcon*, both of which have a rounded vowel in Spence, Walker, Sheridan, Burn, and in PDE. For the other words in which Spence's use of {ɅU} puts him at variance with Walker, Sheridan, and Burn, he is not entirely alone in his recommendation of a rounded vowel. *Salvage* and *salvation* are both learned words and both have {ɅU} in Spence, but the unrounded vowel in Walker, Sheridan, Burn, and PDE. The former, first cited in 1645, should have escaped the ME diphthongization, but not so *salvation*, which was first cited in 1225. Dobson (1957: 544) explains PDE /æ/ in this word by the fact that the vowel is unstressed, but points out that Strong shows ME /au/, possibly under secondary stress. Spence's use of {ɅU} in *salvation* could, then, be a survival of the variant shown by Strong, and *salvage* could have gained the rounded vowel by analogy with the former (*salve*, *salver*, and *salvo*, incidentally, have an unrounded vowel in Spence as well as Walker, Sheridan, and Burn). There are two words *balsamic* and *chalder/chaldron* for which Spence's use of the rounded vowel agrees with PDE as represented in the *CSED*, but not with Walker, Sheridan, and/or Burn. In the case of *balsamic*, the *CSED* gives only /ɔː/, whilst *OED* gives the rounded and unrounded vowels as alternative pronunciations, presumably of equal standing. Since *balsam* has the rounded vowel in all the sources examined here, we can assume that the move towards rounding in *balsamic* shown in Collins is motivated by analogy, as in the *alter-* words discussed above. In the case of *chalder/chaldron*, Spence's use of the rounded vowel is supported by Sheridan, but Walker and Burn have an unrounded vowel. This word appears in several orthographic forms: Spence and Burn give ⟨chalder⟩, ⟨chaldron⟩, whilst Walker and Sheridan use the forms ⟨chaldron⟩, ⟨chaudron⟩. According to the *OED*, all these forms derive from OF forms with OF /au/, which should give NE /ɔː/ in each case, even though the words were adopted after 1500. Dobson, whilst not making direct reference to Walker, does explain his usage when he suggests (1957: 792–3) that 'the Pres E pronunciation [tʃɑːdrn̩] beside [tʃɒːldrn̩] of *chaldron* . . . may be due to lengthening of eModE *ā̆* . . . *OED* records no **chadron* form, but shortening of ME *au* to *ă* may easily occur in the phonetic conditions of this word'.

There is variation between the sources used for Appendix 3*a*(i) in the pronunciation of the word *balm*, for which Spence and Burn recommend the rounded vowel, Walker the unrounded, and Sheridan both. In this environment, ME /au/ from /a/ usually develops to /ɑː/ in PDE, as indeed it does in this word, but we have already seen that variation between /ɑː/ and /ɔː/ was common in the sixteenth century in such words. The continuation of this variation through the eighteenth century is shown not only by the discrepancy between Spence and his two contemporaries here, but perhaps more strikingly in that Sheridan rationalizes the variation by giving /bɔːm/ as meaning 'ointment' and /bæm/ (=[bæːm]?) as meaning the plant. Such rationalizations are fairly common in folk linguistics, where free variation occurs: on Tyneside, for instance, people will tell you that ['plastə] is a sticking plaster, whilst ['plɑːstə] is builder's plaster or plaster of Paris. There is no evidence that anybody consistently differentiates between the two in speech, but the myth persists.

There are only two other words for which Spence has {ʌU}, whilst neither Walker nor Sheridan, nor the *CSED*, records a rounded vowel: these are *scalp* and *pall-mall*. Burn also has the unrounded vowel in both these words, but *Mall* has /ɔː/ for Spence, but not Walker or Sheridan, and is recorded with both /æ/ and /ɔː/ in both Burn and the *CSED*. *Scalp* is one of the cases covered by Dobson and discussed under 2 above, in which failure of late ME diphthongization sometimes occurs where the ⟨al⟩ is followed by a bilabial. Spence's {ʌU} in this case represents the survival of the variant with ME /au/ shown in Daines and Hodges, and as such is possibly conservative, since his contemporaries and PDE have the unrounded vowel. *Mall* and *pall-mall* are obviously related forms, and as such should be dealt with together. According to the *OED*, PDE /ɔː/ is etymologically correct in both cases, since both senses ultimately derive from an alley in which a game of *mall* is played with a *mall* or *maul*—that is, a mallet. However, there must have been some controversy surrounding the pronunciation of *mall* in the late eighteenth century, since Walker devotes one of his notes to the matter:

This word is a whimsical instance of the caprice of custom. Nothing can be more uniform than the sound we give to *a* before double *l* in the same syllable; and yet this word, when it signifies a wooden hammer, has not only changed its deep sound of *a* in *all* into the *a* in *alley*, but has dwindled into the short sound of *e* in *Mall*, a walk in St. James's Park, where they formerly played with malls and balls, and from whence it had its name; and to crown the absurdity, a street parallel to this walk is spelt *Pall Mall*, and pronounced *Pellmell*, which confuses its origin with the French adverb *pêle mêle* . . . That this word was justly pronounced formerly we can scarcely doubt from the rhymes to it

'With mighty *mall*
The monster merciless made him to fall' (SPENCER)

'And give that reverend head a *mall*
Or two or three against a wall' (HUDIBRAS)

As a corroboration of this, we find a large wooden dub used for killing swine called and spelt a *maul*; and the word signifying to beat or bruise is spelt and pronounced in the same manner. The word *mallet*, where the latter *l* is separated from the former, is under a different predicament, and is pronounced regularly.   (Walker 1791)

What emerges here is that the short /æ/ or even /ɛ/ was the fashionable pronunciation in London in the late eighteenth century. Walker bows reluctantly to 'custom' here, even though 'analogy' and history support the use of the rounded vowel, but he would probably have approved of Spence's usage in this case. The then fashionable pronunciations for *The Mall* and *Pall Mall* have survived into PDE, since they are famous places localized in London, but for the common noun *mall* the earlier pronunciation has prevailed, possibly with reinforcement from American English in the recently imported sense of a large covered shopping area. Perhaps Spence used {*AU*} in *mall* because, living as he did so far from the capital, he was unaware of the fashionable pronunciation, and so he would naturally preserve the conservative variant, which could well have been the norm amongst educated and well-bred persons living in the north at that time. The fact that the Scotsman Burn gives the two alternative pronunciations without commenting adversely on either perhaps supports this.[15]

Although, as we have seen, Spence tends to use {*AU*} for the reflexes of ME /a/ before ⟨l⟩ more often than Walker, Sheridan, and Burn use their equivalent symbols for the rounded vowel concerned, Appendix 3*a*(ii) contains a few words in which Spence differs from his contemporaries in using {**}. These are *halberd*, *scallop*, *thraldom*, and *almond*. In the case of *halberd*, the *CSED* agrees with Spence in recording /æ/, whilst Walker, Sheridan, and Burn all show the rounded vowel. The reasons for variation in this word have already been discussed above: suffice it to say that the conflicting evidence of Spence, on the one hand, and Walker, Sheridan, and Burn, on the other, shows that such variation continued at least up to the end of the eighteenth century. It would appear that the rounded variant was favoured in the London standard at that time, but the other variant

---

[15] Indeed, Burn often shows a tolerance which is rare in the late eighteenth century, giving alternative pronunciations where he is aware of them without showing preference or passing judgement. On the word *oblige*, for instance, he writes: 'about forty years ago, the word *oblige* was pronounced thus ob-lige 14 [= /iː/]; then, about twenty years later ob-lige 16 [= /ai/]; and now again, many of the best pronounce, ob-lige 14 . . . There is, indeed, something to be pleaded in behalf of this diversity of pronunciation; for the one is more agreeable to the French, from which it is derived, and the other more agreeable to the English analogy, so that it is hard to say which of these modes is the best: it shall, therefore, be left to the determination of custom' (1786: A2ᵛ).

continued to be used and eventually prevailed. For *scallop* Walker, Sheridan, and Burn all give their short ⟨o⟩ symbol indicating /ɒ/ rather than /ɔː/, but Spence has {ʌ}. In fact, given that the ME /a/ is followed by intervocalic /l/ here, we would expect /æ/ in PDE as in *gallop*, but the *CSED* records both /ɒ/ and /æ/ (with /ɒ/ placed first). Walker (1791) notices this anomaly, and devotes a note to it under his entry for *scallop*: 'This word is irregular, for it ought to have the *a* in the first syllable like that of *tallow*, but the deep sound of *a* is too firmly fixed by custom to afford any expectation of a change'. Jespersen (1909–49: 290) is likewise puzzled by the pronunciation of this word: 'I cannot explain *scallop* [skɔləp], also spelt *scollop*, < F. *escalope*.' Spence's {ʌ} here could well represent an older variant, as the *OED* notes that spellings with ⟨o⟩ do not appear until the sixteenth century, but the variant must have been rare in the eighteenth century, or else Walker would have mentioned it as a more 'analogical' alternative, as he does the rounded variant for *mall*.

Spence also uses {ʌ} in *almond*, but, in this case, Walker, Burn, and PDE as represented in the *CSED* all have a long unrounded vowel, /ɑː/. Sheridan's evidence is unfortunately ambiguous here, for, as we saw in §5.2, he fails to distinguish between the long vowel of, for example, *father*, and the short one of, for example, *man*, using {a¹} for both. His {a¹} in *almond*, could therefore agree either with Spence's {ʌ} or Walker's {a²}, but we have no way of knowing. We would expect the long vowel here, as /ɑː/ is the normal reflex in PDE of ME /au/ from /a/ in this environment (see the discussion of *balm*, above). Furthermore, Spence's full transcription of this word is {ʌMɪN}, showing loss of /l/, which is usually associated with a long reflex of ME /a/ as in *half*, *calf*, *palm*, etc.. However, Spence is not entirely alone in his recommendation of this pronunciation in the late eighteenth century. Jespersen (1909–49: 297) points out that Elphinston has [aˑmənd][16] for *almond* but that he adds 'rather ammon', which suggests, in semi-phonetic spelling, exactly the pronunciation recommended by Spence. Since Elphinston was a Scot, it may be that this pronunciation was acceptable amongst 'good' speakers in the north at that time.

The only remaining word in this lexical set for which Spence's recommended pronunciation differs from those of Walker and Sheridan is *thraldom*, as shown in Appendix 3a(iii): here, Spence uses {ʌ}, whilst Walker, Sheridan, and Burn have the equivalent of /ɔː/ and the *CSED* records /ɔː/ for PDE. Unfortunately, the word *thrall* is not present in Spence's lexicon, but, given his 100 per cent use of {ʌU} in the environment /-⟨ll⟩, as in *call*, *fall*, *gall*, *hall*, etc., it is surprising to see {ʌ} in the derived form here. There is, to my knowledge, no evidence for the development of

---

[16] Here, I have replicated Jespersen's transcription exactly: in the IPA phonemic transcription that I use in this thesis, it would be rendered /ˈɑːmənd/. Jespersen tends to use a half-length mark for 'long' vowels, and does not mark stress.

/au/ from ME /a/ to /ɑː/ in this environment, either before, during, or after the eighteenth century. Moreover, Spence has {ÆU} in *inthrall*, which suggests, as does the tendency to hypercorrection in the 'learned' words discussed above, uncertainty on Spence's part as to the correct pronunciation of ⟨a⟩ before ⟨ll⟩ or ⟨l⟩ followed by a consonant.

What this examination of the lexical set involving ME /a/ before /l/ has revealed, then, is that the variation in the pronunciation of these words in the sixteenth and seventeenth centuries as described by Dobson (1957) continued at least up to the end of the eighteenth century. Many of the discrepancies between Walker, Sheridan, and Burn, on the one hand, and Spence, on the other, can be traced back to the existence of variants in the sixteenth century. More often than not, Spence's pronunciation is the more conservative, except where he appears to show evidence of analogical pronunciations which resurface in the late twentieth century, as in *alternate*, etc. In many cases, though, Spence's apparent overuse of the rounded vowel has the appearance of hypercorrection, especially where the words concerned are learned and of relatively recent adoption. However, 'hypercorrect' does not mean 'artificial': it could well be the case that the pronunciations recommended by Spence were current amongst genteel but provincial speakers in Newcastle at the time, speakers who, like Spence, would be aware of the 'incorrect' nature of Northumbrian [aː] in, for example, *ball*, and who would avoid using this vowel whenever ⟨a⟩ preceded ⟨l⟩, unless they were sure that an unrounded vowel would be acceptable, as in *balcony*[17] and *salmon*, where Spence agrees with his contemporaries and PDE in using the short unrounded vowel.

5.3.3. *Reflexes of ME and later /a/ after /w/*

Let us go on to look at the evidence from Spence and his contemporaries for the pronunciation of ME /a/ after /w/ in, for example, *warm, wharf*. As with the development before /l/, Northumbrian retains unrounded vowels here: Wright (1905) gives, for instance [waːm] as the pronunciation for *warm* and [wasp] for *wasp* in south-east Northumberland (the area around Newcastle). The use of unrounded vowels in such words was not always entirely dialectal in ENE, since rounding after /w/ took place rather later than diphthongization of ME /a/ before /l/ and so variation was still widespread amongst 'good' speakers at least up to the end of the eighteenth century.

The rounded reflexes of ME /a/ after /w/ appear earliest and most consistently when the vowel is followed by /r/.[18] Dobson (1957: 524) writes

[17] *Balcony* was introduced from Italian (first citation 1618 in the *OED*), and so perhaps retains /æ/ from the source language. In Italian, stress would be on the second syllable, but Spence marks it on the first.
[18] Dobson (1957) does not state this explicitly, but he is referring here to preconsonantal and word-final /r/, as in *ward, war*, not to prevocalic /r/, as in *warrior*. The PDE reflexes have a long vowel in the first two cases and a short one in the last, although all three have a rounded vowel.

that, although lengthening of /a/ to /aː/ before /r/ is shown earlier than rounding after /w/, there do not appear to be two separate stages of lengthening and rounding, 'as there is no evidence of an intermediate stage between /a/ and /ɔː/: evidently the lengthening and rounding were simultaneous processes'. The first evidence for this lengthening and rounding is from Daines (1640), followed by Coles (1674) and Cooper (1685). Daines shows the long rounded vowel in *ward, warm, swarm, warn, wharf, dwarf, swarve, warp, wart, quart*, and *thwart*; Coles has this vowel in *ward, dwarf*, and *wharf*, a rounded but short vowel such as /ɒ/ in *warm, swarm, warn, wart, quart, thwart*, and short, unrounded /æ/ in *warp, warble*; and Cooper shows the long rounded vowel in *ward, warden*, and *warm.*

Where the /a/ is followed by a consonant other than /r/, evidence of rounding is much more sporadic in the seventeenth century. The first orthoepist to show a rounded reflex in this environment is Robinson (1617), who has /ɒ/ regularly in *was, wast* and has one instance of /ɒ/ in each of *warrant, want*, but also has one example of /æ/ in *somewhat*. Later in the seventeenth century, Newton (1660–2) has /ɒ/ in *what* but not in *was*; Coles (1674) has /ɒ/ in *what*, and Cooper (1685) has /ɒ/ in *was, watch*, but not in *wan, wasp*, or *quality*. All these authorities are cited by Dobson, who writes: 'The evidence clearly suggests that the rounded pronunciation, which began as a vulgarism . . . made its way into St.E. very slowly indeed. It was most common, and was first accepted in St.E., in the normally weakly stressed *was* and *what*. Unrounded forms apparently still survived in *wan, quality*, etc. in the late eighteenth century' (1957: 717). There are some cases where the rounded vowel is found more regularly in the seventeenth century: these are all words in which the ME /a/ is followed by /t/ or /d/ and then a (syllabic) /r/. The most regular of these is *water*, in which there is early evidence of /ɔː/ from Robinson, Gil (1619), Daines, and Cooper, and in which /ɔː/ is given by eighteenth-century orthoepists from John Jones (1701) onwards.

By the eighteenth century, the rounded reflex of ME /a/ is found regularly between /w/ and /r/, and in certain words like *water* between /w/ and a dental consonant followed by syllabic /r/. In other cases where PDE has /ɒ/ or /ɔː/, there was variation in the eighteenth century between /æ/ and /ɒ/; /aː/ and /ɔː/. This variation was noted by, for example, Jespersen (1909–49: 317), who writes: 'The old unrounded sound seems to have survived till the end of the 18th c. as an occasional or individual pronunciation; Enfield 1790 gives *wash*, etc., in his own pronunciation as equal to the vowel of *hat*, and *water, wart, dwarf* with the vowel of *half, ass*, while Walker 1791 says that 'we frequently hear' *quality* with the vowel of *legality* instead of that of *jollity.*'

Wyld (1936: 202–3) has, as is often the case, interesting anecdotal evidence to add:

By the side of the rounded forms whose existence is fully established among the best speakers . . . for the seventeenth century . . . some seventeenth- and eighteenth-century grammarians suggest the existence of unrounded forms such as [wæz, swæn, kwæl*i*ti, kwænt*i*ti] . . . It looks as if we must assume the existence of a speech community among which *wā* became simply [wæ] and not [wɔ], whose habits of speech have left some slight traces. It is certain . . . that many eighteenth-century speakers said [kwæl*i*ti] and [kwænt*i*ti]. This is asserted by writers on pronunciation and is confirmed by a statement made to me by a lady who died recently, aged eighty-six, that nearly eighty years before, a great aunt of hers, then very old, corrected my informant for saying [kwɔl*i*ti, kwɔnt*i*ti], asserting that these were vulgar pronunciations.[19]

Where the vowel is rounded, PDE has /ɔː/ in words like *water* and those with preconsonantal or word final /r/ after the vowel, but /ɒ/ elsewhere. The long vowel was formerly more widespread: Dobson (1957: 719) cites *was*, *wattle*, *watch*, and *wash* all as being recorded occasionally with the long rounded vowel and *water* as regularly having this in the seventeenth century. There are also circumstances in which rounding does not occur—namely, when the reflex of ME /a/ is followed by a velar consonant, as can be seen in PDE *wag, wax, twang*.

To sum up, this particular sound change appears to have been diffusing gradually from the seventeenth century onwards and to have been subject to phonetic conditioning. The most favourable environment seems to have been that in which a preceding /w/ and a following /r/ exert a combined lengthening and rounding influence; next comes that in which a dental consonant and a syllabic /r/ follow, as in *water*; in other environments, the change appears later and takes longer to regularize, so that, for example, *quality* keeps the unrounded vowel in the speech of the upper classes at least into the nineteenth century. Finally, a following velar consonant seems to block this sound change,[20] so that words like *quack* never have a rounded vowel in RP or its antecedents.

If we now compare the evidence from Spence, Walker, Sheridan, and Burn as presented in Appendix 3*b*(i) and (ii), we shall see that, as we found in §5.2, these four orthoepists appear to represent different stages in the diffusion of this sound change. I included in the lexical set represented in Appendix 3*b*(ii) words in which a velar consonant follows just in case any of the sources used showed rounding in this context, but, as the entries for

---

[19] I quote from the 1936 edition of *A History of Modern Colloquial English*, but as the first edition was dated 1920, the old lady's aunt must have made these remarks in about 1840. I have heard the pronunciation ['kwæliti] used ironically as a stereotype of ultra-conservative RP in the set phrase *the quality* meaning the very highest society. This was used in an episode of *Rumpole of the Bailey* written by John Mortimer QC and appeared sometime in the 1980s.

[20] I had thought that this block on rounding before velar consonants was complete, but the *CSED* gives both /kwæg/ and /kwɒg/ (in that order) for *quag* and *quagmire*: perhaps this last stronghold of unrounded /a/ after /w/ is breaking down.

equangular, quack, quagmire, swag, swagger, thwack, wag, waggish, waggon, and *wax* show, none of our orthoepists has a rounded vowel for any of these words. We should therefore subtract these ten words from the total in any calculations of the extent of rounding shown by these orthoepists, as rounding would appear to be prohibited in this context. We therefore have a total of 106 words from the *Grand Repository* in which a reflex of ME /a/ appears between /w/ and a non-velar consonant: of these, Spence has {ʌ} in 52 and {ʌ} in 54. Walker has 104 of these words (*quarters* and *swath* do not appear in the *Critical Pronouncing Dictionary*), of which 97 have a rounded vowel, 5 have /æ/, and one (*towards*) has /ʌ/; Sheridan, too has 104 matching entries, of which 77 have a rounded vowel, 21 have /æ/, and 6 have /ɛ/ or /eː/; and Burn, too, has 104 matching entries: 65 with a rounded vowel, 38 with /æ/ or /ɑː/, and one with /eː/. In other words, the rounding has become almost categorical in non-velar contexts for the variety described by Walker, whilst those described by Sheridan, Burn, and Spence (in that order) are increasingly conservative with regard to this sound change. (In percentages, Walker has a rounded vowel in 93.26 per cent of the words; Sheridan in 74 per cent; Burn in 62.5 per cent, and Spence in 49 per cent)

If we now look more closely at the phonetic contexts which favour or disfavour rounding of ME /a/ after /w/, we see that the sequence which emerged from our discussion of seventeenth-century evidence is repeated. Wherever preconsonantal /r/ follows, the rounded vowel is given by all four orthoepists, except for three words *dwarf, quarto,* and *thwart,* for which Spence alone has an unrounded vowel. *Dwarf* was one of the words for which Enfield had 'the vowel of *half, ass*' as late as 1790, so it should come as no surprise that the most conservative of our four orthoepists should have an unrounded vowel in this word in 1775. *Thwart* shares certain phonetic characteristics with *dwarf*—notably, an initial dental/alveolar consonant— and so we might be tempted to see the inhibition of rounding in these two cases as due to environmental conditioning, except that *athwart* has the rounded vowel for Spence. On the other hand, a similar pattern emerged in §5.3.2: in Appendix 3*a*, *thraldom* has an unrounded vowel, equivalent to PDE /ɑː/ but *bethrall, inthrall* have the equivalent of PDE /ɔː/. In both these cases, then, if a /θ/ before the /w/ inhibits rounding, it only does so when it is word-initial.

The explanation for Spence's unrounded vowel in *quarto* is probably simpler: as we saw in the discussion of *quality* above, some words beginning with orthographic ⟨q⟩, and therefore with a velar /k/ preceding the /w/, resisted rounding in upper-class speech at least well into the nineteenth century. In the sources cited above, only the words *quality* and *quantity* are cited, but a close inspection of Appendix 3*b* reveals that this phenomenon was more widespread in the eighteenth century, with a number of words in which /k/ precedes the /w/ having an unrounded vowel. Even Walker has some instances of /æ/ in this context—indeed, of the five words for which Walker has /æ/ after /w/ (other than before a velar), four have a preceding /k/: *aquatic, conquassate, dequantitate,* and *quaff* (the fifth, *waft,* like all the other four, has /æ/ in all the other three sources as well, and, like all the others, except *dequantitate,* still has an unrounded vowel in PDE.)[21] It is perhaps worth noting here that Walker explicitly stated as a rule that *a* would be 'broadened' after *w* 'except where the vowel is closed by the sharp or flat guttural *k* or *g,* or the sharp labial *f*' (1791: 11). This would indicate that the phonetic conditioning of this sound change was finer than, for example, Dobson (1957) recognizes: Walker's statement, and the evidence in Appendix 3*b* as well as PDE, show that a following /f/ inhibited rounding, whilst our evidence also shows that a preceding velar, like a following velar, inhibited the rounding in the earlier stages of this sound change, and that the residue of this inhibiting factor is still with us at the end of the twentieth century. If we look at the other, more conservative, orthoepists represented in Appendix 3*b,* we find that, compared with Walker, they have a larger number of words with an unrounded vowel after /kw/, in some cases even in words with other factors favouring the rounded vowel. Spence alone has /æ/ in *quarto,* where the following /r/ should favour rounding, perhaps because, for him, it retained a 'foreign' appearance and so was not associated with *quart* and its derivatives. Sheridan and Burn, on the other hand, have /æ/ and /ɑː/ respectively in *qualm,* for which both Walker and Spence have /ɔː/. In this latter case, the following /lm/ (the /l/ is not vocalized in Spence's or Walker's entry for this word) favours the rounding and, as we saw in §5.3.2, Spence has a rounded vowel in this context more than the other three. (All four have the rounded vowel in *squall,* the other word in which a reflex of /a/ appears between /kw/ and /l/.) Apart from *quart, quarter,* and derivatives, which have /ɔː/ in all four of our sources, *disqualify, equality, quadragessimal, quadrangle, quadrant,*[22] *quadrate, quadrature, quadrennial, quadruped, quadruple, qualification, qualify, quality, quantity, quantum,* have an unrounded vowel for Sheridan, Burn, and Spence, but not Walker; whilst *quadrille, quandary, quarantine, quash, squabble, squadron, squalid, squat,* have the unrounded vowel only in Burn and Spence. Bearing in mind that Burn had 65 'rounded' entries in this set as against Sheridan's 77, the 8 words last cited account for much of the difference between these two orthoepists. It also looks as though the conditioning which accounts for the

[21] In the *CSED, aquatic* is recorded as having /æ/ or /ɒ/ in that order, whilst *quaff* has /ɒ/ or /ɑː/; and *waft* /ɑː/ or /ɒ/ (*conquassate,* marked in the *OED* as 'obs. rare', is, understandably, not included). This, along with the variation in *quagmire,* discussed in n. 20, indicates that this sound change, like that involving /a/ before ⟨l⟩, is still diffusing in RP.

[22] I have treated these items all alike as 'unrounded', but, in fact, Burn and Sheridan have /eː/ rather than /æ/ in *quadrant,* whilst Sheridan also has /eː/ in *quadrate, quadrature.* Walker (1791) remarks in his note to *quadrant:* 'The sound of *a* in this and similar words . . . till lately was always pronounced broad. Some innovators have attempted to give the *a* in this word the slender sound; but the publick ear seems in opposition to it, nor ought it to be admitted.'

difference between these two is lexical rather than just phonetic: all the words for which both Sheridan and Burn as well as Spence have the unrounded vowel contain certain lexical elements: the Latin *quad-* (note, *quadrille*, a recent (1726) loan from French, is not a member of this set, at least for Sheridan: he and Walker actually have forms without /w/ but with a rounded vowel for this word /kɔː/-); *qualify, quant-*, and *quality*.

The information provided in Appendix 3b concerning rounding of ME and later /a/ after /kw/ does seem to suggest that a preceding velar consonant had an inhibiting effect on rounding, but that this phonetic condition gives way to a process of lexical diffusion through the eighteenth century. Spence, Burn, Sheridan, and Walker represent successive stages in this diffusion and, indeed, the diffusion is still going on, as the 'alternative' rounded forms for *aquatic* and *quagmire* in the *CSED* show. Certainly, the evidence from our four pronouncing dictionaries indicates that the pronunciation of ME and later /a/ after /kw/ was much more variable in the eighteenth century than has hitherto been acknowledged.

The only other word for which Sheridan and Burn, as well as Spence, have an unrounded vowel here is *wan*. Walker (1791) notes Sheridan's pronunciation under his entry for this word: 'Mr. Sheridan has given the *a* in this word, and its compounds, the same sound as in *man*. I have always heard it pronounced like the first syllable of *wanton*, and find Mr. Nares, W. Johnston and Mr. Perry, have so marked it.' Walker obviously had not seen the evidence from Mr Burn and Mr Spence, but would probably have dismissed it as 'provincial' even if he had. Burn and Sheridan also have /æ/ in *wasp, waspish*, for which Spence has the rounded vowel, like Walker, whilst Burn alone agrees with Spence in having an unrounded vowel in *swaddle, wad*, and *wadding*. This leaves Spence as the only one of our four orthoepists to have no rounding in *swab, swallow, swamp, swan, swap* (though in this case Spence does have a separate entry for *swop*, spelt with ⟨o⟩ in the conventional spelling and {C} in the New Alphabet) *swath, wabble, waddle, wallet, wand, watch, wattle*, and *wattles*. Although none of the orthoepists represented in Appendix 3b agrees with Spence on the pronunciation of these words, he is not entirely alone, for, according to Jespersen (1909–49: 317), 'Buchanan 1766 has [ɔ] in *ward, warn, want, wasp, wash, watch*, but /æ/ or /a/ in *wabble, wad, wallop* etc.'. The pattern here almost exactly matches that of the *Grand Repository*. Furthermore, in the *British Grammar*, Buchanan (1762: 8) writes: '*A* is short before (ll) as in *tăllow, shăllow, swăllow, ănnually, căsually*, etc.' Viewed in isolation, Spence's distribution of /æ/ and /ɔː/ across the lexical set with initial /w/ may seem erratic, but with this corroboration from Buchanan we see that it simply represents a conservative (for 1775) variety, agreeing, as it does, with that of a Scot writing some nine to thirteen years earlier. Buchanan's evidence also suggests, along with Burn's, that there was a geographical element to the diffusion of this sound change, as pronunciations recommended by northern and Scottish orthoepists tend to be more conservative. (Burn, writing in Glasgow in 1786, is more conservative than Sheridan (albeit an Irishman), writing in London in 1780.)

Perhaps a final remark should be made here about the distribution of long /ɔː/ and short /ɒ/ rounded reflexes of ME and later /a/ in Appendix 3*b*. The lexical sets are those in which Spence has {Ʌ} (rounded) and {ʌ} (unrounded), the equivalents of PDE /ɔː/ (as in *wall*) and /æ/ (as in *man*). He never gives his 'short *o*' symbol {C} (as in *not*) for a word with ⟨a⟩ in the conventional orthography and *vice versa*. I checked this by obtaining a list from OCP of all words with Spence's {C} after /w/: the list was *aquosity, once, one, quoth, swollen, swop* (note the double entry for this word: *swap* also occurs, pronounced /swæp/), *wont, wonted, wot*. I found the same pattern (though with more entries) with words containing {C} and {Ʌ} before ⟨l⟩. As we saw in §4.3, Spence does not have the equivalent of PDE /ɔː/ in any of Wells's sets except the THOUGHT set (and even here, not in *thought* itself, for which Spence has his {O}, equivalent to /oː/). Almost all the words in this set involve reflexes of ME /a/ or /au/, so Spence has no need of a symbol to represent a 'broad *o*': to him, /ɔː/ is evidently a 'broad *a*', to use the terminology of other eighteenth-century orthoepists. Walker, on the other hand, has a symbol {a³} and a symbol {o³}, which he seems to use interchangeably for rounded reflexes of ME /a/: he uses the {o³}, for instance, in *quart, quarter, quarterage, quartern,* and *quarterstaff*. In his list of vowels, Walker has {o³} 'like the broad *a*', and he states that 'the fifth sound of *o* is the long sound produced by *r* final as followed by another consonant as *for, former*. This sound is perfectly equivalent to the diphthong *au* and *for, former* might on account of sound only, be written *faur* and *faurmer*' (1791: 22). Walker's decision to use {o³} rather than an {a³} in *quart*, etc., would appear to be arbitrary. Sheridan, like Spence, seems to use the 'broad *a*' symbol for all rounded reflexes of ME /a/, whilst Burn avoids orthographic confusion by having a single number correspond to a single vowel. Thus the number 5 always stands for /ɔː/, whatever vowel it is placed above.

Taking Spence's transcriptions at face value, there is no difference of length between, for example, *wall* and *warrior*, for both are spelt with {Ʌ} in the New Alphabet, but Sheridan, Walker, and Burn have /ɔː/ in some words and /ɒ/ in others, as Appendix 3*b* shows. Where the vowel is rounded, Burn has more 'long' instances than Walker or Sheridan, with /ɔː/ in *quarrel, quarrelsom, quarry, squander, swallow, swamp, swan, waddle, wanton, warrant, warrantable, warren, was, wash, watch*, but there are even words such as *squadron, warrior*, which are 'long' for all of our eighteenth-century sources, but have short /ɒ/ in RP today. This indicates that, as Dobson (1957: 719) noted for the seventeenth century, variation between short and long vowels in these words continued through the eighteenth century, but Spence's categorical use of what appears to be a long vowel, along with Burn's tendency to use this more than Sheridan or Walker do, might indicate that this, like the use of the unrounded vowel in certain contexts, is a conservative trait of northern and Scots varieties.

In summary, our inspection of the evidence in Appendix 3*b* has revealed that the diffusion of rounding of ME and later /a/ after /w/ is even more complex than has hitherto been acknowledged. The phonetic conditioning is very fine, with preceding /k/ and following /f/, as well as following velars, exerting an inhibiting influence. In the course of the eighteenth century, the effect of the preceding velar seems to weaken, and the sound change diffuses lexically in this context, a diffusion which is still going on in the late twentieth century in words such as *aquatic*, and *quagmire*. Northern varieties seem to be more conservative with regard to this change, as Burn and Spence have less rounding than Sheridan and Walker. As was the case with the lengthening of /a/ discussed in §5.2, Spence's distribution of variants might seem erratic and the work of a 'bad' phonetician when viewed in isolation, but when we compare his realizations with those of Walker, Sheridan, and Burn, we find that the pattern is too consistent to be random: Spence's realizations are the most conservative in both cases, Walker's the most advanced, and the other orthoepists come in between.

5.4. 'SPLITTING' OF ME /ʊ/

5.4.1. *Introduction*

Northern English varieties today are still characterized by what Wells (1982: 356) calls 'the absence of a FOOT-STRUT split'. This 'split', affecting reflexes of ME /ʊ/ as in *cup* and of 'early shortening' of ME /oː/ in, for example, *blood*, was under way by the seventeenth century. Dobson (1957: 585) writes that 'orthoepistical evidence of the unrounding begins *c*.1640' when 'certain orthoepists distinguish the /ʊ/ of *cut* from that of *put*'. By the middle of the eighteenth century the 'unsplit' /ʊ/ was already recognized as a northern characteristic. We have already noted in §2.4 the Cumbrian John Kirkby's (1746) remark that his 'seventh vowel', found in *skull*, *gun*, *supper*, *figure*, *nature*, 'is scarce known to the Inhabitants of the North, who always use the short sound of the eighth vowel instead of it' (quoted in Bergström 1955: 71). (Kirkby's 'eighth vowel' is long in *too*, *woo*, *Food*, etc., short in *good*, *stood*, *Foot*, etc.) Recognition of the salience of this feature becomes more widespread towards the end of the eighteenth century, when Walker (1791: p. xiii) writes: 'If the short sound of the letter *u* in *trunk*, *sunk*, &c., differ from the sound of that letter in the northern parts of England, where they sound it like the *u* in *bull*, and nearly as if the words were written *troonk*, *soonk*, etc., it necessarily follows that every word where that letter occurs must by those provincials be mispronounced.' This suggests that northerners in Walker's time pronounced /ʊ/ where Londoners had /ʌ/, as is the case today, but Kenrick (1773: 36) indicates otherwise:

It is further observable of this sound, that the people of Ireland, Yorkshire, and many other provincials mistake its use; applying it to words which in London are pronounced with the *u* full as in . . . no 3 of the Dictionary: as *bull, wool, put, push*, all of which they pronounce as the inhabitants of the Metropolis do *trull, blood, rut, rush*. Thus the ingenious Mr. Ward of Beverley, has given us in his grammar the words *put, thus* and *rub* as having one quality of sound; but unless by the word *put* he meant the substantive, a Dutch game of cards so called, or the ludicrous appelation given to provincials of *country put*, it is never so pronounced.

Both Walker and Kenrick notice that northerners have 'unsplit' /ʊ/, but, whereas Walker's account suggests that the sound change which caused the split—the unrounding of /ʊ/ from ME /ʊ/ and other sources—has simply not occurred in these northern varieties, Kenrick's observations suggest that it has gone further, spreading to words which retain the rounded vowel in London English. In fact, the variety described by Kenrick is alive and well in cities like Newcastle today: just as Edinburgh has the 'Morningside' accent, and Glasgow the 'Kelvinside', Newcastle has what we might call the 'Jesmond' accent—a modified regional standard heard from middle-class Tynesiders and especially those who have attended the private day schools that abound in Jesmond. One notable characteristic of this accent is a schwa-like vowel in words such as *good, put, puss*, etc. as well as *mud, blood, pus*, etc. (see Wells 1982: 352 for further observations on this phenomenon in 'northern Near-RP'). Perhaps what Walker observed was the 'broad' north-ern accent of his day, whilst Kenrick was referring to the modified one (it is interesting to note that 'Mr Ward' provided evidence of this modified variety in his grammar!).

On the other hand, with regard to Scottish and Irish varieties, Walker (1791: 22–3) suggests that there is 'confusion' as to the correct distribution of the more rounded vowel:

This middle sound of *u* . . . exists only in the following words: *bull, full, pull*; words compounded of *full* as *wonderful, dreadful*, &c, *bullock, bully, push, bush, bushel, pulpit, puss, bullion, butcher, cushion, cuckoo, pudding, sugar, hussar, huzza* and *put* when a verb; but few as they are . . . they are sufficient to puzzle Englishmen who reside at any distance from the capital, and to make the inhabitants of Scotland and Ireland (who, it is highly probable, received a more regular pronunciation from our ancestors), not infrequently the jest of fools.

The suggestion here is that some 'provincials' may fail to use the rounded vowel, Walker's 'middle sound' in the words cited, employing instead what Walker saw as the 'more regular' /ʌ/. This is consistent with Wells's (1982:

400) observation that, whilst the Scottish accent of English has the /ʌ/ phoneme, the distribution of this is different from that of RP: 'it must be noted that many FOOT words have Scots dialect forms with /ʌ/.'

All this would suggest, that where Spence's, Sheridan's, and Burn's distributions of these vowels differ from Walker's, the former are showing northern, Scots, or Irish influences. However, it may well be the case that the situation even in 'polite' London English may not have been as clear-cut as Walker makes out. Walker was a stickler for what he called 'analogy'—that is, regularity—and actually (erroneously, of course), saw the rounded vowel in, for example, *bull* as an irregularity of recent introduction. He states himself that 'some speakers, indeed, have attempted to give *bulk* and *punish* this obtuse sound of *u*, but luckily have not been followed. The words which have already adopted it are sufficiently numerous; and we cannot be too careful to check the growth of so unmeaning an irregularity' (Walker 1791: 23). (Note that Walker does not attribute the use of /ʊ/ in these last two words to any provincial group, but just to 'some speakers'.) Holmberg points out that, 'as late as the latter half of the nineteenth century, Standard-English speakers hesitated on what words to use the normal ME ŭ, i.e. [ʌ] or [ə] and where to use [u]', and goes on to quote Ellis as follows: 'The two sounds . . . coexist in many words. Several careful speakers say (to pət, bətsher), though the majority say (to pʊt, bʊtsher). All talk of a *put* (pət)' (Holmberg 1964: 67).

This would suggest that the sound change concerned was still in progress even in the nineteenth century, and that differences between the accounts of various pronouncing dictionaries might well reflect variable usage *per se* rather than regional variation. On the other hand, what appear to be 'hypercorrect' usages of the unrounded vowel where Walker, or, indeed, present-day RP, has the rounded one, such as those of 'Mr. Ward' described by Kenrick, could well result from the persistence of an 'intermediate' vowel. This is hinted at by Charles Jones (1991) as a possible interpretation of the account given by Sylvester Douglas, in which a 'smothered vocal' is found in a very small lexical set made up of *Tully, scut,* and *rut,* whilst a different vowel is used in words such as *flood, blood, love, dove, come, couplet, punt, hulk, rump, dub,* and *mud.* The latter vowel is described by Douglas as closer to the vowel found long in *prove, tomb, two,* etc., and short in *pull, full, pulpit,* etc. (/ʊ/). Jones suggests that the 'smothered' vowel is perhaps [ʌ] or [ə], and the 'other shade' perhaps [ɣ], and quotes Wells as follows: 'The split of the old short /ʊ/ into two distinct qualities seems to have been established by the middle of the seventeenth century. It may well have originated as an allophonic alternative, with unrounded [ɣ] the forerunner of the modern /ʌ/ in most environments, but a rounded quality (modern /ʊ/) retained after labials' (Wells 1982: 197, quoted in C. Jones 1991: 20). Jones (1991: 20) goes on to point out that, 'if Douglas' observation of a triple development for

Middle English [u] is a correct and accurate one, the existence of some "intermediate" [ɣ] stage is attested by him at a date later than most other observers.' Douglas, then, may well have been describing a variety more conservative than that of Walker, in which lexical diffusion of [ɣ] > [ʌ] had not progressed very far and the phonologization of this originally allophonic split had not occurred. Other observers such as Kenrick may have been describing varieties in which the 'intermediate' [ɣ] had spread throughout the lexical set without developing to [ʌ].

5.4.2. *Reflexes of ME (and later) /ʊ/ in eighteenth-century pronouncing dictionaries*

As I explained in §5.1, Spence's *Grand Repository* shows no evidence of a phonemic split of ME /ʊ/, having no symbol equivalent to /ʌ/ in the New Alphabet. It would not be profitable to compare every entry with Spence's { U} with the same words in Walker, Sheridan, and Burn, partly because the number of entries is so great (1,199 words with this vowel in stressed position), and partly because we can expect variation in only a small number of these words. I did, however, compare Burn's entries for all the words concerned in order to discover whether the 'misuse' of /ʌ/ cited by Walker as typical of Scots (and Irish) usage would be apparent. In fact, the comparison confirmed that the vowel equivalent to RP /ʌ/ was, for Burn as well as for Walker, the most common reflex of ME and later /ʊ/: out of the 1,199 words for which Spence had the equivalent of /ʊ/, only forty had the same vowel for Burn. The vast majority of these forty were words cited by Walker as having 'the middle sound' (i.e. /ʊ/), or compounds including those elements: for instance, Burn has /ʊ/ in *bull, bullock, bully, bullion, bulrush, bullet, bulwark, pull, pulpit,* and *pullet.* As we might have expected, there are a few words for which Burn has /ʌ/ but Walker has /ʊ/, notably *huzza, cushion, woman,*[23] and Burn shows variation between /ʌ/ and /ʊ/ in *butcher* and its derivatives. I have chosen to compare in Spence, Walker, Sheridan, and Burn those words cited by Walker as having 'the middle sound', those additional words with /ʊ/ in Burn, those which in present-day RP form minimal pairs, and a few others which had variable usage in the late eighteenth century. The distribution of /ʊ/ and /ʌ/ (and other vowels in some cases) across this subset in the four dictionaries is shown in Appendix 4. Walker's usage is the same as present-day RP, with distinct vowels for *put* (vb.) and *put* (n.); *puss* (cat) and *pus* (matter). Spence, as we might expect from a northerner, shows no evidence of a phonemic split whatsoever: he uses the symbol {U}, described in his New Alphabet as 'u as in *tun*', in all these

---

[23] Walker gives as his rule 169: 'There is a sixth sound of *o* exactly corresponding to the *u* in *bull, full, pull,* &c. which, from its existing only in the following words, may be called its irregular sound. These words are, *woman, bosom, worsted, wolf,* and the proper names, *Wolsey, Worcester* and *Wolverhampton*' (1791: 22).

words. Since Spence does not comment on the articulation or quality of the sounds represented in his alphabet, it is futile to speculate on how this {ʟ} was pronounced: it could represent the [ə] of the 'modified' variety, like present-day Jesmond; the 'intermediate' [ɣ]; or, indeed, the [ʊ] of broad northern varieties. What is significant is that there is no phonemic split in the variety described by Spence. Burn and Sheridan, on the other hand, do show evidence of a phonemic split. Burn's system of notation shows five 'sounds of u' represented in his numerical system as: 1 as in *tun*; 3 as in *bush*; 4 as in *full, do*; 6 as in *tune*; and 15 as in *busy*. The vowels that concern us in this section are 1 and 3, which we have treated in Appendix 4 as equivalent to /ʌ/ and /ʊ/ respectively. Appendix 4 shows that Burn does indeed have minimal pairs: *puss* has /ʊ/ whilst *pus* has /ʌ/; *could* has /ʊ/, whilst *cud* has /ʌ/; but that Burn's distribution of /ʌ/ is not the same as that of Walker's, for Burn has /ʊ/ in both *put* (vb.) and *put* (n.), as well as in *currier* ('a dresser of leather'), *fulgent, housewife* (= /ˈhʊzwif/), *tush*, and *tut*, but he has /ʌ/ in *woman*, *cushion*, and *huzza*, whilst for *butcher* he has /ʌ/ or /ʊ/. Burn's use of /ʌ/ in these cases, as well as in *soot, sooty*, which will be discussed in §5.5, brings to mind Wells's (19982: 400) observation (quoted in §5.1.) that 'many FOOT words have Scots dialect forms with [ʌ]', and might suggest Scots influence in Burn's system, but the acknowledged variable usage in *butcher* would appear, in the light of the quote from Ellis (see §5.4.1), to be no more than an honest reflection of the variation that really existed at the time even in London English. Sheridan's distribution of /ʊ/ and /ʌ/ is much closer to Walker's, the only differences being that Sheridan alone of the four orthoepists here has *full* ('replete') and *full* ('to cleanse cloth') as a minimal pair, and that he, like Burn, has /ʌ/ in *huzza*. This would indicate that, if the tendency to use /ʌ/ for words which should, in 'correct' speech, have /ʊ/ was, as Walker suggests, an Irish as well as a Scottish trait, Sheridan is showing little influence from his native dialect here. *Huzza*, like *tush* and *tut*, is an exclamation, probably used informally, and likely to be variable, and, in differentiating *full* ('replete') from *full* ('to cleanse cloth'), Sheridan is more likely to be making an artificial distinction than showing Irish influence.

Looking at 'split' versus 'unsplit' /ʊ/, then, has shown us that Spence does indeed reveal northern influence in his lack of any split. Sheridan also shows the split, with a distribution very similar to that of Walker and present-day RP. Burn, having the split, but with the two phonemes distributed differently from Walker, may be showing what Walker saw as the Scots tendency to 'confuse' these vowels, but evidence into the nineteenth century of continued variation in *butcher* indicates that he could simply be giving a more realistic picture of the variation that still existed with regard to reflexes of ME /ʊ/.

5.5. LATER SHORTENING OF ME /oː/

5.5.1. *Introduction*

The next sound change under consideration here is what Dobson (1957) calls the 'later shortening' of ME /oː/, which accounts in present-day RP for the pronunciation of *good, foot, hook*, etc., with /ʊ/, as against *blood, flood* with /ʌ/ from earlier shortening and *moon, fool*, etc. with unshortened /uː/. Dobson (1957: 511–12) points out that evidence for this later shortening first appears sporadically:

> In the seventeenth century only the best observers give evidence of the development of [ʊ] by later shortening of . . . [uː] . . . But there is sufficient evidence of [ʊ] by later shortening in the following cases. (*a*) Before [d] in *good* . . . in *hood* . . . and in *stood* . . . (*b*) Before [t] in *foot* . . . and in *soot* . . . but, as in PresE, not in *boot, root* and *shoot*. (*c*) Before [θ] Coles gives [ʊ] in *sooth* and *tooth*, which in PresE have normally [uː], though [ʊ] exists as a variant in *tooth*. (*d*) Before [v] there is no evidence of later shortening to [ʊ]. (*e*) Of other consonants, only [k] regularly causes later shortening; it seems by contrast only rarely to have caused early shortening . . . In *book*, [ʊ] is recorded by Hodges, Cole and possibly Cooper . . . in *hook, look* and *took* by Hodges and Coles; in *cook* by Hodges; and in *brook, crook* and *shook* by Coles. But Coles has [uː] in *nook* and *rook*, which have [ʊ] in PresE . . . Before other consonants the shortening is sporadic; Hodges has [ʊ] in *hoop*, and Cocker seems to have [ʊ] beside [uː] in *fool*.

It is apparent from Dobson's summary of seventeenth-century evidence that this later shortening is a sound change which is both phonetically conditioned and subject to lexical diffusion in the seventeenth century. It also seems to have been diffusing socially and/or geographically, since different orthoepists show the shortening in different words. To add to the complications, both this and the earlier shortening which gives us /ʌ/ today in *blood, flood, glove*, were, in the terms used by Wang (1969), 'competing' for the same lexical items so that, as Dobson (1957: 508) points out, 'in the later seventeenth century, any one word may have [ʌ], [uː] or [ʊ].'

This variability is still, to a certain extent, in evidence today. For the most part, RP shows later shortening in words in which the vowel is followed by /d/, /t/, /k/, as in the above examples, but there is variation. This is evident within lexical sets, thus *food, mood* retain the long vowel, whilst *good, stood*, show later shortening, and, of course, *blood, flood* show earlier shortening; but some individual words also have variable pronunciations: *room* usually has the long vowel in RP, but certain (conservative?) RP speakers have a short vowel /ʊ/.[24] In some northern varieties of English, the long vowel is retained before /k/, whilst, of course, in educated Scots usage, the effects of

---

[24] Daniel Jones (1967: 405) gives *room* as [rum] with [ruːm] as an alternative, followed by a note to the effect that 'the use of the variant [ruːm] appears to be much on the increase'.

the Scottish Vowel Length Rule will be evident. According to McDavid (1949) and Bronstein and Sheldon (1951), considerable variation also exists in American English.

5.5.2. *Reflexes of ME /oː/ in eighteenth-century pronouncing dictionaries*

Given this history of continued variability in words with reflexes of ME /oː/, we might expect the distribution of /ʌ/, /ʊ/, and /uː/ across this lexical set to differ significantly in the accounts of Spence, Walker, Sheridan, and Burn respectively. Appendix 5*a* shows the vowel used by Walker, Sheridan, and Burn for each word in which Spence has {ⓞ} except where this is a result of 'yod-dropping' (these latter instances will be discussed separately in §5.6). The list includes not only words with reflexes of ME /oː/, but also those with later /uː/, sometimes varying with /oː/ in later loanwords such as *pontoon* (1676, from French), *hecatomb* (1592, from Latin, and still varying between /uː/ and /əʊ/ according to the *CSED*, and *monsoon* (1584, from Dutch). Variation between /oː/ and /uː/ in words such as *gold* and *blackamoor* was widespread in the eighteenth century, and Walker comments upon it in many cases.[25] However, we are here primarily concerned with variation between /uː/ (no shortening), /ʊ/ (later shortening), and /ʌ/ (early shortening).

As we might expect, Spence, a northerner who, as we have already seen in §§5.2, 5.3, and 5.4, has a tendency to be conservative with regard to his pronunciations, has less evidence of later shortening than the other three orthoepists examined here (and, of course, no evidence at all of early shortening, as he does not have a phoneme equivalent to /ʌ/.) Appendix 5*a*, words with Spence's {ⓞ} (= /uː/), is considerably longer than Appendix 5*b*, words with Spence's {ʟ} (= /ʊ/) from ME /oː/. Moreover, there are only four words in Appendix 5*b*, all containing the elements *hood* or *soot*, for which any of the other orthoepists have /uː/ where Spence has /ʊ/, but 37 in Appendix 5*a* where one or more of the other three have /ʊ/ contrasting with Spence's /uː/. However, the pattern that we have seen in §§5.2 and 5.3, with Walker as the most advanced, and Spence as the most conservative, with Sheridan/Johnston and Burn in between, is not followed here. Surprisingly, Walker tends to agree with Spence in having /uː/ more often than Sheridan or Burn, the only exceptions being words with the element *good*, for which only Burn and Spence have /uː/, and *wool*, for which Spence alone has (unhistorical) /uː/.

Most of the variation in Appendix 5*a* involves words in which ME /oː/ is followed by /k/, an environment which we have noted in §5.5.1 as being variable in the seventeenth century, and in which the shortening is still

---

[25] Justifying his different pronunciations for *moor* and *blackamoor*, Walker (1791) writes: '*Moor*, a black man, is regular in polite conversation, and like *more* in vulgar. *Moor*, a marsh, is sometimes heard rhyming with *store* but more correct speakers pronounce it regularly, rhyming with *poor.*'

diffusing in northern English today. Spence has /uː/ in all the words with final /k/, but Walker agrees with him in this, whilst Burn and Sheridan have this set split, but in different ways. Bronstein and Sheldon (1951) carried out an exercise involving the comparison of a smaller number of words with ME /oː/ in seven eighteenth-century dictionaries including Sheridan (1789) and Walker (1791) and fifteen from the nineteenth century. They conclude:

Most variation of all appears in the -ook words, now, in American dictionaries, stabilized to [ʊ]. The pronunciation [u] predominates slightly for most of these words in the eighteenth century, although *look, shook* and the disyllable *crooked* favor [ʊ]. By the nineteenth century [u] is passing out and [ʊ] has become the favored sound in all the *ook* words exept *nook*. This shift seems to have occurred without occasioning much comment, favorable or adverse, among dictionary editors. In the eighteenth century, Walker gives [u] for all the *ook* words. Jones, who in almost all other respects follows Walker, protests mildly that 'Mr. Walker has marked as similar sounds the double *o* in *look* and *tooth, took* and *tool,* though in strictness there is no smaller difference between them than between *long* and *short* ... (Preface, p. iii)   (Bronstein and Sheldon 1951: 89)

In Appendix 5*a* we see that Burn has the most instances of /ʊ/, showing this pronunciation in *book* and all its derivatives, *brook, cook, cookery, look, nook, overlook,* and *partook* (he also has it in *took,* which does not appear in the *Grand Repository*). He has /uː/ in *betook, crook, crooked, flook, hook,* and *hooked.* The only inconsistency here is between *took* and *partook* with /ʊ/ as against *betook* with /uː/. Sheridan has fewer instances of /ʊ/ before /k/ and is more consistent, with *look, overlook, betook, partook, took,* and *shook* (not present in Burn's dictionary) all having /ʊ/. When we look at the evidence provided by Bronstein and Sheldon,[26] we see that such variation is very common in the eighteenth century, for Kenrick (1773) and Perry (1788) both have /ʊ/ in *book, brook, cook, hook, look,* and *shook,* whilst Perry also has it in *crook, crooked,* and *took.* Significantly, the earliest dictionary examined by Bronstein and Sheldon, Johnston (1772), shows no evidence of /ʊ/ before /k/. This suggests that Walker was here recommending what might well have been conservative usage in London at the time, probably because it satisfied his feeling for analogy (/uː/ was, for him, the normal pronunciation of ⟨oo⟩), and that /uː/ in *hook, cook,* etc. was not yet diagnostically northern. Spence's categorical use of /uː/ in this context accords with that of his nearest contemporary Johnston (1772), and is likewise probably conservative rather than specifically northern.

If we look at the other contexts in which variation between /ʊ/ and /uː/ occurs, once again Burn shows more instances of /ʊ/ than Sheridan. He has /ʊ/ before nasals in *coom, coomb,* and *loom;* before fricatives in *loose* (adj.), *loose* (vb.), *lose, looseness, sooth, soothsayer* (but not *forsooth*); and word-/

[26] Bronstein and Sheldon (1951) used later editions of some of the eighteenth-century dictionaries than those to which I have referred.

morpheme-finally in *ado* (but not *outdo*), *to*, *into*, *together*, *toward*, *towardly*, *towards*. Sheridan, on the other hand, has /ʊ/ in *forsooth* but not in *sooth*, *soothsayer*, *to*, and *together*. (In *toward*, *-s -ly*, Sheridan, like Walker, has the pronunciation /toːrdz/ etc.) Bronstein and Sheldon show no evidence of /ʊ/ before nasals or fricatives, and it is possible that Burn is showing genuine uncertainty as to the distribution of long and short variants here, especially when we consider that he actually gives *coom* in his Introduction (1786: 4) as an example of his vowel 4 (/uː/). The variation in *to-* words could perhaps be explained another way: in a pronouncing dictionary, words are cited in isolation, whereas in continuous speech they may vary according to context. Walker (1791) says as much in his note under *to*: 'What has been observed of the word *the*, respecting the length of the *e* before a vowel, and its shortness before a consonant, is perfectly applicable to the preposition and the adverb *to*.' On the other hand, these inconsistencies, as well as that in Appendix 5*b* (*hood* and *manhood* with /uː/ but *falsehood* with /ʊ/) could be the result of 'interference' from Scots in Burn's case. It would appear that eighteenth-century observers such as Walker were already aware of the effects of the Scottish Vowel Length Rule. As Aitken (1979: 101–2) points out: 'This is a very pervasive and very characteristically Scottish rule . . . Among the effects are the opposition in Scots and Scottish Standard English between such pairs as *brewed* [bruːd] and *brood* [brud] . . . most Scots speakers operate it in their everyday Standard English, *as one of those provincial factors which the eighteenth-century anglicisers failed to eliminate*' (emphasis added). English observers, today as in the eighteenth century, tend to perceive the effects of this rule as a failure on the part of Scots to differentiate vowels which are phonemically long or short in English usage. Amongst those who commented on this aspect of Scots usage in the eighteenth century is Kenrick, who commented that 'one of the chief differences between the Scotch and English gentlemen in the pronunciation of English (is) laying the accent on the vowel, instead of the consonant, by which means they make syllables long, that are short with us' (1773: 42). Likewise, Walker (1791: p. xi) includes the following observation in his section on 'Rules to be Observed by the Natives of Scotland':

With respect to quantity, it may be observed that the Scotch pronounce almost all their accented vowels long. Thus, if I am not mistaken they would pronounce . . . *subject*, *soobject*. . . . In addition to what has been said, it may be observed that *oo* in *food*, *mood*, *moon*, *soon*, &c. which ought always to have a long sound, is generally shortened in Scotland to that middle sound of the *u* in *bull*, and it must be remembered that *wool*, *wood*, *good*, *hood*, *stood*, *foot* are the only words where this sound of *oo* ought to take place.

Burn's distribution of long /uː/ and short /ʊ/ is too inconsistent to show the effects of the Scottish Vowel Length Rule *per se*, but, if this rule was operative in his own speech and yet not in the 'correct' variety which he was attempting to describe, the kind of confusion hinted at by Walker might occur.

Turning to Appendix 5*b*, we see that all the words which involve 'early shortening' have /ʌ/ for Walker, Sheridan, and Burn, as we might have expected from our discussion in 5.4. The only anomalous cases here are *soot* and *sooty*, which, as Bronstein and Sheldon show, were notoriously variable in the eighteenth century and later. Here, Burn and Sheridan have /ʌ/ in *soot*, Burn also has /ʌ/ in *sooty*, where Sheridan has /uː/, Spence has /ʊ/ in both, and Walker has /uː/ in both. According to Bronstein and Sheldon, Kenrick (1773), Perry (1788), and P.D. (1796) all show the same pattern as Burn. This pronunciation of *soot* is thus not necessarily a scotticism: in this case, the unrounded vowel could well have resulted from early shortening of ME /oː/ in this word, just as in *blood*, and *flood*. Wyld (1936: 237) gives evidence of early shortening to [ʊ] or even [ʌ] from Daines (1640), whilst Walker explicitly condemns this pronunciation as a vulgarism rather than a scotticism in his rule 309, thus: '*Soot* is vulgarly pronounced so as to rhyme with *but*, *hut*, etc., but ought to have its long regular sound, rhyming with *boot* as we always hear it in the compound *sooty*' (1791: 35). However, Wyld (1936: 239) observes 'within my own memory, some old-fashioned speakers of RS still sound [sat][27] instead of the now universally-received [sut]'. This suggests that, as with *butcher*, Burn is not so much showing evidence of Scottish influence here as attesting a pronunciation which existed in the usage of educated speakers in London as well as in Glasgow, but which Walker, with his predilection for analogy, refuses to sanction.

What this examination of words involving ME /oː/ has shown us, then, is that much variation existed in the eighteenth century, especially between /uː/ and /ʊ/. Walker's pronunciations seem very conservative when we see from the evidence in Burn and Sheridan, as well as from Bronstein and Sheldon (1951), that the shortening before /k/ particularly seemed to be diffusing lexically at the time. Apart from the possible influence of the Scottish Vowel Length Rule, though, there is no evidence that continued use of /uː/ was seen as a northern characteristic in the eighteenth century: in this respect, Spence's usage, like that of Johnston (1772) and, indeed, of Walker, is simply conservative.

5.6. YOD-DROPPING, OR 'SINKING THE LIQUEFACTION'

5.6.1. *Introduction*

The next sound change that I wish to consider here is the dropping of /j/ before /uː/ in reflexes of ME /yː, iu, ɛu/ and /eu/. According to Dobson, by the beginning of the sixteenth century, reflexes of all of these varied between

---

[27] Wyld's [a] is the equivalent of RP [ʌ].

[iu] and [yː]. Dobson (1957: 712) goes on to say that in ENE, the following changes take place:

(a) The more common pronunciation [iu] gradually changes to [juː].
(b) Towards the end of the seventeenth century, there is a tendency for the second element of [iu] or more likely [juː] to be fronted in the direction of [yː]; this tendency still persists in PresE.
(c) After the development of [juː], combinative changes occur as a result of which the [j] disappears and the vowel remains as [uː], as in *sure*; similarly after the consonant [j] the diphthong [iu], in tending to become [juː], is reduced to [uː] by the coalescence of the two [j]'s; and after certain consonants or combinations of consonants there is a tendency to eliminate the [j] for greater ease of pronunciation, as in *chute, Jew, rheum, rude, sewer, lute*, and (in some forms of seventeenth-century English and present American English) in *duke* and *tune*.
(d) The variant pronunciation [yː] remains unchanged during the sixteenth and seventeenth centuries in stressed syllables, but becomes increasingly rarer.

In unstressed syllables, alongside the development to /juː/, there existed a variant pronunciation with /ɪ/ or /ə/. Particularly before final /r/, evidence for this becomes increasingly common in the homophone lists of late-seventeenth-century orthoepists such as Cooper (1687), who has, for example, *centaury, century; ordure, order; pastor, pasture;* and *picture, pick't her* as homophones. In this context, the pronunciation with /ɪ/ or /ə/ is not stigmatized in the seventeenth century, but in other environments it is less common in the sevententh century. Cooper gives *scrupelous* in his Latin text (1685) as 'facilitas causa', but in the English edition (1687) as 'barbarous speaking'.[28] As we move into the eighteenth century, though, criticism of the pronunciation /ɪr/ or /ər/ becomes more widespread: according to Sheldon (1938: 275). 'Swift . . . writes creeter to indicate vulgar pronunciation' in his *Polite Conversations*.

Likewise, much of the seventeenth-century evidence for the palatalization of preceding alveolar consonants in (*c*) is from 'vulgar' or dialectal sources: Cooper, for instance, in his semi-phonetic notation, lists *shugar* with the [j] assimilated, as a 'barbarous' pronunciation. By the end of the eighteenth century, this palatalization, with its subsequent assimilation of the /j/, is accepted even by Walker in *sugar* and with palatalization but not assimilation in *sure*, but elsewhere it is heavily stigmatized, at least in stressed syllables.

Yod-dropping is a sound change (or perhaps a set of sound changes) which is still diffusing in the twentieth century. The most extreme case of yod-dropping exists in the dialects of East Anglia, where even *human* and

---

[28] The same could be said of all the pronunciations which Cooper designates 'barbarous' in his English edition. I do not believe that Cooper had a sudden attack of prescriptivism between 1685 and 1687: it is more likely that the phrase *facilitas causa* loses (or gains) something in the translation. After all, one man's *facilitas* is another man's laziness.

beautiful are pronounced /'huːmən/ and /'buːtifəl/, but yod-dropping after /d/ and /n/ in, for example, *duke* and *new*, like other 'Cockney' features, has passed into the 'Estuary English'[29] of young middle-class persons, particularly (though not exclusively) in the south and east. Looking at works written earlier in the century, we see variant pronunciations or, indeed, pronunciations with /juː/ or /ju/ only, given for words which more recent dictionaries record with only /uː/ or /ʊ/. Jespersen (1909–49: 382) states that after /r/ 'the [j] now is only heard in weak syllables: *erudite* ['erjudait], *querulous* ['kwerjuləs] . . . Note the difference between *garrulous* ['gærjuləs] and *garrulity* [gə'ruːliti].' As we shall see, this rule is followed in the eighteenth century by Sheridan, but Collins (1992) gives only /'ɛrʊdait/, /'gærʊləs/, /gæ'ruːlɪtɪ/, and for *querulous* has the first pronunciation given as /'kwerʊləs/, with /'kwɛrjʊləs/ as a variant. Both Jespersen (1909–49: 382) and Strang (1970: 118) write of variation in words with preceding /l/, such as *luminous, lute, salute, revolution*;[30] yet again, the *CSED* gives only /uː/ for all these words.

5.6.2. *Evidence from eighteenth-century pronouncing dictionaries*

Since this sound change seems not to have worked its way fully through the lexicon today, and since the usage is still variable even with regard to some individual words, such as *querulous*, we might expect to find even more variability in eighteenth-century usage. Comparing the pronunciations given by Spence, Walker, Sheridan, and Burn for words with ME /yː, iu, ɛu/, and /eu/, I found that variation only occurred:

1. When the vowel in question was unstressed, and the variation referred to in §5.6.1 between 'full' pronunciations with /juː/ and 'reduced' ones with /ə/ or /ɪ/ persisted.

2. In words recently borrowed from French, such as *connoisseur* (1732), for which Spence has /kɒnɪz'juːr/, Walker has /kɒnɪ'seːr/, Sheridan has /kɒnɪ'ʃuːr/, and Burn /kɒnɪ'sʊr/. Walker (1791) has a note to this word which probably indicates that the extreme variation here is due to uncertainty about how to pronounce what was still a 'foreign' word: 'This word is perfectly French and, though in very general use, is not naturalised. The pronunciation of it given here is but a very awkward one, but perhaps as good a one as we have letters in our language to express it; for the French *eu* is not to be found among any of our English vowel or diphthongal sounds.'

3. Where the preceding consonant is either already palatal, as in *june*,

---

[29] Mugglestone (1995: 96) writes: 'Estuary English, first described in 1984 in the *Times Educational Supplement*, is usually characterized as a "classless" blend of RP and "Cockney" spoken in the area around London and the Thames valley and marked by a range of "proscribed" (though common) articulations such as the use of the glottal stop or the use of /t, d/ deletion.'

[30] I can vividly recall Barbara Strang herself using the pronunciation /'ljuːnətɪk/.

juice, or is an alveolar which becomes palatalized, as in *super, luxurious*, etc. Here, there is variation between those who give pronunciations with the /j/ assimilated into the palatal and those who do not, as well as between those who do and do not show palatalization of preceding alveolars.

4. The only other context in which a substantial amount of variation is found is that in which the vowel follows /r/. (Dobson (1957: 707) includes /r/ in a list of palatal consonants after which /j/ tends to be assimilated, but, because not all pronunciations of /r/ are or were palatal, and because variation after this consonant is so widespread in the eighteenth century, I shall deal with it separately.) Referring to the period 1570–1770, Strang (1970: 118) writes: 'The closing decades of this period also saw a tendency to drop /j/ before /uː/. After /r/ usage varied in the 1760's, but the /j/ has now completely vanished (*rude, crude, crew, fruit*, etc.)' As we shall see, this variation persisted throughout the eighteenth century and is displayed very clearly in the comparison between our four pronouncing dictionaries.

In other contexts, there is little variation between our four sources: Strang (1970: 118) refers to 'divided usage' after /l/, but Spence, Walker, Sheridan, and Burn show /juː/ regularly in this environment. Likewise, there is no sign of yod-dropping after /n/ or /d/, perhaps not surprisingly, as this was already highly stigmatized: Walker (1791: 32) writes of the 'diphthong' ⟨ew⟩: 'This diphthong is pronounced like long *u* and is almost always regular. There is a corrupt pronunciation of it like *oo* chiefly in London, where we sometimes hear *dew* and *new*, pronounced as if written *doo* and *noo*.'

5.6.3. *Variation in final unstressed syllables*

As we shall see in §5.7, the representation of unstressed vowels in the *Grand Repository* is a very complicated matter, and it would be beyond the scope of this book to deal with it exhaustively. Here, I can only point out areas of variation both within Spence's *Grand Repository* and between this and the other three pronouncing dictionaries examined here. As I have already indicated in §5.6.1, the use of /ə/ or /ɪ/[31] rather than /juː/ in unstressed syllables was beginning to be stigmatized by the early eighteenth century. Later in the century, opinions vary, but on the whole, the 'reduced' pronunciations are viewed as informal at the best, and vulgar at the worst. Kenrick (1773: 32), writing of the tendency 'even among the politest speakers, of giving the *t* alone the sound of *ch*' in words such as *nature, creature*, goes on to add: 'For my own part, nevertheless, I cannot discover the euphony; and though the contrary mode be reprobated, as vulgar, by certain mighty fine speakers, I think it more conformable to the general scheme of English pronunciation.' Kenrick, then, suggests that the palatalization in

---

[31] As we shall see, Spence varies between {ɫ} and {ʟ} in his representation of unstressed vowels: this variation is a complex matter, which I shall attempt to deal with in §5.7.

words like *nature* is 'a species of affectation that is to be discountenanced; unless we are to impute it to the tendency in the metropolitan pronunciation of prefacing the sound of *u* with a *y* consonant; or, which is the same thing, converting the *t* or *s* preceding into *ch* or *zh*, as in *nature, measure* etc'. Kenrick's use of terms such as *mighty fine* and *affectation* suggest here a reluctant acknowledgement that /ˈneːtjuːr/ or /ˈneːtʃuːr/ are the more fashionable pronunciations, but that he prefers /ˈneːtər/.

Walker (1791: 23), as might be expected, is less equivocal on this matter: his 'Principle 179' states:

There is an incorrect pronunciation of this letter [= ⟨u⟩] when it ends a syllable, not under the accent which prevails, not only among the vulgar, but is sometimes found in better company; and that is giving the *u* an obscure sound, which confounds it with vowels of a very different kind. Thus we not infrequently hear *singular, regular* and *particular* pronounced as if written *sing-e-lar, reg-e-lar,* and *par-tick-e-lar.*

Under *nature*, Walker writes 'there is a vulgar pronunciation of this word as if written *na-ter*, which cannot be too carefully avoided'. In fact, the balance tips in favour of the pronunciation with /juː/: where pronunciations with /ə/ are mentioned as acceptable, this is as an alternative to what was seen by some as the equally if not more vulgar pronunciation involving palatalization of the preceding consonant. Thus the author of *A Caution to Gentlemen Who Use Sheridan's Dictionary* (1790: 6, quoted in Sheldon 1938: 306–7) admits that 'the natural propensity is to abbreviate -u- and to pronounce the word thus nètŭr' (= ['netər]: Sheldon.) However, Sheldon (1938: 307) adds 'the author goes on to observe that in polite pronunciation, the u̱ is long and a y̱ is sounded before it, ['netjur]. But -TSHUR and -TSHOUS cannot be tolerated, and if a foreigner or native "be ambitious for passing for an English gentleman, let him avoid with utmost care, Mr. Sheridan's -SH-" '. Thus pronunciations like /ˈneːtər/ are, on the whole, regarded as vulgar, but are preferable to the palatalization of /t/ and subsequent assimilation of /j/ involved in, for example, /ˈneːtʃər/.

To find out Spence's representation of every word in which reflexes of ME /yː, iu, ɛu/ or /eu/ are unstressed would be very difficult using OCP, as he uses several different symbols in these words ({U}, {Ʊ}, and {Ŧ}). Instead, I have made a manual search for all the words ending in ⟨ure⟩ in traditional orthography. These words, with their representations in the four pronouncing dictionaries, appear in Appendix 6*a*. There are 78 words in the list here, one of which (*dorture*[32]) appears only in the *Grand Repository*, and a further two of which (*decocture, defeature*) do not appear in Burn. For purposes of comparison here, we shall exclude the words which either already have a palatal consonant before the vowel (*injure, perjure*), and those which have a

---

[32] The *OED* marks this as 'obs. ex. hist'; after 1700, the more usual spelling is ⟨dorter⟩.

preceding consonant which tends not to be palatalized (*epicure, failure, figure, transfigure, tenure*). This means that we can compare the four dictionaries according to how many words have yod-dropping, reduction to /ə/, and no palatalization (the /ˈneːtər/ pattern); those which have no palatalization, yod-dropping, or reduction (the /ˈneːtjuːr/ pattern), and those which have palatalization, yod-dropping, and reduction (the pattern most common in PDE: the /ˈneːtʃər/ pattern). In addition, Walker has a strange 'compromise' pattern, involving palatalization but no yod-dropping or reduction (the /ˈneːtʃjuːr/ pattern.) Out of 71 words for Spence, 70 for Walker and Sheridan, and 68 for Burn, the pattern is as shown in Table 5.2. With regard to yod-dropping and palatalization of the preceding consonant, Sheridan is by far the most advanced of the four orthoepists, showing a pronunciation close to that of PDE in the vast majority of cases. Burn and Spence are both conservative, but in different ways: Burn appears to favour a pronunciation (the /ˈneːtər/ type), which was accepted in the seventeenth century but was becoming stigmatized in the eighteenth. However, when we look at Burn's (1786: 5–6) introductory remarks, we see that he is not entirely happy with his representations of these words in the dictionary:

Wherever the termination -*ure* is marked according to the first class of vocal sounds above given, the *u* takes the sound of *y* consonant before it; as in na[12]ture[1], which is pronounced na[12]tyur[1]; meas[13]ure[1],–meas[13]yure[1] &c. And the same pronunciation is to be observed in their derivatives, as nat[11]ur[1]al[11]–natyur-al; meas[13]ur[1]a[11]ble[0]–meas-yur-a-ble.There is another peculiarity in the pronunciation of the word *nature* and several others where *u* or *eau* follow *t* or *d*, as *education, situate, situation, piteous,* &c, which are pronounced as if a faint sound of ch or j came between the *t* or *d* and *u*. Thus na-tchure, ed-chu-ca-*ti*-on, sit-chu-a-*ti*-on, or ed-ju-ca-*ti*-on &c, but this is so delicately pronounced, that it is almost impossible to represent it by characters.

The clue here is in the last sentence: Burn transcribes *nature* etc as na[12] ture[1] (= /ˈneːtər/) etc., because, whilst his system of placing numbers over the

Table 5.2. *Comparison of words with <ure> ending from Appendix 6a*

Dictionary	Pattern				Total words
	/ˈneːtər/	/ˈneːtjuːr/	/ˈneːtʃər/	/ˈneːtʃjuːr/	
Spence	3	56	12	0	71
Walker	0	12	0	58	70
Sheridan	0	2	61	0	63
Burn	47	19	2	0	68

Note: The figures do not add up to 70 for Sheridan because he has a small number of words with different patterns: 3 words with /tʃuːr/ and 4 with /tʃʊr/, showing palatalization and yod-dropping but not reduction In each case, I suspect that the lack of reduction is due to secondary stress.

vowels of the actual dictionary entry (as opposed to respelling), is perfectly adequate for the representation of the vowels themselves, he runs into difficulties when 'extra' consonants are pronounced, or the consonants are modified. We cannot really tell from the above statement whether Burn really wishes the words in Appendix 6a which he has transcribed as {-ture[1]}, etc., to be pronounced /tər/, /tjər/, or /tʃər/: his transcriptions are only really reliable as an indication of whether the vowel has been reduced to schwa (vowel 1) or not (vowel 6 = /juː/). Spence, of course, has no such problems regarding the capabilities of his transcription system: he clearly favours a pronunciation that avoids assimilation, yod-dropping, *and* reduction (the /ˈneːtjuːr/ pattern). This pronunciation would have been beyond reproach in the late eighteenth century: all three of the other orthoepists studied here use it for at least a few words and, indeed, something very like it is still recorded today in, for instance *ordure*, for which *CSED* gives /ˈɔːdjʊə/. This is almost certainly the pronunciation that Spence would have heard in the rhetorical style used by the clergymen who seem to have provided his model of 'correct' speech.

So Sheridan is the most advanced of our four orthoepists with regard to the pronunciation of the words in Appendix 6a, and Spence is the most conservative, but what are we to make of Walker's favoured pattern, in which palatalization occurs without consequent assimilation or reduction? The extent of palatalization in Walker's representations of these words might seem surprising, given the extent to which this is condemned by, for example, the author of *A Caution*. However, Walker (1791) saw this as allowable if not preferable, in post-tonic syllables: under *nature*, he notes: 'The sibilation and aspiration of *t* in this and similar words, provided they are not too coarsely pronounced, are so far from being a deformity to our language, by increasing the number of hissing sounds, as some have insinuated, that they are a real beauty; and by a certain coalescence and flow of the sound, contribute greatly to the smoothness and volubility of pronunciation.' In fact, Walker here is standing by one of his principles of analogy: that assimilations, or departures from the 'true' sound of a letter, may occur only when the sound concerned is not under the main stress. So we can expect to find palatalization in these unstressed contexts. But the retention of /j/, or even a diphthong /iu/ after the palatalized consonant, here does seem rather artificial, and it is noticeable that Walker is the only one of our four orthoepists to show this pronunciation. In Appendix 6a, I have marked with an asterisk words for which Walker actually gives the transcription {yu[1]r}, i.e. /jjuːr/ or posibly /jiur/. Even if Walker's {u[1]} is intended to be /iu/ rather than /juː/, these pronunciations sound very stilted. The most likely explanation for them is that Walker's recommended pronunciation is a compromise, allowing palatalization, because his rule of analogy states that this can happen in post-tonic syllables, but not allowing yod-dropping or reduction, which are viewed as 'incorrect'.

5.6.4. *Palatalization and variation after palatal consonants in stressed syllables*

In words with palatal consonants not derived from alveolars—for example, those with initial /dʒ/—Spence, Walker, and Sheridan regularly show the yod 'dropped' or, rather, assimilated into the palatal: thus all three have the pronunciations /dʒuːn, dʒuːs/ for *June, juice,* but Burn has /dʒjuːn, dʒjuːs/. Once again, Burn is the most conservative of the four orthoepists, but, as we shall see in our discussion of variation after /r/ in this case, it is probably an instance in Burn of a particularly Scottish hypercorrection.

We have already seen that the author of *A Caution to Gentlemen Who Use Sheridan's Dictionary* attacked Sheridan for his palatalizations. and, in our discussion of the words in Appendix 6*a*, that Sheridan had more instances of palatalization than Spence or Burn before the unstressed ⟨ure⟩ ending. It is certainly the case that Sheridan admitted this palatalization of alveolars before earlier /juː/ to an extreme degree: he has palatalization of /s/ to /ʃ/ with consequent loss of following /j/ in all words with the prefix *super-*, whereas Spence, Walker, and Burn all have /sjuː/ here, and in all similar words except *sugar, sure* and *surety,* in which /ʃ/ occurs in PDE. Likewise, the author of *A Vocabulary of Such Words in the English Language as are of Dubious or Unsettled Accentuation* (1797) writes under *tune*: 'I have followed Mr. Walker in the pronunciation of this word [= /tjuːn/]; Mr. Sheridan shounds it tsho³n [= /tʃuːn/]; and this sound he gives also to the *tu* in *Tuneful, Tuneless, Tuner, Tunick, Tunicle, Tutelage, Tutelary, Tutelar, Tutor, Tutorage,* and *Tutoress,* while Mr. Walker preserves the pure sound of the *tu* as in *Tune,* above marked' (quoted from Sheldon 1938: LXXX). Indeed, as this suggests, Walker, but also Spence and Burn, have /tjuː/ in all of the above words that occur in their dictionaries. The author of *A Caution* and, indeed, Jespersen (1909–49: 344, 347) attribute Sheridan's pronunciation of words such as *tune* and *suicide* to interference from Irish English. In many cases, the accusation of 'Irishism' is a knee-jerk reaction from critics who simply did not agree with Sheridan's recommendations, but, in this case, there may be some substance in it. Jespersen (1909–49: 347) points out that 'B. Shaw writes *Choosda* and *schoopid* as Irish for *Tuesday* and *stupid* (John Bull's Isl. 12, 38)'.[33] On the other hand, initial /tʃ/ and /ʃ/ for /tj/ and /sj/ are attested in

---

[33] I am informed (Karen Corrigan, personal communication) that this palatalization does occur in Irish, but only in the Ulster dialects, so that it is very unlikely that the Dublin-born Sheridan would have been influenced by it. What is more likely is that the palatalization was a colloquialism common in London, which may well have been widely used in less careful speech, then as now. Another Irish author who uses the same semi-phonetic spelling to signal the same pronunciation is Samuel Beckett. In his novel *Watt*, we find the following: 'We are the Galls, father and son, and we are come, what is more, all the way from town, to *choon* the piano' (1972: 67; 1st edn., 1953; emphasis added). Beckett deals with such linguistic issues as the arbitrary nature of the sign in this novel, which has a great deal of linguistic experimentation. However,

seventeenth-century English (as opposed to Irish) sources: Dobson (1957: 706–7) shows *suit: Shute: shoot* as homophones in Hodges; and *tulip: julip*[34] as well as *dew: due: jew* in Brown (none of our sources shows initial /dj/ becoming /dʒ/). These instances are, however, few and far between and in homophone lists, which, as Dobson explains, often give more colloquial pronunciations. If Sheridan's palatalizations in *supreme, tune*, etc. are not Irishisms, perhaps they represent a more colloquial kind of London English.

What we discover from comparing Spence, Walker, Sheridan, and Burn with regard to words in which a palatal consonant occurs or is created by palatalization is that Burn, with /juː/ even after palatals like /dʒ/, is at one end of the spectrum, Sheridan, with his palatalization even in initial position before a stressed vowel, is at the other end, and Walker and Spence, with some instances of palatalization, notably before unstressed vowels, lie in between.

5.6.5. *Variation after /r/*

As indicated above, the greatest degree of variation between /juː/ and /uː/, both within certain pronouncing dictionaries and between the four studied here, is in the environment with a preceding /r/ as in *rude, peruse*, etc. Whilst Walker sees /juː/ as the regular sound of long ⟨u⟩,[35] as well as ⟨ew⟩ and ⟨eu⟩, he finds the pronunciation /uː/ acceptable after /r/, for he writes of the 'diphthong' ⟨ui⟩ : 'When this diphthong is preceded by *r*, it is pronounced like *oo*, thus *bruise, cruise, fruit, bruit, recruit* are pronounced as if written *broose, crooze, broot, froot, recroot*' (1791: 39) This categorical statement refers only to orthographic ⟨ui⟩: in other cases where earlier /juː/ or /iu/ follows /r/, Walker's usage varies: he has /uː/ in e.g. *brute, intrude, prune* but /juː/ in *frugal, peruse, quadruple*, so that Jespersen (1909–49: 382) is probably right in identifying Batchelor (1809) as the first to state categorically that 'the long *u* (yuw), properly pronounced, never immediately follows *r* in the same syllable'. In fact, as Strang (1970: 182) suggests, there was much uncertainty and variation between /juː/ and /uː/ after /r/ in the late eighteenth century. According to Jespersen, Sheridan has /uː/ after /r/ in *crude, crucify, cruet, cruise, crew, true, fruit, rue*, etc., and Johnston (1764) shows some inconsistency in that he has a rule that /uː/ should be used after /d/, /l/, /n/, /r/, /s/, and /t/, and gives *rude* as an example of this, but, in his dictionary

although the number of characters with Irish names (O'Meldon, MacStern, Fitzwein) suggests an Irish setting, it is not clear whether *choon* is intended to be specifically Irish.

[34] *Julip* here presumably means *julep* 'a sweet drink, variously prepared and sometimes medicated' *CSED*. Spence has *Julap* (pronounced /ˈdʒuːlɪp/) with this meaning. Dobson here gives this without comment as evidence that *tulip* was pronounced with initial /tʃ/, but since *julip* is only ever shown with a voiced initial consonant, the pairing can only be 'near alike'.

[35] The expected 'spelling pronunciation' of ⟨u⟩ when long would be /juː/ or /iu/, because this is the name of the letter: according to Dobson (1957: 703), the name of ⟨u⟩ had been so pronounced since 1528.

entry for *rude*, the pronunciation indicated is /juː/. On the other hand, Johnston gives no indication that /uː/ is 'vulgar'. When we turn to the Scottish orthoepist Elphinston, however, a different attitude is apparent: Jespersen (1909–49: 382) quotes him as writing in 1787 that it is 'vulgar indolence or bluntness' to 'sink the liquefaction' in *peruse*, *rule*, making them *per-ooz*, *rool*. If the dropping of /j/, which Elphinston refers to as 'sinking the liquefaction', was most advanced in London, where in vulgar usage it had progressed to words such as *dew* and *new*, perhaps in Scotland a more conservative norm prevailed, in which /j/ was retained even after /r/ in the polite, educated usage of the 'provincial' middle classes. Sylvester Douglas provides further enlightenment on this issue: he has /juː/ in *excuse*, *use*, *profuse*, *humility*, *Hume*, *human*, *curious*, *unity*, *pure*, *pew*, *dew*, and *hue* as well as in a handful of words in which present-day RP has /uː/: *Bruce*, *spruce*, *truce*, *recluse* (notice that three out of these last four have /r/ before the vowel). Charles Jones (1991: 63) points out that Douglas regards the Scots tendency to use /juː/ in the items *blue*, *pursue*, and *luxury* as well as *build* and *burial* as 'an unacceptable hypercorrection', and goes on to quote Sir Walter Scott's observation in *The Heart of Midlothian* (first published 1818):

The Magistrates were closely interrogated before the House of Peers concerning the particulars of the Mob, and the *patois* in which these functionaries made their answers, sounded strange in the ears of the southern nobles. The Duke of Newcastle having demanded to know with what kind of shot the guard which Porteous commanded had loaded their muskets, was answered naively: 'Ow, just sic as ane shoots *dukes* and *fools* with'. This reply was considered as a contempt of the House of Lords, and the Provost would have suffered accordingly, but that the Duke of Argyll explained, that the expression properly rendered into English meant *ducks and water fowls*. (Scott 1971: 207 n., quoted in C. Jones 1991: 63–4)

If Burn and Spence were representing conservative varieties such as might well have been used by modified speakers in eighteenth-century Scotland and northern England, we might expect to find evidence for the conservative or even hypercorrect use of /juː/ in contrast to Walker's /uː/. The examples quoted by Jespersen might suggest that Sheridan, on the other hand, tends to go further than Walker in his use of /uː/. In order to discover whether this is the case, I have taken all the words in the *Grand Repository* in which ME /yː, iu, ɛu/ or /eu/ (or, indeed /iu/ from later sources[36]) occur after /r/. These appear in Appendices 6b–d.

   Out of 110 words in Appendices 6b–d, Sheridan has only 13 with /juː/, Walker has 29, Spence has 59, and Burn has a near-categorical 102. If we discount the words marked n.a., which do not occur in one or more of the

---

[36] According to Dobson (1957: 703) 'the English pronunciation of Latin *u* in an open syllable . . . develops with ME [yː], with which it is identical'. Thus relatively late latinate coinages like *eruginous* (1646) belong here.

other dictionaries, Burn retains the /j/ in 102 out of 108 words, or 94.44%; Spence himself retains it in 53.6%; Walker in 29 out of 107 or 27.1%, and Sheridan in 13 out of 107 or a mere 12.14%. This shows a reluctance to 'sink the liquefaction' which seems to increase with distance from the capital, with Spence having almost twice as many instances of /juː/ as Walker, and Burn almost twice as many as Spence. The difference between Walker and Sheridan is less striking, and probably indicates that Sheridan was, in this instance, less conservative than Walker. If we look at the few instances in which Sheridan does have /juː/, we find that he never has /juː/ where Walker or Burn have /uː/. The words concerned are: *congruence*, *congruent*, *congruous*, *erudition*, *eruginous*, *ferula*, *garrulity*, *garrulous*, *peruke*, *peruse*, *purulency*, *purulent*, and *virulent*. In all but *eruginous*, *garrulity*, *peruke*, and *peruse*, the /juː/ is unstressed, and it is noteworthy that, whilst Sheridan has /juː/ in *congruence*, *congruent*, and *congruous*, he has /uː/ in *congruity* when the vowel is stressed. Thus, Sheridan comes closest of all our four orthoepists to the distribution described by Jespersen (1909–49: 385): 'Before a completely unstressed vowel, [j] in [juː] is not left out.' In many of these words, /juː/ was still possible until relatively recently: the fact that Jespersen sees /juː/ as the norm in words such as *erudition*, *garrulous*, *purulency*, *purulous*, and *virulent*, whilst the *CSED* has /juː/ in none of them, perhaps indicates that, whilst stress was once a conditioning factor in the diffusion of this sound change, it no longer is. In fact, Burn never has his vowel 4 (/uː/) in any of the words in Appendices 6*b* or *c*: in the few cases in which his vowel 6 (/juː/) is not used, he has his short vowel 3—for example, in *fruit* and *truth*. Certainly, our findings show that Shields (1974: 59) was not quite correct in stating that Spence had 'maximal distribution of /juː/'.

The results from Burn and, to a lesser extent, Spence do suggest here that these northern English and Scots orthoepists are recommending a pronunciation which by Walker's standards would be conservative or even hypercorrect, but, by the standards of a Scottish orthoepist like Elphinston, avoids the 'vulgar indolence' of 'sinking the liquefaction'. Sheridan, on the other hand, has a very advanced pronunciation, with a distribution of /uː/ and /juː/ close to that of earlier twentieth-century English. Perhaps here, as with the palatalization of /s/ and /t/, he was giving evidence of a more colloquial pronunciation current in London in the eighteenth century.

5.7. UNSTRESSED VOWELS

5.7.1. *Introduction*

The pronunciation of unstressed vowels was a potential minefield for eighteenth-century speakers who aspired to 'correct' pronunciation. Walker (1791: 23) states this quite clearly:

It may, indeed, be observed, that there is scarcely any thing more distinguishes a person of mean and good education than the pronunciation of the unaccented vowels. When vowels are under the accent, the prince and the lowest of the people, with very few exceptions, pronounce them in the same manner; but the unaccented vowels in the mouth of the former have a distinct, open and specific sound, while the latter often totally sink them, or change them, into some other sound. Those, therefore, who wish to pronounce elegantly, must be particularly attentive to the unaccented vowels; as a neat pronunciation of these, forms one of the greatest beauties of speaking.

If further testimony is needed to the salience of unstressed vowels at this time, we need look no further than *A Caution to Gentlemen Who Use Sheridan's Dictionary* (1790), in which, according to Sheldon (1938: 308), 'Sheridan's critic disapproves of the fact that Sheridan makes no distinction in the pronunciation of unstressed syllables, writing <u>cavurn</u>, <u>comunur</u>, <u>culpuble</u>, all with the same sound'. Remarks like these have led scholars such as Sheldon (1938, 1947) and Shields (1973, 1974) to conclude that Walker was against the 'reduced' pronunciation of unstressed vowels. Sheldon (1947: 135) specifically sets Walker and Sheridan against each other as representing respectively 'idealized' and 'realistic' pronunciations: 'Not only does Walker want unstressed vowels pronounced, but he generally wants the full sound given to vowels which Sheridan, often properly, represents as reduced or obscure in value. Frequently, Walker tries to make the pronunciation of the unstressed syllable accord more closely with the spelling'. Shields (1973: 78) goes further in suggesting that 'the full, spelling pronunciation of unstressed syllables' was 'recommended by virtually all 18c writers (for example, of great importance, Sheridan 1780), who are on the whole unwilling to recommend anything like a schwa'. As we shall see, this overstates the case: the distribution of 'full' and 'reduced' pronunciations actually recommended in eighteenth-century pronouncing dictionaries was much more complex.

Contrary to Shields's suggestion, Jespersen (1909–49: 249) writes that 'from the 18th c. we have more or less unambiguous testimonies to the tendency towards obscuration' citing John Jones (1701), de Castro (1751), Johnston (1764), Elphinston (1765), and Walker (1791). However, evidence of a 'reduced' or 'obscure' pronunciation of unstressed vowels goes back at least to the sixteenth century and, if Wyld's (1936: 258) evidence from occasional spellings is to be believed, 'at least as early as the middle of the fifteenth century'. In these fifteenth-century spellings, the existence of a 'reduced' vowel is, according to Wyld, often signalled by a lack of consistency in the spelling of a vowel, such as the four different spellings of *staple* as ⟨stapell⟩, ⟨stapyll⟩, ⟨stapal⟩, ⟨stapul⟩ in the Cely Papers. It is very difficult to ascertain the value of the 'reduced' vowel from such evidence: does ⟨stapyll⟩, for instance, indicate indecision and suggest that all unstressed vowels were levelled under /ə/, or should we take it at face value as representing something like /steːpɪl/? As we shall see, both pronunciations were possible then and in the eighteenth century.

Wyld's early evidence is thus, like all evidence from 'occasional spellings', difficult to interpret and not necessarily reliable (see §3.2.2 for discussion of this). When we move on to the orthoepistic evidence from the sixteenth century, the picture is not much clearer, but there is, as Dobson (1957: 827 ff.) suggests, enough to indicate that reduction to /ə/ was general, at least in everyday, colloquial speech. With the sixteenth-century orthoepists, the evidence again seems to take the form of a tendency to substitute various spellings for each other: for instance 'Bullokar clearly used [ər] for ME *ĕr* (unstressed), for he confuses the sufixes *-er*, *-or* and *-our* (i.e. *-ŭr*), and uses the 'half-vowel' *r* to represent both ME unstressed *ĕr* and the combination [ə]-glide plus *r* (e.g. in *fire*)' (Dobson 1957: 868). Clearer, more direct evidence only becomes available from the seventeenth century onwards, for, as Dobson (1957: 867) points out, 'the identity of the vowel [ə] is not recognized by any orthoepist before Wallis'.

By the end of the seventeenth century, an identification of unstressed vowels with the 'obscure' or 'guttural' sound of ⟨u⟩ (i.e. /ʌ/?) is becoming common, and this continues to be the most usual description of them in the eighteenth century. That something like /ə/ was intended, at least for the 'reduced' vowel, is suggested by descriptions such as that of Abraham Tucker (1773: 14), quoted in Abercrombie (1965: 66):

This short '*u*' . . . is easiest pronounced of all the vowels . . . and therefore is a great favourite with my countrymen, who tho not lazy are very averse to trouble, wishing to do as much work with as little pain as possible. We can draw it out to a great length on particular occasions, as when the watchman calls 'past ten *u-u-u* clock', or when a man hesitates till he hits upon some hard name, as 'This account was sent by Mr *u-u-u* Schlotzikoff, a Russian.'

This is not to say that /ʌ/ and /ə/ did not exist as separate phonemes in the eighteenth century, merely that orthoepists had difficulty distinguishing between these two vowels, which, after all, are both central and unrounded.[37] Walker acknowledges the existence of an 'obscure' pronunciation of some unstressed vowels, and identifies it in his transcriptions with the 'short ⟨u⟩' of *but*, etc, but his descriptions of this sound suggest that he is not entirely happy with this identification. He first writes: 'The unaccented termination in *-ace*, whether nouns or verbs, have the *a* so short and obscure as to be nearly similar to the *u* in *us*', and then goes on as follows: 'The *e* in

---

[37] A coalescence of these two vowels occurs in some accents of present-day English. Wells (1982: 132) writes that 'in Wales and in some (higher-prestige) midlands and north-of-England accents, STRUT words have stressed [ə], in consequence of the STRUT-Schwa merger . . . Even in GenAm it may well be considered that stressed [ʌ] and unstressed [ə] are co-allophones of one phoneme.'

her is pronounced nearly like short *u*; and as we hear it in the unaccented terminations of *writer*, *reader*, &c, where we may observe, that the *r* being only a jar, and not a definite and distinct articulate like the other consonants, instead of stopping the vocal efflux of voice, lets it imperfectly pass, and so corrupts and alters the true sound of the vowel' (1791: 12–13). Here, Walker's use of the word *nearly* suggests that the unstressed vowel is not exactly the same as that in *us*, but that he can think of no better way of representing it. Elsewhere, his description of 'irregular and unaccented sounds' suggests the kind of arbitrary substitution of one spelling for another that provided the fifteenth- and sixteenth-century evidence from 'occasional spellings'.

But besides the long and short sounds common to all the vowels, there is a certain transient indistinct pronunciation of some of them, when they are not accented, that cannot so properly be called obscure, as imperfect: for it seems to have no more of the sound of the vowel to which it corresponds than what is common to the rest; that is a simple guttural tone, entirely unmodified by the organs which distinguish the sound of one vowel from another, and is really no more than a commencement of the vowel intended to be pronounced. When the accent is not upon it, no vowel is more apt to run into this imperfect sound than *a* . . . If the accent be kept strongly on the first syllable of the word *tolerable*, as it always ought to be, we find scarcely any distinguishable difference to the ear, if we substitute *u* or *o* instead of *a* in the penultimate syllable. Thus *tolerable*, *toleroble*, and *toleruble*, are exactly the same word to the ear, if pronounced without premeditation or transposing the accent, for the real purpose of distinction.   (Walker 1791: 12)

Thus we see that, despite the use of loaded terms such as *corrupt*, *obscure*, and *imperfect*, all of which suggest a certain distaste for this pronunciation, Walker does acknowledge the existence of unstressed vowels and identifies the sound as almost, but not exactly, that of /ʌ/.

Most eighteenth-century pronouncing dictionaries, like Walker's, represent the unstressed vowel equivalent to schwa with a 'short ⟨u⟩' symbol identical to that used for /ʌ/. A swift glance at any page of the *Grand Repository* would suggest that this is the exception here, for Spence often represents vowels in unstressed syllables with his symbol {Ɨ}, otherwise used for the /ɪ/ of *sit*, etc. On the first page of the dictionary proper (reproduced as the frontispiece to this book), we see the following words with the vowels here underlined represented in this way: *abacus*, *abaft*, *abaisance*, *abandon*, *abasement*, *abatement*, *abbacy*, *abbess*, *abbot*, *abbreviation*, *abbreviature*, *abdicate*, *abdication*, *abdomen*, *abdominous*, *abecedarian*, *abecedary*, *aberrance*, *aberrant*, *aberring*, *aberration*, *abetment*. Only the presence on this page of the word *abdominous*, with the underlined vowel sound represented as {ʊ}, suggests that Spence has any other way of representing unstressed vowels. Spence's widespread use of a symbol apparently equivalent to /ɪ/ for unstressed vowels other than reflexes of

ME and later /ɪ/ has been remarked upon before. Abercrombie (1965: 73) suggests that the presence of this vowel in, for example, *sycophant, haddock, haggle, swallow,* represented by Spence as being pronounced /'sɪkɪfɪnt, 'hædɪk, 'hægɪl, 'swælɪ/, is one of the 'traces of Spence's northern origins' to be found in the *Grand Repository*. Certainly /'swælɪ/ is a strikingly similar pronunciation to that used in present-day Glaswegian (where it is used as a euphemism for 'alcoholic beverage'), and I have heard /'hædɪk/ in fish and chip shops on Tyneside, but we shall have to look very carefully at the distribution of /ɪ/ in unstressed syllables in the *Grand Repository* and other eighteenth-century pronouncing dictionaries to see if Spence's usage was particularly 'northern' in the eighteenth century.

Before we look at the distribution in detail, though, it is worth reminding ourselves that, even in present-day RP, some unstressed vowels (other than those spelt ⟨i⟩) are pronounced as /ɪ/ rather than /ə/: the *CSED* gives *damage, sausage, village* all with /ɪdʒ/ as the final syllable, and *harmless, hopeless,* and, indeed, *abbess,* as well as *menace, furnace, palace,* and *solace,* all with /ɪs/.[38] Walker recognizes variation in some of these unstressed endings, recommending /ɪ/ for some words and /ə/ for others.Thus, for the *-ace* ending, he writes '*menace, palace, pinnace, populace, solace,* might, without any great departure from their common sound, be written *pallus, sollus,* &c, while *furnace* almost changes the *a* into *i* and might be written *furnis*' (1791: 12–13). Later, he writes '*eo,* when unaccented, has the sound of *u* short in *surgeon, sturgeon, dudgeon, luncheon, puncheon, truncheon, burgeon, habergeon;* but in *scutcheon, escutcheon, pidgeon* and *widgeon,* the *eo* sounds like short *i*' (1791: 31). He also suggests that *marchioness* should be pronounced as if written *marshunes,* but *cushion* as if written *cushin* (1791: 33). Could it be, then, that Spence's use of /ɪ/ in unstressed syllables is not so far out of line, or as peculiarly northern, as has been suspected?

Evidence for variation between /ə/ and /ɪ/ in unstressed syllables is provided by both Wyld (1936) and Dobson (1957). Wyld provides evidence for /ɪ/ in *-est, -en, -el, -less, -ness, -le(d)ge, -et, -age, -as (purchase, Thomas), -on, -ot.* In some places, he suggests that a change from /ɪ/ to /ə/ has been taking place in his lifetime: for instance, on *purchase,* he writes 'I remember hearing [pʌtʃɪs] in my boyhood from excellent speakers who preserved the habits of an earlier generation' (1936: 263),[39] whilst on the spelling ⟨stomick⟩ for *stomach,* he writes 'I have heard the latter word so pronounced by very old speakers whose speech was merely old-fashioned though it contained no vulgarisms' (1936: 263). (It is perhaps worth noting that Spence transcribes both *purchase* and *stomach* as pronounced exactly in the way suggested by

---

[38] In recent years, a pronunciation with schwa has begun to take over in these words, particularly in the speech of relatively young modified or 'near RP' speakers. The speech of Prime Minister Tony Blair is particularly noticeable in this respect, with pronunciations like /'ɒfəs/ for *office,* etc.

[39] In fact, the *CSED* (1992) still gives /pɜːtʃɪs/.

Wyld.) Dobson (1957: 915) explains this variation in the realization of unstressed syllables as resulting from two distinct sound changes: the first occurs in ME and affects only words with ME /e/, whilst the second affects back vowels and, according to Dobson, could not have occurred before the fifteenth century, as it is not until then that back vowels are reduced to schwa. Dobson also suggests that the first change, that involving ME /e/, was not affected by the following consonant, but that, in the case of the second change, involving /ə/ from ME back vowels, the raising to /ɪ/ was environmentally conditioned, with /n/ (as in *pigeon*) and /dʒ/ (as in *courage*) favouring the change. Dobson further suggests that variation was present up to the end of his period (1700) and that extensive use of /ɪ/, particularly for ME /e/, seems to have been a northern feature. There are a few indications from sixteenth-century orthoepists that this use of /ɪ/ for /ə/ from ME /e/ was northern: 'Mulcaster, (a Northerner) says that unstressed *e* as in *written*, *saieth*, sounds like short *i*. Coote (1596) includes *-id* for *-ed* among the characteristics of "the barbarous speech of your country people", and adds that it is Scottish' (Dobson 1957: 916). On /ɪ/ from late ME /ə/ before /l/ and /n/ as in *people*, *happen*, Dobson tells us that 'the Northerner Levins regularly has *il* for original *le*' and in a footnote that '*OED*'s spellings show *-il* for *-le* (as in *people*) and *-in* for *-en* (as in *happen, hearken*) from the fourteenth-century onwards, the fourteenth-century instances being Scottish and Northern' (1957: 917).

There is thus enough evidence to suggest that Spence's use of a symbol representing /ɪ/ for unstressed vowels, even where his contemporaries use a symbol representing /ʌ/ or /ə/, could reflect actual pronunciation in the eighteenth century, particularly in the north. This pronunciation does not seem to have been stigmatized in the eighteenth century: it is not included in Walker's 'rules to assist the natives of Scotland', and, when Walker mentions variation between /ɪ/ and /ə/, he points out in which words the reader should use which sound, but gives no dire warnings about getting this wrong. Contrast his remarks on the use or non-use of syllabic /r̩/ and /l̩/ in *swivel*, *chicken*, etc.: 'This diversity in the pronunciation of these terminations ought the more carefully to be attended to, as nothing is so vulgar and childish as to hear *swivel* and *heaven* pronounced with the *e* distinctly, or *navel* and *chicken* with the *e* suppressed' (Walker 1791: 104). Walker is here concerned with whether a vowel is pronounced in the final syllable of the word or not, rather than with the quality of that vowel. Likewise, in his note under *cushion*, for which he, most unusually for Walker, gives two alternative pronunciations, Walker shows no inclination to condemn either variant: 'I have given this word two sounds: not that I think they are equally in use. I am convinced that the first [/ˈkʊʃɪn/] is the more general, but because the other is but a trifling departure from it, and does not contradict the universal rule of pronouncing words of this termination.' This is hardly the way that Walker would write if the use of /ɪ/ in unstressed syllables was a really salient northern characteristic. On the other hand, Emsley (1933: 1157) points out that, whilst he can find little in Buchanan's works to justify the accusation of contemporary critics in the *Monthly Review* that, as a Scot, Buchanan was not 'a competent judge of English pronunciation', he feels that 'credit should be given the critics . . . for noting . . . his most outstanding fault, the tendency to overuse the 'short i' sound in final syllables as in *martial, filial, human.*' Perhaps this was recognized as a Scots or northern characteristic in the eighteenth century, but, especially towards the end of the century, its salience was overshadowed by the much more important issue of whether the vowel should be pronounced 'full' or 'obscure'.

The only indications we have of Spence's attitude to the pronunciation of unstressed vowels (apart from the transcriptions in the *Grand Repository* themselves, of course), are such as can be gleaned from the changes that he makes on his errata page, and those that he makes in the versions of his alphabet used in his later works. It is striking that, in neither case, does he change /ɪ/ to /ə/ or vice versa: of the 104 items on his errata page in the *Grand Repository*, 38 involve changes to or, more likely, from {Ɨ} (= /ɪ/), but in every case except that of *aquafortis*, where the underlined vowel is changed from {A} (=/eː/) to {Ɨ}, the {Ɨ} is changed to the symbol representing the 'full' value of the vowel concerned. Thus, for example, *advocate, aphorism, apothem, apozem, apposite, apposition, composition, controversy, controvert, decorate, decoration, decorous, desolate, diastole, indisposition,* and *percolate,* all have {Ɨ} changed to {C} (= /ɒ/) for the underlined vowel.[40] The changes in his later works appear to be of the same nature: Shields (1973: 78) points out that, in the later texts, 'Spence moves steadily towards the full, spelling pronunciation of unstressed syllables recommended by virtually all 18c. writers'. Where Spence shows variation between /ɪ/ and /ə/, as we have already seen from the discussion of the words ending in *-ure* in §5.6.3, this is unlikely to indicate uncertainty on his part as to which is 'correct': variation of this kind was present from the fourteenth century onwards, was acknowledged (but not condemned) in the eighteenth century by the likes of Walker, and, to some extent, is still present today.

5.7.2. *Evidence from eighteenth-century pronouncing dictionaries*

Obviously, the number of unstressed vowels present in the *Grand Repository* entries is likely to be huge, so, as I have already explained in §5.1, it would be beyond the scope of this book to analyse the full extent of variation between

[40] Interestingly, one of the few changes that Walker would like to have made in the *Critical Pronouncing Dictionary* is in the opposite direction. After his errata, he writes: 'There is but one class of words I could have wished had been differently marked, and that is, some of those ending in *-wards*, with the accent on a preceding syllable. When the accent is on this termination, as in *rewards*, the *a* has the broad sound; but when the accent precedes, this letter goes into its obscure sound, and *wards* has exactly the sound of *words*.' (1791: p. xvi).

/ɪ/, /ə/, and the 'full' pronunciation of vowels in the *Grand Repository* and between this and other pronouncing dictionaries. Instead, I have taken (Appendix 7*b*) a selection of words, which are mentioned by Walker and/or Wyld and added some which I have noticed as showing variation. Before considering these, though, we should perhaps look at the words beginning with *per-*, which Shields (1973) examined for evidence of variation in the *Grand Repository*. I have provided the list of words in Appendix 7*a*, along with the pronunciation of the vowel of the first syllable given by Spence, Walker, Sheridan, and Burn. Out of 86 words beginning with *per-*, Spence has {Ɨ} (/ɪ/) in 62, {Ɇ} (/ɛ/) in 22, and {E} (/iː/) in 2: in this context, then, there is no variation between /ɪ/ and /ə/ in the *Grand Repository*, only between /ɪ/ and 'full' values. Shields's list as reproduced in Appendix 7*a* has some words in which *per-* is stressed, and, indeed, all the words for which Spence has either {Ɇ} or {E}, such as *perry*, *pericardium*; *period*, *periodical*, would have either full or secondary stress on this syllable. However, there are also words with {Ɨ} in this list in which the syllable is equally likely to be under secondary stress (contrast *pericranium* with {Ɨ} and *pericardium* with {Ɇ}), as well as some, like *perforate*, which have {Ɨ} in a syllable with primary stress. Walker, Sheridan, and Burn each show less internal variation, but the contrast between them is interesting: Walker and Sheridan each have 'full' values, usually /ɛ/ in all cases, almost certainly because the rule followed by Walker (and, in this case, Sheridan too) is that vowels may be reduced only in syllables following the main stress. Burn has the 'reduced' /ə/ in almost all cases, with some instances of /ɛ/ or /iː/, and, in the one case of *periwig*, /ɪ/. Shields concludes from her study of the *per-* words in the *Grand Repository* 'that Spence had a sound in some words that he could not identify, and therefore adopted a variable pattern of representation, with little linguistic meaning' (1973: 82). The comparison with Walker and Burn, as well as the discussion of /ɪ/ in unstressed syllables in §5.7.1, would, however, suggest that Spence is not alone in showing variation here, and this variation is caused, not by uncertainty as to what the sound is, but as to whether the 'full' or 'reduced' pronunciation should be used.

Given the evidence discussed in §5.7.1 that the 'overuse' of /ɪ/ in unstressed syllables was a recognizably northern or Scots feature in the eighteenth century, it is strange that Burn has /ə/ or /ɛ/ so consistently. The only explanation that I can think of is that this feature (use of /ɪ/) was salient in Scotland, and therefore studiously avoided by Burn, but less so in England, where more attention was paid to variation between 'full' and 'reduced' syllables. If this was the case, Spence may well have heard variation between /ɪ/ and 'full' values of the vowels concerned from the northern clergymen who provided his model of good speech.

Spence does show variation between /ɪ/ and /ə/ elsewhere, though, as we can see from Appendix 7*b*. These words have been hand-picked to demonstrate variation, and so Spence's pronunciations seem less unusual here than in Appendix 7*a*. However, it is noticeable that, once again, Burn shows only one instance of /ɪ/, in *assemblage*: even where /ɪ/ is given in all the other three pronouncing dictionaries, as in *ribbon/riband*. Where /ɪ/ is still used in present-day RP, as in *furnace*, *advantage*, as with the words in Appendix 6*a*, Burn varies between /ə/ and the 'full' pronunciation, with one example, in *wagon* of a syllabic /n̩/. It would be interesting to carry out a fuller study of this feature in Burn (and, indeed, other Scottish orthoepists of the late eighteenth century): here, I can only say that Burn's distribution of /ə/ and 'full' vowels, together with his very sparing use of /ɪ/ in unstressed syllables, suggests a 'hypercorrect' avoidance of the 'northern' /ɪ/.

Spence and Sheridan both have a notation representing /ɪ/ for ME and later /ɛ/, confirming Dobson's statement (quoted in §5.7.1) that the raising from /ə/ was more general here than with ME back vowels. Both Walker and Burn have the 'full' vowel /ɛ/ for all the words in the list beginning with *barren* in Appendix 7*b*. Spence likewise has {ɫ} (/ɪ/) in the termination ⟨-er⟩, in *barker*, *barrister*, *barter*, etc. (not in Appendix 6*b*), but varies between {ɫ} (/ɪ/) and {ʊ} (/ə/) for the ending ⟨-or⟩, with {ɫ} in *anchor*, *major*, but {ʊ} in *bachelor*, *servitor*, whilst the other three dictionaries have their notation for /ə/ in all of these (except that Burn does not mark the vowel in the final syllable of *servitor*). In fact, the other words with ⟨o⟩ in traditional orthography almost all have {ɫ} in the *Grand Repository*, with some instances of {ʊ}, and occasional 'full' pronunciations, as in *zealot*, whereas, for Walker and Sheridan, /ə/ seems to be the norm and /ɪ/ the exception, where a 'reduced' pronunciation is given. Spence is alone here in his /ɪ/ pronunciation of the final syllable of *follow*, *swallow*, etc., but the pronunciation explicitly condemned by Walker for this class of words is that with /ə/. Walker (1791: 37) writes of ⟨ow⟩: 'The vulgar shorten this sound and pronounce the *o* obscurely and sometimes as if followed by *r*, as *winder* and *feller* for *window* and *fellow*; but this is almost too despicable for notice.' Once again, the primary sociolinguistic variable is /ə/: Walker is condemning a reduced, and prescribing a full, pronunciation and has nothing to say on the possibility of /ɪ/, which, in the case of these words, is almost certainly a northernism on Spence's part, but perhaps not one that was heavily stigmatized at the time.

It is difficult to reach firm conclusions from such a small amount of evidence, but I would tentatively put forward the following suggestions. First, Walker's reputation as an arch-prescriptivist who prescribed 'unnatural' pronunciations is not entirely justified. He recommends a pronunciation which is very like, if not identical to, the /ə/ of present-day English in many cases where the vowel falls after the main stress, and, in the case of *afterwards*, etc. states a wish to change his 'full' pronunciations to /ə/. Secondly, the extensive use of /ɪ/ in unstressed syllables that we find in the

Grand Repository is almost certainly a northern feature, but it represents the continuation of a late ME sound change which seems, at least in the case of back vowels, to have been environmentally conditioned, and to have been more extensive in the north in all contexts. Variation between /ɪ/ and /ə/ is attested at all stages from the fifteenth century to the present day, with a reversal of the original sound change (back to /ə/) seeming to gather momentum from the eighteenth century, and still continuing today. 'Over-use' of /ɪ/ is, however, condemned much less than the 'incorrect' use of reduced vowels, and so the /ɪ/ realizations in the *Grand Repository* may well represent the usage of 'good' (modified) speakers in the Newcastle of the late eighteenth century. In Scotland, the /ɪ/ may well have been more stigmatized, which could explain Burn's avoidance of this pronunciation even where it occurs in present-day RP. Finally, what are we to make of Spence's variation between {ʟ} and {Ɨ} in *bachelor*, *major*, etc? Are we dealing with genuine variation here, perhaps involving lexical diffusion, or is Spence aware of two possible pronunciations in this context and vacillating between the two? I would suggest that the total lack of changes from /ə/ to /ɪ/ or vice versa on the errata page of the *Grand Repository*, together with the absence of such changes in Spence's later works, argues against the latter. However, to discover patterns of variation which might indicate lexical diffusion we would have to carry out a much more thorough study of unstressed vowels in the *Grand Repository* than is possible within the scope of this book.

I have, throughout this section, treated Spence's {Ɨ} as representing /ɪ/ in unstressed syllables, and his {ʟ} as representing /ə/. Given that Spence provides no information concerning the articulation of the sounds repres-ented by his symbols, it is difficult to be precise on this matter. Shields (1973: 83) concludes that 'Spence at no time identified any central vowel as a separate "letter"'. It is possible that {Ɨ} represents /ə/ as well as /ɪ/ and/or {ʟ} represents not only /ə/ in, for example, *bachelor*, but also /ʊ/ in, for example, *put*. If so, then this represents a failure on Spence's part to adhere to his principle that 'to read what is printed in this alphabet, nothing is required but to apply the same sound immutably to each character (in whatever position) that the alphabet directs'. In this case, his reputation as the author of the first 'phonetic' dictionary of English is slightly diminished, but, there again, no eighteenth-century orthoepist produced a separate symbol for /ə/. There is also the possibility that {ʟ} did stand for a single phoneme, with a quality nearer to [ɣ], which we mentioned in §5.4. It is certainly the case that in the modified near-RP used by middle-class Tynesiders, the vowels in the two syllables of, for example, *putter* (= a golf club) are very similar to each other. Perhaps a similar situation existed in the Newcastle of 1775, but, in the absence of more specific information on articulation in the *Grand Repository*, this would be difficult to establish.

5.8. WEAKENING AND/OR LOSS OF WORD FINAL AND PRECONSONANTAL /r/

5.8.1. *Introduction*

We have touched upon this subject already in §5.2, where we saw that lengthening of /a/ in, for example, *bar, bard* was initially triggered by a weakening of /r/, first in preconsonantal, and later in word final positions. By the end of the eighteenth century, /r/ has been lost in these positions, at least in the most advanced dialect of London described (but not approved of) by Walker, and lengthening of /a/ before this vocalized *r* has become categorical. In other dialects though, notably those of Scotland and Ireland, /r/ was neither weakened nor lost and, since loss of /r/ was actually stigmatized, there was no incentive for the 'polite' speakers of Dublin or Edinburgh to adopt this sound change. In the varieties described by Spence and Burn, in which there is little or no likelihood of /r/ being vocalized, lengthening of /a/ before /r/ seems to have been introduced on a purely lexical basis, as an 'imported' sound change without a phonetic trigger.

The history of weakening/loss of /r/ is complex and intertwined with that of the effect of this /r/ on preceding vowels. By the eighteenth century, orthoepists are reluctant to admit to loss of /r/ because of the stigma by then attached to any deviation from the written word.[41] Thus, /r/ is always indicated as being pronounced in the transcriptions or respellings provided in pronouncing dictionaries: to discover whether /r/ really was pronounced, and whether it was weakened or not, in the 'correct' usage described in pronouncing dictionaries, we therefore have to 'read between the lines'. This means gleaning information from the comments provided in introductory material and, particularly in the case of the *Grand Repository* where no such introductory material exists, looking at the vowels preceding /r/ for any evidence of the modifications that are linked with weakening/loss of /r/.

First, though, let us recap on the history of weakening/loss of /r/ up to the end of the eighteenth century. We have already seen in §5.2 that weakening of /r/ in medial and final positions is first attested by Jonson (1640), but that this distinction between a 'strong' /r/ in initial position and a 'weak' /r/ in medial (particularly preconsonantal) and final positions is more widely commented on in the eighteenth century. Jespersen (1909–49: 358) identifies this 'strong' /r/ as 'probably a trilled point- /ʀ/ (like the Scotch) before a vowel, and before a consonant an untrilled consonantal /r/ very much like the sound now given to *r* before a vowel in South England'. Certainly, Jonson's designation of *r* as 'the dog's letter' (i.e. sounding like a dog's

---

[41] Mugglestone (1995: 97–8) shows how the statement of Johnson that 'for pronunciation the best general rule is, to consider those as the most elegant speakers, who deviate least from the written word' (1755: a2ᵛ i.) was taken up and used as a precept by many orthoepists and grammarians of the later eighteenth and the nineteenth centuries.

growl; cf. *s*, which is 'the snake's letter') suggests some kind of trilled consonant, and the 'weakening' in medial and final positions would take /r/ further towards the vocalic end of what Charles Jones (1991: 6) calls the 'sonority hierarchy', to a continuant. Walker's remarks (1791: 50) on the difference between the English and Irish pronunciations of /r/ suggest that, for the Irish, /r/ is always trilled; for Londoners, it is a continuant [ɹ] in initial and intervocalic positions, but fully vocalized in preconsonantal and final positions (in *bar, bard, card, regard*); in the 'correct' English which he is recommending, though, /r/ should be 'as forcible as in Ireland' in initial position, but 'nearly as soft as in London' in preconsonantal and final positions. The Irish, 'correct' English, and London pronunciations described by Walker are the synchronic correlates of three diachronic stages in the vocalization of /r/: the Irish pronunciation of the late eighteenth century probably corresponds to the English pronunciation of the sixteenth century and earlier, with no vocalization or weakening; the 'correct' English pronunciation prescribed in 1791 by Walker, with a trilled /r/ word-initially, but a continuant preconsonantally and finally, shows the first stage of weakening attested by Jonson (1640); and the 'London' English of 1791 is much closer to present-day RP, with a continuant in initial position, and vocalization of /r/ in preconsonantal and final positions.

There is earlier evidence of loss of /r/: Wyld (1936: 298) shows evidence from rhymes (such as *first: dust* in Surrey) and spellings (e.g. ⟨wosted⟩ for *worsted*) from the fifteenth century onwards. Wyld (1936: 299) notes that this early evidence almost always involves words with /s/ or /ʃ/ after the /r/ and sees this as the first stage in the weakening and subsequent vocalization of /r/:

> To summarize . . . it would appear that the weakening and disappearance of *r* before another consonant, especially, at first, before [s, ʃ], had taken place by the middle of the fifteenth century at any rate in Essex and Suffolk; that a hundred years later London speakers of the humbler sort (Machyn), as well as more highly placed and better educated persons in various walks of life, pronounced the sound but slightly, if at all; that the tendency is more and more marked, not only before [s, ʃ], but before other consonants also, until by the middle of the next century it seems that the pronunciation among the upper classes (the Verneys and their relatives) was very much the same as at present.

Wyld's evidence is thus much earlier than the orthoepistic evidence cited above, but, as we saw in §3.2, this is usually the case with indirect evidence from rhymes and spellings. Wyld points out (1936: 299) that 'these pronunciations . . . have been ousted by another type . . . in which the *r* was not lost until lengthening had taken place'. That such early loss of /r/ existed, at least in colloquial English, is attested by the survival into PDE of informal/formal doublets such as *bust*: *burst*; *cuss*: *curse*, in which the more informal item shows early loss of /r/ with no lengthening of the preceding vowel (/bʌst, kʌs/), whilst the formal one shows later loss with its associated lowering and lengthening (/bɜːst, kɜːs/).[42] As we have seen in §5.2, the later, orthoepistic evidence for weakening/loss of /r/, notably that of Flint and Walker, associates this change in the realization of /r/ with lengthening of the preceding vowel. It would appear that we have two different sound changes here: an early one in which /r/ is assimilated to the following /s/ or /ʃ/, with no effect on the preceding vowel, and a later one in which /r/ is weakened or vocalized, with 'compensatory lengthening' of the preceding vowel. The first was almost certainly confined to colloquial English, despite Wyld's assertion that it is found in upper-class speech in the eighteenth century, and evidence for it is sporadic, whilst the later change is of a much more general nature and finds its way into 'correct' speech, for the prestige accent of present-day British English, RP, is non-rhotic. It is this later change that we are concerned with here, for evidence of the earlier change would certainly be considered 'vulgar' by the last quarter of the eighteenth century.

As I have already indicated, all the pronouncing dictionaries studied here indicate /r/ as being realized in all positions in their respellings. In the case of other consonants which have been vocalized or, in what were once consonant clusters like initial /kn/, lost by simplification, eighteenth-century pronouncing dictionaries indicate the vocalization or loss by using a different font (usually italic) or, in the case of the *Grand Repository*, by simply missing them out. Thus Spence writes {NO} (= /noː/) for *know*, and {KᴧF} (= /kɑːf/) for *calf*; Walker and Sheridan, like Spence, omit the ⟨k⟩ from *know* and the ⟨l⟩ from *calf* in their respellings, whilst Burn has an italic {*k*} and {*l*} in these instances, indicating a silent letter.

In Spence's case, we can probably take his inclusion of word final and preconsonantal /r/ at face value, for Northumbrian English would, like Scots, have been rhotic in the late eighteenth century.[43] Walker's respellings, with /r/ always realized, are harder to interpret, for, whilst he asserts (1791: 50) that 'this letter is never silent', he elsewhere writes that '*r*, being only a jar, and not a definite and distinct articulation like the other consonants, instead of stopping the vocal efflux of voice, lets it imperfectly pass' (1791: 13). Walker has been cited by Jespersen (1909–49: 360) as being 'the oldest Englishman to admit the muteness' of preconsonantal and word final /r/. As

---

[42] The *CSED* gives *bust, cuss* as 'informal', whilst the *OED* cites them as 'US'. Both exist in my own dialect, and not as US imports. They have each developed a range of senses distinct from their more formal counterparts: to *cuss* is to swear, whilst to *curse* is to wish somebody ill; *cussed* means 'bad-tempered', and a *bust* (in this sense more probably US) can be a raid by the police. Bailey (1996: 99) also notes the existence of these doublets as one of the 'characteristics of seventeenth-century folk speech as used by the first permanent English-speaking settlers in North America'.

[43] Kolb (1966) shows retention of preconsonantal /r/ (realized as [ʁ]) in the twentieth century in traditional dialects of Northumberland, whilst Påhlsson (1972) shows it as still occurring, but recessive.

we have seen in §2.4, the 'oldest Englishman' to admit this was in fact Tucker (1773) and (see §5.2) Walker 'admits' to this 'muteness' rather grudgingly, asserting that /r/ should be pronounced, albeit more weakly even preconsonantally and word finally. Thus it is not surprising that Walker indicates the /r/ as being realized in all positions, for this was 'correct' in his view. Mugglestone (1995: 98–103), shows that, throughout the nineteenth century, vocalization of /r/ was as highly stigmatized as 'h-dropping': as late as 1880, Gerard Manley Hopkins criticized Keats for his 'rhyming open vowels to silent *r*s, as *higher* to *Thalia*: as long as the *r* is pronounced by anybody, and it is by a good many yet, the feeling that it is there makes this rhyme most offensive, not indeed to the ear, but to the mind' (Abbott 1935: 37, quoted in Mugglestone 1995: 101). As Mugglestone points out, Hopkins' words here suggest that he *thinks* the /r/ is pronounced rather than that he actually *hears* it: given that non-rhoticity is a feature of RP, and that rhotic accents, at least in England, are now viewed as 'rustic' and of low prestige, it is unlikely that /r/ was still pronounced in preconsonantal and word final position as late as 1880, except perhaps in a highly artificial 'stage' pronunciation. A century earlier, though, a 'weakened' /r/ could well have still been realized in these positions in 'careful' speech, as indicated by Walker.

Shields (1973: 87–8) suggests that, whilst Spence's retention of /r/ is genuine, Walker's is not 'retained' but self-consciously 'restored'. Her reasoning here is that Walker's retention of /r/ in, for example, *farther* cannot be natural, because he marks the first vowel of this word as the 'long Italian *a*', and she believes that this lengthening is consequent on vocalization of /r/. We have already seen in §5.2 that this is not the case: lengthening of /a/ before /r/ predates the complete loss of the consonant and is more likely to be caused by weakening, a movement along the sonority hierarchy from the more 'consonant-like' trill, to the more 'vowel-like' continuant. Thus Walker's combination of lengthened /a/ and a weakened but still realized /r/ is perfectly natural. Shields also fails to notice that Spence himself has more than a few instances of the long {ʌ} (= /ɑː/) before /r/ in the *Grand Repository* (179 in all: see Appendices 2*c*(i) and (ii)).

5.8.2. *Evidence from pronouncing dictionaries*

Before we go on to look in detail at the realization of vowels before /r/ in Spence, Walker, Sheridan, and Burn, perhaps we should consider what kind of /r/ is represented by Spence's {R} in the *Grand Repository*. Spence's own pronunciation of /r/ was almost certainly realized as [ʀ] or [ʁ]—that is, one of the articulations known as the 'Northumbrian burr'. This pronunciation was first noticed by Defoe (1724–7: iii. 232–3), who wrote:

I must not quit *Northumberland* without taking notice, that the Natives of this Country, of the antient original Race or Families, are distinguished by a *Shibboleth* upon their Tongues in pronouncing the Letter *R*, which they cannot utter without a hollow Jarring in the Throat, by which they are as plainly known, as a foreigner is in pronouncing the *Th*: this they call the *Northumberland R*, or *Wharle*; and the Natives value themselves upon that Imperfection, because, forsooth, it shews the Antiquity of their Blood.

Later in the eighteenth century, this 'Northumberland R' becomes subject to criticism—for example, from Kenrick, who describes it (1773: 31) as 'very aukwardly pronounced, somewhat like a *w* or *oau*' and Stephen Jones (1798: 49) who writes of 'the rough sound of *r*, as it is pronounced by the natives of Durham, who sound it in their throats with a disagreeable rattling'. This would appear to contradict Defoe's statement to the effect that Northumbrians were proud of the burr, but they were and are an independent-minded people with a high degree of 'accent loyalty',[44] and, more than a century after Jones, Heslop (1903: 16) could write of the 'burr' as being 'the birthright of people of every station in life'. Heslop also writes of Lord Eldon (a native of Newcastle and Lord Chancellor at the beginning of the nineteenth century) using the 'burr' on the Woolsack. This would indicate that, by the end of the nineteenth century, the 'Northumberland R' was a highly salient feature of Northumbrian speech, and was criticized as such by orthoepists, but that Northumbrians themselves were not minded to modify this feature towards the 'weaker' /r/ of London speech. If Lord Eldon did not see fit to lose his 'burr', then the working-class Thomas Spence would almost certainly have retained it, as is suggested by Place, who writes that 'he had a strong northern 'burr in his throat' and a slight impediment in his speech' (BL Add. MS 27,808, fo. 154, quoted in Shields 1973: 75).

What evidence can we find in the *Grand Repository* for the existence of the 'burr'? In present-day Northumbrian, and even in the urban dialect of Tyneside, vowels before ⟨r⟩ show the effects of what Påhlsson (1972: 20) terms 'burr-modification': 'Burr-modified vowels are vowels that have become retracted and lowered (in most cases) due to a following posterior /r/, e.g. "first" [fɔːst], "word" [wɔːd], irrespective of its more precise realization'. There is no evidence of such 'burr-modification' in the *Grand Repository*: *first* is here transcribed as {FꟾRST}, i.e. /fɪrst/; *word* is transcribed as {WꞱRD}, i.e. either /wʊrd/ or /wərd/; and the words beginning with *per-* in Appendix 7*a* are transcribed as either {PER} (e.g. *permanent*) or {PꟾR} (e.g. *perfect*), whereas in present-day broad Tyneside the first syllable of both these words would be pronounced /pɔː/. Especially in the case of *word*, in which the traditional spelling has ⟨o⟩, Spence could easily have represented a burr-modified vowel with his {ᴁU} (= /ɔː/) or {C} (= /ɒ/)

---

[44] The Northumbrian Language Society takes the stance that Northumbrian has the status of a separate language rather than a dialect of English. Each April, at the Morpeth Gathering, a kind of Northumbrian Eisteddfod, prizes are given for the best story and poem in Northumbrian.

symbol, had such modification been present in the pronunciation that he was representing. We must draw one of two conclusions from the lack of any evidence for burr-modification in the *Grand Repository*: either the variety described therein did not realize /r/ as a 'burr', or it may have done, but burr-modification, like lengthening of /a/ before /r/, is a sound change triggered by the weakening of the following consonant. All the negative remarks about the burr's harshness quoted above suggest that, in the late eighteenth century, it had not been weakened. The *Grand Repository* thus provides us with no evidence about the articulation of /r/ in the variety described therein, only that it is realized in all positions.

Leaving aside the question of the 'Northumbrian burr', let us examine the vowels before /r/ in Spence, Walker, Sheridan, and Burn for signs of the modifications associated with weakening and/or loss of word final and preconsonantal /r/. We have seen in §4.3 that most of the differences in inventory between the phonemic system of the *Grand Repository* and that of RP as described in Wells (1982) are due to innovations which are associated with loss of rhoticity in the latter system. Thus Spence has no phonemic equivalent of the diphthongs /ɪə/ (NEAR), /ɛə/ (SQUARE), and /ʊə/ (CURE), nor does he have a distinct phoneme equivalent to RP /ɜː/ (NURSE). These three diphthongs developed as a result of what Wells (1982: 213–18) calls 'Pre-R Breaking', whilst the vowel in NURSE is the result of two sound changes: what Wells (1982: 199–203) calls the 'NURSE Merger' followed by the lengthening also found before a (weakened) /r/ in *car, cart, nor, north*. The 'NURSE Merger' itself does not depend on weakening or loss of the following /r/, for a partial merger has occurred in some rhotic accents like Scots, in which, according to Wells (1982: 200), '*word* and *bird* have [ər] but *heard* [ɛr]'. However, the emergence of a separate phoneme in NURSE words would only occur after the lengthening to /ɜː/, which is associated with weakening of the following /r/. 'Pre-R Breaking' is associated in PDE with non-rhotic varieties such as RP, but historically this change, like lengthening before /r/, is associated with weakening rather than full vocalization of the following /r/.

Evidence of either breaking or lengthening of vowels before /r/ in Spence, Walker, Sheridan, or Burn should thus indicate that the following /r/ is weakened. Appendix 8 shows a selection of words in which lengthening or breaking occurs in RP, with the IPA equivalent of the vowel given by Spence, Walker, Sheridan, and Burn for each word. The words are listed in alphabetical order in Appendix 8: *bird, birth,* and *burden; fern, fir,* and *fur* have been chosen as words which show the result of the 'NURSE Merger' in PDE; *for* and *north* to provide evidence for lengthening (since lengthening of /a/ has already been discussed in §5.2), and *beer, chair, fire, flour, flower, sure,* and *tower* to provide evidence for breaking.

Let us consider first the evidence for the 'NURSE Merger' provided by Appendix 8. The pronunciations of *bird, birth, burden, fern, fir,* and *fur* show no evidence at all for this merger in Spence, where even the /ə/ which I have given here for *burden* and *fur* could, as we have seen in §5.7, be /ʊ/, for Spence's {ʟ} represents both. Spence's transcriptions show no modification of the vowels preceding /r/ in these words. The other three orthoepists represented here do, however, provide evidence of the 'NURSE Merger': Burn, surprisingly for a Scot, seems to have the full merger, with all six words considered here having the same vowel. Walker and Sheridan, on the other hand, each show a partial merger, like the one found, according to Wells (1982), in present-day Scots: for Walker, *bird*, *burden*, and *fur* have /ə/ but *birth*, *fern*, and *fir* have /ɛ/, whilst for Sheridan *bird*, *burden*, *fir*, and *fur* all have /ə/, whilst *birth* and *fern* have /ɛ/. If we remember that the same representation is given for both /ə/ and /ʌ/ in Sheridan and Walker, then it would appear that orthographic ⟨u⟩ before /r/ remains as what was perceived as a ⟨u⟩ sound (/ə/ or /ʌ/), orthographic ⟨e⟩ remains unmodified as /ɛ/, but ⟨i⟩ before /r/ is variably modified to either /ɛ/ or /ə/. Walker attempts to explain the pronunciation of ⟨i⟩ before /r/ as follows:

When this letter is succeeded by *r*, and another consonant in a final syllable, it has exactly the sound of *e* in *vermin, vernal* &c, as *virtue, virgin* &c, which approaches to the sound of short *u*; but when it comes before *r*, followed by another consonant in a final syllable, it acquires the sound of *u* exactly, as *bird, dirt, shirt, squirt* &c. *Mirth, birth* and *firm*, are the only exceptions to this rule; where *i* is pronounced like *e*.   (1791: 108)

The letter *r*, in this case, seems to have the same influence on the vowel, as it evidently has on *a* and *o*. When these sounds come before double *r*, or single *r*, followed by a vowel, as in *arable, carry, marry, orator, horrid, forage* &c, they are considerably shorter than when *r* is the final letter of the word, or when it is succeeded by another consonant, as in *arbor, car, mar, or, nor, for*. In the same manner, the *i* coming before either double *r*, or single *r*, followed by a vowel, preserves its pure, short, sound, as in *irritate, conspiracy*, &c, but when *r* is followed by another consonant, or is a final letter of a word with the accent upon it, the *i* goes into a deeper and broader sound, equivalent to short *e*, as heard in *virgin, virtue*. So *fir*, a tree, is perfectly similar to the first syllable of *ferment*, though often corruptly pronounced like *fur*, a skin. *Sir* and *stir* are exactly pronounced, as if written *sur* and *stur*.   (1791: 109)

In Walker's view, the modification of ⟨i⟩ in *bird, birth, fir*, etc. is caused by the 'influence' of the following /r/. We have already seen in §5.2 that Walker describes preconsonantal and word final /r/ as more weakly articulated than intervocalic /r/, and so his remarks provide fairly clear evidence that the modification and/or lengthening of vowels before /r/ is associated with the weakening of that consonant. The distinction between the vowel in the first syllable of *virtue* and that of *bird* is less clear: the former is 'exactly the sound of *e* in *vermin*' and 'approaches to the sound of short *u*', whilst the latter is 'the sound of *u* exactly'. It is possible that Walker here perceives a distinction which his system of notation cannot express: perhaps the sound that 'approaches' short *u* is [ə], or a centralized [ë], whilst 'short *u* exactly' is [ʌ]. Elsewhere, Walker shows uncertainty as to the exact pronunciation of *earth*, which he gives as pronounced /ɛrθ/, but adds that it 'is very often liable to a coarse vulgar sound, as if written *urth*; there is indeed but a delicate difference between this and the true sound; but quite sufficient to distinguish a common from a polite speaker'. In the light of Walker's remarks concerning the 'vulgarity' of pronouncing *fir* like *fur* and the subtlety of the distinction between the two, perhaps what we see in Appendix 8 as represented in the pronunciations given by Spence, Walker, Sheridan, and Burn are four stages in the modification of vowels before /r/: Spence has no modification, suggesting that his /r/ is not weakened, Walker has some vowels modified to /ɛ/ and others to /ə/ with what looks like a lexical distribution of variants; Sheridan's system is similar to Walker's, but with more instances of /ə/, and Burn's shows the complete 'NURSE Merger', with all the vowels realized as /ə/. This would suggest a sequence, at least for ME /ɪ/, of /ɪ/ ⟩ /ɛ/ ⟩ /ə/, an idea which has been put forward by Luick (1914–40), but dismissed by Dobson (1957: 752–4), and which should perhaps be re-examined in the light of more detailed evidence from eighteenth-century pronouncing dictionaries. Spence's total lack of even a partial 'NURSE Merger' certainly suggests that he has no weakening of /r/; Walker's and Sheridan's evidence suggests weakening, with a resistance to the 'vulgar' /ə/ found with the total merger. What are we to make, though of a Scot, Burn, showing the full 'NURSE Merger'? I would suggest that, in this case, Burn is not representing even a 'polite', modified Scots pronunciation. He acknow-ledges in his Introduction his debt to other pronouncing dictionaries, notably that of Kenrick, whose system of notation he took over wholesale. It is possible that, in this case, Burn is using Kenrick's pronunciation rather than his own.[45]

Appendix 8 shows what at first sight appears to be evidence of breaking before /r/ in *flower* and *tower*, which seem to have triphthongs in all four pronouncing dictionaries. However, Burn and Spence, the only two who have a separate entry for *flour*, show no breaking in this word, which is in fact an alternative spelling of one sense of *flower*, and none of our orthoepists shows any breaking in *beer*, *chair*, *fire*, or *sure*. The difference between *flour* and *flower* in particular suggests that all four orthoepists are led by the spelling here: the /ɪr/ (Spence) and /ər/ (Walker, Sheridan, Burn) represent the ⟨er⟩ ending, a separate syllable, rather than /ə/ from breaking before /r/. This is not to say that breaking did not exist in any of the varieties described by these orthoepists: it would be strange if it did not, since there is

---

[45] Kenrick seems to have two ways of marking 'reduced' or unstressed syllables: the superscripted 1 is used for 'reduced' vowels as well as for /ʌ/, whilst the superscripted 0 is used for syllabic consonants and syllables in which the vowel is entirely 'sunk'. Burn uses the 0 only for syllabic consonants.

evidence for breaking in, for example, *fire* from as early as the sixteenth century in the works of reputable orthoepists such as Hart (see Dobson 1957: 760). All that we can conclude from Appendix 8 is that these pronouncing dictionaries provide no evidence for breaking.

Lengthening of /a/ before /r/ has already been dealt with in §5.2, but Appendix 8 provides some evidence for the parallel lengthening of /o/. Spence has no lengthening in either *for* or *north*, Walker, Sheridan, and Burn all have a long vowel in *north*, but only Walker has a long vowel in *for*. We saw in §5.2. that Walker showed the most 'advanced' lengthening of /a/ before /r/, as he had the long vowel categorically before word final as well as preconsonantal /r/. The two examples here would suggest a similar pattern for /o/ before /r/: an investigation on the scale of that carried out for /a/ in §5.2 would make a very interesting comparison, but is beyond the scope of this book. Such evidence as we have here confirms that the variety described in the *Grand Repository* shows no weakening of word final or preconsonantal /r/; that described by Walker shows a good deal of evidence for weakening, but not necessarily loss, of /r/ in these positions; whilst those described by Sheridan and Burn show some evidence for weakening, but less than we find in Walker, probably because the Irish and Scots varieties actually spoken by these two orthoepists had no weakening, so that the lengthenings and modifications of vowels before /r/ indicated by them are the result either of influence from another variety or, as I suspect in the case of Burn, copying from another pronouncing dictionary.

5.9. LOSS OF INITIAL /h/

5.9.1. *Introduction*

Wells (1982: 254) describes 'H-dropping' as 'the single most powerful pronunciation shibboleth in England' and, with regard to present-day English, he is almost certainly right. However, although there is evidence for h-dropping from EME onwards (Lass 1987: 96; Milroy 1983), Mugglestone (1995: 109) points out that 'the rise of /h/ as a social symbol does not antedate the eighteenth century, and, more specifically, it becomes prominent only towards its end'.

Milroy (1983) argues that h-dropping is not a Germanic trait, but was introduced to English via French after the Norman Conquest. Loanwords from French, such as *herb*, *host*, would be introduced with the French pronunciation without initial /h/, and spellings such as *erb* are common enough in ME. However, many of these words had Latin cognates with initial ⟨h⟩ and, especially towards the end of the ME/beginning of the ENE period, consciousness of their ultimate Latin origins led scholars to adopt spellings with initial ⟨h⟩ for these words: for instance, the *OED* tells us that *herb* was increasingly spelt with ⟨h⟩ from about 1475 onwards. The ⟨h⟩ was, however, still silent in these words of French/Latin origin, providing a pattern of variation in the realization of initial ⟨h⟩. From the thirteenth century onwards, there is evidence that /h/ varies with zero, particularly at the beginning of words: Charles Jones (1989: 266–74) examines evidence from the early thirteenth-century *Laȝamon's Brut*, and the sixteenth-century *Diary of Henry Machyn*, both of which show dropping and, conversely, insertion of /h/ (or rather ⟨h⟩, as we are dealing with spellings here). Jones suggests that the dropping or insertion of /h/ might be used as a means of attaining the 'ideal' syllable shape: in an example from Machyn, ⟨gohyng⟩ for *going*, the /h/ allows for an 'overlap', and can be interpreted as a segment which both terminates the first syllable and initiates the second. In word-initial position, the insertion of /h/ would allow for the kind of onset, less vowel-like than the vocalic peak, that an 'ideal' syllable should have in Jones's model. Because /h/ is so neutral with regard to labiality or palatality, taking on as it does the articulatory quality of the following vowel, it is ideal as a sort of 'floating' segment, to be added or deleted as the syllable shape dictates.[46] Jones admits that this explanation, attractive though it seems, is not wholly satisfactory, especially with regard to the data from Machyn, which is too 'patchy' or inconsistent to allow for such a neat solution. However, given that there is no direct evidence earlier than the eighteenth century that either dropping or insertion of /h/ was stigmatized, Jones's explanation is certainly better than any relying on 'hypercorrection'.

Mugglestone suggests that Sheridan was the first orthoepist to voice disapproval of h-dropping when he states: 'There is one defect which more generally prevails in the counties than any other, and indeed is gaining ground among the politer part of the world, I mean the omission of the aspirate in many words by some, and in most by others' (Sheridan 1762: 34, quoted in Mugglestone 1995: 113). According to Dobson (1957: 991), some seventeenth-century orthoepists provide evidence of loss of /h/ before vowels, but such evidence, at least when it concerns stressed syllables, is from 'vulgar or dialectal speech'. He bases this judgement on the fact that the evidence comes from northerners (Lily and Brown) and in homophone lists. However, there is no direct evidence that this loss of /h/ was recognized as a vulgarism in the seventeenth century: it is notably absent from Cooper's (1687) list of 'barbarous' pronunciations, for example. By the end of the eighteenth century, h-dropping is recognized as a particular failing of the Cockneys: Walker (1791: pp. xii–xiii) includes in his list of the 'peculiarities'

---

[46] Charles Jones's description of the 'neutrality' of /h/ here tallies perfectly with those of eighteenth-century orthoepists. Sheridan (1780: 16), for instance, writes of ⟨h⟩: 'This character is no mark of any articulate sound, but is a mere sign of aspiration, or effort of the breath. This is the only power it has when simple.' Walker (1791: 46), in a similar vein, writes that 'this letter is no more than breathing forcibly before the succeeding vowel is pronounced'.

of his 'countrymen, the Cockneys' the fault of 'not sounding *h* where it ought to be sounded, and inversely'. Thus Walker sees as particularly reprehensible, not only h-dropping, but also h-insertion. He goes on to give a list of words in which it is correct to 'sink' the initial ⟨h⟩. These are: *heir, heiress, herb, herbage, honest, honestly, honesty, honour, honourable, honourably, hospital, hostler, hour, hourly, humble, humbly, humbles, humour, humourist, humourous, humourously, humoursome*. Other eighteenth-century orthoepists provide similar lists, though none is as extensive as Walker's: Buchanan (1762: 48) tells us that '*h* is written, but not pronounced in *honour, hour, herb, heir, honest, humour, host*'; Sheridan (1780: 16) lists *heir, honest, honour, hospital, hostler, hour, humour, humble, humbles*; and Elphinston (1790: 7) writes that *h* is to be missed from *heir, herb, hour, honour, homage, hostler, hospital, Humphrey, Helen, honest*, and *humble*. Elphinston then goes on to provide a mnemonic (in his reformed spelling) to help the reader remember where /h/ should or should not be omitted:

Dhe onnest hoast is evver hospitabel, practising constant hospitallity; az doz not evvery founder of an ospital. Dhe eir claims dhe erritage, dho dhe inheritor inherit dhe inheritance. So dhe erritabel ov won dialect proves the herreditary ov anoddher. Dhe horary is doutles dhe cirkel of dhe ours; but hue, hew and hewer cannot keep too clear ov u, yoo, yew and ewer.

There is a good deal of overlap between these lists: all three include *heir, honour, hour,* and *honest* (all of which still have a silent ⟨h⟩ in RP), but only Buchanan includes *host* and Elphinston omits *humour*. Elphinston's mnemonic also shows us that words with the same root may be treated differently with regard to presence or absence of /h/: *hospital* with silent ⟨h⟩ is here contrasted with *hospitable* and *hospitality*, for instance. This would suggest that, along with the stigmatization of h-dropping in words which were not of French (or Latin) origin, uncertainty was beginning to creep in as to exactly where ⟨h⟩ should be pronounced. Pronouncing dictionaries such as Walker's condemn the addition of /h/ to words in which it is either not present in the spelling or silent, but Walker's method for correcting this 'fault of the Londoners' involves first getting the pupil to pronounce /h/ wherever ⟨h⟩ appears, at least word-initially, and only then teaching him or her where to drop it. Elphinston (1786: 15) seems to sanction the restoration of /h/ when he writes: 'Dhey dhat think *uman, umor* and dhe like, look too *umbel*, may innocently indulge the seeming aspiration.' It is worth noting here that *human* is absent from Elphinston's list of words with silent ⟨h⟩ four years later in 1790. The sensitization to h-dropping as a social shibboleth seems already by the end of the eighteenth century to have led to the recommendation that ⟨h⟩ be pronounced in certain words where it had formerly been silent. Garrett (1910: 403) provides evidence from a grammar written in Latin and German in either the late seventeenth or early eighteenth century. Here, the rule is given under *h* that this letter is silent in the French words *humble, hour, hospital, honest*, but that in Latin words beginning with *hum-*, the ⟨h⟩ is pronounced as /j/, thus *human, humect, humid, humility, humour* are transcribed in this grammar as beginning with *juh*, which is almost certainly to be interpreted as /juː/. Of the second list, only *humour* survives into lists of words with silent ⟨h⟩ written at the end of the eighteenth century (*human* having been dropped by Elphinston from such lists between 1786 and 1790). From the mid-eighteenth century onwards, consciousness of the 'vulgarity' of h-dropping leads to a tendency to realize the orthographic ⟨h⟩ as /h/ in some words in which it had been silent. This process was a very gradual one, certainly involved lexical diffusion, and carried on through the nineteenth and into the twentieth centuries. In 1846 Smart explicitly states that it is better to err on the side of pronouncing ⟨h⟩ where it could be silent than vice versa: 'In some pronouncing dictionaries, *herb* and *hospital* are included among the words whose initial *h* is silent; but the *h* may be aspirated in these and their derivatives without the least offence to polite ears; and even in *humble* and *humour*, the sounding of *h* is a fault, far less grating than it would be in *heir, honest* and the other words stated above' (quoted in Mugglestone 1995: 148). Wyld (1936: 295) writes of the words *humour, humoured* that 'the restoration of the aspirate . . . is a trick of yesterday, and I never observed it until a few years ago, and then only among speakers who thought of every word before they uttered it'. Even in the twentieth century, there is variation in, for example, *hotel*, which the *CSED* gives only with initial /h/, but for which I have certainly heard h-less pronunciations, at least from older/more conservative RP speakers.[47] Apart from this, the only words in which initial ⟨h⟩ is now silent in RP are *heir, honest, honour, hour* and their derivatives (but not, for instance, *inheritance*).

5.9.2. *Evidence from pronouncing dictionaries*

Appendix 9 shows all the words with initial ⟨h⟩ which appear in the *Grand Repository* and which have been mentioned by seventeenth- and/or eighteenth-century orthoepists as having silent ⟨h⟩. The pronunciation recorded in the dictionaries of Spence, Walker, Sheridan, and Burn is marked as + (with /h/) or − (without /h/) in each case.

The number of items here is very small, depending as it does on words

---

[47] I remember being told by a particularly formidable teacher (*c.*1962) that /ən əˈtɛl/ was more correct than /ə həuˈtɛl/. This preyed on my mind, as we were otherwise being constantly reprimanded for h-dropping. The continuing prestige of the h-less form in this case is perhaps related to a desire, on the part of the English educated middle classes, to display their knowledge of French. As well as *hotel, historic* and *historical* are sometimes heard without initial /h/ from RP speakers, and, with or without /h/, may be preceded by the indefinite article *an* as in 'An historic occasion'.

appearing in the *Grand Repository*, and so differences between the four sources are necessarily slight. However, it is noticeable that Spence has the smallest number of words with /h/ in this list, 7 as opposed to 11 in Walker and Burn and 13 in Sheridan. The difference between Sheridan, on the one hand, and Walker and Burn, on the other, is slight, and depends entirely on his consistent use of /h/ in *herb* and its derivatives, as opposed to Walker's uncharacteristically inconsistent pattern with /h/ in *herbal* and *herbalist* but not in *herb* or *herbage*. Spence, on the other hand, has no /h/ where all three of the others have it in *heritable*, *host*, *hostess*, and only pronounces /h/ where Walker and Sheridan have it silent in one word, *humble*, for which Burn, too, has the /h/. The *Grand Repository* is, of course, the earliest of the four pronouncing dictionaries examined here and so Spence's paucity of words with 'restored' /h/ could simply be typical of his time: we saw above, for instance, that Buchanan (1762) included *host* in his list of h-less forms. However, I would argue for another explanation: we have seen above that 'restoration' of /h/ to words in which ⟨h⟩ had formerly been silent was caused by a reaction to the stigmatization of h-dropping. Spence in 1775 would probably not have been aware of any such stigma, as his native dialect, then as now, did not delete /h/ at the beginning of words of non-French origin, at least not in stressed positions. Wright (1905: 254) writes of the traditional dialects of Britain: 'Initial *h* has remained before vowels in Sh & Or I, Sc, Irel, Nb and perhaps also in portions of n. Dur and n. Cum. In the remaining parts of England it has disappeared.' Heslop (1892: p. xvii), writing about Northumbrian, observes that '*h* is invariably used correctly, and is never omitted where it ought to be sounded'. Spence does mention h insertion in '*A Horange*' as a vulgarism in *The Giant Killer* (1814), but by then he had been living in London for at least twenty-two years, ample time to become accustomed to the 'faults of the Cockneys'. Spence's lack of forms with 'restored' /h/ in Appendix 9 is probably best explained by the lack of any awareness on the part of a native of Newcastle in 1775 that h-dropping was stigmatized, and therefore the lack of any need for 'hypercorrect' restoration.

Of course, h-dropping is not found in Scots either, and yet Burn has as many words with 'restored' /h/ as Walker and Sheridan. This could be explained by the later date of Burn's dictionary. By 1786, even though h-dropping was not found in the Scots vernacular, awareness of London prestige norms would have been fairly high in Scotland, after, for example, Sheridan's lecturing tour of 1761, and, as we have seen in §5.8, Burn studied and was influenced by other pronouncing dictionaries, notably Kenrick's. It is perhaps this transference of London norms that has caused the restoration of /h/ in, for example, *herb* in Scots (and, indeed, Tyneside), as opposed to its continued silence in this word in American English.

5.10. MERGER OF /ʍ/ AND /w/

In §4.3, we compared the phonological system represented in the *Grand Repository* with that of RP and found that the only difference of inventory that involves consonants rather than vowels is that Spence, unlike RP, contrasts /ʍ/ and /w/—that is, *which* and *witch*, *Whig* and *wig* form minimal pairs. The sound represented by ⟨wh⟩ in accents which preserve this contrast (e.g. Scots, American English) has been analysed as either a 'fortis labio-velar fricative [ʍ]' (Gimson 1970: 217) or as consonant cluster [hw]. Gimson sees this pronunciation, and the issue of its phonemic status, as parallel with that found at the beginning of words like *hue*, which could be represented phonetically as either [hj] or [ç], but concludes that 'the fact that the stock of words in which /ʍ/ may be opposed to /w/ . . . is greater than those in which [ç] is opposed to /j/, provides some argument in favour of a monophonemic rather than a biphonemic solution for /ʍ/' (1970: 217). I have followed Gimson here in representing the initial phoneme of *which* as /ʍ/, even though, as we shall see, most eighteenth-century orthoepists describe this sound as /hw/ and treat the pronunciation /wɪtʃ/ for *which* as a special kind of h-dropping.

Words with initial ⟨wh⟩ in English are mostly derived from Old English words with initial ⟨hw⟩, originally pronounced [χw] but becoming [hw], at least in southern dialects. According to Dobson (1957: 974), 'in the South and South-east Midlands, from the twelfth century onwards there was simplification to [w] by loss of the initial [h], and this pronunciation had currency in vulgar London speech'. Dobson (1957: 974) goes on to demonstrate that most sixteenth- and seventeenth-century orthoepists 'normally retain [hw] or [w]' and that 'the pronunciation [w] is shown only by sources which are influenced by vulgar or dialectal speech'. Wyld provides evidence from spellings with ⟨w⟩ rather than ⟨wh⟩ or ⟨hw⟩ from early ME in the South and West, and further instances in the fifteenth, sixteenth, and seventeenth centuries. He notes, though, that the evidence is sparser than one might have expected had this change been widespread and concludes that the change (which he describes as voicing of [ʍ] to [w]) 'was not unknown in the fifteenth century, and that this became more widespread, though for a long time not universal in London and the surrounding counties. There were perhaps always, as now, a certain number of speakers who prided themselves on "pronouncing the *h*"' (1936: 312).

In words like *who*, and its derivatives, RP now has initial /h/ rather than /w/ or /ʍ/.[48] Dobson (1957: 980–1) describes this as loss of [w] 'by vocalization and aphesis before ME *ō*' and states that *who* and related

---

[48] Some words now spelt with ⟨wh⟩ had initial ⟨h⟩ originally, the ⟨w⟩ being added in Late ME. Examples are *whole*, *whore*, and *whoop*. Most of these now have initial /h/, but, whilst the *OED* has /h/ for *whoop*, the *CSED* gives initial /w/. Both sources have initial /h/ in *whooping cough*.

forms are found without *w* in the thirteenth and fourteenth centuries, but that sixteenth- and seventeenth-century orthoepists show variation and concludes that 'StE normally kept pronunciations developed from the ME form which retained [w] until about 1650; [huː], &c. entered educated speech, it would seem, about 1640.' By the late eighteenth century, this change to /h/ in *who* etc. is accepted by the likes of Walker and Sheridan. The latter gives a 'simple rule' for the pronunciation of ⟨wh⟩, that 'it never stands for the simple aspirate *h*, except before the vowel *o*; when it precedes any of the other vowels, the *w* forms diphthongs with them, preceded by the aspirate' (Sheridan 1780: 22).[49] The change to /w/ before other vowels is mentioned without any unfavourable comment in the earlier part of the eighteenth century: Jespersen (1909–49: 374) tells us that it was mentioned in the eighteenth century first by John Jones, who notes (1701: 118) '*what, when,* etc., sounded *wat, wen,* etc., by some', and later by Johnston (1764) who states that in *wh-* the *h* is 'very little heard'.[50] By the end of the century, though, 'dropping' the ⟨h⟩ of the ⟨wh⟩ is stigmatized just as much as the dropping of initial /h/ discussed in §5.9. As Jespersen points out, Elphinston in 1787 'mentions *wat* and *wen* as bad pronunciations heard in England' and Walker includes 'not sounding *h* after *w*' in his list of the 'faults of Londoners' (1791: p. xiii, quoted in Jespersen 1909–49: 374), On the letter ⟨h⟩, Walker (1791: 46) writes:

This letter is often sunk after *w*, particularly in the capital, where we do not find the least distinction of sound between *while* and *wile, whet* and *wet, where* and *wear*. Trifling as this difference may appear at first sight, it tends greatly to weaken and impoverish the pronunciation, as well as sometimes to confound words of a very different meaning. The Saxons, as Dr. Lowth observes, placed the *h* before the *w*, as *hwat*, and this is certainly its true place; for in the pronunciation of all words, beginning with *wh*, we ought to breath forcibly before we pronounce the *w*, as if the words were written *hoo-at, hoo-ile* &c. and then we shall avoid that feeble, cockney pronunciation, which is so disagreeable to a correct ear.

The pronunciation of ⟨wh⟩ as /w/ is stigmatized towards the end of the eighteenth century even though it had probably found its way into at least the colloquial usage of educated southerners by then. Looking carefully at what Walker has to say above, we see that it is stigmatized because it creates homophones, and because it is associated with Cockney, but, above all, it is stigmatized because, like h-dropping, it involves a deviation from the written word and, what is worse, the 'loss' of a letter. Although Walker does not state this explicitly, I presume that the pronunciation of ⟨wh⟩ as /h/ in *who*

---

[49] Sheridan here analyses the sound represented by ⟨wh⟩ in *when* as [hu], suggesting that, for him at least, it was [hw] rather than [ʍ].

[50] What Johnston (1764: 9) writes is: '*Wh* sounds *whee* before *a, e* and *i* . . . where the *h* is very little heard: when *o* follows it, the *h* only and not the *w* is heard.' This suggests, not that few people pronounce the /h/ in ⟨wh⟩, but that the aspiration is faint.

etc. is exempted from this condemnation, because what was then regarded as the 'true' sound of ⟨wh⟩—i.e. [huː]—is still present.

We have already noted that Elphinston saw the change of /ʍ/ to /w/ in *what*, *when*, etc. as a fault of the English, whilst Walker saw it more specifically as a fault of the Cockneys. This change began in the south of England and, like h-dropping, it has never affected Scots. This is probably because, as late as the end of the eighteenth century, the pronunciation of ⟨wh⟩ in Scots was [χw] rather than the 'weaker' [hw]. We are told as much by Sylvester Douglas, who writes under *W*: 'The Scotch pronounce the *wh* like their guttural *ch*, followed in like manner by a *u*, losing itself in the succeeding vowel' (Douglas 1779, quoted in C. Jones 1991: 141). Douglas goes on to observe that 'when they endeavour to correct this fault they are apt to omit the *h*, so as to pronounce *whit* and *wit*, *whig* and *whig* in the very same manner' (Douglas 1779, quoted in C. Jones 1991: 141). This suggests that, in the eighteenth century, some Scots speakers might pronounce /ʍ/ as /w/ thinking it to be more correct than the very un-English sounding [χw]. Charles Jones (1997) suggests that there may be evidence of this tendency in James Robertson's *The Ladies' Help to Spelling*, a book published in Glasgow in 1722. Robertson pairs together as words that 'sound alike' *while/wile*; *whore/woer* [= *wooer*]; *white/Wight*; *who/woe*. Jones (1997: 448–9) writes of this:

It is difficult to imagine [hw] onsets in items like ⟨woe⟩, ⟨woer⟩ and ⟨wile⟩. We might therefore tentatively suggest that [h]-less forms are being recommended by Robertson to the young Ladies of Glasgow, a female usage directly opposed to that of London. Since [hw] forms were regarded as particularly Scottish (especially their 'Commonly Pronounced' ⟨chot⟩ '*what*' and ⟨chuen⟩ '*when*' types with their syllable initiating [χ]/[ç]) then their replacement by [w] might be expected in a work recommending at least local prestige usage.

The Scots who wished to pronounce correctly would thus wish to avoid the 'provincial' [χw] and may not have realized that [w] was regarded in England as 'vulgar': indeed, in the early part of the century when the *Ladies' Help* was written, there is no evidence that it was stigmatized in England. By the end of the eighteenth century, Scottish orthoepists who, like Elphinston, were familiar with polite London usage, would have been aware that [w] was just as 'incorrect' as [χw], but those who were confined to Scotland might not have been. There is no evidence of [w] being recommended by orthoepists from the north of England. In present-day Tyneside English, *what*, *when*, etc. are pronounced with initial [w]: this change has reached further north than h-dropping. However, Kolb (1966: 347) shows [hw] even in *who*, *whose* in the traditional dialects of Northumberland, and Wright (1905: 209) tells us that 'initial hw has generally remained in Sh & Or I, Sc (except in n.e.) Irel., Nhb., n. Dur., Cum., Wm., n. Yks., IMa. . . . In the remaining parts of England initial hw has become w'. We might, therefore, expect to find [hw] or [ʍ] even in the 'polite' usage of educated, middle-class Novocastrians in the late eighteenth century, for with no 'Scotch' [χw] to avoid, the good citizens of Newcastle would have had no need or wish to veer towards the 'Cockney' [w].

Let us now look at the pronunciation of words with initial ⟨wh⟩ in our four pronouncing dictionaries, as listed in Appendix 10. As with the appendices discussed in §§5.2–5.9, the list here is confined to all the items with initial ⟨wh⟩ in traditional orthography which appear in the *Grand Repository*. Although, as we have seen in the above discussion, pronunciations of ⟨wh⟩ in the eighteenth century were usually described as [hw], I have represented the pronunciations phonemically as either /ʍ/, /w/, or /h/ in Appendix 10 and shall continue to do so in the ensuing discussion. What is most striking about Appendix 10 is the preponderance of words with /w/ in Burn. This pronunciation is signalled in Burn's dictionary by printing the ⟨h⟩ in italic, thus *whip* appears as ⟨W*h*ip⟩. Similarly, the /h/ in *who* is signalled by italicizing the initial ⟨w⟩. There are only three words in Appendix 10 which Burn prints without italicizing either the ⟨w⟩ or the ⟨h⟩, thus indicating that neither is silent: these are *whitlow*, *whitsuntide*, and *whizz*. Burn also has this ⟨Wh⟩ representation for *whiffler* (but not *whiffle*), *whitster*, and *whittle*, none of which appears in the *Grand Repository*. Apart from *whiffler*, all the words for which Burn has ⟨Wh⟩ appear consecutively, from *whitlow* to *whizz* inclusive, even though this means that some words with the element ⟨whit⟩ meaning 'white', have initial /w/ (*whitleather*, not in Appendix 10) and others, such as *whitster* and *whitsuntide*, have /ʍ/. This might suggest that Burn, like Robertson in the *Ladies' Help*, is recommending a 'polite' Scots pronunciation with initial /w/ in the majority of cases, but that he occasionally lapses into the more natural (for a Scot) /ʍ/.

Appendix 10 shows that Walker and Sheridan have the same pronunciation for ⟨wh⟩ in every case, but Spence differs from these two in having /w/ in *wharf* and *wharfage* and differs from all three of the other orthoepists here in having /ʍ/ rather than /h/ in *who*, *whole*, *wholesale*, *wholesome*, *wholly*, *whom*, *whoop*, and *whose*. The first of these differences is hard to explain: Spence actually invented a ligatured letter for ⟨wh⟩, his {WH}, which indicates that he was well aware of the 'phonemic' status of /ʍ/. His decision to invent a single character for this rather than represent it as a sequence of /h/ and /w/ also perhaps indicates that the pronunciation represented by Spence's {WH} was [ʍ] rather than [hw]. When he departs from this representation for *wharf*, *wharfage*, it is unlikely to be a mistake. Perhaps Spence, as a resident of the quayside, had heard pronunciations of these nautical terms with /w/ from visiting southerners? This is a fanciful observation, but the only one I can offer. Spence's /ʍ/ in words with ⟨o⟩ after ⟨wh⟩ could easily be dismissed as 'spelling pronunciation' were it not for his {H} in *whore, whoredom*. These words were generally spelt with initial ⟨h⟩ until the sixteenth century,[51] and have never been pronounced with initial [ʍ] or [hw], but if Spence had been recording an artificial spelling pronunciation for *who*, etc., we might have expected to find it here as well. *Whole*, like *whore*, was originally spelt with initial ⟨h⟩, but in this case *OED* tells us that dialectal pronunciations with [ʍ] do appear. Likewise, for *who* and its derivatives, pronunciations with initial [hw] are recorded in Northumberland by the SED: Orton and Halliday (1962–3) show instances of *who* pronounced [hweː, hwiː] and *whose* pronounced [hweːz, hwiːz] in Northumberland. Presumably, the [w] has not been assimilated in these dialects because the following vowel is [iː] or [eː] rather than [uː]. Spence was no doubt aware that the 'correct' vowel was [uː] in these words, but may also have been aware that his native [ʍ] or [hw] was prestigious (he would almost certainly have heard this rather than initial /w/ in *which*, etc., from the clergymen who provided his model of 'correct' speech). Spence's use of /ʍ/ in *who*, etc., was a northernism, but not one that was stigmatized: Walker and Sheridan tell us that ⟨wh⟩ is pronounced /h/ before ⟨o⟩ but make no adverse comment about the retention of /ʍ/ in such words, and it is quite possible that educated middle-class speakers in the Newcastle of 1775 did use a 'compromise' pronunciation with the 'northern' but usually 'correct' /ʍ/ but with the 'southern' vowels which would normally trigger assimilation to /h/.

---

[51] According to the *OED*, they could even be spelt with initial ⟨w⟩ in the sixteenth century, but there is no direct evidence that these words could be pronounced with initial /w/ at the time.

6. Conclusion

We saw in Chapter 2 that, if the eighteenth century is one of 'the Cinderellas of English historical linguistic study' (Charles Jones 1989: 279), then phonology is the Cinderella of eighteenth-century studies, and Spence is the Cinderella of eighteenth-century phonology. I hope that the detailed study in Chapter 5 of information from Spence's *Grand Repository* and other eighteenth-century pronouncing dictionaries has been enough to show that such scholarly neglect is unjustified and, in particular, that Dobson's dismissive remark about eighteenth-century orthoepists (quoted in §3.2.2) is misconceived. C. Jones (1993: 96) suggests that one explanation for 'this state of affairs' is 'the still resonant perception of the period as normative and prescriptive, negative characteristics which have somehow come to imply at worst a lack of reliability in the accounts of contemporary observers', yet we have seen that even the arch-prescriptivist Walker deserves far more credit than he is given by the likes of Sheldon for the acuteness of his observations. Even where Walker condemns a proscribed pronunciation such as 'h-dropping', his remarks provide valuable information concerning the sociolinguistic situation in late-eighteenth-century Britain. Instead of ignoring these pronouncing dictionaries because they offend our late-twentieth-century sense of political correctness, we should, like Crowley (1991), pay attention to them, not least for the window they provide onto the socio-political significance of linguistic issues in the eighteenth century.

When we take seriously the evidence provided by eighteenth-century pronouncing dictionaries, we find a wealth of information on the diffusion of sound changes in this period. In Chapter 5, I have been able to deal only with a small number of sound changes and with evidence from Spence's *Grand Repository* and three other pronouncing dictionaries of his time in each section: in terms of the resources available, I have hardly scratched the surface, yet I believe that there are significant findings.

In §5.2, a large lexical set was examined, comprising words with reflexes of ME and later /a/, for evidence of the lengthening of this vowel. Where there were differences between the four pronouncing dictionaries studied in terms of the distribution of long and short reflexes of this vowel, it was found that these were not discrepancies which could be written off as revealing inaccuracy or inconsistency on the part of the orthoepists/lexicographers concerned, but that the four dictionaries represented different stages in the evolution of the sound change. Walker's distribution represents that of the most advanced variety and Spence's that of the most conservative, with Johnston and Burn coming in between. This gradation from advanced to conservative applies not only to the proportion of long reflexes in the four dictionaries, but also to the nature of the lengthening rule in the four 'grammars' represented by them: in Walker's phonology, the rule has been fully phonemicized and is categorical, whilst in Johnston's, Burn's, and, to a lesser extent, Spence's, the rule is still to a certain extent subject to phonological constraints (though less so than in the earlier grammars of Flint and Cooper), and to lexical diffusion. This pattern is entirely compatible with the account of the life-cycle of a sound change given by Harris (1989: 37) and the fact that patterns such as this have been revealed in Chapter 5 is in itself enough to justify the decision to take seriously the evidence of eighteenth-century pronouncing dictionaries.

The pattern found in §5.2 shows the Scots (Johnston?, Burn) and northern (Spence) orthoepists as more conservative than the Londoner, Walker. This is only to be expected at a time when London was acknowledged to be the hub of polite society: many sound changes (such as jod-dropping, loss of rhoticity, the merger of /ʍ/ and /w/) had originated in the capital, and the provinces were considered behind the times in linguistic as well as sartorial fashions. However, as we saw in Chapter 1, Newcastle in the eighteenth century was a thriving intellectual centre in its own right, and the same could certainly be said for the major cities of 'North Britain', Glasgow and Edinburgh. Today, Glasgow and Edinburgh each have their own prestigious local accents, 'Kelvinside' and 'Morningside' respectively, and I have argued in §5.4 that Newcastle has a similar phenomenon in what I have called the 'Jesmond' accent. We saw in §5.3.3.4 that provincial orthoepists such as Spence and Buchanan recommended the usage of clergymen and barristers in their own cities as models of 'correct' pronunciation, and I suggested that these upper-middle-class professionals might well exemplify a kind of 'modified' local standard. Some of the findings in Chapter 5 certainly point to the existence of standards of pronunciation in Scotland and in Newcastle which were not always identical with those of London. We saw in §5.6 that jod-dropping, or 'sinking the liquefaction' as Elphinston called it, was stigmatized to a greater extent in Scotland than in London, and that the Glaswegian, Burn, showed significantly less evidence of jod-dropping than Walker, Sheridan, or Spence. In §5.10, Burn's indication that ⟨h⟩ is silent in words with initial ⟨wh⟩, except for the subset including words like *who* in which the ⟨w⟩ is silent, seems puzzling, given that this particular instance of 'h-dropping' (or, in the terms used in this work, the merger of /ʍ/ and /w/) was condemned as a cockneyism by Walker, and is not found in present-day Scots. However, when we compare the data examined in §5.10 with the material presented in Charles Jones (1997) we see a real possibility that, in Glasgow at least, /w/ was the more 'refined' pronunciation, avoiding as it does any possibility of the speaker falling into the 'harsh' Scottish pronunciation with initial [ç] or [χ].

Because northern orthoepists have had less attention paid to them than Scottish ones, there is little in the way of similar corroborative evidence where Spence's 'northernisms' are concerned. However, the examination of material from the *Grand Repository* in Chapter 5 has uncovered nothing to support Place's accusation (quoted in §1.2.3) that Spence 'spelled the words, according to the Northumbrian idiom'. We saw in §5.8 that, whilst Spence's phonology is undoubtedly rhotic, this would be viewed as 'correct' in 1775 and that the *Grand Repository* shows no evidence of the effects of the 'Northumbrian burr' which Spence is described as having used himself. Other 'northern' features, such as the lack of a phoneme corresponding to RP /ʌ/, are just as likely, then as now, to have been found in the 'modified' local standard of the Newcastle clergymen used as models by Spence, whilst others, like the retention of /ʍ/ in *which*, etc., would actually be viewed as 'correct' even in London. Where Spence differs from the other orthoepists examined here, it is sometimes not in the direction of Northumbrian usage but in a, possibly 'hypercorrect', tendency to avoid such usage. One example of this was found in §5.2, where we saw Spence's extension of the change of ME /a/ to /ɔː/ before /l/ to recent neoclassical formations like *altitude.* This, like Burn's use of /w/ in *which*, etc., could be explained as an avoidance of a local pronunciation deemed 'incorrect'—in this case, the Northumbrian [aːl] in words like *all, ball*, etc.

The material examined in Chapter 5 shows, above all, that eighteenth-century pronouncing dictionaries in general, and Spence's *Grand Repository* in particular, are worthy of our attention. The scholarly neglect of the past is perhaps understandable though, because a study such as this would not have been possible without resources and technology that have only become available relatively recently. The availability of Alston's microfiche collection *English Linguistics 1500–1800* has made access to the works of eighteenth-century orthoepists/lexicographers much easier, whilst OCP has allowed me to deal with the large amounts of data needed to reveal the complex patterns of diffusion described in, for instance, §5.2. It is only when we work on this scale, looking at the distribution of a sound change across the whole lexicon rather than at a few isolated examples, that a pattern emerges from what might otherwise be seen as chaos and inconsistency. Of course, there are drawbacks to the approach taken here: even with the use of OCP, there has been a great deal of groundwork to be done in preparing the lists provided in Appendices 2–10. Recoding and entering the data from even such a small dictionary as the *Grand Repository* was painstaking and time-consuming, as was the task of looking up in the other dictionaries the words from the lists output from OCP. In some cases, notably that of the unstressed vowels discussed in §5.7, limitations even in Spence's otherwise 'phonetic' system made the task of obtaining a suitable word-list from OCP impossible. On the whole, though, I would assert that the findings of Chapter 5 vindicate the method used here, and, indeed, given that the idea of lexical diffusion has been around since Wang (1969) introduced it, and given that a pronouncing dictionary provides us with a kind of lexicon, it is surprising that there have not been more studies of this kind.

6.2. POINTERS TO FUTURE WORK

I have already indicated that the studies in Chapter 5 barely scratch the surface in terms of the wealth of phonological evidence available in eighteenth-century pronouncing dictionaries. There are many other dictionaries, such as those of Kenrick and Perry, the investigation of which would bear fruit, particularly with an approach similar to that used here. Although this study has been primarily concerned with Spence's *Grand Repository,* the other pronouncing dictionaries used for comparison have proved just as fascinating. Burn has hardly been studied at all elsewhere, except for references to him in, for example, Charles Jones (1991), yet, within the limitations of his notation, he provides a great deal of important evidence, not least of which is that pointing towards the existence of a sort of 'Proto-Kelvinside' local standard in eighteenth-century Glasgow. The production of a monograph on Burn would be an interesting and valuable task in itself, but perhaps has become even more timely with the upsurge of interest in Scottish orthoepists of the eighteenth century heralded by Jones (1995). Even Walker and Sheridan, who have had a relatively large share of scholarly attention lavished upon them by, for example, Sheldon (1938, 1947, 1967) and Benzie (1972) would merit further attention of the detailed nature applied here.

Quite apart from the study of individual pronouncing dictionaries, there is a need for work on northern grammarians and orthoepists to complement that being carried out by, for example, Charles Jones (1991, 1993, 1995, 1997) on the Scottish ones. I pointed out in Chapter 1 that more grammars were printed in Newcastle in the eighteenth century than in any other anglophone city except London: surely this phenomenon of northern grammarians and orthoepists needs to be examined? Hitherto, there have been isolated monographs on northerners such as John Kirkby, Granville Sharp, and Mather Flint but no work drawing these together to compare with that of Jones (1995) on the Scots.

More specifically, there is much work yet to be done on the *Grand Repository.* I have been able to look at only nine sound changes, or nine areas of the phonology, in Chapter 5, and even here there are matters left unresolved. The distribution of the different pronunciations of unstressed vowels in the *Grand Repository* would yield a volume in itself and the comparison of Spence's patterns with those of present-day Tyneside English (which are quite different from those of RP) would be a fascinating task for a phonetician. Quite apart from the phonology, there are other aspects of the *Grand Repository* which would be well worth investigating. The lexicographical aspects have not been discussed here, yet, in searching through word-lists and looking up words from these lists in the other dictionaries, it becomes apparent that some words (those marked with a dash in Appendices 2–10) are not found in some or even any of the other dictionaries here: examples are *antarctic, magna carta*, and *dorture*. If we found a dictionary published before 1775 which contained all these words, we might be nearer to finding a source for the *Grand Repository*. There again, some of the definitions (such as *whig*: 'a friend to civil and religious liberty') bear the hallmark of Spence as clearly as Dr. Johnson's do his, and some of the words could equally be Spence's own in the sense of having been collected in the course of his eclectic reading, rather than taken from another dictionary. Either way, there is some fascinating detective work to be done.

I have concentrated throughout on the *Grand Repository*, but, in Chapter 1 and in §5.7, I refer to Spence's later works written in modified versions of his New Alphabet. Shields (1973, 1974) has carried out some work on the comparison of Spence's different alphabets, but this is on a small scale and only suggests, as we saw in §5.7, that the later versions involve a certain amount of compromise towards spelling pronunciation on Spence's part. Spence's remarks on 'vulgar' pronunciations in his last work *The Giant Killer* (1814, quoted in §1.2.1) indicate that Spence had become aware of Cockney vulgarisms by then, and it would be interesting to see if a more thorough comparison of the *Grand Repository* with later works such as the 'phonetic' versions of *The Important Trial of Thomas Spence* and *The Constitution of Spensonia* reveal any change in the actual pronunciations suggested by the notation.

6.3. CLOSING REMARKS

Although I have referred to various phonological theories in Chapters 2 and 5, this work has been essentially pretheoretical. I pointed out in Chapter 3 that, in the past, scholars had tended to make *a priori* assumptions about the evidence provided by orthoepists, tending to ignore or dismiss anything that did not fit in with whatever theory they espoused. Given the neglect of eighteenth-century phonology demonstrated in Chapter 2, I felt from the outset that the most important thing to do in this work would be to take the data seriously, examine them closely, and then to seek an explanation for what might seem random or inconsistent patterns of distribution. It should come as no surprise that the most satisfactory explanations have been afforded by lexical phonology, a theory which takes account of lexical diffusion as a process which occurs at certain stages in the evolution of a sound change, but, in some cases, more 'sociolinguistic' explanations, involving the existence of different norms in Newcastle, Glasgow and London, have been more appropriate. To a phonological theorist, this method might seem unfashionably empirical and deductive, but, as Charles Jones (1989: 265–74), did when dealing with data from Henry Machyn's diary I have found that a close examination of such detailed information as can be found in eighteenth-century pronouncing dictionaries 'will remind us of the complexity of actual historical data and warn us against the temptation of too readily accepting "neat" and all-embracing solutions for the phonological variation they provide' (C. Jones 1989: 268). Finally, I would like to think that, along with Abercrombie (1948) and Shields (1973, 1974), I have ensured that there will never again be reason to refer to Spence as a 'forgotten phonetician'.

APPENDIX 1

Sample of output from OCP: all words containing the recoded character ⟨3⟩ (= Spence's {ɑ})

(aDR3'TNiS)	1	(e'KWiP3Z)	1	(K3'N)	1
(aDR3'T)	1	(F3'BiL)	1	(K3')	1
(aJ3'N)	1	(F3'L)	1	(L3'iL)	1
(aN3'iNS)	1	(F3'N)	1	(L3'NZ)	1
(aN3'iR)	1	(F3'ST)	1	(L3'N)	1
(aN3'NT)	1	(F3'ZiN)	1	(L3'TiR)	1
(aP3'NT)	1	(F3')	1	(MeM3'R)	1
(aV3'DiBiL)	1	(GR3'N)	1	(M3'DOR)	1
(aV3'D)	1	(HE'R3N)	1	(M3'iTE)	1
(BR3'DiR)	1	(He'MiR3DZ)	1	(M3'L)	1
(BR3'L)	1	(H3'ST)	1	(M3'STUR)	1
(BuRJ3'S)	1	(H3')	1	(M3'ST)	1
(B3'iNSE)	1	(J3'FuL)	1	(N3'SuM)	1
(B3'is)	1	(J3'NiR)	1	(N3'ZE)	1
(B3'L)	1	(J3'NTUR)	1	(N3'Z)	1
(B3'STiRuS)	1	(J3'N)	1	(O'ViRJ3)	1
(B3')	2	(J3'ST)	1	(PaRa'BiL3D)	1
(C3'S)	1	(J3')	1	(PuRL3'N)	1
(DiK3')	1	(iNJ3'N)	1	(P3'NTiD)	1
(DiSaP3'NTMiNT)	1	(iNJ3')	1	(P3'NT)	1
(DiSaP3'NT)	1	(i'NV3S)	1	(P3'NYiRD)	1
(DiSJ3'NT)	1	(KL3'STiR)	1	(P3'ZiN)	1
(DiSj3'N)	1	(KL3'STRiS)	1	(P3'Z)	1
(DiSL3'iL)	1	(KoNJ3'NT)	1	(RiJ3'N)	1
(DiV3'D)	1	(KoNJ3'N)	1	(RiJ3'S)	1
(DiV3'R)	1	(KoNV3')	1	(RiK3'L)	1
(D3'T)	1	(KoN3'D)	1	(RiZe'RV3'R)	1
(eKSPL3'T)	1	(KoRiL3'DiL)	1	(RoMB3'DiS)	1
(eMBR3'DiRE)	1	(Ko'NV3)	1	(R3'iLiST)	1
(eMBR3'DiR)	1	(Ko'RiL3D)	1	(R3'iLTE)	1
(eMBR3'L)	1	(KW3'N)	1	(R3'iL)	1
(eMPL3'iR)	1	(K3NiR)	1	(SA'NF3N)	1
(eMPL3')	1	(K3'FiD)	1	(SFER3'D)	1
(eMP3'ZiN)	1	(K3'F)	2	(SP3'L)	1
(eSKRi'T3R)	1	(K3'L)	1	(S3'L)	1
(eS3'N)	1	(K3'NiJ)	1	(TRE'F3L)	1

(TR3′WAT)	1	(T3′)	1	(V3′S)	1
(TuRM3′L)	1	(VIS-R3′)	1	(3′L)	1
(T3′LiT)	1	(V3′DiR)	1	(3′NTMiNT)	1
(T3′L)	1	(V3′D)	1	(3′STiR)	1

Total words read	17,031
Total words selected	17,031
Total words picked	122
Total words sampled	122
Total words kept	122
Total vocabulary	120

APPENDIX 2*a*

Nares's list of words with 'Open A' spelt ⟨a⟩ compared with the same entries in the *Grand Repository* and three other pronouncing dictionaries

Entry	Spence	Walker	Johnston	Burn	RP
ADAGIO	short	/eː/	—	/eː/	long
ADVANCE	short	short	short	long	long
ADVANTAGE	short	short	short	short	long
AFTER	short	short	short	long	long
AGHAST	short	short	—	long	long
AH	long	long	long	long	long
AHA	long	long	—	long	long
ALABASTER	short	short	short	long	variable*
ALAS	short	short	/eː/	short	short
ALEXANDER	short	short	short	short	long
ALMOND	short	long	long	long	long
ALMS	long	long	long	long	long
(AMEN)	long	/eː/	/eː/	/eː/	long/ /eː/
ANSWER	short	short	long	long	long
ANT	short	short	long	short	short
ASK	short	short	short	short	long
ASP	short	short	short	long	short
ASS	short	short	short	long	short
BALM	/ɔː/	long	long	/ɔː/	long
BASK	short	short	short	long	long
BASKET	short	short	short	long	long
BASTARD	short	short	short	long	variable*
BATH	short	long	short	long	long
BLANCH	long	short	long	long	long
BLASPHEME	short	short	short	short	short
BLAST	short	short	short	long	long
BOMBAST	short	short	short	long	short
BRANCH	long	short	long	long	long
BRASS	short	short	short	long	long
(BRAVADO)	/eː/	/eː/	/eː/	/eː/	long
CALF	long	long	long	long	long
CALM	long	long	long	long	long
(CANTATA)	/eː/	/eː/	—	/eː/	long
CASCADE	short	short	short	short	short
CASK	short	short	short	long	long
CASKET	short	short	short	long	long

Entry	Spence	Walker	Johnston	Burn	RP
CAST	short	short	short	long	long
CASTLE	short	short	short	long	long
CATHOLIC	short	short	short	short	short
CHAFF	short	short	short	long	long
CHALDRON	short	long	long	long	/ɔː/
CHANCE	short	short	short	long	long
CHANDLER	short	long	long	long	long
CHANT	short	short	long	long	long
CLASP	short	short	short	long	long
CLASS	short	short	short	short	long
COMMAND	short	long	long	long	long
COMPLAISANT	/ɪ/	short	long	long	/ə/
CONTRAST	short	short	short	variable	long
COUNTERMAND	short	long	long	long	long
COURANT	short	long	short	long	long
CRAFT	short	short	short	long	long
DANCE	short	short	short	long	long
DASTARD	short	short	short	long	short
DEMAND	short	long	long	long	long
DISASTER	short	short	short	long	long
DRAFF	short	short	—	long	short
DRAMA	short	short/ /eː/	short	long	long
ELASTIC	short	short	short	short	short
ENCHANT	short	short	long	long	long
ENHANCE	short	short	short	long	long
ENSAMPLE	short	—	long	long	long
EXAMPLE	short	short	long	short	long
FAST	short	short	short	long	long
FATHER	long	long	long	long	long
FLASK	short	short	short	long	long
FRANCE	—	—	long	—	—
GALLANT	short	short	short	variable	short
GANTLET	short	short	short	short	short/ /ɔː/
GAPE	/eː/	long	/eː/	long	/eɪ/
GASP	short	short*	short	long	long
GHASTLY	short	short	—	long	long
GLANCE	short	short	short	long	long
GLANDERS	short	short	—	long	short
GLASS	short	short	short	long	long
GRAFF	short	short	short	long	—
GRANT	short	short	long	long	long
GRASP	short	short	short	long	long
GRASS	short	short	short	long	long

Entry	Spence	Walker	Johnston	Burn	RP
HA	long	long	—	long	long
HALF	long	long	long	long	long
HASP	short	short	short	long	long
JANTY	short	long	—	long	—
JASPER	short	short	short	short	short
LANCE	short	short	short	long	long
LANCH	—	short	long	long	—
LASS	short	short	short	short	short
LAST	short	short	short	short	long
LATH	short	long	short	long	long
MAMMA	long	long	long	long	long
MASCULINE	short	short	short	short	short
MASK	short	short	short	long	long
MASS	short	short	—	short	variable**
MAST	short	short	short	long	long
MASTER	long	long	long	long	long
MASTIFF	short	short	short	long	short
NASTY	short	short	short	short	long
PALM	long	long	long	long	long
PAPA	long	long	long	long	long
PARAGRAPH	short	short	short	long	variable*
PASCHAL	short	short	short	short	short
PASS	short	short	short	long	long
PASQUIN	—	short	short	short	—
PAST	short	short	short	long	long
PASTERN	—	short	short	short	short
PASTOR	short	short	short	long	long
PASTURE	short	short	short	long	long
PASTY	/eː/	short	short	long	short
PATH	short	short	short	long	long
PILASTER	short	short	short	long	short
PLANCHED	short	—	—	short	—
PLANT	short	short	long	short	long
PLASTER	short	short	—	long	long
PLASTIC	short	short	short	short	variable**
POETASTER	—	short	short	short	short/ /eɪ/
PRANCE	short	long	short	long	long
PSALM	long	long	long	long	long
QUAFF	short	short	/ɔː/	short	/ɒ/ /long
QUALM	/ɔː/	/ɔː/	/ɔː/	long	long
RAFT	short	short	short	long	long
RAFTER	short	short	short	long	long
RASCAL	short	short	short	short	long

Entry	Spence	Walker	Johnston	Burn	RP
RATH	—	short	—	—	short
RASP	short	short	short	long	long
REMAND	—	long	long	long	long
REPAST	short	short	short	long	long
REPRIMAND	short	long	long	long	long
SALAMANDER	—	long	short	long	short
SALVE	long	long	long	long	variable**
SAMPLE	short	short	short	short	long
SCATH	short	short	—	long	—
SHAFT	short	short	long	long	long
SLANDER	short	short	long	long	long
SLANT	short	short	long	long	long
(SONATA)	—	/eː/	—	/eː/	long
STAFF	long	short	short	long	long
TASK	short	short	short	long	long
TRANCE	short	short	short	short	long
TRANSIT	short	short	short	short	short
TRANSACT	short	short	short	short	short

Notes: Words in parentheses are those for which Nares notes that the 'regular' sound of ⟨a⟩ (/eː/) is equally acceptable.
   * = variable with long first (i.e. more usual); ** = variable with short first.

APPENDIX 2*b*

Incidence of 'long' and 'short' reflexes of ME /a/ before word-final /r/ in the *Grand Repository* and three other pronouncing dictionaries

Entry	Spence (1775)	Walker (1791)	Johnston (1764)	Burn (1786)
AFAR	short	long	short	short
BAR	short	long	short	short
CAR	short	long	short	short
FAR	short	long	long	short
JAR	short	long	short	long
MAR	short	long	short	long
PAR	short	long	short	short
SPAR	short	long	short	short
STAR	short	long	short	short
TAR	short	long	short	long

APPENDIX 2c(i)

Words with {Λ} in stressed syllables in the *Grand Repository* compared with the same entries in two other pronouncing dictionaries

Entry	Johnston (1764)	Burn (1786)	Entry	Johnston (1764)	Burn (1786)
ALARM	long	long	BARLEY	long	long
ALARMING	—	long	BARLEYBRAKE	—	long
APART	long	long	BARLEYCORN	—	long
APARTMENT	—	long	BARM	long	long
ARC	—	long	BARN	long	long
ARCH	long	long	BARNACLE	long	long
ARCHED	—	long	BARNACLES	—	—
ARCHER	long	long	BARTER	long	short
ARCHERY	short	long	CARD	long	long
ARCHWISE	—	long	CARDINAL	long	long
ARK	long	long	CARPENTRY	short	long
ARM	long	long	CARPENTER	long	long
ARMED	—	long	CARPER	—	—
ARMISTICE	—	long	CARPET	long	long
ARMOURY	long	long	CARPING	—	long
ARMOURER	—	long	CART	long	long
ARMOUR	long	long	CARTE BLANCHE	—	long
ARMPIT	—	long	CARTEL	long	long
ARMS	long	long	CARTER	—	long
ARMS-END	—	long	CARTRIDGE	short	long
ARMY	long	long	CARVE	long	long
ART	long	long	CARVER	long	long
ARTFUL	long	long	CARVING	—	long
ARTICLE	long	long	CHARGE	long	long
ARTIST	long	long	CHARGEABLE	long	long
ARTLESS	—	long	CHARGER	long	long
BARBARISM	short	long	CHARM	long	long
BARBAROUS	long	long	CHARMER	long	long
BARBERRY	long	long	CHARMING	long	long
BARD	long	long	CHARNEL	long	long
BARGAINER	—	—	CHART	long	long
BARGE	long	long	CHARTER	long	long
BARK	long	long	CHARTERED	—	long
BARKER	—	long	CHARTER (party)	—	long
BARKY	—	long	COMPART	—	long

Entry	Johnston (1764)	Burn (1786)	Entry	Johnston (1764)	Burn (1786)
COPARTNER	long	long	MARGARET	—	long
DARK	long	long	MARGIN	long	long
DARKLY	—	long	MARGINAL	long	—
DARKNESS	long	long	MARGRAVE	long	long
DARKSOME	long	long	MARJORY	—	—
DARKEN	long	long	MARK (n.)	long	long
DARLING	—	long	MARK (vb.)	long	long
DARN	long	long	MARKET	long	long
DART	long	long	MARKSMAN	long	long
DEPART	long	long	MARL	long	long
DEPARTMENT	—	long	MARLINE	—	long
DEPARTURE	long	long	MARMADUKE	—	—
DISARM	long	long	MARQUESS	long	long
DISBARK	long	long	MARQUISATE	long	long
DISCARD	long	long	MARSHALL	short	long
DISCHARGE	long	long	MART	long	long
DISEMBARK	long	long	MARTHA	long	—
DISREGARD	/e:/	long	MARTIAL	long	long
EARL MARSHALL	—	long	MARTIN	—	long
ENARCH	—	—	MARTINGALE	long	long
FOOLHARDY	—	long	MARTINMAS	—	long
GUARD	long	long	MARTYR	long	long
GUARDIAN	long	long	MARTYRDOM	long	long
GUARDSHIP	—	long	MARVEL	long	long
HARM	long	long	PARK	long	long
HARP	long	long	PARLEY	long	long
HARPING IRON	—	long	PARLIAMENT	long	long
HART	—	long	PARLOUR	long	long
HUSSARS	—	—	PARSLEY	long	—
IMPART	long	long	PARSNIP	long	—
INTERLARD	long	long	PARSON	long	long
LARCENY	long	long	PART	long	long
LARD	long	long	PARTNERSHIP	—	long
LARDER	long	long	PARTNER	long	long
LARGE	long	long	PARTRIDGE	long	long
LARGELY	—	long	PARTS	—	long
LARGESSE	long	long	PARTY	long	long
LARK	long	long	PROTOMARTYR	short	long
MARCH	long	long	REGARD	long	long
MARCHES	—	long	REMARK	long	long
MARCHIONESS	long	long	RETARD	long	long
MARCID	—	long	SARK	—	long

Entry	Johnston (1764)	Burn (1786)	Entry	Johnston (1764)	Burn (1786)
SHARP	long	long	STARCH	long	long
SHARPEN	long	long	SURCHARGE	long	long
SHARPER	—	long	YARD	long	long
SMART	long	long	YARN	long	long

Here. 'long' and 'short' refer to the symbols used by Burn and Johnston which are the equivalent of Spence's {Λ} and {λ} respectively. Where a different vowel is used by either Burn or Johnston in a particular word, this is indicated either by the use of the appropriate IPA symbol, or by the use of the symbol employed in that particular dictionary. In unstressed syllables, Johnston often, but not always, uses an unaccented vowel symbol: this is referred to here as 'unstressed a'.

APPENDIX 2*c*(ii)

Words with {Λ} in unstressed syllables in the *Grand Repository* compared with the same entries in two other pronouncing dictionaries

Entry	Johnston (1764)	Burn (1786)	Entry	Johnston (1764)	Burn (1786)
ADVANCE GUARD	—	—	COUNTERPART	—	long
ARCHBISHOP	short unstressed	long	FIRE ARMS	—	long
ARCHDEACON	short unstressed	long	LANDMARK	short unstressed	long
ARCHDEACONSHIP	short unstressed	long	PARLIAMENTARY	short	long
ARCHDEACONRY	—	long	PLACART	long	long
ARCHDUCHESS	short unstressed	long	RAMPART	short unstressed	short
ARCHDUKE	short unstressed	long	SAILYARD	—	long
AVANT GARDE	—	—	VANGUARD	long	long
(charter) PARTY	—	long	VINEYARD	short unstressed	short

Here. 'long' and 'short' refer to the symbols used by Burn and Johnston which are the equivalent of Spence's {Λ} and {λ} respectively. Where a different vowel is used by either Burn or Johnston in a particular word, this is indicated either by the use of the appropriate IPA symbol, or by the use of the symbol employed in that particular dictionary. In unstressed syllables, Johnston often, but not always, uses an unaccented vowel symbol: this is referred to here as 'unstressed a'.

APPENDIX 2*d*(i)

Words with {ʌ} in stressed syllables in the *Grand Repository* compared with the same entries in two other pronouncing dictionaries

Entry	Johnston (1764)	Burn (1786)	Entry	Johnston (1764)	Burn (1786)
ANARCHIAL	—	—	BARB	long	long
ANASARCA	—	—	BARBARA	—	—
ANICATHARTIC	—	—	BARBECUE	—	short
ANTARCTIC	short	long	BARBED	—	long
ANTIMONARCHIAL	short	short	BARBER	long	long
ARBITER	short	long	BARBLE	—	long
ARBITRARY	short	long	BARGAIN	long	long
ARBITRATE	—	long	BARNABY	—	—
ARBOROUS	—	—	BOMBARD	short	long
ARBOUR	long	long	CARBONADE	—	short
ARCHETYPE	short	long	CARBUNCLE	short	short
ARCHIBALD	—	—	CARCASS	short	long
ARCHITECT	short	long	CARCELAGE	—	—
ARCHIVES	short	long	CARDIAC	long	long
ARCTIC	short	—	CARGO	long	long
ARCUATE	—	long	CARMINE	—	short
ARDENCY	short	long	CARNAGE	long	long
ARDENT	long	long	CARNAL	long	long
ARDOUR	long	long	CARNALLY	—	long
ARDUOUS	long	long	CARNEOUS	—	long
ARGILOUS	—	long	CARNIVAL	short	long
ARGIL	—	long	CARP	long	long
ARGUE	long	long	CARTILAGE	short	long
ARGUER	—	long	CARTRUT	—	long
ARGUMENT	long	long	CARTULARY	—	—
ARNOLD	—	—	CATHARTIC	/ɔː/	short
ARQUEBUSE	short	long		('broad	
ARSE	—	long		a')	
ARSENAL	short	long	CHARCOAL	short	short
ARSENIC	short	long	CHARLATAN	—	long
ARTERY	short	long	CHARLES	long	long
ARTICHOKE	short	long	CHARLOTTE	long	—
ARTIFICE	short	long	COPARCENARY	—	long
ARTISAN	short	long	COPARCENER	—	—
ARTHUR	—	—	COPARCENY	—	—

Entry	Johnston (1764)	Burn (1786)	Entry	Johnston (1764)	Burn (1786)
DEBARK	long	long	INCARCERATE	—	short
DWARF	/ɔː/	/ɔː/	INCARNATE	short	short
EMBARGO	long	short	JARGON	long	long
EMBARK	long	long	LARBOARD	long	long
ENLARGE	long	long	LETHARGIC	long	long
FARCE	short	long	MAGNA CARTA	—	—
FARCY	short	short	MARBLE	long	long
FARDEL	short	short	MARSH	short	long
FARFETCHED	—	short	MONARCHAL	—	long
FARM	long	long	MONARCHIAL	long	—
FARMER	—	long	PARBOIL	short	short
FARTHER	short	long	PARCEL	short	long
FARTHEST	—	long	PARCENERY	—	short
FARTHING	long	long	PARCHMENT	short	long
GARB	long	long	PARDON	short	long
GARBAGE	long	long	PARGET	short	short
GARBLE	long	long	PARSE	—	long
GARDEN	long	long	PARSIMONY	short	short
GARDENING	—	long	PARTERRE	short unstressed	long
GARGLE	long	long	PARTIAL	long	long
GARLAND	long	long	PARTIALLY	—	long
GARLIC	long	long	PARTICLE	long	long
GARMENT	long	long	PARTISAN	short	long
GARNER	long	long	PARVITUDE	—	long
GARNET	long	long	PERICARDIUM	—	long
GARNISH	long	long	PHARMACY	short	long
GARTER	long	long	QUARTO	/ɔː/	/ɔː/
HARBINGER	short	long	SARCASM	short	short
HARBOUR	long	long	SARCENET	short	short
HARD	long	long	SCARFSKIN	—	long
HARDEN	long	long	SCARLET	long	long
HARDLY	—	long	SHARD	—	long
HARDWARE	—	long	SCARP	long	long
HARDY	long	long	SNARL	long	long
HARLEQUIN	short	long	SPARK	long	long
HARLOT	long	long	SPARKLE	long	long
HARMONY	long	long	STARBOARD	—	short
HARNESS	long	long	STARK	long	long
HARPSICHORD	short	long	START	long	long
HARSH	long	long	STARTLE	long	long
HARVEST	long	long	STARVE	long	long
IMPARTIAL	long	long	SUPERCARGO	long	long

Entry	Johnston (1764)	Burn (1786)	Entry	Johnston (1764)	Burn (1786)
TARDY	short	long	TART	long	long
TARGE	—	—	TARTAR	long	short
TARGET	short	long	THWART	/ɔː/	/ɔː/
TARGUM	—	long	VARLET	long	long
TARNISH	short	long	VARNISH	long	long

APPENDIX 2*d*(ii)

Words with {ʌ} in unstressed syllables in the *Grand Repository* compared with the same entries in two other pronouncing dictionaries

Entry	Johnston (1764)	Burn (1786)	Entry	Johnston (1764)	Burn (1786)
ARBITRATOR	short	long	ARTICULATE	short	long
ARCADE	—	long		unstressed	
ARCANUM	—	long	ARTICULATION	short	long
ARCHANGEL	short	long	ARTIFICIAL	short	long
	unstressed		ARTIFICER	short	short
ARCHBISHOPRIC	short	long		unstressed	
	unstressed		ARTILLERY	short	long
ARCHETYPAL	—	long		unstressed	
ARCHIEPISCOPAL	—	—	BARBARIAN	short	short
ARCHIPELAGO	—	—		unstressed	
ARCHITECTURE	short	long	BARBARIC	short	short
ARCUATION	—	long		unstressed	
ARGILATIOUS	—	—	BARBARITY	short	short
ARGUMENTATION	—	long		unstressed	
ARMADA	—	short	BARGAINEE	—	—
ARMIGEROUS	—	—	BARTHOLOMEW	short	—
ARMILORY	—	long		unstressed	
ARMIPOTENT	—	long	BULWARK	short	/ʌ/
ARMORIAL	short	short		unstressed	
	unstressed		CARDIACAL	—	—
ARTHRITICAL	—	short	CARNATION	short	long
ARTICULAR	—	long		unstressed	

Entry	Johnston (1764)	Burn (1786)	Entry	Johnston (1764)	Burn (1786)
CARNIVOROUS	short unstressed	long	PARTIALITY	short	short
			PARTICIPANT	—	short
CARNOSITY	—	long	PARTICIPATE	short unstressed	short
CARTOUCHE	short unstressed	short	PARTICIPIAL	—	short
CARTOON	short unstressed	long	PARTICIPLE	long	long
			PARTICULAR	short unstressed	short
COUNTERMARCH	—	long			
COUNTERSCARP	short unstressed	long	PARTICULARISE	short unstressed	short
HARMONEOUS	short unstressed	long	PARTICULARLY	short	short
			PARTITION	short unstressed	short
HARPOON	short unstressed	long	PARTOOK	—	long
HARPOONEER	short	long	PATRIARCH	short unstressed	short
HIERARCH	—	short			
HIERARCHY	short unstressed	short	SARCASTIC	—	short
			SARCOTIC	—	short
INARTICULATE	short unstressed	short	SARDONYX	—	short
			TARPAULING	short unstressed	long
INCARNATION	short unstressed	short	TARTARIAN	—	long
MARTYROLOGY	short	long	TETRARCH	short unstressed	short
NARCOTIC	short unstressed	short	TETRARCHY	short unstressed	—
OLIGARCHY	short unstressed	short	UPSTART	short unstressed	long
PARTAKE	short unstressed	long			

APPENDIX 3*a*(i)

Words with {*ʌ*U} (= /ɔː/) before orthographic ⟨l⟩ in the *Grand Repository* compared with the same entries in three other pronouncing dictionaries

Entry	Walker (1791)	Sheridan (1780)	Burn (1786)	Entry	Walker (1791)	Sheridan (1780)	Burn (1786)
AFTERALL	ɔː	ɔː	ɔː	ALTERNATIVE	æ	æ	æ
ALB	eː	æ	æ	ALTERNATIVELY	æ	æ	æ
ALBUGINEOUS	æ	æ	—	ALTERNITY	æ	æ	æ
ALCHEMIST	æ	æ	æ	ALTHOUGH	ɔː	ɔː	ɔː
ALCHEMY	æ	æ	æ	ALTIMETRY	æ	æ	æ
ALCOHOL	æ	æ	æ	ALTITUDE	æ	æ	æ
ALCOVE	æ	æ	æ	ALTOGETHER	ɔː	ɔː	ɔː
ALDER	ɔː	ɔː	ɔː	ALUMINOUS	æ	æ	æ
ALDERMAN	ɔː	ɔː	ɔː	ALWAYS	ɔː	ɔː	ɔː
ALGEBRA	æ	æ	æ	APALL	ɔː	—	—
ALGEBRAICAL	æ	æ	æ	BALD	ɔːw	ɔː	ɔː
ALGID	æ	æ	—	BALDERDASH	ɔːw	ɔː	ɔː
ALGIDITY	æ	æ	—	BALDNESS	ɔːw	ɔː	ɔː
ALGIFIC	æ	æ	—	BALL	ɔːw	ɔː	ɔː
ALKALI	æ	æ	æ	BALM	ɑː	ɔː/æ	ɔː
ALKALINE	æ	æ	æ	BALSAM	ɔːw	ɔː	ɔː
ALKERMIS	æ	æ	æ	BALSAMIC	æ	æ	æ
ALKORAN	æ	æ	æ	BEFALL	ɑːw	ɔː	ɔː
ALL	ɔː	ɔː	ɔː	BESTIALITY	æ	æ	æ
ALL-HALLOWS	ɔː	ɔː	ɔː	BETHRAL	ɔː	ɔː	ɔː
ALMIGHTINESS	ɔː	ɔː	—	CABAL	æ	æ	æ
ALMIGHTY	ɔː	ɔː	ɔː	CABALLER	æ	æ	ɑː
ALMANAC	ɔː	ɔː	ɔː	CALDRON	ɔːw	ɔː	ɔː
ALPHA	æ	æ	æ	CALEFACTION	æ	æ	—
ALPHABET	æ	æ	æ	CALEFACTORY	æ	æ	—
ALPHABETICAL	æ	æ	æ	CALEFY	æ	æ	—
ALREADY	ɔː	ɔː	ɔː	CALK	ɔːw	ɔː	ɔː
ALSO	ɔː	ɔː	ɔː	CALKER	ɔːw	ɔː	ɔː
ALTER	ɔː	ɔː	ɔː	CALL	ɔːw	ɔː	ɔː
ALTERATION	ɔː	ɔː	ɔː	CALLING	ɔːw	ɔː	ɔː
ALTERATIVE	ɔː	ɔː	ɔː	CATCALL	ɔː	ɔː	ɔː
ALTERCATE	—	—	—	CHALDER	—	—	ɑː
ALTERCATION	æ	æ	æ	CHALDRON	ɑː	ɔː	ɑː
ALTERNATE	æ	æ	æ	CHALK	ɔːw	ɔː	ɔː
ALTERNATION	æ	æ	æ	CHALKY	ɔːw	ɔː	ɔː

Entry	Walker (1791)	Sheridan (1780)	Burn (1786)	Entry	Walker (1791)	Sheridan (1780)	Burn (1786)
CRESTFALLEN	ɔː	ɔː	ɔː	PIEBALD	ɔː	ɔː	ɔː
EXALT	ɔː	ɔː	ɔː	PSALTER	ɔːw	ɔː	ɑː
FALCATED	æ	æ	æ	PSALTERY	ɑːw	ɔː	ɑː
FALCHION	ɔː	ɔː	ɔː	QUALM	ɔː	æ	ɑː*
FALCON	ɔːw*	ɔː*	ɔː	RECALL	ɔː	ɔː	ɔː
FALL	ɔː	ɔː	ɔː	REINSTALL	ɔː	ɔː	ɔː
FALSE	ɔː	ɔː	ɔː	SALT	ɔː	ɔː	ɔː
FALSEHOOD	ɔː	ɔː	ɔː	SALTERN	ɔː	ɔː	ɔː
FALSIFY	ɔː	ɔː	ɔː	SALTPETRE	ɔː	ɔː	ɔː
FALTER	ɔː	ɔː	ɔː	SALVAGE	æ	æ	æ
FOOTBALL	ɔː	ɔː	ɔː	SALVATION	æ	æ	æ
FORESTALL	ɔːw	ɔː	ɔː	SCALD	ɔː	ɔː	ɔː
FUZZBALL	ɔː	ɔː	ɔː	SCALP	æ	æ	æ
GALL	ɔːw	ɔː	ɔː	SMALL	ɔː	ɔː	ɔː
HALL	ɔː	ɔː	ɔː	SMALL-COAL	ɔː	ɔː	ɔː
HALM*	ɔːw	ɔː	ɔː	SMALL-CRAFT	ɔː	ɔː	ɔː
HALSER*	ɔːw	ɔː	ɔː	STALK*	ɔːw	ɔː	ɔː (=stem)
HALT	ɔː	ɔː	ɔː	STALK	ɔːw*	ɔː*	ɔː* (=walk)
HALTER	ɔː	ɔː	ɔː	STALL	ɔː	ɔː	ɔː
INSTALL	ɔː	ɔː	ɔː	SUBALTERN	æ	æ	æ
INTHRALL	ɔːw	ɔ	ɔː	TALK*	ɔːw	ɔː	ɔː
MALL	æ	æ	ɔː/æ	TALKATIVE	ɔːw*	ɔː*	ɔː
MALT	ɔː	ɔː	ɔː	TALL	ɔː	ɔː	ɔː
MISCALL	ɔːw	ɔː	ɔː	WALK*	ɔː	ɔː	ɔː
OFFALS	ə	ə	æ	WALL	ɔː	ɔː	ɔː
PALL	ɔː	ɔː	ɔː	WITHALL	ɔː	ɔː	ɔː
PALL-MALL	ɛ/ɛ	ɛ/ɛ	æ/æ				
PALSY	ɔː	ɔː	ɔː				
PALTRY	ɔː	ɔː	ɔː				

Note: *denotes that the ⟨l⟩ is silent, either in a particular dictionary or, if marked on the headword, in all four (including the *Grand Repository*).

APPENDIX 3*a*(ii)

Words with {ʌ} (= /æ/) before orthographic ⟨l⟩ in the *Grand Repository* compared with the same entries in three other pronouncing dictionaries

Entry	Walker (1791)	Sheridan (1780)	Burn (1786)	Entry	Walker (1791)	Sheridan (1780)	Burn (1786)
ALMOND*	ɑː	æ	ɑː	HALCYON	æ	æ	æ
ALMONDS*	ɑː	æ	ɑː	MALVERSATION	æ	æ	æ
BALCONY	æ	æ	æ	PALFREY	æ	æ	ɔː
CALCEATED	æ	æ	—	PALMIPEDE	æ	æ	æ
CALCINATION	æ	æ	æ	PALMISTRY	æ	æ	ɑː
CALCINE	æ	æ	æ	PAPLPABLE	æ	æ	æ
CALCULATE	æ	æ	æ	PALPITATE	æ	æ	æ
CALCULATOR	æ	æ	æ	SALMON*	æ	æ	æ/æl
CALCULUS	æ	æ	æ	SALVER	ɑː	æ	æ
CALCULOUS	æ	æ	æ	SALVO	æ	æ	æ
CALX	æ	æ	æ	SCALLOP	ɒ	ɒ	ɒ
CHALKOGRAPHER	æ	æ	æ	TALMUD	æ	æ	æ
HALBERD	ɔː	ɔː	ɔː	VALVE	æ	æ	æ

Note: *denotes that the ⟨l⟩ is silent, either in a particular dictionary or, if marked on the headword, in all four (including the *Grand Repository*).

APPENDIX 3*a*(iii)

Words with {Λ} (= /ɑː/) before orthographic ⟨l⟩ in the *Grand Repository* compared with the same entries in three other pronouncing dictionaries

Entry	Walker (1791)	Sheridan (1780)	Burn (1786)	Entry	Walker (1791)	Sheridan (1780)	Burn (1786)
ALMONER	ɑː	æ	ɑː	HALF*	ɑː	æ	ɑː
ALMS	ɑː*	æ*	ɑː*	HALVE*	ɑː	æ	ɑːl
ALMSDEEDS	ɑː*	æ*	—	HALVES*	ɑː	æ	ɑːl
ALMSHOUSE	ɑː*	æ*	ɑː*	PALM*	ɑː	æ	ɑː
CALF*	ɑː	æ	ɑː	SALVE*	ɑːl	æl	ɑːl
CALM*	ɑː	æ	ɑː	THRALDOM	ɔː	ɔː	ɔː
CALMLY*	ɑː	æ	ɑː				

Note: * denotes that the ⟨l⟩ is silent, either in a particular dictionary or, if marked on the headword, in all four (including the *Grand Repository*).

APPENDIX 3*b*(i)

Words with {ᴁ} (= /ɔː/) after /w/ in Spence's *Grand Repository* compared with the same entries in three other pronouncing dictionaries

	Walker (1791)	Sheridan (1780)	Burn (1786)		Walker (1791)	Sheridan (1780)	Burn (1786)
ATHWART	ɔː	ɔː	ɔː	REARWARD	ɔː	ɛ	ɑː
AWARD	ɔː	ɔː	ɔː	REWARD	ɔː	ɔː	ɔː
FORWARN	ɔː	ɔː	ɔː	SOMEWHAT	ɒ	ɒ	ɒ
LUKEWARM	ɔː	ɔː	ɔː	SQUALL	ɔː	ɔː	ɔː
QUALM	ɔː	æ	ɑː	SWARD	ɔː	ɔː	ɔː
QUART	ɔː	ɔː	ɔː	SWARM	ɔː	ɔː	ɔː
QUARTER	ɔː	ɔː	ɔː	SWARTHY	ɔː	ɔː	ɔː
QUARTERAGE	ɔː	ɔː	ɔː	TOWARD	toːrd	toːrd	ɑː
QUARTERN	ɔː	ɔː	ɔː	TOWARDLY	ʌ	ɛ	ɑː
QUARTERS	—	—	—	TOWARDS	toːrdz	toːrdz	ɑː
QUARTERSTAFF	ɔː	ɔː	ɔː	WALK	ɔː	ɔː	ɔː

Entry	Walker (1791)	Sheridan (1780)	Burn (1786)	Entry	Walker (1791)	Sheridan (1780)	Burn (1786)
WALL	ɔː	ɔː	ɔː	WARNING	ɔː	ɔː	ɔː
WANDER	ɒ	ɒ	ɒ	WARP	ɔː	ɔː	ɔː
WANT	ɒ	ɒ	ɒ	WARRANT	ɒ	ɒ	ɔː
WANTON	ɒ	ɒ	ɔː	WARRANTABLE	ɒ	ɒ	ɔː
WAR	ɔː	ɔː	ɔː	WARREN	ɒ	ɒ	ɔː
WARBLE	ɔː	ɔː	ɔː	WARRIOR	ɔː	ɔː	ɔː
WARD	ɔː	ɔː	ɔː	WART	ɔː	ɔː	ɔː
WARDEN	ɔː	ɔː	ɔː	WAS	ɒ	ɒ	ɔː
WARDMOTE	ɔː	ɔː	ɔː	WASH	ɒ	ɒ	ɔː
WARDROBE	ɔː	ɔː	ɔː	WASP	ɒ	æ	æ
WARFARE	ɔː	ɔː	ɔː	WASPISH	ɒ	æ	æ
WARLIKE	ɔː	ɔː	ɔː	WATER	ɔː	ɔː	ɔː
WARM	ɔː	ɔː or eː	ɔː	WHARF	ɔː	ɔː	ɔː
WARMTH	ɔː	ɔː	ɔː	WHARFAGE	ɔː	ɔː	ɔː
WARN	ɔː	ɔː	ɔː	WHAT	ɒ	ɒ	ɒ

APPENDIX 3*b*(ii)

Words with {ʌ} (= /æ/) after /w/ in the *Grand Repository* compared with the same entries in three other pronouncing dictionaries

Entry	Walker (1791)	Sheridan (1780)	Burn (1786)	Entry	Walker (1791)	Sheridan (1780)	Burn (1786)
AQUATIC	æ	æ	æ	QUADRATURE	ɒ	eː	æ
CONQUASSATE	æ	æ	æ	QUADRENNIAL	ɔː	æ	æ
DEQUANTITATE	æ	æ	æ	QUADRILLE	kɔː	kɔː	æ
DISQUALIFY	ɒ	æ	æ	QUADRUPED	ɒ	æ	æ
DWARF	ɔː	ɔː	ɔː	QUADRUPLE	ɒ	æ	æ
EQUALITY	ɒ	æ	æ	QUAFF	æ	æ	æ
EQUANGULAR	æ	æ	—	QUAGMIRE	æ	æ	æ
QUACK	æ	æ	æ	QUALIFICATION	ɒ	æ	æ
QUADRAGESIMAL	ɒ	æ	æ	QUALIFY	ɒ	æ	æ
QUADRANGLE	ɒ	æ	æ	QUALITY	ɒ	æ	æ
QUADRANT	ɔː	eː	eː	QUANDARY	ɒ	ɒ	æ
QUADRATE	ɔː	eː	æ	QUANTITY	ɒ	æ	æ

Entry	Walker (1791)	Sheridan (1780)	Burn (1786)	Entry	Walker (1791)	Sheridan (1780)	Burn (1786)
QUANTUM	ɒ	æ	æ	SWATH	—	—	ɔː
QUARANTINE	ɒ	ɒ	æ	THWACK	æ	æ	æ
QUARREL	ɒ	ɒ	ɔː	THWART	ɔː	ɔː	ɔː
QUARRELSOME	ɒ	ɒ	ɔː	WAFT	æ	æ	æ
QUARRY	ɒ	ɒ	ɔː	WAG	æ	æ	æ
QUARTO	ɔː	ɔː	ɔː	WABBLE	ɒ	ɒ	—
QUASH	ɒ	ɒ	ɑː	WAD	ɒ	ɒ	æ
SQUAB	ɒ	ɒ	ɒ	WADDING	ɒ	ɒ	æ
SQUABBLE	ɒ	ɒ	æ	WADDLE	ɒ	ɒ	ɔː
SQUADRON	ɔː	ɔː	ɑː	WAGGISH	æ	æ	æ
SQUALID	ɒ	ɒ	æ	WAGGON	æ	æ	æ
SQUANDER	ɒ	ɒ	ɔː	WALLET	ɒ	ɒ	ɒ
SQUAT	ɒ	ɒ	æ	WALLOW	ɒ	ɒ	ɒ
SWAB	ɒ	ɒ	ɒ	WAN	ɒ	æ	æ
SWADDLE	ɒ	ɒ	æ	WAND	ɒ	ɒ	ɒ
SWAG	æ	æ	æ	WATCH	ɒ	ɒ	ɔː
SWAGGER	æ	æ	æ	WATTLE	ɒ	ɒ	ɒ
SWALLOW	ɒ	ɒ	ɔː	WATTLES	ɒ	ɒ	ɒ
SWAP	ɒ	ɒ	ɒ	WAX	æ	æ	æ

APPENDIX 4

Reflexes of ME /ʊ/ in the *Grand Repository* and three other pronouncing dictionaries

Entry	Spence (1775)	Walker (1791)	Sheridan (1780)	Burn (1786)
BOSOM	ɔː	ʊ	uː	ʊ
BULL	ʊ	ʊ	ʊ	ʊ
BULLET	ʊ	ʊ	ʊ	ʊ
BULLION	ʊ	ʊ	ʊ	ʊ
BULLOCK	ʊ	ʊ	ʊ	ʊ
BULLY	ʊ	ʊ	ʊ	ʊ
BULRUSH	ʊ	ʊ	ʊ	ʊ
BULWARK	ʊ	ʊ	ʊ	ʊ
BUSH	ʊ	ʊ	ʊ	ʊ
BUSHEL	ʊ	ʊ	ʊ	ʊ
BUTCHER	ʊ	ʊ	ʊ	ʊ or ʌ
COULD	ʊ	ʊ	ʊ	ʊ
CUD	ʊ	ʌ	ʌ	ʌ
CUCKOO	ʊ	ʊ	ʊ	ʊ
CURRIER	ʊ	ʌ	ʌ	ʊ
CUSHION	ʊ	ʊ	ʊ	ʌ
FULL (ad.)	ʊ	ʊ	ʊ	uː
FULL (vb.)	ʊ	ʊ	ʌ	uː
FULGENT	ʊ	ʌ	ʌ	ʊ
HOUSEWIFE	ʊ	ʌ	ʌ	ʊ
HUSSAR	ʊ	ʊ	—	—
HUZZA	ʊ	ʊ	ʌ	ʌ
PUDDING	ʊ	ʊ	ʊ	ʊ
PULL	ʊ	ʊ	ʊ	ʊ
PULLET	ʊ	ʊ	ʊ	ʊ
PULPIT	ʊ	ʊ	ʊ	ʊ
PUS (matter)	ʊ	ʌ	ʌ	ʌ
PUSS (cat)	ʊ	ʊ	ʊ	ʊ
PUSH	ʊ	ʊ	ʊ	ʊ
PUT (vb.)	ʊ	ʊ	ʊ	ʊ
PUT (n.)	ʊ	ʌ	ʌ	ʊ
SUGAR	ʊ	ʊ	ʊ	ʊ
TUSH	ʊ	ʌ	ʌ	ʊ
TUT	ʊ	ʌ	ʌ	ʊ
WOLF	ʊ	ʊ	ʊ	ʊ
WOMAN	ʊ	ʊ	ʊ	ʌ
WORSTED	ʊ	ʊ	ʊ	ʊ

Note: I have departed from strict alphabetical order where necessary in order to keep what are minimal pairs in RP adjacent to each other.

APPENDIX 5*a*

Words with {ᴕ} in the *Grand Repository* (other than those involving 'yod-dropping') compared with the same entries in three other pronouncing dictionaries

Entry	Walker (1791)	Sheridan (1780)	Burn (1786)	Entry	Walker (1791)	Sheridan (1780)	Burn (1786)
ADO	uː	uː	ʊ	BROOK	uː	uː	ʊ
AFTERNOON	uː	uː	uː	BROOM	uː	uː	uː
ALOOF	uː	uː	uː	BUFFOON	uː	uː	uː
ALTOGETHER	ɔː	ɔː	ɒ	BUFFOONERY	uː	uː	uː
APPROVABLE	uː	uː	—	CANOE	uː	uː	uː
APPROVE	uː	uː	uː	CARTOON	uː	uː	uː
APPROVER	uː	uː	uː	COMMOVE	uː	uː	uː
BABOON	uː	uː	uː	CHOOSE	uː	uː	uː
BAMBOOZLE	uː	uː	—	CONTOUR	uː	uː	uː
BEFOOL	uː	uː	uː	COO	uː	uː	uː
BEHOOF	uː	uː	uː	COOK	uː	uː	ʊ
BEHOOVE	uː	uː	uː	COOKERY	uː	uː	ʊ
BETOOK	uː	ʊ	uː	COOL	uː	uː	uː
BLACKAMOOR	ɔː	uː	ɔː	COOLER	uː	uː	uː
BLOOM	uː	uː	uː	COOLLY	uː	uː	uː
BOOBY	uː	uː	uː	COOLNESS	uː	uː	uː
BOOK	uː	uː	ʊ	COOM	uː	uː	ʊ
BOOKISH	uː	uː	ʊ	COOMB	uː	uː	ʊ
BOOK-KEEPING	uː	uː	ʊ	COOP	uː	uː	uː
BOOKWORM	uː	uː	ʊ	COOPER	uː	uː	uː
BOOM	uː	uː	uː	COOPERAGE	uː	uː	uː
BOON	uː	uː	uː	COPY-BOOK	uː	uː	ʊ
BOOR	uː	uː	uː	CROOK	uː	uː	uː
BOORISH	uː	uː	uː	CROOKED	uː	uː	uː
BOOT	uː	uː	uː	CUCKOO	uː	uː	uː
BOOTED	uː	uː	uː	DISAPPROVE	uː	uː	uː
BOOTH	uː	uː	uː	DISPROOF	uː	uː	uː
BOOTLESS	uː	uː	uː	DISPROVE	uː	uː	uː
BOOTY	uː	uː	uː	DO	uː	uː	uː
BORROWER	ɔː	ɔː	ɔː	DOER	uː	uː	uː
BOUGH	ɔʊ	ou	ɔː *or* au	DOINGS	uː	uː	uː
BRIDEGROOM	uː	uː	uː	DOOM	uː	uː	uː
BROOCH	uː	uː	ɔː	DOOMSDAY	uː	uː	uː
BROOD	uː	uː	uː	DRAGOON	uː	uː	uː

Entry	Walker (1791)	Sheridan (1780)	Burn (1786)	Entry	Walker (1791)	Sheridan (1780)	Burn (1786)
DRAWING-				LOOSENESS	uː	uː	ʊ
ROOM	uː	uː	uː	LOSE	uː	uː	ʊ
DROOP	uː	uː	uː	MONSOON	uː	uː	uː
ENTOMB	uː	uː	uː	MOOD	uː	uː	uː
FESTOON	uː	uː	uː	MOON	uː	uː	uː
FLOOK	uː	uː	uː	MOONSHINE	uː	uː	—
FOOD	uː	uː	uː	MOOR	uː	uː	oː
FOOL	uː	uː	uː	MOORY	uː	uː	oː
FOOLHARDY	uː	uː	uː	MOOSE	uː	uː	uː
FOOLISH	uː	uː	uː	MOOT	uː	uː	uː
FORENOON	uː	uː	uː	MOVE	uː	uː	uː
FORSOOTH	uː	ʊ	uː	MOVEABLE	uː	uː	uː
GLOOM	uː	uː	uː	MOVEABLES	uː	uː	uː
GOLD	oː *or* uː	uː	oː *or* uː	MOVEMENT	uː	uː	uː
GOLDEN	oː *or* uː	uː	oː *or* uː	MOVING	uː	uː	uː
GOLDSMITH	oː *or* uː	uː	oː *or* uː	NOOK	uː	uː	ʊ
GOOD	ʊ	ʊ	uː	NOON	uː	uː	uː
GOODLY	ʊ	ʊ	uː	NOONDAY	uː	uː	uː
GOODNESS	ʊ	ʊ	uː	NOONTIDE	uː	uː	uː
GOODS	ʊ	ʊ	uː	NOOSE	uː	uː	uː
GOOSE	uː	uː	uː	OOZE	uː	uː	uː
GROOM	uː	uː	uː	OUTDO	uː	uː	uː
GROOVE	uː	uː	uː	OVERLOOK	uː	ʊ	ʊ
HALOO	uː	uː	uː	PARAMOUR	uː	oː	uː
HARPOON	uː	uː	uː	PARTOOK	uː	ʊ	ʊ
HECATOMB	uː	oː	uː	PICAROON	uː	uː	uː
HITHERTO	uː	uː	uː	PLATOON	uː	uː	uː
HOOF	uː	uː	uː	POLTROON	uː	uː	uː
HOOK	uː	uː	uː	PONTOON	uː	uː	—
HOOKED	uː	uː	uː	POOL	uː	uː	uː
HOOP	uː	uː	uː	POOP	uː	uː	uː
HOOT	uː	uː	uː	POOR	uː	uː	uː
IMPROVE	uː	uː	uː	PROOF	uː	uː	uː
INTOMB	uː	uː	uː	PROVE	uː	uː	uː
INTO	uː	uː	ʊ	RAGOUT	uː	uː	uː
LAMPOON	uː	uː	uː	RENDEZVOUS	uː	uː	uː
LOO	uː	uː	uː	REMOVAL	uː	uː	uː
LOOK	uː	ʊ	ʊ	REMOVE	uː	uː	uː
LOOM	uː	uː	ʊ	REPROOF	uː	uː	uː
LOOSE (adj.)	uː	uː	ʊ	REPROVE	uː	uː	uː
LOOSE (vb.)	uː	uː	ʊ	ROOD	uː	uː	uː
LOOSEN	uː	uː	ʊ	ROOF	uː	uː	uː

Entry	Walker (1791)	Sheridan (1780)	Burn (1786)	Entry	Walker (1791)	Sheridan (1780)	Burn (1786)
ROOK	uː	uː	uː	TOMB	uː	uː	uː
ROOM	uː	uː	uː	TOO	uː	uː	uː
ROOST	uː	uː	uː	TOOL	uː	uː	uː
ROOT	uː	uː	uː	TOOTH	uː	uː	uː
SCHOOL	uː	uː	uː	TOOTHSOME	uː	uː	uː
SCOOP	uː	uː	uː	TOWARD	ɔː	ɔː	ʊ
SHALOON	uː	uː	—	TOWARDLY	ɔː	ɔː	ʊ
SHOOK	uː	ʊ	—	TOWARDS	ɔː	ɔː	ʊ
SHOOT	uː	uː	uː	TROOP	uː	uː	uː
SLOOP	uː	uː	uː	TROOPER	uː	uː	uː
SMOOTH	uː	uː	uː	TWO	uː	uː	uː
SOON	uː	uː	uː	UNDO	uː	—	uː
SOOTH	uː	uː	ʊ	UNMOOR	uː	uː	uː
SOOTHE	uː	uː	uː	UNROOF	uː	uː	uː
SOOTHSAYING	uː	uː	ʊ	UNTO	uː	uː	—
SPOON	uː	uː	uː	WHIRLPOOL	uː	uː	uː
STOOK	—	—	—	WHO	uː	uː	uː
STOOL	uː	uː	uː	WHOM	uː	uː	uː
STOOP	uː	uː	uː	WHOOP	uː	uː	uː
SWOON	uː	uː	uː	WHOSE	uː	uː	uː
SWOOP	uː	uː	uː	WIDOWER	ɔː	ɔː	ʌ
TATOO	uː	uː	uː	WOMB	uː	uː	uː
THROUGH	uː	uː	uː	WOO	uː	uː	uː
THROUGHOUT	uː	uː	uː	WOOER	uː	uː	uː
TO	uː	ʊ	ʊ	WOOF	uː	uː	uː
TOGETHER	ɔː	ʊ	ʊ	WOOL	ʊ	ʊ	ʊ
TOLL-BOOTH	uː	uː	—				

APPENDIX 5*b*

Words with {ʊ} from ME /oː/ in the *Grand Repository* compared with the same entries in three other pronouncing dictionaries

Entry	Walker (1791)	Sheridan (1780)	Burn (1786)	Entry	Walker (1791)	Sheridan (1780)	Burn (1786)
AFOOT	ʊ	ʊ	ʊ	FOOTING	ʊ	ʊ	ʊ
BAREFOOTED	ʊ	ʊ	ʊ	FOOTPAD	ʊ	ʊ	ʊ
BLOOD	ʌ	ʌ	ʌ	GLOVE	ʌ	ʌ	ʌ
BLOODILY	ʌ	ʌ	ʌ	HOOD	ʊ	ʊ	uː
BLOODSHED	ʌ	ʌ	ʌ	MANHOOD	ʊ	ʊ	uː
BLOODSHOT	ʌ	ʌ	ʌ	SHOULD	ʊ	ʊ	ʊ
BLOODY	ʌ	ʌ	ʌ	SOOT	uː	ʌ	ʌ
FALSEHOOD	ʊ	ʊ	ʊ	SOOTY	uː	uː	ʌ
FLOOD	ʌ	ʌ	ʌ	WEBFOOTED	ʊ	ʊ	ʊ
FOOT	ʊ	ʊ	ʊ	WOULD	ʊ	ʊ	ʊ
FOOTBALL	ʊ	ʊ	ʊ				

APPENDIX 6a

Words with the ending ⟨-ure⟩ (unstressed) in the *Grand Repository* and three other pronouncing dictionaries

Entry	Spence (1775)	Walker (1791)	Sheridan (1780)	Burn (1786)
ADVENTURE	tɪr	tʃjuːr	tʃər	tər
CALENTURE	tjuːr	tʃjuːr	tjuːr	tjuːr
CAPTURE	tjuːr	tʃjuːr	tʃər	tjuːr
CENSURE	sɪr	ʃjuːr	ʃər	sər
COMPOSURE	ʒər	ʒjʊːr	ʒər	zər
COMPRESSURE	ʃər	ʃjuːr	ʃər	ʃər
DEBENTURE	tjuːr	tʃjuːr	tʃər	tər
DECOCTURE	tjuːr	tʃjuːr	tʃər	—
DEFEATURE	tjuːr	tʃjuːr	tʃər	—
DEFLEXURE	kʃər	kʃjuːr	kʃər	kʃər
DEPARTURE	tjuːr	tʃjuːr	tʃər	tər
DEPASTURE	tjuːr	tʃjuːr	tʃər	tər
DISCOMFITURE	tjuːr	tjuːr*	tʃər	tər
DISCOMPOSURE	ʒər	ʒjuːr	ʒər	zər
DISPLEASURE	ʒər	ʒjuːr	ʒər	zər
DORTURE	tjuːr	—	—	—
EMBRASURE	ʒər	zjuːr	ʒər	zjuːr
ENCLOSURE	ʒər	ʒjuːr	ʒər	zər
EPICURE	kjuːr	kjuːr	kjuːr	kjuːr
EXPOSURE	ʒər	ʒjuːr	ʒər	zər
FAILURE	ljuːr	ljuːr*	ljər	lər
FEATURE	tjuːr	tʃjuːr	tʃər	tər
FIGURE	gər	gjuːr	gjuːr	gər
FISSURE	sjuːr	ʃjuːr	ʃər	sjuːr
FLEXURE	kʃər	kʃjuːr	kʃər	ksjuːr
FORFEITURE	tjuːr	tjuːr*	tjuːr	tər
FRACTURE	tjuːr	tʃjuːr	tʃər	tər
FURNITURE	tjuːr	tjuːr	tʃər	tər
FUTURE	tjuːr	tʃjuːr	tʃər	tər
GESTURE	tjuːr	tʃjuːr	tʃər	tər
ILLNATURE	tjuːr	tʃjuːr	tʃər	tər
IMPOSTURE	tjuːr	tʃjuːr	tʃər	tər
INJURE	dʒər	dʒər	dʒər	dʒər
JOINTURE	tjuːr	tʃjuːr	tʃər	tər
JUDICATURE	tjuːr	tjuːr	tʃuːr	tjuːr
JUNCTURE	tjuːr	tʃjuːr	tʃər	tər
LECTURE	tɪr	tʃjuːr	tʃər	tər
LEGISLATURE	tjuːr	tjuːr	tʃər	tər
LIGATURE	tjuːr	tjuːr	tʃuːr	tjuːr
LITERATURE	tjuːr	tjuːr	tʃuːr	tjuːr

Entry	Spence (1775)	Walker (1791)	Sheridan (1780)	Burn (1786)
MANUFACTURE	tjuːr	tʃjuːr	tʃər	tər
MEASURE	ʒər	ʒjuːr	ʒər	zər
MINIATURE	tjuːr	tjuːr	tʃər	tjuːr
MOISTURE	tjuːr	tʃjuːr	tʃər	tər
NATURE	tjuːr	tʃjuːr	tʃər	tər
NOMENCLATURE	tjuːr	tʃjuːr	tʃər	tər
NURTURE	tjuːr	tʃjuːr	tʃər	tər
ORDURE	djuːr	dʒjuːr	dʒər	djuːr
OVERTURE	tjuːr	tʃjuːr	tʃʊr	tjuːr
PASTURE	tjuːr	tʃjuːr	tʃər	tjuːr
PERJURE	dʒər	dʒjuːr	dʒər	dʒər
PLEASURE	ʒər	ʒjuːr	ʒər	zər
POSTURE	tjuːr	tʃjuːr	tʃər	tər
PRESSURE	sjuːr	ʃjuːr	ʃər	sər
PROCEDURE	djuːr	dʒjuːr	dʒər	dər
PUNCTURE	tjuːr	tʃjuːr	tʃər	tər
QUADRATURE	tjuːr	tjuːr	tʃʊr	tjuːr
RAPTURE	tjuːr	tʃjuːr	tʃər	tər
RAZURE	zjuːr	ʒjuːr	ʃər	zjuːr
RUPTURE	tjuːr	tʃjuːr	tʃər	tər
SCISSURE	sjuːr	ʒjuːr	ʃər	sjuːr
SCRIPTURE	tjuːr	tʃjuːr	tʃər	tər
SCULPTURE	tjuːr	tʃjuːr	tʃər	tjuːr
SEIZURE	zjuːr	ʒjuːr	ʒər	zər
SEPULTURE	tjuːr	tjuːr	tʃər	tər
SIGNATURE	tjuːr	tjuːr	tʃʊr	tjuːr
STATURE	tjuːr	tʃjuːr	tʃʊr	tjuːr
STRICTURE	tjuːr	tʃjuːr	tʃər	tər
STRUCTURE	tjuːr	tʃjuːr	tʃər	tər
SUTURE	tjuːr	tʃjuːr	tʃər	tər
TENURE	juːr	juːr	jər	juːr
TINCTURE	tjuːr	tʃjuːr	tʃər	tər
TORTURE	tjuːr	tʃjuːr	tʃər	tər
TRANSFIGURE	gər	gjuːr*	gjər	gər
TREASURE	ʒər	ʒjuːr	ʒər	zər
VENTURE	tjuːr	tʃjuːr	tʃər	tər
VERDURE	djuːr	dʒjuːr	dʒər	djuːr
VESTURE	tjuːr	tʃjuːr	tʃər	tər

Notes: I have interpreted the ⟨u⟩ as in *luck* of Walker, Sheridan, and Burn, along with the {ʊ̷} of Spence, as /ə/ and the {ɨ̵} of Spence as /ɪ/. (See §5.7 for discussion of this.)

Where the representations of Walker's pronunciations are marked *, this is to indicate that Walker had {yuˡ}: since we have interpreted Walker's {uˡ} as /juː/, this would give /jjuː/, which does not seem likely. It is, of course, possible that Walker's {uˡ} represented /iu/ rather than, or as well as, /juː/, but even /jiu/ seems unlikely.

APPENDIX 6*b*

Words with {U}(=/juː/) after {R} in the *Grand Repository* compared with the same entries in three other pronouncing dictionaries

Entry	Walker (1791)	Sheridan (1780)	Burn (1786)
BREW	uː	uː	juː
BREWER	uː	uː	juː
BREWING	uː	uː	juː
BREWIS	uː	uː	juː
BRUISE	uː	uː	juː
BRUIT	uː	uː	juː
BRUMAL	uː	uː	juː
BRUNETTE	uː	uː	juː
CREW	uː	uː	juː
ERUDITION	juː	juː	juː
ERUGINOUS	juː	juː	juː
EXCRUCIATE	uː	uː	juː
EXTRUDE	uː	uː	juː
FERULA	juː	juː	—
FERULE	—	—	juː
FRUGAL	juː	uː	juː
FRUGALITY	juː	uː	juː
GARRULITY	juː	juː	juː
GARULOUS	juː	juː	juː
GREW	juː	uː	juː
GRUEL	juː	uː	juː
IMPRUDENT	uː	uː	juː
INSCRUTABLE	juː	uː	juː
INTRUDE	uː	uː	juː
INTRUSION	uː	uː	juː
JURISPRUDENCE	juː	uː	juː
OBTRUDE	uː	uː	juː
OBTRUSION	uː	uː	juː
PERUKE	juː	juː	juː
PERUSE	juː	juː	juː
PROTRUDE	juː	uː	juː
PURULENCY	juː	juː	juː
PURULENT	juː	juː	juː
RECRUIT	uː	uː	juː
RHEUM	uː	uː	juː

Entry	Walker (1791)	Sheridan (1780)	Burn (1786)
RHEUMATIC	uː	uː	juː
RHEUMATISM	uː	uː	juː
RHUBARB	uː	uː	juː
RUBRIC	uː	uː	juː
RUBY	uː	uː	juː
RUDE	uː	uː	juː
RUDIMENTS	uː	uː	juː
RUE	uː	uː	juː
RUEFUL	uː	uː	juː
RUGINE	—	—	juː
RUIN	uː	uː	juː
RULE	uː	uː	juː
RUMINATE	uː	uː	juː
RUMOUR	uː	uː	juː
RURAL	uː	uː	juː
SCREW	uː	uː	juː
SCRUPLE	uː	uː	juː
SCRUTINISE	uː	uː	juː
SCRUTINY	uː	uː	juː
SCRUTOIR	uː	uː	juː
SHREW	uː	uː	juː
SHREWD	uː	uː	juː
STREW	oː	uː	juː *or* oː
VIRULENT	juː	juː	ju

APPENDIX 6*c*

Words with {ⓌⒹ} after {R} by yod-dropping in the *Grand Repository* compared with the same entries in three other pronouncing dictionaries

Entry	Walker (1791)	Sheridan (1780)	Burn (1786)
ABSTRUSE	juː	uː	juː
ABSTRUSENESS	juː	uː	juː
ACCRUE	uː	uː	juː
BRUTAL	uː	uː	juː

Entry	Walker (1791)	Sheridan (1780)	Burn (1786)
BRUTALITY	uː	uː	juː
BRUTE	uː	uː	juː
BRUTISH	uː	uː	juː
CONGRUE	—	—	juː
CONGRUENCE	juː	juː	juː
CONGRUENT	juː	juː	juː
CONGRUITY	juː	uː	juː
CONGRUOUS	juː	juː	juː
CREWEL	uː	uː	juː
CRUCIAL	uː	uː	juː
CRUCIATE	uː	uː	—
CRUCIFEROUS	uː	uː	juː
CRUCIFIXION	uː	uː	juː
CRUCIFY	uː	uː	juː
CRUDE	uː	uː	juː
CRUDITY	uː	uː	juː
CRUEL	uː	uː	juː
CRUELLY	uː	uː	juː
CRUELTY	uː	uː	juː
CRUET	uː	uː	juː
CRUISE	uː	uː	juː
CRURAL	uː	uː	juː
DETRUDE	uː	uː	juː
DETRUSION	uː	uː	juː
DRUID	uː	uː	juː
FEBRUARY	juː	ʊ	juː
FRUIT	uː	uː	ʊ
FRUITION	juː	uː	juː
MENSTRUAL	juː	ʊ	juː
MENSTRUUM	juː	ʊ	ʊ
PRUDE	uː	uː	juː
PRUDENCE	uː	uː	juː
PRUDENT	uː	uː	juː
PRUNE	uː	uː	juː
PRUNELLO	uː	uː	juː
PRURIENCE	uː	uː	juː
QUADRUPED	juː	ʊ	juː
QUADRUPLE	juː	ʊ	juː
RUTH	uː	uː	uː
TRUANT	uː	uː	juː
TRUCE	uː	uː	juː
TRUCIDATION	uː	uː	juː

Entry	Walker (1791)	Sheridan (1780)	Burn (1786)
TRUCULENT	uː	uː	juː
TRUE	uː	uː	juː
TRUTH	uː	uː	ʊ

APPENDIX 6*d*

Words with {ɭ} after {R} by yod-dropping in the *Grand Repository* compared with the same entries in three other pronouncing dictionaries

Entry	Walker	Sheridan	Burn
RUTHFUL	uː	uː	uː
RUTHLESS	uː	uː	uː

APPENDIX 7*a*

Words beginning with ⟨per-⟩ in the *Grand Repository* and three other pronouncing dictionaries (adapted from Shields 1973: 123)

Entry	Spence (1775)	Walker (1791)	Sheridan (1780)	Burn (1786)
PERADVENTURE	I	ɛ	ɛ	ə
PERCEIVE	I	ɛ	ɛ	ə
PERCEPTIBLE	I	ɛ	ɛ	ə
PERCEPTION	I	ɛ	ɛ	ə
PERCH	ɛ	ɛ	ɛ	ə
PERCHANCE	I	ɛ	ɛ	ə
PERCIPIENT	I	ɛ	ɛ	ə
PERCOLATE	ɛ	ɛ	ɛ	ə
PERCUSSION	I	ɛ	ɛ	ə
PERCUTIENT	I	ɛ	ɛ	ə
PERDITION	I	ɛ	ɛ	ə
PERDUE	I	ɛ	ɛ	ə
PEREGRINATE	I	ɛ	ɛ	ə
PEREGRINE	I	ɛ	ɛ	ɛ
PEREMPTORILY	I	ɛ	ɛ	ɛ
PEREMPTORY	I	ɛ	ɛ	ɛ
PERENNIEL	I	ɛ	ɛ	ə
PERENNITY	I	ɛ	ɛ	ə
PERFECT	I	ɛ	ɛ	ə
PERFECTION	I	ɛ	ɛ	ə
PERFIDIOUS	I	ɛ	ɛ	ə
PERFIDY	ɛ	ɛ	ɛ	ə
PERFORATE	I	ɛ	ɛ	ə
PERFORCE	I	ɛ	ɛ	ə
PERFORM	I	ɛ	ɛ	ə
PERFUME	I	ɛ	ɛ	ə
PERFUSE	I	ɛ	ɛ	ə
PERHAPS	I	ɛ	ɛ	ə
PERICARDIUM	ɛ	ɛ	ɛ	ɛ
PERICRANIUM	I	ɛ	ɛ	ɛ
PERIL	ɛ	ɛ	ɛ	ə
PERILOUS	ɛ	ɛ	ɛ	ə
PERIPHERY	I	iː	eː	iː
PERISH	ɛ	ɛ	ɛ	ɛ
PERISHABLE	ɛ	ɛ	ɛ	ɛ

Entry	Spence (1775)	Walker (1791)	Sheridan (1780)	Burn (1786)
PERIWIG	ɛ	ɛ	ɛ	ɪ
PERIWINKLE	ɛ	ɛ	ɛ	ɛ
PERIOD	iː	iː	iː	iː
PERIODICAL	iː	iː	eː	iː
PERJURY	ɛ	ɛ	ɛ	ə
PERJURE	ɛ	ɛ	ɛ	ə
PERMANENT	ɛ	ɛ	ɛ	ə
PERMISSION	ɪ	ɛ	ɛ	ə
PERMIT	ɪ	ɛ	ɛ	ə
PERMUTE	ɪ	ɛ	ɛ	—
PERNICIOUS	ɪ	ɛ	ɛ	ə
PERORATION	ɪ	ɛ	ɛ	ə
PERPENDICULAR	ɛ	ɛ	ɛ	ə
PERPETRATE	ɪ	ɛ	ɛ	ə
PERPETUAL	ɪ	ɛ	ɛ	ə
PERPETUATE	ɪ	ɛ	ɛ	ə
PERPETUITY	ɪ	ɛ	ɛ	ə
PERPLEX	ɪ	ɛ	ɛ	ə
PERPLEXED	ɪ	ɛ	ɛ	ə
PERQUISITE	ɛ	ɛ	ɛ	ə
PERRY	ɛ	ɛ	ɛ	ɛ
PERSECUTE	ɪ	ɛ	ɛ	ə
PERSEVERE	ɪ	ɛ	ɛ	ə
PERSIST	ɪ	ɛ	ɛ	ə
PERSON	ɪ	ɛ	ɛ	ə
PERSONABLE	ɪ	ɛ	ɛ	ə
PERSONALLY	ɪ	ɛ	ɛ	ə
PERSONATE	ɪ	ɛ	ɛ	ə
PERSPECTIVE	ɪ	ɛ	ɛ	ə
PERSPICACIOUS	ɪ	ɛ	ɛ	ə
PERSPICUOUS	ɪ	ɛ	ɛ	ə
PERSPIRATION	ɪ	ɛ	ɛ	ə
PERSPIRE	ɪ	ɛ	ɛ	ə
PERSUADE	ɪ	ɛ	ɛ	ə
PERSUASION	ɪ	ɛ	ɛ	ə
PERSUASIVE	ɪ	ɛ	ɛ	ə
PERT	ɛ	ɛ	ɛ	ə
PERTAIN	ɪ	ɛ	ɛ	ə
PERTINACIOUS	ɛ	ɛ	ɛ	ə
PERTINENT	ɛ	ɛ	ɛ	ə
PERTURBATION	ɛ	ɛ	ɛ	ə
PERUKE	ɪ	ɛ	ɛ	ɛ

Entry	Spence (1775)	Walker (1791)	Sheridan (1780)	Burn (1786)
PERUSE	ɪ	iː	eː	ɛ
PERVADE	ɪ	ɛ	ɛ	ɛ
PERVERSE	ɪ	ɛ	ɛ	ɛ
PERVERSION	ɪ	ɛ	ɛ	ɛ
PERVERT	ɪ	ɛ	ɛ	ɛ
PERVICACIOUS	ɛ	ɛ	ɛ	ə
PERVIOUS	ɛ	ɛ	ɛ	ə

Note: I have interpreted Spence's {ɪ̵} as /ɪ/, because it has that value in stressed syllables. Shields (1973) concludes that {ɪ̵} in some cases represents a vowel closer to schwa (see §5.7.2).

APPENDIX 7*b*

Vowels in unstressed syllables: a selection of words from the *Grand Repository* and three other pronouncing dictionaries

Entry	Spence (1775)	Walker (1791)	Sheridan (1780)	Burn (1786)
⟨eon⟩, ⟨ion⟩				
BLUDGEON	ɪ	ə	ə	ə
CURMUDGEON	ɪ	ə	ə	ə
CUSHION	ɪ	ɪ *or* ə	ə	ə
DUDGEON	ɪ	ə	ə	ə
DUNGEON	ɪ	ə	ə	ə
ESCUTCHEON	ɪ	ɪ	ə	ə
GUDGEON	ɪ	ə	ə	ə
HABERGEON	ə	—	—	ə
LUNCHEON	ɪ	ə	ə	ə
MARCHIONESS	ɪ	ə	ɪ	ə
PIGEON	ɪ	ɪ	ə	ə
PUNCHEON	ɪ	ə	ə	ə
RIBBON/RIBAND	ɪ	ɪ	ɪ	æ
SCUTCHEON	ɪ	ɪ	ə	ə
STURGEON	ɪ	ə	ə	ə
SURGEON	ɪ	ə	ə	ə
TRUNCHEON	ɪ	ə	ə	ə
WAGON	ɪ	ə	ə	ŋ̩

Entry	Spence (1775)	Walker (1791)	Sheridan (1780)	Burn (1786)
⟨o⟩				
FAGGOT	ɪ	ə	ə	ə
ZEALOT	ɒ	ə	ə	ɒ
ACCOMMODATION	ɪ	oː	oː	oː
FOLLOW	ɪ	oː	oː	oː
HOLLOW	ɪ	oː	oː	oː
PILLOW	ɪ	oː	oː	oː
SORROW	ɪ	oː	oː	oː
SWALLOW	ɪ	oː	oː	oː
WALLOW	oː	oː	oː	oː
WIDOW	ɪ	oː	oː	ə
ANCHOR	ɪ	ə	ə	ə
BACHELOR	ə	ə	ə	ə
MAJOR	ɪ	ə	ə	ə
SERVITOR	ə	ə	ə	not marked
⟨ace⟩				
FURNACE	ɪ	ɪ	ɪ	æ
MENACE*	ɪ	eː	ɛ	eː
PALACE*	ɪ	æ	æ	æ
PINNACE*	ɪ	æ	ɛ	eː
POPULACE*	eː	æ	ɛ	eː
SOLACE*	eː	æ	ɛ	eː
⟨age⟩				
ASSEMBLAGE	ɪ	eː	ɛ	ɪ
DISADVANTAGE	ɪ	eː	æ	æ
⟨e⟩				
BARREN	ɪ	ɛ	ɪ	ɛ
BONNET	ɪ	ɛ	ɪ	ɛ
BRACELET	ɪ	ɛ	ɪ	ɛ
BRAINLESS	ɪ	ɛ	ɪ	ɛ
BUCKET	ɪ	ɛ	ɪ	ɛ
CALENDAR	ɪ	ɛ	ɪ	ɛ
CHALLENGE	ɪ	ɛ	ɪ	ɛ
CLOSET	ɪ	ɛ	ɪ	ɛ
DIABETES	ɪ	ɛ	ɪ	ɛ
GAUNTLET	ɪ	ɛ	ɪ	ɛ
GRUEL	ɪ	ɛ	ɪ	ɛ
INTERPRET	ɪ	ɛ	ɪ	ɛ

Entry	Spence (1775)	Walker (1791)	Sheridan (1780)	Burn (1786)
PATRONESS	I	ɛ	I	ɛ
SORCERESS	I	ɛ	I	ɛ

Notes: The vowel concerned is that of the last syllable, except where underlined.

In the entries marked * Walker gives transcriptions with 'full' vowels, even though he admits elsewhere (1791: 12–13) that they 'might without any great departure from their common sound, be written *pallus, sollus,* etc.'.

APPENDIX 8

Vowels before /r/ in the *Grand Repository* and three other pronouncing dictionaries

Entry	Spence (1775)	Walker (1791)	Sheridan (1780)	Burn (1786)
BEER	iː	iː	iː	iː
BIRD	ɪ	ə	ə	ə
BIRTH	ɪ	ɛ	ɛ	ə
BURDEN	ə	ə	ə	ə
CHAIR	eː	eː	eː	eː
FERN	ɛ	ɛ	ɛ	ə
FIR	ɪ	ɛ	ə	ə
FIRE	ai	ai	ai	ai
FLOUR	au	—	—	au
FLOWER	auɪ	auə	auə	auə
FOR	ɒ	ɔː	ɒ	ɒ
FUR	ə	ə	ə	ə
NORTH	ɒ	ɔː	ɔː	ɔː
SURE	uː	juː	uː	juː
TOWER	auɪ	auə	auə	auə

APPENDIX 9

Words of French/Latin origin with initial ⟨h⟩ in the *Grand Repository* and three other pronouncing dictionaries

Entry	Spence (1775)	Walker (1791)	Sheridan (1780)	Burn (1786)
HEIR	−	−	−	−
HEIRESS	−	−	−	−
HERB	−	−	+	−
HERBAL	−	+	+	−
HERBAGE	−	−	+	−
HERBALIST	−	+	+	−
HERITABLE	−	+	+	+
HERITAGE	+	+	+	+
HOMAGE	+	+	+	+
HONEST	−	−	−	−
HONESTY	−	−	−	−
HONOUR	−	−	−	−
HONOURABLE	−	−	−	−
HONORARY	−	−	−	−
HOSPITAL	−	−	−	+
HOSPITALITY	+	+	+	+
HOST	−	+	+	+
HOSTESS	−	+	+	+
HOSTLER	−	−	−	−
HOUR	−	−	−	−
HOURLY	−	−	−	−
HUMAN	+	+	+	+
HUMBLE	+	−	−	+
HUMID	+	+	+	+
HUMILITY	+	+	+	+
HUMOUR	−	−	−	−
HUMORIST	−	−	−	−
HUMOROUS	−	−	−	−
HUMOURSOME	−	−	−	−

Note: + means that /h/ is pronounced; − means that /h/ is not pronounced.

APPENDIX 10

Words with initial ⟨wh⟩ (in traditional orthography) in the
Grand Repository and three other pronouncing dictionaries

Entry	Spence (1775)	Walker (1791)	Sheridan (1780)	Burn (1786)
WHALE	ʍ	ʍ	ʍ	w
WHARF	w	ʍ	ʍ	w
WHARFAGE	w	ʍ	ʍ	w
WHAT	ʍ	ʍ	ʍ	w
WHEAT	ʍ	ʍ	ʍ	w
WHEATEN	ʍ	ʍ	ʍ	w
WHEEDLE	ʍ	ʍ	ʍ	w
WHEEL	ʍ	ʍ	ʍ	w
WHEELBARROW	ʍ	ʍ	ʍ	w
WHEELWRIGHT	ʍ	ʍ	ʍ	w
WHEEZE	ʍ	ʍ	ʍ	w
WHELM	ʍ	ʍ	ʍ	w
WHELP	ʍ	ʍ	ʍ	w
WHEN	ʍ	ʍ	ʍ	w
WHENCE	ʍ	ʍ	ʍ	w
WHERE	ʍ	ʍ	ʍ	w
WHEREAS	ʍ	ʍ	ʍ	w
WHEREBY	ʍ	ʍ	ʍ	w
WHEREFORE	ʍ	ʍ	ʍ	w
WHEREIN	ʍ	ʍ	ʍ	w
WHEREOF	ʍ	ʍ	ʍ	w
WHEREUPON	ʍ	ʍ	ʍ	w
WHERRY	ʍ	ʍ	ʍ	w
WHET	ʍ	ʍ	ʍ	w
WHETHER	ʍ	ʍ	ʍ	w
WHETSTONE	ʍ	ʍ	ʍ	w
WHEY	ʍ	ʍ	ʍ	w
WHICH	ʍ	ʍ	ʍ	w
WHIFF	ʍ	ʍ	ʍ	w
WHIFFLE	ʍ	ʍ	ʍ	w
WHIG	ʍ	ʍ	ʍ	w
WHILE	ʍ	ʍ	ʍ	w
WHILES	ʍ	—	—	w
WHILST	ʍ	ʍ	ʍ	w
WHIM	ʍ	ʍ	ʍ	w
WHIMPER	ʍ	ʍ	ʍ	w

Entry	Spence (1775)	Walker (1791)	Sheridan (1780)	Burn (1786)
WHIMSICAL	ʍ	ʍ	ʍ	w
WHIMSY	ʍ	ʍ	ʍ	w
WHIN	ʍ	ʍ	ʍ	w
WHINE	ʍ	ʍ	ʍ	w
WHIP	ʍ	ʍ	ʍ	w
WHIRL	ʍ	ʍ	ʍ	w
WHIRLPOOL	ʍ	ʍ	ʍ	w
WHISK	ʍ	ʍ	ʍ	w
WHISKERS	ʍ	ʍ	ʍ	w
WHISPER	ʍ	ʍ	ʍ	w
WHIST	ʍ	ʍ	ʍ	w
WHISTLE	ʍ	ʍ	ʍ	w
WHIT	ʍ	ʍ	ʍ	w
WHITE	ʍ	ʍ	ʍ	w
WHITEN	ʍ	ʍ	ʍ	w
WHITHER	ʍ	ʍ	ʍ	w
WHITLOW	ʍ	ʍ	ʍ	ʍ
WHITSUNTIDE	ʍ	ʍ	ʍ	ʍ
WHIZ	ʍ	ʍ	ʍ	ʍ
WHO	ʍ	h	h	h
WHOLE	ʍ	h	h	h
WHOLESALE	ʍ	h	h	h
WHOLESOME	ʍ	h	h	h
WHOLLY	ʍ	h	h	h
WHOM	ʍ	h	h	h
WHOOP	ʍ	h	h	h
WHORE	h	h	h	h
WHOREDOM	h	h	h	h
WHOSE	ʍ	h	h	h
WHY	ʍ	ʍ	ʍ	w

References

Aarsleff, H. (1983), *The Study of Language in England 1780–1860* (2nd edn., London: Athlone Press).

Abbott, C. C. (1935) (ed.), *The Correspondence of Gerard Manley Hopkins and Richard Watkins Dixon* (London: Oxford University Press).

Abercrombie, D. (1948), 'Forgotten Phoneticians', *Transactions of the Philological Society*, 1–34.

——(1965), 'Forgotten Phoneticians', in *Studies in Phonetics and Linguistics* (London: Oxford University Press).

——(1981), 'Extending the Roman alphabet: Some Orthographic Experiments of the Past Four Centuries', in R. E. Asher and E. Henderson (eds.), *Towards a History of Phonetics* (Edinburgh: Edinburgh University Press).

Adams, J. (1799), *The Pronunciation of the English Language Vindicated from Imputed Anomaly and Caprice* (Edinburgh: J. Moir for the Author).

Aitchison, J. (1981), *Language Change: Progress or Decay?* (London: Fontana).

Aitken, A. J. (1979), 'Scottish Speech: A Historical View, with Special Reference to the Standard English of Scotland', in A. J. Aitken, and T. McArthur (eds.), *Languages of Scotland* (Edinburgh: Chambers).

Alston, R. C. (1965–73), *A Bibliography of the English Language from the Invention of Printing to the Year 1800*, vols. i–xvii, (Leeds: Arnold).

——(1972). (ed.), *English Linguistics 1500–1800* (London: The Scolar Press).

Anderson, J. M., and Jones, C. (1977), *Phonological Structure and the History of English* (Amsterdam: North Holland Publishing Company).

Anon. (1763), *The Alphabet of Reason* (London: The Author).

Anon. (1790), *A Caution to Gentlemen Who Use Sheridan's Dictionary* (3rd edn., London: G. Bourne and R. & T. Turner).

Anon. (1797), *A Vocabulary of Such Words in the English Language as are of Dubious or Unsettled Accentuation* (London: F. and C. Rivington, G. and T. Wilkie (*et al.*)).

Ashraf, P. M. (1983), *The Life and Times of Thomas Spence* (Newcastle: Frank Graham).

Bailey, N. (1727), *The Universal Etymological English Dictionary* (London: T. Cox).

Bailey, R. W. (1996), *Nineteenth-Century English* (Ann Arbor: University of Michigan Press).

Baldi, P., and Werth, R. N. (1978) (eds.), *Readings in Historical Phonology* (Philadelphia: Pennsylvania State University Press).

Barber, C. (1993), *The English Language: A Historical Introduction* (Cambridge: Cambridge University Press).

Batchelor, T. (1809), *An Orthoëpical Analysis of the English Language* (London) (see Zettersten 1974).

Baugh, A. C., and Cable, T. (1978), *A History of the English Language* (3rd edn., London: Routledge & Kegan Paul).

Beal, J. C. (1985) 'Lengthening of *a* in Tyneside English', *Current Issues in Linguistic Theory* 41: 31–44.

—— (1993*a*), 'The Grammar of Tyneside and Northumbrian English', in J. Milroy and L. Milroy (eds.), *Real English: The Grammar of English Dialects in the British Isles*, (London: Longman).

—— (1993*b*), 'Lengthening of *a* in Eighteenth-Century English: A Consideration of Evidence from Thomas Spence's *Grand Repository of the English Language* and Other Contemporary Pronouncing Dictionaries', *Newcastle and Durham Working Papers in Linguistics*, 1: 2–17.

—— (1994), 'The Jocks and the Geordies: Modified Standards in Eighteenth-Century Pronouncing Dictionaries', *Newcastle and Durham Working Papers in Linguistics*, 2: 1–19.

Beattie, J. (1783), *Dissertations Moral and Critical* (London).

Beckett, S. (1972), *Watt* (London: Calder & Boyars).

Bendix, W. (1921), *Englische Lautlehre nach Nares (1784)* (Darmstadt: K. F. Bender).

Benzie, W. (1972), *The Dublin Orator* (Menston: The Scolar Press).

Bergström, F. (1955), 'John Kirkby (1746) on English Pronunciation', *Studia Neophilologica*, 27: 65–104.

Bewick, T. (1862), *A Memoir of Thomas Bewick Written by Himself* (Newcastle: Ward).

Bindman, D. (1989), *The Shadow of the Guillotine: Britain and the French Revolution* (London: British Museum Publications).

Bloomfield, M. W., and Newmark, L. (1963), *The English Language: A Historical Introduction* (Westport, Conn.: Greenwood).

Bolton, W. F. (1972), *A Short History of Literary English* (2nd edn., London: Arnold).

—— (1982), *A Living Language: The History and Structure of English* (New York: Random House).

Boswell, J. (1934), *Life of Johnson*, ed. G. Birkbeck Hill; revised and enlarged by L. F. Powell (6 vols.; Oxford: Clarendon Press).

Bourcier, G. (1981), *An Introduction to the History of the English Language*, English adaptation by Cecily Clark (Cheltenham: Stanley Thornes).

Bronstein, A. J. (1986), 'The History of Pronunciation in English Language Dictionaries', in R. R. K. Hartmann (ed.), *The History of Lexicography* (Amsterdam: Benjamins).

Bronstein, A. J., and Sheldon, E. K. (1951), 'Derivatives of Middle English O in Eighteenth- and Nineteenth-Century Dictionaries', *American Speech*, 24: 81–9.

Brook, G. L. (1958), *A History of the English Language* (London: Deutsch).

Bryant, M. M. (1962), *Modern English and its Heritage* (2nd edn., New York: Macmillan).

Buchanan, J. (1757), *Linguae Britannicae Vera Pronunciatio* (London: A. Millar).

—— (1762), *The British Grammar* (London: A. Millar).

—— (1766). *An Essay Towards Establishing a Standard for an Elegant and Uniform Pronunciation of the English Language* (London: Edward & Charles Dilly).

Burn, J. (1786), *A Pronouncing Dictionary of the English Language* (2nd edn., Glasgow: Alex. Adam for the Author and James Duncan; 1st edn., 1777).

Butler, M. (1984), *Burke, Paine, Godwin and the Revolution Controversy* (Cambridge: Cambridge University Press).

Castro, J. de (1751), *Grammatica Lusitano-Anglica* (London: W. Meadows and E. Comyns).

Cercignani, F. (1981), *Shakespeare's Works and Elizabethan Pronunciation* (Oxford: Clarendon Press).

Chomsky, N., and Halle, M. (1968), *The Sound Pattern of English* (New York: Harper & Row).

Cocker, E. (1796), *Cocker's Accomplished School-Master* (London: J. Back).

Cohen, M. (1977), *Sensible Words: Linguistic Practice in England 1640–1785* (Baltimore: Johns Hopkins University Press).

Coles, E. (1674), *The Compleat English Schoolmaster* (London: Peter Parker).

Collins (1992), *Collins Softback English Dictionary* (4th edn., Glasgow: Harper Collins).

Cooper, C. (1685), *Grammatica Linguæ Anglicanæ*: see Sundby (1953).

——(1687), *The English Teacher*: see Sundby (1953).

Coote, E. (1596). *The English School-Maister* (London: Widow Olwin for Ralph Jackson and Robert Dexter).

Crowley, T. (1991), *Proper English? Readings in Language, History and Cultural Identity* (London: Routledge).

Daines, S. (1640), *Orthoepia Anglicana* (London: Robert Young and Richard Badger for the Company of Stationers).

Davies, C. (1934), *English Pronunciation from the Fifteenth to the Eighteenth Centuries* (London: J. M. Dent & Sons).

Davis, N. (1954), 'The Language of the Pastons', in *Proceedings of the British Academy*, xl: 119–44.

Defoe, D. (1724–7), *A Tour Thro' the Whole Island of Great Britain* (London: G. Straham, W. Mears, R. Francklin, S. Chapman, R. Stags, and J. Graves).

Dix, H. (1633), *The Art of Brachygraphy* (London: The Author).

——(1641), *A New Art of Brachygraphy* (3rd edn.; London: the Author).

Dobson, E. J. (1955),'Early Modern Standard English', in *Transactions of the Philological Society*, 25–54.

——(1957), *English Pronunciation 1500–1700* (Oxford: Oxford University Press).

Douglas, S. (1779), *A Treatise on the Provincial Dialect of Scotland*, ed. C. Jones (1991).

Dyche, T. (1723), *A Dictionary of all Words Commonly Used in the English Tongue* (London: Samuel Butler & Thomas Butler).

——and Pardon, W. (1735), *A New General English Dictionary* (London: Richard Ware).

Ekwall, E. (1975), *A History of Modern English Sounds and Morphology*, trans. and ed. A. Ward (Oxford: Blackwell; 1st edn., 1914).

Elliott, R. W. V. (1954), *Modern Language Review*, 49: 5–12.

Ellis, A. J. (1869), *On Early English Pronunciation*, part I (London: Asher & Co. for the Philological Society, Trübner & Co. for the Early English Text Society).

Elphinston, J. (1765), *The Principles of the English Language Digested, English Grammar Reduced to Analogy* (London: James Bettenham).

——(1786), *Propriety Ascertained in her Picture. Volume I* (London: John Water).

——(1787), *Propriety Ascertained in her Picture. Volume II* (London: John Water).

——(1790), *Inglish Orthoggraphy Epittomized* (London: W. Ritchardson, J. Deighton and W. Clark (*et al.*)).

Emsley, B. (1933), 'James Buchanan and the Eighteenth-Century Regulation of English Usage', *PMLA* 18: 1154–66.

——(1940), 'Progress in Pronouncing Dictionaries', *American Speech*, 15: 55–9.

——(1942), 'The First "Phonetic" Dictionary', *Quarterly Journal of Speech*, 28: 202–206.

Fisher, A. (1787), *A Practical New Grammar* (23rd edn., Newcastle: S. Hodgson).

Flasdieck, H. M. (1932), 'Studien zur schriftsprachlichen Entwicklung der Neuenglischen Velar-Vokale in Verbindung mit R', *Anglia*, 56: 113–264, 321–420.

Flint, J. Mather (1740), *Pronunciation de la langue Angloise* (Paris: Didot).

Franklin, B. (1768), 'A Scheme for a New Alphabet and Reformed Mode of Spelling', in *Letters and Papers on Philosophical Subjects* (London).

——(1806), *Letters and Papers on Philosophical Subjects* (London).

Freeborn, D. (1992), *From Old English to Standard English* (London: Macmillan).

Garrett, R. M. (1910), 'English Pronunciation in a German Grammar of the Eighteenth Century', *Englische Studien*, 42: 393–405.

Gil, A. (1621), *Logonomia Anglica* (2nd edn.; London: Iohannis Beale).

Gimson, A. C. (1970), *An Introduction to the Pronunciation of English* (2nd edn., London: Arnold).

Görlach, M. (1988), 'The Study of Early Modern English Variation—the Cinderella of English Historical Linguistics?', in J. Fisciak (ed.), *Historical Dialectology, Regional and Social* (Berlin: Mouton de Gruyter).

——(1991), *Introduction to Early Modern English* (Cambridge University Press).

H, the Hon. Henry (1854–66), *Poor Letter H: Its Use and Abuse* London.

Harris, J. (1989), 'Towards a Lexical Analysis of Sound Change in Progress', *Journal of Linguistics*, 25: 35–56.

Heslop, R. O. (1892), *Northumberland Words* (London: English Dialect Society).

——(1903), 'Dialect Notes from Northernmost England', *Transactions of the Yorkshire Dialect Society*, 5: 7–31.

Holder, W. (1669), *Elements of Speech* (London: T.N. for J. Martyn).

Holmberg, B. (1956), *James Douglas on English Pronunciation c.1740* (Lund: Gleerup).

——(1964), *On the Concept of Standard English and the History of Modern English Pronunciation* (Lund: Gleerup).

Hopkins, W. (1670), *The Flying Pen-man* (London: Samuel Lee).

Horn, W. (1925–6), 'Die Entwicklung des mittelenglischen kurzen *u* im Neuenglischen', *Englische Studien*, 60: 121–9.

——and Lehnert, M. (1954), *Laut und Leben: Englische Lautgeschichte der neueren Zeit (1400–1950)* (2 vols.; Berlin: Deutsche Verlag der Wissenschaften).

Horsley, P. M. (1971), *Eighteenth-Century Newcastle* (Newcastle: Oriel Press).

Jespersen, O. (1909–49), *A Modern English Grammar on Historical Principles* (Heidelberg: Winter; Copenhagen: Munksgaard).

Johnson, S. (1755), *A Dictionary of the English Language* (London: W. Strahan for J. & P. Knapton, T. & T. Longman *et al.*).

Johnston, W. (1764), *Pronouncing and Spelling Dictionary* (London: The Author).

—— (1772), *Pronouncing and Spelling Dictionary* (2nd edn.; London: the Author).

Jones, C. (1989), *A History of English Phonology* (London: Longman).

—— (1991) (ed.), *Sylvester Douglas: A Treatise on the Provincial Dialect of Scotland (1779)* (Edinburgh: Edinburgh University Press).

—— (1993), 'Scottish Standard English in the Late Eighteenth Century', *Transactions of the Philological Society*, 91/1: 95–131.

—— (1995), *A Language Suppressed* (Edinburgh: John Donald).

—— (1997), 'An Early 18th Century Scottish Spelling Book for Ladies', *English Studies*, 78/5: 430–50.

Jones, D. (1967), *Everyman's English Pronouncing Dictionary*, ed. A. C. Gimson (13th edn,. London: Dent).

Jones, J. (1701), *Practical Phonography* (London: Richard Smith).

Jones, S. (1798), *Sheridan Improved: A General Pronouncing and Explanatory Dictionary of the English Language* (3rd edn., London: Vernor and Hood, J.Cushell, Ogilvie and Son and Lackington, Allen & Co.).

Jonson, B. (1640), 'The English Grammar', in *The Works of Benjamin Jonson* (London: Richard Bishop), ii. 31–84.

Kenrick, W. (1773), *A New Dictionary of the English Language* (London: John and Francis Rivington, William Johnston (*et al.*)).

—— (1784), *A Rhetorical Grammar of the English Language* (London: R. Cadell and W. Longman.

Kern, K. (1913), *Die englische Lautlentwicklung nach Right Spelling (1704) und anderen Grammatiken um 1700* (Darmstadt: K. F. Bender).

Kiparsky, P. (1988), 'Phonological Change', in F. J. Newmeyer (ed.), *Linguistics: The Cambridge Survey*, i. *Linguistic Theory—Foundations* (Cambridge: Cambridge University Press).

Kökeritz, H. (1944), *Mather Flint on Early Eighteenth-Century Pronunciation* (Uppsala and Leipzig: Almqvist & Wiksell.

—— (1953), *Shakespeare's Pronunciation* (New Haven: Yale University Press).

Kolb, E. (1966), *Phonological Atlas of the Northern Region* (Bern: Francke Verlag).

Labov, W. (1966), *The Social Stratification of English in New York City* (Washington: Center for Applied Linguistics).

—— (1972), *Sociolinguistic Patterns* (Oxford: Basil Blackwell).

—— (1978), 'On the Use of the Present to Explain the Past', in P. Baldi and R. N. Werth, (eds.), *Readings in Historical Phonology* (Philadelphia: Pennsylvania State University Press).

—— (1994), *Principles of Linguistic Change*, i. *Internal Factors* (Oxford: Basil Blackwell).

Lass, R. (1987), *The Shape of English* (London: Dent).

Leith, D. (1983), *A Social History of English* (London: Routledge).

Leonard, S. A (1929), *The Doctrine of Correctness in English Usage 1700–1800* (Wisconsin: Madison).

Lehmann, W. P. (1967) (ed.), *A Reader in Nineteenth-Century Historical Indo-European Linguistics* (Bloomington, Ind.: Indiana University Press).

Lounsbury, T. R. (1894), *History of the English Language* (rev. edn., New York: Henry Holt & Co.; 1st edn., 1879).

Luick, K. (1914–40). *Historische Grammatik der Englischen Sprache* (Leipzig: Fauchnitz).

McCalman, I. (1988), *Radical Underworld: Prophets, Revolutionaries and Pornographers in London, 1795–1840* (Cambridge: Cambridge University Press).

McDavid, R. I. (1949), 'Derivatives of Middle English [oː] in the South Atlantic Area', *Quarterly Journal of Speech*, 35: 496–504.

Mackenzie, E. (1827), *A Descriptive and Historical Account of the Town and County of Newcastle upon Tyne* (Newcastle upon Tyne: Mackenzie and Dent.

McKnight, G. H. (1928), *Modern English in the Making* (New York: Dover Publications).

McMahon, A. (1991), 'Lexical Phonology and Sound Change: The Case of the Scottish Vowel Length Rule', *Journal of Linguistics*, 27: 29–53.

Malone, K. (1924), 'Granville Sharp (1767) on English Pronunciation', *Philological Quarterly* 3: 208–27.

Martin, B. (1749), *Lingua Britannica Reformata* (London: J. Hodges, J. Austen, J. Newberry (et. al.)).

Matthews, W. (1937), 'Some Eighteenth-Century Vulgarisms', *Review of English Speech*, 13: 307–25.

Meyer, E. (1940), *Der englische Lautbestand in der zweiten Hälfte des 18. Jahrhunderts nach James Buchanan* (Berlin: Diss).

Michael, I. (1970), *English Grammatical Categories and the Tradition to 1800* (Cambridge: Cambridge University Press).

Milroy, J. (1983), 'On the Sociolinguistic History of /h/ Dropping in English', in M. Davenport *et al.* (eds.), *Current Topics in English Historical Linguistics* (Odense: Odense University Press).

——(1993), 'Some New Perspectives on Sound Change: Sociolinguistics and the Neogrammarians', *Newcastle and Durham Working Papers in Linguistics*, 1: 181–205.

—— and Harris, J. (1980), 'When is a Merger not a Merger? The MEAT/MATE Problem in a Present-Day English Vernacular', *English World-Wide*, 1/2: 199–210.

—— and L. Milroy (1985), *Authority in Language* (London: Routledge & Kegan Paul).

Moore, S. (1951), *Historical Outlines of English Sounds and Inflections*, revised by A. H. Marckwardt (Ann Arbor: George Wahr).

Mugglestone, L. (1995), *Talking Proper* (Oxford: Clarendon Press).

Müller, E. (1914), *Englische Lautlehre nach James Elphinston (1765, 1787, 1790)* (Heidelberg: Carl Winter).

Nares, R. (1784), *Elements of Orthoepy* (London: T. Payne & Son).

Newton, I. (1660–2), unpublished notes in R. W. V. Elliott (1954).

Nist, J. (1966), *A Structural History of English* (New York: St Martin's).

Orton, H. and Halliday, W. J. (1962–3) (eds.), *Survey of English Dialects (B): The Basic Material: The Six Northern Counties and the Isle of Man*, i–iii (Leeds: E. J. Arnold & Co.).

Påhlsson, C. (1972), *The Northumbrian Burr* (Lund: C. W. K. Gleerup).

Partridge, A. C. (1969), *Tudor to Augustan English* (London: Andre Deutsch).

Payne, A. C. (1980), 'Factors Controlling the Acquisition of the Philadelphia Dialect by Out-of-State Children', in W. Labov (ed.), *Locating Language in Time and Space* (New York: Academic Press).

P.D. (1796), *Pronouncing Dictionary of the English Language* (London: J. W. Myers).

Perry, W. (1775), *The Royal Standard English Dictionary* (Edinburgh: David Willison for the Author).

——(1788), *The Royal Standard English Dictionary* (1st American edn.; Worcester: Isaiah Thomas).

Peters, R. A. (1965), 'Linguistic Differences between Early and Late Modern English', *Studia Neophilologica*, 37: 134–8.

——(1968), *A Linguistic History of English* (Boston: Houghton Mifflin).

Pollner, C. (1976), *Robert Nares: 'Elements of Orthoepy' (1784)* (Frankfurt: Peter Lang).

Prins, A. A. (1972), *A History of English Phonemes* (Leiden: Leiden University Press).

Pyles, T., and Algeo J. (1982), *The Origins and Development of the English Language* (3rd edn. New York: Harcourt Brace Jovanovich).

Rigg, A. G. (1968), *The English Language: A Historical Reader* (New York: Appleton-Century-Crofts).

Robertson, J. (1722), *The Ladies' Help to Spelling* (Glasgow: James Duncan).

Robertson, S. (1954), *The Development of Modern English* (2nd edn., rev. by Frederic G. Cassidy, Englewood Cliffs, NJ: Prentice-Hall).

Robinson, R. (1617), *The Art of Pronuntiation* (London: Nicolas Okes).

Robinson, R. (1887), *Thomas Bewick: His Life and Times* (Newcastle: The Author).

Rohlfing, H. (1984), *Die Werke James Elphinstons (1721–1809) als Quellen der englischen Lautlehre* (Heidelberg: Heidelberg University Press).

Ronberg, G. (1992), *A Way with Words: The Language of English Renaissance Literature* (London: Arnold).

Rudkin, O. (1927), *Thomas Spence and his Connections* (London: Augustus M. Kelley).

Samuels, M. L. (1965), *Linguistic Evolution with Special Reference to English* (Cambridge: Cambridge University Press).

Schlauch, M. (1959), *The English Language in Modern Times (since 1400)* (Warsaw: Państwowe Wydawnictwo Naukowe).

Scott, Sir Walter (1971), *The Heart of Midlothian*, ed. W. M. Parker (London: Dent).

Sheldon, E. K. (1938), 'Standards of English Pronunciation according to the Grammarians and Orthoepists of the 16th, 17th, and 18th Centuries, (dissertation, Wisconsin).

——(1946), 'Pronouncing Systems in Eighteenth-Century Dictionaries', *Language*, 22: 27–41.

——(1947), 'Walker's Influence on the Pronunciation of English', *PMLA* 62: 130–46.

——(1967), *Thomas Sheridan of Smock Alley 1719–1788* (Princeton, NJ: Princeton University Press).

Shelton, T. (1630), *Short-Writing* (2nd edn., London: I.D. for S.C.).

Sheridan, T. (1756), *British Education; or The Source of the Disorders of Great Britain* (London: R. J. Dodsley).

——(1761), *A Dissertation on the Causes of the Difficulties which Occur in Learning the English Tongue* (London: R. and J. Dodsley).

——(1762), *A Course of Lectures on Elocution* (London: W. Straham for A. Miles, R. & J. Dodsley, T. Davies, *et al.*).

——(1775), *Lectures on the Art of Reading* (London: J. Dodsley, J. Wilkie, *et al.*).

——(1780), *A General Dictionary of the English Language* (London: R. & J. Dodsley, C. Dilly, and J. Wilkie).

——(1789), *A General Dictionary of the English Language* (3rd edn.; London: Charles Dilly).

Shields, A. F. (1973), 'Thomas Spence and the English Language, (MA dissertation, University of Newcastle).

——(1974), 'Thomas Spence and the English Language', *Transactions of the Philological Society*, 33–64.

Smalley, D. S. (1855), *The American Phonetic Dictionary of the English Language* (Cincinnati: Longley Brothers).

Smart, B. H. (1846), *Walker's Pronouncing Dictionary of the English Language, Adapted to the Present State of Literature and Science* (London: Longman, Brown & Co.).

Smith, C. W. (1866), *Mind Your H's and Take Care of Your R's* (London).

Spence, T. (1775), *The Grand Repository of the English Language* (Newcastle: T. Saint).

——(1782*a*), *A Supplement to the History of Robinson Crusoe* (Newcastle: T. Saint).

——(1782*b*), *The Real Reading Made Easy* (Newcastle: T. Saint).

——(1792), *The Case of Thomas Spence, Bookseller* (London: printed for the Author).

——(1793), *The Rights of Man* (London: printed for the Author).

——(1793–5), *One Pennyworth of Pigs' Meat or Lessons for the Swinish Multitude* (2nd edn., 3 vols.; London: printed for the Author).

——(1795*a*), *The Meridian Sun of Liberty* (London: printed for the Author).

——(1795*b*), *The Coin Collector's Companion* (London: printed for the Author).

——(1795*c*), *The End of Oppression* (London: printed for the Author).

——(1796), *The Reign of Felicity* (London: printed for the Author).

——(1797), *The Rights of Infants* (London: printed for the Author).

——(1798), *The Constitution of a Perfect Commonwealth* (London: printed for the Author).

——(1801), *The Restorer of Society to its Natural State* (London: printed for the Author).

——(1803), *Dhĕ Impŏrtănt Triăl ŏv Tŏmĭs Spĕns* (London: printed for the Author).

——(1807), *The Important Trial of Thomas Spence* (2nd edn., London).

——(1814), *The Giant Killer, or Anti-Landlord*, Numbers. 1, 2. London.

Starnes, De W., and Noyes G. E. (1991), *The English Dictionary from Cawdrey to*

Johnson 1604–1755, repr. 1991 with an introduction by Gabriele Stein (Amsterdam: John Benjamins, 1st edn., 1946).

Steel, L. (1678), *Short Writing* (Bristol: The Author; London: Charles Allen and Benjamin Clark).

Stevick, R. D. (1968), *English and its History: the Evolution of a Language* (Boston: Allyn & Bacon).

Stichel, H. (1915), *Die englische Aussprache nach den Grammatiken Peytons (1756, 1765)* (Darmstadt: K. F. Bender).

Strang, B. M. H (1968), *Modern English Structure* (2nd edn., London: Arnold).

——(1970), *A History of English* (London: Methuen).

Sundby, B. (1953), *Christopher Cooper's English Teacher* (Lund: Gleerup).

Sweet, H. (1888), *A History of English Sounds from the Earliest Period* (2nd edn., Oxford: Clarendon Press).

Toller, J. N. (1900), *Outlines of the History of the English Language* (Cambridge: Cambridge University Press).

Toon, T. (1976), 'The Variationist Analysis of Early Old English Manuscript Data', in W. M. Christie, Jnr. (ed.), *Proceedings of the Second International Conference on Historical Linguistics* (Amsterdam: North Holland).

Tucker, A. (1773), *Vocal Sounds* (London: T. Jones).

Tucker, S. (1967), *Protean Shape: A Study in Eighteenth-Century Vocabulary and Usage* (London: Athlone).

——(1972), *Enthusiasm: A Study in Semantic Change* (Cambridge: Cambridge University Press).

Wakelin, M. F. (1988), *The Archaeology of English* (London: Batsford).

Walker, J. (1791), *A Critical Pronouncing Dictionary* (London, G. G. J. and J. Robinson, and T. Cadell).

Wang, W. S.-Y. (1969), 'Competing Sound Changes as a Cause of Residue', *Language*, 45: 9–25.

Warden, J. (1753), *A Spelling Book* (Edinburgh: the Author).

Waters, A. W. (1917), *The Trial of Thomas Spence in 1801* (Leamington Spa: Courier Press).

Weinreich, U., Labov, W., and Herzog, M. (1968), 'Empirical Foundations for a Theory of Language Change', in W. Lehmann and Y. Malkiel (eds.), *Directions for Historical Linguistics* (Austin, Tex.: University of Texas Press).

Weinstock, H. (1976),'The Aims, Problems and Value of A Dictionary of Modern English Pronunciation 1500–1800', in *DEMEP: English Pronunciation 1500–1800* (Stockholm: Almquist & Wiksell International).

Welford, R. (1895), *Men of Mark 'Twixt Tyne and Tweed* (Newcastle: Walter Scott).

Wells, J. C. (1982), *Accents of English* (3 vols.; Cambridge: Cambridge University Press).

Willis, J. (1602), *The Art of Stenographie* (London: Cuthbert Burbie).

Wright, J. (1905), *The English Dialect Grammar* (Oxford: Henry Frowde).

Wyld, H. C. (1923), *Studies in English Rhymes from Surrey to Pope* (London: Murray).

——(1927), *A Short History of English* (3rd edn., London: Murray; 1st edn., 1914).

——(1936), *A History of Modern Colloquial English* (3rd edn.; Oxford: Basil Blackwell, (1st edn., 1920).

Zettersten, A. (1974), *A Critical Facsimile Edition of Thomas Batchelor* (Lund: Gleerup).

Index